U0920861

统计年鉴

HANGZHOU STATISTICAL YEARBOOK

杭 州 市 统 计 局
国家统计局杭州调查队　编
杭州市社会经济调查局

2010

（京）新登字041号

图书在版编目（CIP）数据

杭州统计年鉴. 2010/杭州市统计局 国家统计局杭州调查队 杭州市社会经济调查局编. -- 北京:
中国统计出版社，2010.8
ISBN 978-7-5037-6023-5

Ⅰ. ①杭… Ⅱ. ①杭… Ⅲ. ①统计资料-杭州市-

2010-年鉴 Ⅳ. ①C832.551-54

中国版本图书馆CIP数据核字(2010)第148844号

杭州统计年鉴—2010

作者/杭州市统计局 国家统计局杭州调查队 杭州市社会经济调查局
责任编辑/余竞雄 郭 栋
责任校对/俞伟锋 陈小国
封面设计/杭州云鼎广告有限公司
出版发行/中国统计出版社
通信地址/北京市西城区三里河月坛南街57号 中国统计出版社
邮编/100826
电话/（010）63376907
E-mail/yearbook@gj.stats.cn
印刷/浙江新中商务印刷有限公司
经销/新华书店
开本/890×1240 毫米 1/16
字数/85万
印张/26
印数/1-1200册
版别/2010 年 8 月第 1 版
版次/2010 年 8 月第 1 次印刷
书号/ISBN 978-7-5037-6023-5/C·2380
定价/300.00元

《杭州统计年鉴－2010》编委会和编辑人员

Editorial Board and Staff

编者说明

一、《杭州统计年鉴—2010》是一部信息密集的资料工具书。本书通过大量统计数据，真实地记录了在改革开放中杭州的经济、科技、社会的发展变化。本年鉴在前几年年鉴的基础上作了进一步的调整和改进，充实了数据信息量，并与前几年在版本内容、指标数据等方面基本保持连贯性。

二、本年鉴内容包括：综合；人口、劳动力；农业；工业、能源；建筑业；交通运输、邮电；固定资产投资；国内商业；对外经济、旅游；财政、金融、保险；城市建设、环境保护；科技、教育、文化、卫生、体育；人民生活、物价、民政等十三部分。

三、本年鉴辑入的统计数字，以2009年为主，为方便读者使用，主要指标还列入了1978年以来有关年度的统计数字。根据国家统一规定，本年鉴按第二次全国经济普查结果对2005年以来的生产总值和社会消费品零售额数据进行了同步调整。

四、2001年3月起，萧山、余杭撤市建区，市区数据为新市区口径，增长速度按同比口径计算。

五、本年鉴表中符号使用说明：“－”表示这一栏没有数字；“…”表示该数字极小，不足计量单位；“#”表示其中的主要项；空白栏表示未掌握资料；“*”表示表下有注解。

六、读者在使用统计资料时，凡与本年鉴有出入的，均以本年鉴为准。

七、《杭州统计年鉴》公开出版以来，受到了广大读者的关心和支持，对此我们深表谢意。欢迎广大读者对年鉴内容、编排等方面提出宝贵意见，以利于我们进一步提高年鉴的编辑工作水平，更好地为广大读者服务。

Editorial Note

Ⅰ. *Hangzhou Statistical Yearbook 2010* covers comprehensive data series of Hangzhou's social and economic development. Through the statistical data, it reflects the changes and development of Hangzhou's economy, science, technology and society since China adopted the policy of reform and opening to the outside world. This book is adjusted and progressed on basis of last years' books. It enriches the data, and keeps the consistency with last years' book in content and indicators.

Ⅱ. The book contains the following twelve chapters: 1. General Survey; 2. Population and Labor Force; 3. Agriculture; 4. Industry and Energy; 5. Construction; 6. Transportation, Post and Telecommunication Services; 7. Investment in Fixed Assets; 8. Domestic Trade; 9. Foreign Trade and Tourism; 10. Finance, Banking and Insurance; 11. Urban Construction and Environmental Protection; 12. Science and Technology, Education, Culture, Public Health and Sports; 13. People's Livelihood, Price Indices and Civil Administration.

Ⅲ. The book mainly reflects statistical data in 2009. And it also contains some selected data series in important years after 1978. According to state regulations, the GDP and total retail sales of social consumer goods data in the yearbook are adjusted simultaneously since 2005 on the basis of the Second National Economic Census.

Ⅳ. The administrative of area urban district has been adjusted since March 2001, the new administrative area is composed of eight district including Xiaoshan and Yuhang. Data of urban district belong to new administrative area, while indices are calculated at comparable coverage.

Ⅴ. Notations used in this book:"—" indicates that the column has no figure;"…" indicates that the figure is not large enough to be measured with the smallest unit in the table;"blank" indicates that the data not available;"#" indicates the major items of the total;" * " indicates"see footnotes below".

Ⅵ. In any case the data of this book shall be deemed as the authoritative ones.

Ⅶ. Previous editions of Hangzhou Statistical Yearbook have won wide acclaim among the readers. In order to excel, we welcome all candid comments and criticism from our readers.

目　录
Contents

第一篇　综合
Chapter 1　General Survey

第二篇 人口、劳动力
Chapter 2 Population and Labor Force

第三篇　　农业
Chapter 3　Agriculture

第四篇　工业、能源
Chapter 4　Industry and Energy

第五篇　建筑业
Chapter 5　CONSTRUCTION

第六篇　交通运输、邮电
Chapter 6　Transportation, Post and Telecommunications

第七篇　固定资产投资

Chapter 7　Investment in Fixed Assets

第八篇　国内商业
Chapter 8　Domestic Trade

第九篇　对外经济、旅游
Chapter 9　Foreign Trade and Tourism

第十篇　财政、金融、保险
Chapter 10　Finance, Banking and Insurance

第十一篇　城市建设、环境保护
Chapter 11　Urban Construction and Environmental Protection

第十二篇　科技、教育、文化、卫生、体育
Chapter 12　Science and Technology, Education, Culture, Public Health and Sports

第十三篇 人民生活、物价、民政

Chapter 13 People's Livelihood, Price Indices and Civil Administration

2009年杭州市国民经济和社会发展统计公报

杭 州 市 统 计 局
国家统计局杭州调查队
杭州市社会经济调查局

（2010年2月）

2009年，是新世纪以来杭州经济发展最为困难的一年，面对百年不遇国际金融危机的严重冲击和极其复杂的国内外形势，全市人民在市委、市政府的正确领导下，以科学发展观为统领，全力保增长、扩内需、调结构、增活力、重民生、抓稳定，各项工作取得了明显成效，经济实现稳步回升，社会事业协调发展，现代产业体系建设迈出新步伐，市域网络化大都市建设加快推进，市民生活品质进一步提高。

一、综　　合

经济总量

初步核算，全市实现生产总值（GDP）5087.55亿元，按可比价格计算，比上年增长10.0%，连续19年保持两位数增长。其中：第一产业增加值190.51亿元，第二产业增加值2387.12亿元，第三产业增加值2509.92亿元，比上年分别增长3.1%、6.5%和14.2%。三次产业结构由上年的3.8∶48.5∶46.7调整为3.8∶46.9∶49.3。全市按常住人口计算的人均GDP为63333元，按户籍人口计算的人均GDP为74761元，分别增长8.4%和9.1%，按国家公布的2009年平均汇率计算，分别达到9271美元和10944美元。

非公经济

初步测算，在全市生产总值中，非公有制经济所占比重已达到64.5%，其中个体私营经济占全市生产总值的比重为52.5%。2009年末，全市共有私营企业14.09万户，从业人员130.93万人；个体工商户28.46万户，从业人员59.78万人。

财政收支

全年完成财政总收入1019.43亿元，比上年增长12.0%，其中地方财政一般预算收入520.79亿元，比上年增长14.4%。在税收收入中，增值税342.52亿元，增长12.1%；营业税176.45亿元，增长22.8%；企业所得税186.81亿元，下降8.3%；个人所得税80.27亿元，增长17.8%。全年地方财政支出490.40亿元，比上年增长16.9%。其中：教育、科学技术支出108.35亿元，增长16.8%；社会保障和就业支出48.55亿元，增长20.4%；医疗卫生支出32.36亿元，增长24.7%；环境保护支出9.75亿元，增长30.3%。市本级预算内民生支出89.93亿元，增长20.5%，支出增量占新增财力的76.8%。

市场价格

市区居民消费价格总水平比上年下降1.4%。八大类商品和服务项目价格呈“五升三降”格局（见下表）。

市区居民消费价格指数

项　　目	2009年	2008年
市区居民消费价格指数（上年=100）	98.6	104.9
1.食品	101.7	114.6
2.烟酒及用品	100.7	102.5
3.衣着	100.6	98.6
4.家庭设备用品及维修服务	100.9	105.0
5.医疗保健和个人用品	100.6	105.3
6.交通和通信	95.2	94.7
7.娱乐教育文化用品及服务	96.9	99.4
8.居住	91.8	102.4

全市工业品出厂价格下降4.9%；原材料、燃料、动力购进价格下降7.8%。市区房屋销售价格平均上涨2.8%，其中新建房销售价格上涨2.0%，二手房销售价格上涨4.6%。12月，市区房屋销售价格比上年同期上涨11.5%。

劳动就业

全年城镇新增就业人员23.52万人；安置失业人员再就业15.56万人，分别比上年增长17%和23.6%。年末城镇登记失业率由上年的3.02%下降为2.99%。

二、人口、人民生活和社会保障

人口

年末全市常住人口达810万人，比上年末增加13.4万人。其中户籍人口683.38万人，比上年末增加5.74万人。在户籍人口中，农业人口328.9万人，非农业人口354.48万人。按公安部门统计的全市人口出生率为9.18‰，人口自然增长率为3.42‰。

人民生活

据抽样调查，市区城镇居民人均可支配收入26864元，比上年增长11.5%。人均生活消费性支出18595元，比上年增长11.2%，恩格尔系数（食品占消费支出比重）由上年的38.3%下降至37.5%。年末人均住房建筑面积30.85平方米，比上年末增加1.02平方米。每百户居民家庭拥有汽车21.65辆、空调器203.87台、移动电话178.5部、家用计算机86.87台、微波炉74.62台、热水器94.95台。

全市农村居民人均纯收入11822元，比上年增长10.6%；人均生活消费性支出9065元，增长7.3%。恩格尔系数由上年的35.9%下降至33.8%。年末人均居住面积达70.74平方米，比上年末增加1.04平方米。每百户农村居民家庭拥有洗衣机82台、电冰箱95台、空调器100台、热水器81台、微波炉23台、移动电话194部、家用计算机36台，生活用汽车12辆。

年末城乡居民储蓄存款余额达4286.92亿元，比上年末增长23.3%。

社会保障

至2009年末，全市参加基本养老保险342.24万人，参加失业保险215.68万人，参加工伤保险274.15万人，参加生育保险199.25万人，参加基本医疗保险298.31万人，分别比上年末净增24.13万人、13.27万人、28.33万人、17.57万人和23.72万人。市区最低月工资标准为960元。市区失业保险金标准为768元/月。

社会福利

年末全市拥有各类福利院、敬老院208所（不含社会办农村敬老院），床位22430张，收养人员13600人。全市城镇享受最低生活保障人数17510人，农村享受最低生活保障人员71242人。农村五保户和城镇“三无”人员集中供养率分别为93.99%和99.60%。开展第九次“春风行动”，共募集社会帮扶资金4085.50万元。

三、城市建设、环境保护和安全生产

城市基础设施建设

全年完成基础设施投资601.84亿元，比上年增长11.2%。地铁一二期36个站点全部开工，20个站点完成主体施工。“十纵十横”道路综合整治工程全面完工。萧山机场公路改造、钱江通道及南接线（钱江大道）、杭新景高速公路延伸线（之江大桥）、庆春路过江隧道、杭长高速公路等重大交通项目开工，申嘉湖杭高速建成。中山路综保工程顺利开街。市区完成47条河道综保工程。七格污水处理厂三期建成试通水。

公用事业

全年累计投产110千伏及以上变电容量448.7万千伏安，35千伏5.8万千伏安，新增110千伏及以上线路262.27千米。全市用电量达到459.70亿千瓦时，比上年增长6.9%，其中城乡居民生活用电56.4亿千瓦时，增长10.1%。市区自来水日供水能力达到320万立方米，比上年增加21万立方米。年末市区居民家庭天然气用户达到51.84万户，比上年末增长19.0%；城区新辟公交线路15条，更新公交车855辆，公交空调车比例达93%以上。新增停车泊位9704个，累计停车泊位数达60129个。至年末，市区免费单车布点2150个，投放自行车50000辆。富阳、临安与主城区实现了公交一体化。

环境保护

2009年全市化学需氧量和二氧化硫排放量较上年分别减少4.1%和3.7%；工业废气二氧化硫排放达标率、

工业废水排放达标率分别达到99.48%和96.21%。全市城市污水集中处理率由上年的83.2%提高到88.9%;主要水系监测断面水质三类以上比例由上年的57.1%提高为60.7%。市区空气质量达到二级和好于二级的天数达到327天,比上年增加26天。市区扩绿面积1395公顷。至年末,市区人均公园绿地面积15.48平方米,市区建成区绿化覆盖率为39.94%。

安全生产

2009年,全市发生各类事故次数、死亡人数、受伤人数和直接经济损失分别比上年下降16.7%、8.7%、17.4%和16.1%。亿元GDP安全生产事故死亡人数为0.18人,比上年下降14.3%。全市流通领域食品快速检测合格率为99%。

四、农　　业

全年完成农林牧渔业总产值289.74亿元,比上年增长5.8%。其中农业产值149.74亿元,增长6.3%;林业产值36.23亿元,增长13.1%;牧业产值63.29亿元,增长1.0%;渔业产值32.56亿元,增长5.3%。全年粮食总产量107.24万吨,比上年下降2.6%;水产品19.65万吨,增长6.4%;肉类30.92万吨,增长4.7%;禽蛋14.31万吨,增长8.1%;水果77.27万吨,增长6.3%。

全年茶叶、花卉苗木、水产品、节粮型畜禽、蔬菜和竹业等"六大优势产业"实现产值161.60亿元,比上年增长5.0%;水果、干果、蚕桑、药材和蜂业等"五大特色产业"实现产值37.18亿元,比上年增长16.7%,合计占农林牧渔业总产值比重为68.6%,比上年提高0.7个百分点。

五、工业和建筑业

工业生产

2009年全市实现工业增加值2101.14亿元,按可比价计算增长5.5%。实现工业销售产值10720.99亿元,增长0.9%。其中规模以上工业销售产值9261.73亿元,增长0.6%。在规模以上工业中:轻工业实现销售产值3944.78亿元,增长4.3%,重工业实现销售产值5316.96亿元,下降2.0%。全年规模以上工业实现新产品产值1567.05亿元,增长18.8%。新产品产值率由上年的14.20%提高到16.73%。

工业效益

全市规模以上工业企业实现主营业务收入9026.32亿元,比上年增长0.6%;实现利税882.62亿元,比上年增长10.0%,其中利润510.97亿元,增长12.6%。工业产品产销衔接良好,全年规模以上工业产品产销率为98.6%。

建筑业

全年实现建筑业增加值285.98亿元,比上年增长15.3%。全市有总承包和专业承包资格的建筑企业1230家,完成建筑业产值2110.17亿元,比上年增长17.2%;房屋建筑施工面积19434万平方米,增长21.0%;房屋建筑竣工面积6610万平方米,增长14.0%。

六、固定资产投资和房地产开发

固定资产投资

全年完成全社会固定资产投资 2291.65 亿元，其中限额以上固定资产投资 2195.17 亿元，分别比上年增长 15.7%和 16.6%。在限额以上固定资产投资中，第一产业投资 3.13 亿元，比上年增长 1.7%；第二产业投资 611.55 亿元，增长 7.2%；第三产业投资 1580.49 亿元，增长 20.8%。

房地产业

2009 年全市完成房地产开发投资 704.68 亿元，比上年增长 14.5%。房屋施工面积 5121.49 万平方米，比上年增长 2.7%；竣工面积 763.95 万平方米，下降 25.9%。全年商品房销售面积 1441.18 万平方米，比上年增长 86.0%，其中住宅销售 1300.99 万平方米，增长 92.2%。市区公开销售经济适用房 7002 套，建筑面积 50.09 万平方米。

七、国内贸易

全年实现社会消费品零售总额 1804.93 亿元，比上年增长 14.4%。其中城市消费品零售额 1716.49 亿元，增长 14.4%；县以下农村消费品零售额 88.44 亿元，增长 13.6%。分行业看，批发零售贸易业零售额 1597.26 亿元，增长 14.5%；餐饮业零售额 203.28 亿元，增长 13.8%；其他行业零售额 4.39 亿元，增长 3.5%。

八、对外经济

对外贸易

受国际金融危机影响，全年完成外贸进出口总额 404.17 亿美元，比上年下降 15.9%。其中进口总额 132.37 亿美元，下降 8.4%；出口总额 271.8 亿美元，下降 19.1%。按出口贸易方式分，一般贸易 211.55 亿美元，下降 17.7%；加工贸易 59.03 亿美元，下降 23.8%。出口国别和地区中，对欧盟出口 76.71 亿美元，下降 17.3%；对美国出口 57.74 亿美元，下降 23.1%；对日本出口 24.82 亿美元，下降 11.0%。

对外合作

至 2009 年末，全市累计设立各类境外投资企业（机构）69 个，比上年增长 43.8%，其中非贸易企业 27 个。全年境外协议出资 1.53 亿美元，其中非贸易性投资 1.06 亿美元，比上年分别增长 15.4%和 14.0%。完成对外承包工程和劳务合作营业额 3.70 亿美元。

利用外资

全年批准外商直接投资 554 项，合同利用外资 69.65 亿美元，比上年增长 11.8%；实际到位外资 40.14 亿美元，增长 21.2%。全年总投资在 1000 万美元以上大项目 288 个，投资总额和合同外资分别占全市的 96.7%和 92.7%。至 2009 年末，共有 70 家世界 500 强企业来杭投资 117 个项目。

引进内资

全年共引进内资项目 5451 个，协议资金 1287.02 亿元，比上年增长 18.0%；到位资金 560.55 亿元，比上年增长 18.5%。

开发区建设

杭州经济技术开发区、杭州高新技术产业开发区、萧山经济技术开发区和杭州之江国家旅游度假区等4个国家级开发区全年合同引进外资24.93亿美元，实际利用外资15.45亿美元，分别占全市的35.8%和38.5%。全年实现技工贸总收入3282.83亿元，比上年下降8.3%，实现利税153.9亿元。

九、交通运输、邮电和旅游

交通运输

全市货物运输总量2.24亿吨，比上年下降0.8%；旅客运输量3.01亿人次，比上年增长3.5%。至年末，萧山国际机场已开通航线160条，其中国际航线25条，港、澳、台航线8条；全年民航旅客进出港达到1494.47万人次，比上年增长17.9%。道路建设快速发展。全年新增公路里程999千米，至年末，全市境内公路总里程达到14266千米，其中高速公路503.28千米。全市公路通村率为99.2%，行政村客运班车通达率由上年的97.5%提高到98.5%。机动车辆持续增长，年末全市社会机动车拥有量达157.89万辆，其中私人汽车71.87万辆，比上年末分别增长13.1%和27.2%。

邮电通讯

全市完成邮政业务总量12.80亿元，比上年增长17.1%。邮政特快专递辐射221个国家和地区，全年完成国内特快业务1167.81万件，比上年增长35.3%；国际特快业务46.28万件，比上年增长71.0%。完成电信业务收入126.17亿元，比上年增长8.5%。年末固定电话用户为390.38万户，移动电话用户为1011.93万户；计算机宽带用户达到162.40万户，比上年增长22.9%。

旅游业

全年接待入境旅游者230.40万人次，比上年增长4.1%；接待国内游客5093.72万人次，增长11.9%。旅游总收入达到803.12亿元，增长13.6%，其中旅游外汇收入13.8亿美元，增长6.5%。市民出境旅游人数为41.7万人次，比上年增长47.6%。旅游基础设施日趋完善。至年末，全市各类旅行社达427家；星级宾馆达到250家，其中五星级酒店16家；A级景区29个，其中5A景区1个，4A景区20个。

十、金融、证券和保险

金融

2009年末，全市金融机构本外币存款余额14284.21亿元，比上年末增长26.0%；贷款余额13113.3亿元，比上年末增长30.3%，其中个人消费贷款余额1967.88亿元，比上年末增长56.6%。

资本市场

2009年新增上市公司10家，共募集资金30.46亿元。至年末，全市上市公司累计64家，实现上市融资560.03亿元。

保险

全市保费收入159.7亿元,比上年增长9.2%;其中,财产险保费收入59.6亿元,增长24.2%,人身险保费收入100.1亿元,增长1.9%。共支付各类保险赔款49.9亿元,增长4.4%,其中财产险30.1亿元,增长3.6%,人身险19.8亿元,增长5.6%。

十一、教育和科技

教育

全市学前三年幼儿入园率为97.4%。年末共有小学417所,在校学生44.51万人;初中252所,在校学生24.19万人;普通高中75所,在校学生11.81万人。全市小学入学率和初中升学率均达到100%,初中毕业生升入各类高中比例由上年的98.7%提高到99.1%,其中优质高中招生比例由上年的76.6%上升到78.5%。普通高等院校36所,在校学生42.98万人,比上年增长4.9%,其中在校研究生3.57万人。高等教育毛入学率由上年的51.94%提高到53.58%。全市义务教育阶段接收进城务工人员子女17.46万人。全年义务教育免收杂费、课本费、作业本费3.61亿元。

科技

2009年全市专利申请量达到26077件,专利授权量15507件,分别比上年增长40.6%和57.7%。2009年新增国家重点扶持的高新技术企业302家,累计达到1236家;累计培育认定研发中心521家,其中省级182家;企业技术中心454家,其中国家级14家,省级132家。年内新增12个中国驰名商标,累计已达78个。

十二、文化、卫生和体育

文化

2009年全市获国家级、省级文艺、广播影视、动漫类奖131项。年末有各类专业艺术表演团体20个,公共图书馆16个,文化馆13个,博物馆、纪念馆62个,全国重点文物保护单位24处(群)。全市有线电视用户203.62万户,其中数字电视104.39万户。电视、广播综合覆盖率分别达到99.8%和99.83%。广播电视"村村通"实现全覆盖。成功举办第五届中国国际动漫节、第十一届西湖博览会等重大文化活动。蚕桑丝织技艺、西泠印社"篆刻"列入联合国教科文组织"人类非物质文化遗产代表作"名录。

卫生

2009年末,全市拥有各类医疗卫生机构2687个,其中医院144个;拥有床位4.02万张,其中医院床位3.31万张。有各类专业卫生技术人员5.63万人,其中执业(助理)医师2.28万人,注册护士2.10万人。农村卫生服务得到改善。农村自来水普及率由上年的99.48%提高到99.72%,自来水受益人数达437.07万人。参加新型农村合作医疗参合率为97.62%,乡镇覆盖率达100%。全市婴儿死亡率及5岁以下儿童死亡率分别由上年的4.43‰、6.2‰下降到3.81‰、5.1‰,每十万孕产妇死亡率由上年的7.77人下降为7.26人。

体育

2009年,杭州籍运动会员获第十一届全运会5金12银15铜奖牌。成功举办第十七届市运会、冲浪中国高峰论坛、国际冲浪嘉年华活动、世界汽车飘移大赛杭州站比赛、汽车“王中王”争霸赛等有影响力的大型赛事。群众体育活动深入开展。完成新建各类体育健身场所2088个。组织举办了市冬泳表演赛、传统武术锦标赛、市桥牌联赛、羽毛球俱乐部联赛、全国门球邀请赛、全国桥牌邀请赛等活动。

国民经济和社会发展存在的主要困难和薄弱环节是:受国际金融危机影响,工业、出口指标增长没有达到预期目标;经济回稳的基础尚不牢固,调整经济结构难度加大;城乡和区域发展不平衡状况尚未根本改变;经济发展质量有待提升,企业自主创新能力有待增强;民生保障和就业压力仍然较大。这些矛盾和问题需要采取更加有效的措施加以解决。

公报注释:

本公报中增加值为现价,增加值增长速度按可比价格计算。

Statistical Communiqué of Hangzhou on the 2009 National Economic and Social Development

Hangzhou Municipal Bureau of Statistics

Hangzhou Survey Office of National Bureau of Statistics

Hangzhou Socio－economic Investigation Bureau

February, 2010

In 2009, the year was the most difficult year of Hangzhou's economic development in the new century. Facing with the severe impact of the international financial crisis and the extremely complicated domestic and international situation, under the correct leadership of Hangzhou Municipal Party Committee of the Communist Party of China (CPC) and Hangzhou Municipal Government, guided by the scientific development concept, ensured growth fully, expanded domestic demand, adjusted the structure, increased vitality, emphasized people's livelihood and grasped stability, all works had achieved remarkable results, the economy recovered steadily, the social undertakings developed coordinately, the construction of modern industrial system had taken new steps, the construction of network metropolitan of the city speeded up, and the quality of life further improved.

I. General Outlook

Economic Aggregate

According to the preliminary statistics, the Gross Domestic Product (GDP) of Hangzhou was 508.755 billion yuan, up by 10.0% over the previous year at comparable price, which had maintained an annual economic growth rate of over 10% for consecutive 19 years. Of the total, the value－added of the primary industry was 19.051 billion yuan; that of the secondary industry was 238.712 billion yuan; and that of the tertiary industry was 250.992 billion yuan, up by 3.1%, 6.5% and 14.2% respectively. The proportion of the 3 Industries was adjusted from 3.8%, 49.5% and 46.7% of the previous year into 3.8%, 46.9% and 49.3% respectively. The GDP per capita calculated by permanent residents was 63,333 yuan and that by the people through household register was 74,761 yuan, up by 8.4% and 9.1% respectively. According to the average exchange rate published by the government in 2009, the GDP per capita calculated by permanent residents and that by the people through household register reached 9,271 US dollars and 10,944 US dollars respectively.

Figure 1: Gross Domestic Product and Its Growth, 2000－2009

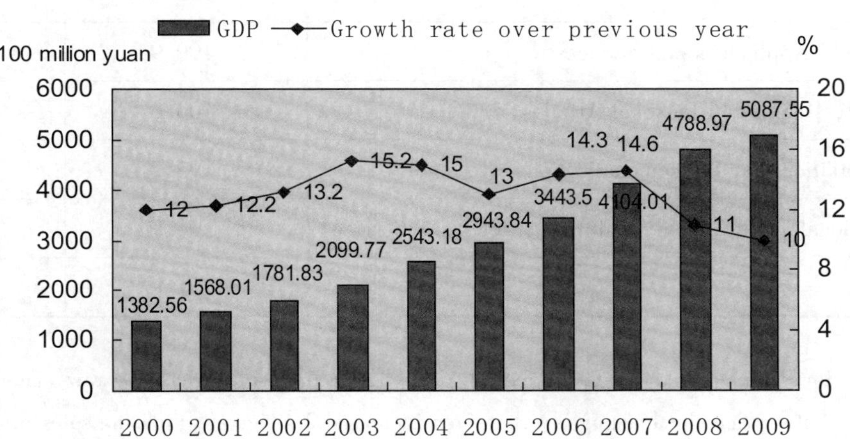

Non - state - owned Economic

According to the preliminary statistics, the non - state - owned economic accounted for 64.5% of the Hangzhou's GDP, in which the self - employed and private - owned economic was 52.5%. At the end of 2009, there were 140,900 private - owned enterprises, employing 1.3093 million laborers and 284,600 households of individual business, employing 597,800 laborers.

Fiscal Revenue and Expenditure

The general fiscal revenue of the city totaled 101.943 billion yuan, up by 12.0% over the previous year. Of the total, the general budgetary revenue of the local government was 52.079 billion yuan, up by 14.4%. In the tax income, the value - added tax amounted to 34.252 billion yuan, up by 12.1%; the business tax numbered 17.645 billion yuan, up by 22.8%; the enterprises' income tax was 18.681 billion yuan, down by 8.3%; the individual income tax reached 8.027 billion yuan, up by 17.8%. The fiscal expenditure of the local government was 49.04 billion yuan, up by 16.9%. Of which, the expenditure for education, science & technology numbered 10.835 billion yuan, up by 16.8%; the expenditure for the social security and employment amounted to 4.855 billion yuan, up by 20.4%; the expenditure for health and hygiene reached 3.236 billion yuan, up by 24.7%; the expenditure for the environment protection totaled 0.975 billion yuan, up by 30.3%. The expenditure of city level budget in people's livelihood totaled 8.993 billion yuan, up by 20.5%, the incremental expenditure accounted for 76.8% in additional financial resources.

Commodity Price

In 2009, the general level of consumer prices in urban area dropped 1.4% compared with the previous year. The prices of 8 major kinds of commodity and service items presented the layout of "5 Raising and 3 Dropping".

Table1 : Consumer Prices in 2008 and 2009 Unit: %

Item	2009	2008
The general level of consumer prices in urban area (the previous year = 100)	98.6	104.9
1. Food	101.7	114.6
2. Tobaccos and Alcohols	100.7	102.5
3. Clothing	100.6	98.6
4. Household Appliances and Services	100.9	105.0
5. Medical, Health and Personal Articles	100.6	105.3
6. Transportation and Telecommunications	95.2	94.7
7. Recreational, Educational, Cultural Articles and Services	96.9	99.4
8. Housing	91.8	102.4

The producer prices for manufactured goods dropped 4.9%. The purchasing prices for raw materials, fuels and power dropped 7.8%. The sales prices for housing in urban area increased 2.8%, of which the sales prices of new commercial building rose by 2.0% and that of second - hand housing went up by 4.6%. In December, housing sales price in urban district rose 11.5% over the same period the previous year.

Employment

In 2009, net increase of job positions reached 235,200 and a total of 155,600 unemployed people were re – employed, up by 17% and 23. 6% respectively over the previous year. The year – end registered rate of urban unemployment dropped from 3. 02% of the previous year to 2. 99%.

II. Population, Living Conditions and Social Security

Population

At the end of 2009, the total number of permanent residents in Hangzhou reached 8. 10 million, an increase of 134,000 in number over the end of the previous year. Of the total, that of population through household register numbered 6. 8338 million, an increase of 57,400 in number. In the registered people, the agriculture population amounted to 3. 289 million and the non – agriculture population reached 3. 5448 million. The data form the public security department show that the birth rate was 9. 18 per mill and the natural growth rate was 3. 42 per mill.

Living Conditions

According to the sampling survey, the disposable income per capita for urban residents was 26,864 yuan, up by 11. 5% over the previous year. The living expense per capita for urban residents was 18,595 yuan, up by 11. 2%. The Engle coefficient dropped from 38. 3% to 37. 5%. The usable floor space per capita for urban residents was 30. 85 square meters, increased 1. 02 square meters over the previous year. There were 21. 65 cars, 203. 87 air – conditions, 178. 5 mobile phones, 86. 87 PC, 74. 62 microwave ovens, 94. 95 water heaters per 100 urban households.

The net income per capita for rural residents in Hangzhou was 11,822 yuan, up by 10. 6% over the previous year. The living expense per capita for rural residents was 9,065 yuan, up by 7. 3%. The Engle coefficient dropped from 35. 9% to 33. 8%. The usable floor space per capita for rural residents was 70. 74 square meters, increased 1. 04 square meters over the previous year. By the end of 2009, there were 82 washing machines, 95. 0 refrigerators, 100 air – conditions, 81. 0 water heaters, 23. 0 microwave ovens, 194 mobile phones, 36 PC and 21. 65 cars per 100 rural households.

By the end of 2009, the balances of urban and rural residents′savings totaled 428. 692 billion yuan, up by 23. 3% over the end of the previous year.

Social Security

By the end of 2009, a total of 3. 4224 million people participated in the basic pension programs, a total of 2. 1568 million people participated in the unemployment insurance programs, a total of 2. 7415 million people participated in the work accident insurance programs, a total of 1. 9925 million people participated in the birth insurance programs, and a total of 2. 9831 million people participated in the basic health insurance programs, which increased 241,300, 132,700, 283,300, 175,700 and 237,200 persons compares with the end of the previous year respectively. The lowest salary standard in urban enterprises was 960 yuan / month. The unemployment insurance standard in urban adjusted was 768 yuan / month.

Social Welfare

By the end of the year, there are 208 welfare institutions and old people′s institutions of various kinds, providing 22,430 beds and accommodating for 13,600 inmates. A total of 17,510 urban residents and a total of 71,242 peasants benefited from the minimum living relief system. The centralized support rate for 5 kinds of rural perfected households and 3 kinds of urban non – working – ability residents reached 93. 99% and 99. 6% respectively. Carried out the ninth "Spring Action", a total of 40. 855 million yuan social funds raised.

III. Urban Construction, Environment Protection and Work Safety

Urban Infrastructure Construction

In 2009, the investment in construction of urban infrastructure reached 60. 184 billion yuan, up by 11. 2%. The 36 stations of metro of the first – stage and second – stage started, of which 20 completed the main part. The road comprehensive improvement project of "10 vertical and 10 horizontal" completed fully. The major transport projects started such as the Xiaoshan airport highway transformation, Qianjiang channel and southern connection (Qianjiang Boulevard), the extension of Hang – XIn – Jing expressway (Zhijiang Bridge), Qingchun Road river tunnel and Hang – Chang expressway. The Shen – Jia – Hu – Hang expressway had completed. The comprehensive protection of Zhongshan Road opened smoothly. The 47 river comprehensive protection projects completed fully. The construction of Qige 3 – stage sewage treatment plant completed and carried out water testing.

Public Utilities

A total of 4. 487 million kVA of 110 kV and above transformer capacity and 580,000 KVA of 35 KV completed, 262. 27 kilometers cables of 110 KV or above lines were increased. The power consumption in the city reached 45. 970 billion KWH, up by 6. 9% over the previous year. Of the total, the power consumption of urban and rural residents was 5. 64 billion KWH, up by 10. 1%. A total of 3. 20 million cubic meters of tap water was supplied in the urban area, increased 210,000 cubic meters over the previous year. By the end of the year, the number of households used pipeline coal – gas reached 518,400, up by 19. 0% compared with the end of the previous year. 15 new bus routes opened, 855 bus updated and the proportion of air – conditioned car in urban district public transport was over 93%. 9,704 new parking berths added, and totaled 60,129. By the end of the year, 2,150 free bicycle service networks were launched, and 50,000 public bikes delivered. Fuyang and Lin'an realized the integration of public transport with the main district of the city.

Environment protection

In 2009, the amount of the total emission of industrial chemical oxygen demand (COD) and that of the sulfur dioxide discharge was dropped 4. 1% and 3. 7% compared with the previous year respectively. 99. 48% of the sulfur dioxide discharge in the industrial emissions and 96. 21% of the industrial wastewater comprehensive discharge reached the standard respectively. The centralized disposal rate of city sewage rose from 83. 2% of the previous year to 88. 9%. The proportion of supervised break – face water quality above third level was rose from 57. 1% of the previous year to 60. 7%. The number of days which air quality in the urban area reached Ⅰ – level or above Ⅱ – level were 327, 26 days added over the previous year. An area of 1,395 hectares green belt was increased. By the end of the year, the green land area of urban gardens and parks per capita in the urban area reached 15. 48 square meters. The green coverage rate of built – up area was 39. 94%.

Work Safety

In 2009, the accident number, the death toll and the injuring toll and the direct economical loss of accidents decreased 16. 7%, 8. 7%, 17. 4% and 16. 1% compared with the previous year respectively. The death toll from work accidents every 100 million yuan worth of GDP was 0. 18 persons, a decline of 14. 3% compared with the previous year. The passed rate of food rapid detection in city's circulation area was 99%.

IV. Agriculture

The total output value of farming, forestry, animal husbandry and fishery achieved 28. 974 billion yuan, up by 5. 8% over the previous year. Of the total, the output value of planting sector was 14. 974 billion yuan, up by 6. 3% , that of forestry sector was 3. 623 billion yuan, up by 13. 1% , that of animal husbandry sector was 6. 329 billion yuan, up by 1. 0% and that of fishery sector was 3. 256 billion yuan, up by 5. 3%. The total output of grain in 2009 was 1. 0724 million tons, down by 2. 6% over the previous year; that of aquatic products was 0. 1965 million tons, up by 6. 4% ; that of meat products was 0. 3092 million tons, up by 4. 7% ; that of poultry egg products was 0. 1431 million tons, up by 8. 1% and that of fresh fruits amounted to 0. 7727 million tons, up by 6. 3%.

The " 6 Advantageous Industries" of tea, seedling plants, aquatic products, grains – saving livestock & poultry, vegetables and bamboos achieved an output value of 16. 160 billion yuan, up by 5. 0% over the previous year. The "5 Featured Industries" of fresh fruits, dried fruits, silkworm cocoons & mulberry, medicinal materials and honey achieved an output value of 3. 7. 18 billion yuan, up by 16. 7%. They accounted for 68. 6% of the total agricultural output value, increased 0. 7 percentage points over the previous year.

V. Industry and Construction

Industry Production

In 2009, the total Industrial added value was 210. 114 billion yuan, up by 5. 5% over the previous year at comparable price. The total sales value of the industrial enterprises was 1,072. 099 billion yuan, up by 0. 9%. Of which the total sales value of the industrial enterprises above designated size reached 926. 173 billion yuan, up by 0. 6%. In the industrial enterprises above designated size, the sales value of light industry numbered 394. 478 billion yuan, up by 4. 3% and that of heavy industry amounted to 531. 696 billion yuan, down by 2. 0%. The output value of new products achieved 156. 705 billion yuan, up by 18. 8 and the sales ratio of them rose from 14. 2% of the previous year to 16. 73% of this year.

Industrial Benefit

The sales income of the industrial enterprises above designated size achieved 902. 632 billion yuan, up by 0. 6% over the previous year and the amount of their profits & taxes were 88. 262 billion yuan, up by 10. 0%. Of the total, the profits numbered 51. 097 billion yuan, up by 12. 6%. The production and marketing situation was good and the sales rate of industrial enterprises above designated size reached 98. 6%.

Construction

The total value – added of the construction sector achieved 28. 598 billion yuan, up by 15. 3% over the previous year. The number of construction enterprises with the qualification of general contract and special contract was 1,230 and the annual construction value amounted to 211. 018 billion yuan, up by 17. 2%. The floor space under construction was 194. 34 million square meters, up by 21. 0% and the completed floor space was 66. 10 million square meters, up by 14. 0%.

VI. Investment in Fixed Assets and Investment in Real Estate

Investment in Fixed Assets

In 2009, the completed investment in fixed assets was 229. 165 billion yuan and of which, the super – scale investment in fixed assets was 219. 517 billion yuan, increased 15. 7% and 16. 6% over the previous year respectively. According to the direction of the investment in fixed assets, the investment in the primary industry was 0. 313 billion yuan, up by 1. 7%. The investment in the secondary industry was 61. 155 billion yuan, up by 7. 2%. The investment in the tertiary industry was 158. 049 billion yuan, up by 20. 8%.

Investment in Real Estate

In 2009, the development investment of real estate in the whole year totaled 70. 468 billion yuan, up by 14. 5% over the previous year. The total floor space of the commercial buildings under construction reached 51. 2149 million square meters, up by 2. 7% and that of completed commercial buildings amounted to 7. 6395 million square meters, down by 25. 9%. The floor space of the sold ones reached 14. 4118 million square meters, up by 86. 0% and of which the floor space of the sold commercial residential buildings stood at 13. 0099 million square meters, up by 92. 2%. The floor space of economic and suitable houses by publicly shaking to sale in urban was 7,002 houses with 0. 5009 million square meters.

VII. Domestic Trade

Total retail sales of the consumer goods in the whole city achieved 180. 493 billion yuan, up by 14. 4% over the previous year. Of the total, that of the urban area was 171. 649 billion yuan, up by 14. 4% and that of the rural area reached 8. 844 billion yuan, up by 13. 6%. In terms of the different sectors, the retail sales value of wholesale and retail sector was 159. 726 billion yuan, up by 14. 5%; that of the catering sector 20. 328 billion yuan, up by 13. 8% and that of other sector 0. 439 billion yuan, up by 3. 5%.

VIII. Foreign Economic

International Trade

Under the influence of the international financial crisis, the annual value of import and export totaled 40. 417 billion US dollars, down by 15. 9% over the previous year. Of the total, the total value of import reached 13. 237 billion US dollars, down by 8. 4% and that of export amounted to 27. 18 billion US dollars, down by 19. 1%. In term of trading type, the total value of general trading stood at 21. 155 billion yuan, down by 17. 7% and that of processing trading numbered 5. 903 billion yuan, down by 23. 8%. In term of exporting countries, the export value to EU was 7. 671 billion yuan, down by 17. 3%, that to USA was 5. 774 billion yuan, down by 23. 1% and that to Japan 2. 482 billion yuan, down by 11. 0%.

International Cooperation

By the end of 2009, the number of establishment enterprises (or institutions) by foreign investment accumulated 69, up by 43. 8%. Of which non – trading enterprises reached 27. The contractual value of the foreign investment reached 153 million US dollars and of which the value of non – trading investment was 106 million US dollars, up by 15. 4% and 14. 0% over the previous year respectively. The accomplished business revenue through contracted overseas engineering projects and overseas labor contracts amounted to 370 million US dollars.

Utilization of Foreign Capital

There were 554 new foreign direct – funded projects signed in the year. The contractual value of foreign investment totaled 6. 965 billion US dollars, up by 11. 8% over the previous year and the foreign investment actually utilized reached 4. 014 billion US dollars, up by 21. 2%. The projects of total investment over 10 million US dollars amounted to 288. The total investment value and the contractual value shared 96. 7% and 92. 7% of the whole – city investment. By the end of 2009, there were 117 projects built in Hangzhou funded by 70 companies of the World Top 500 Companies.

Utilization of Domestic Capital

There were 5,451 domestic investment projects in the year. The contractual value of the domestic investment was 128. 702 billion yuan, up by 18. 0% and the actually utilized investment was 56. 055 billion yuan, up by 18. 5%.

Development Zone Construction

In 2009, the contractual value of the foreign investment reached 2. 493 billion US dollars and the actually utilized investment was 1. 545 billion US dollars, accounted for 35. 8% and 38. 5% respectively in 4 state – level development zones, such as Hangzhou Economic and Technological Development Zone, Hangzhou High – Tech Development Zone, Xiaoshan Economic & Technological Development Zone and Hangzhou Zhijiang National Holiday Resort Zone. The total revenue of technology, industry and trade from the 4 development zones achieved 328. 283 billion yuan in the year, dwon by 8. 3% , taxes and profits 15. 39 billion yuan.

IX. Transportation, Post & Telecommunications and Tourism

Transportation

In 2009, the annual transported cargo totaled 22,400 million tons, down by 0. 8% over the previous year. The volume of passenger transportation in the whole year reached 30,100 million person – trips, up by 3. 5% over the previous year. By the end of the year, there were 160 flight routes built in the Xiaoshan International Airport, including 25 international routes and 8 routes of Hongkong, Macau and Taiwan. The volume of passenger transportation handled by civil aviation amounted to 14. 9447 million person – trips, up by 17. 9%. The construction of road sped up. The length of increased roads totaled 999 kilometers. By the end of 2009, the total length of level roads in Hangzhou reached 14,266 kilometers, including 503. 28 kilometers expressway. The rate of the roads through villages was 99. 2% and the communication rate of passenger buses to administrative villagers rose from 97. 5% of the previous year to 98. 5%. The motor vehicles of the city continued to increase drastically. The year – end amount of motor vehicles reached 1. 5789 million and of which the private cars were 718,700, up by 13. 1% and 27. 2% respectively.

Post & Telecommunications

The volume of post totaled 1. 093 billion yuan, up by 17. 1% over the previous year. The radiant network of EMS reached 221 countries and areas. During the year, 11. 6781 million copies of domestic EMS were completed and 462,800 copies of international EMS were delivered, up by 35. 3% and 71. 0% respectively. The revenue of telecommunications totaled 12. 617 billion yuan, up by 8. 5%. By the end of 2009, local telephone users numbered 3. 9038 million and there were 10. 1193 million mobile phone users. The registered users in international internet amounted to 1. 624 million, up by 22. 9%.

Tourism

In 2009, the number of oversea visitors to Hangzhou totaled 2. 304 million person – trips, up by 4. 1% over the previous year and the domestic tourists to Hangzhou reached 50. 9372 million person – trips, up by 11. 9%. The income from tourism totaled 80. 312 billion yuan, up by 13. 6%. Of which the tourism foreign exchange earnings was 1. 380 billion US dollars, up by 6. 5%. The number of Hangzhou visitors went abroad was 417,000 person – trips, up by 47. 6%. The tourist infrastructure facilities had been further perfected. By the end of the year, there were 427 travel agencies of various kinds in the city, and the number of star – level hotels reached 250, including 16 5 – star hotels. There were 29 Sceneries above A – level in urban and of which, 1 scenery was AAAAA – level and 20 Sceneries was AAAA – level.

X. Banking, Securities and Insurance

Banking

By the end of 2009, the saving deposits of RMB and foreign exchange from all financial institutions in Hangzhou amounted to 1,428. 421 billion yuan, up by 26. 0% compared with the end of the previous year and loans of RMB and foreign exchange from all financial institutions stood at 1311. 33 billion yuan, up by 30. 3%. Of which, the loads for individual consumption reached 196. 788 billion yuan, up by 56. 6%.

Capital Marketing

In 2009, there were 10 increased listed companies than those in the end of the previous year in Hangzhou, raising 3. 046 billion yuan. By the end of the year, the number of listed companies in Hangzhou accumulated 64 and money raised through stock markets totaled 56. 003 billion yuan.

Insurance

In 2009, the premiums of insurance companies in the city gained 15. 97 billion yuan, up by 9. 2% over the previous year. Of the total, the property insurance premiums were 5. 96 billion yuan, up by 24. 2% and the life insurance premiums were 10. 01 billion yuan, up by 1. 9%. The insurance companies paid an indemnity worth of 4. 99 billion yuan, up by 4. 4%. Of which, the indemnity for the property insurance was 3. 01 billion yuan, up by 3. 6%, and that for the life insurance was 1. 98 billion yuan, up by 5. 6%.

XI. Education, Science and Technology

Education

In 2009, the enrollment rate of the kindergartens for the children 3 years before school age reached 97. 4%. By the end of the year, the number of elementary schools totaled 417 in the city with 445,100 students, 252 junior middle schools with 241,900 students as well as 75 senior secondary schools with 118,100 students. The students from junior middle schools enrolled into senior secondary schools of various sorts rose from 98. 7% of the previous year to 99. 1% and of which, the enrollment proportion of excellent senior secondary schools rose from 76. 6% of the previous year to 78. 5%. There were 36 general colleges and universities with 429,800 students, up by 4. 9% and included 35,700 graduate students. The gross enrollment rate of general colleges and universities rose from 51. 94% of the previous year to 53. 58%. The whole city received 174, 600 children of non – local workers in the compulsory education. The exempted fee of incidental expenses, textbook expenses and homework – book expenses by the compulsory education stood at 361 million yuan.

Science and Technology

In 2009, a total of 26,077 patent applications were submitted and 15,507 patents were authorized, up by 40. 6% and 57. 7% over the previous year respectively. There were 302 new enterprises authorized as national support high – tech enterprises, added up to 1,236. The cultivated and authorized R&D centers reached 521, including 182 province – level centers. Enterprise technology centers reached 454, including 14 state – level and 132 province – level. 12 well – known trademarks in China increased, and reached a total of 78.

XII. Culture, Public Health and Sports

Culture

In 2009, Hangzhou won 131 awards of state – level, provincial arts, radio and television, Cartoon. By the end of the year, there were 19 performing art ensembles, 16 public libraries, 13 cultural stations, 62 museums & memorial halls and 24 state – level protection units of key cultural relics. A number of 2. 0362 million households had used cable television services and of which the number of using digital television was 1. 0439 households. The coverage rate of TV and that of Broadcasting all reached 99. 8% and 99. 83% respectively. The coverage rate of the rural broadcasting and television project of "Extending Radio and TV Coverage to Every Village" reached 100%. A series of important cultural activities were successfully held, such as the 5th China International Animation Festival, the 11th China Hangzhou West Lake Expo and so on. Sericulture and silk weaving techniques and Xiling " Seal" were listed " intangible cultural heritage of mankind" in the UNESCO.

Public Health

By the end of 2009, there were altogether 2,687 medical treatment institutions of various kinds, including 144 hospitals and a total of 40,200 beds, including 33,100 hospital beds. There were 56,300 health workers in the city, including 22,800 licensed doctors and 21,000 registered nurses. The condition of health care in rural area was improved. The popularization rate of tap water in the rural area rose from 99.48% of the previous year to 99.72%, supplying 4.3707 million benefited people. A total of 3.6918 million peasants participated n. The participating rate of ew – type rural medical cooperative service was 97.62% and the township coverage rate reached 100%. The mortality rate of newborns and that of children below 5 year age dropped from 4.43‰ and 6.2‰ of the previous year to 3.81‰ and 5.1‰. The death rate per 100,000 pregnant women dropped from 7.77 persons of the previous year to 7.26 persons.

Sports

In 2009, Hangzhou membership athletes won 5 gold, 12 silver and 15 bronze medals in the Eleventh National Sports Games. The 17th City Sports Games, Surfing Forum in China, International Surf Carnival, Hangzhou World Championship Race Car Drift, Car " King of King" Competition and other influential big events held successfully. Mass Sports went depth, and all types of 2088 new fitness centers completed. Winter swimming exhibition, Traditional Wushu Championships, City Bridge League, Badminton Club League, National Invitational Croquet Tournament and National Bridge Tournament and other activities organized.

The major difficulties and problems in economic and social development as follows: under the influence of international financial crisis, the growth of industry and export did not meet the expectations; the basis of the economic recovery was not strong and the adjustment of the economic structure was more difficult; urban and rural development imbalance had not fundamentally changed; the quality of economic development should be improved and the Independent innovation capability should be enhanced; livelihood security and employment pressure were still large. These contradictions and problems should take more effective measures to solve.

Notes:

Gross domestic product (GDP) and value – added as quoted in this Communiqué are calculated at current prices, whereas their growth rates are at comparable prices.

第一篇
CHAPTER-1

综合
GENERAL SURVEY

综　　合
General Survey

主要统计指标
Major Statistical Indicators

全市生产总值	Gross Domestic Product	5087.55	亿元	(100 million yuan)
为上年	As Compared with the Preceding Year	110.0	%	(%)
第一产业	Primary Industry	190.51	亿元	(100 million yuan)
为上年	As Compared with the Preceding Year	103.1	%	(%)
第二产业	Secondary Industry	2387.12	亿元	(100 million yuan)
为上年	As Compared with the Preceding Year	106.5	%	(%)
#工业	Industry	2101.14	亿元	(100 million yuan)
为上年	As Compared with the Preceding Year	105.5	%	(%)
第三产业	Tertiary Industry	2509.92	亿元	(100 million yuan)
为上年	As Compared with the Preceding Year	114.2	%	(%)
全市户籍人均生产总值	Per Capita GDP	74761	元	(yuan)
为上年	As Compared with the Preceding Year	109.1	%	(%)
2009 年生产总值构成	Composition of Gross Domestic Product	100	%	(%)
第一产业	Primary Industry	3.8	%	(%)
第二产业	Secondary Industry	46.9	%	(%)
#工业	Industry	41.3	%	(%)
第三产业	Tertiary Industry	49.3	%	(%)

1-01 行政区划(2009年末)

Division of Administrative(End of 2009)

单位:个 (unit)

地区	Region	乡镇 Towns and Townships	#镇 Towns	街道 Subdistrict Offices	村、居委会 Villages and Neighborhood Committees	#村 Villages
全市	**Whole Municipality**	**130**	**99**	**70**	**3003**	**2093**
市区	Urban District	40	39	57	1479	690
上城区	Shangcheng	–	–	6	52	–
下城区	Xiacheng	–	–	8	71	–
江干区	Jianggan	4	4	6	146	14
拱墅区	Gongshu	2	2	8	92	–
西湖区	Xihu	2	2	10	192	61
高新(滨江)区	Hi-Tech(Binjiang)	–	–	3	43	15
萧山区	Xiaoshan	17	17	11	562	411
余杭区	Yuhang	15	14	5	321	189
桐庐县	Tonglu	11	7	2	201	183
淳安县	Chun'an	23	11	–	436	425
建德市	Jiande	13	12	3	273	232
富阳市	Fuyang	21	15	4	302	276
临安市	Lin'an	22	15	4	312	287

1－02　土地面积和人口密度(2009年末)

Land Area and Population Density(End of 2009)

地　区	Region	土地面积(平方公里) Land Area (sq. km)	年末总人口(万人) Population (10000 persons)	人口密度(人/平方公里) Population Density (person/sq. km)
全　市	**Whole Municipality**	**16596**	**683.38**	**412**
市　区	Urban District	3068	429.44	1400
上城区	Shangcheng	18	32.52	18067
下城区	Xiacheng	31	39.84	12852
江干区	Jianggan	210	44.28	2109
拱墅区	Gongshu	88	30.74	3494
西湖区	Xihu	263	61.78	2349
高新(滨江)区	Hi－Tech(Binjiang)	73	14.47	1982
萧山区	Xiaoshan	1163	120.99	1040
余杭区	Yuhang	1222	84.84	694
桐庐县	Tonglu	1780	40.07	225
淳安县	Chun'an	4452	45.27	102
建德市	Jiande	2364	51.34	217
富阳市	Fuyang	1808	64.67	358
临安市	Lin'an	3124	52.59	168

1-03 平均每天主要社会经济活动

Selected Indicators on Average Daily Social and Economic Activities

指 标 Item	1995	2000	2005	2006	2007	2008	2009
全市生产总值 (万元) Gross Domestic Product (10000 yuan)	20877	37878	80621	94288	112333	130991	139385
工业增加值 (万元) Value - Added of Industry (10000 yuan)	10023	16670	36427	42715	50752	58630	57565
规模以上工业企业利税总额 (万元) Total Pre - tax Profits of Industrial Enterprises above Designated Size (10000 yuan)	1728	4428	12347	15432	20010	21976	24181
农林牧渔业总产值(现价) (万元) Gross Output Value of Farming, Forestry, Animal Husbandry and Fishery (Current Price) (10000 yuan)	2730	4182	6013	6175	6771	7500	7938
全社会固定资产投资 (万元) Total Investment in Fixed Assets (10000 yuan)	6365	14123	37991	40015	46138	54260	62785
住宅竣工面积 (平方米) Floor Space of Residential Buildings Completed (sq. m)	8751	11501	19327	15876	21153	24472	15949
社会消费品零售总额 (万元) Total Retail Sales of Consumer Goods (10000 yuan)	8201	14101	26724	30476	35515	42695	49450
城乡居民储蓄新增额 (万元) The Increased Amount of Residents´Savings Deposits (10000 yuan)	2819	1223	9767	9961	2181	23062	22195
财政收入合计 (万元) Total Financial Revenue (10000 yuan)	1510	3914	14268	17109	21601	24947	27930

注:本表按当年价计算。2003 年起城乡居民储蓄新增额为本外币合并数据。

a) Figures in value terms in this table are calculated at current prices. The increased amount of residents´savings deposits include both RMB and foreign currencies.

1-04 国民经济
Major Indicators of

指　　标		Item	
年末常住人口	(万人)	Long - term Residents(End of 2009)	(10000 persons)
年末户籍人口	(万人)	Honsehold Registration Population(End of 2009)	(10000 persons)
#非农业人口	(万人)	Non - agriculture Population	(10000 persons)
年末从业人员数	(万人)	Total Number of Employed Persons(End of 2009)	(10000 persons)
全市生产总值	(亿元)	Gross Domestic Product	(100 million yuan)
第一产业	(亿元)	Primary Industry	(100 million yuan)
第二产业	(亿元)	Secondary Industry	(100 million yuan)
第三产业	(亿元)	Tertiary Industry	(100 million yuan)
人均生产总值(户籍)	(元)	Per Capita GDP(Household)	(yuan)
主要农产品产量		Output of Major Farm Products	
粮食	(万吨)	Grain	(10000 tons)
棉花	(吨)	Cotton	(ton)
油菜籽	(吨)	Rapeseeds	(ton)
茶叶	(吨)	Tea	(ton)
蚕茧	(吨)	Silk - worm Cocoons	(ton)
猪年末存栏	(万头)	Hogs in Stock at Year End	(10000 heads)
肉类产量	(万吨)	Output of Meat	(10000 tons)
淡水产品产量	(吨)	Freshwater Aquatic Products	(ton)
规模以上工业总产值	(亿元)	The Output Valne of Industrial Enterprises Above Designated Size	(100 million yuan)
规模以上工业企业利税总额	(亿元)	Total Pre - tax Profits of Industrial Enterprises Above Designated Size	(100 million yuan)
全社会交通运输客运量	(万人次)	Total Passenger Traffic	(10000 person - times)
全社会交通运输货运量	(万吨)	Total Freight Traffic	(10000 tons)
限额以上固定资产投资	(亿元)	Total Investment in Fixed Assets Above Designated Size	(100 million yuan)
社会消费品零售总额	(亿元)	Total Retail Sales of Consumer Goods	(100 million yuan)

注:1. 交通运输客货运输量 1990 年起为全社会数,1990 年以前为交通系统数。
2. 境外旅游者人数 1995 年开始为全市数,1994 年及以前系市区数。
3. 规模以上工业的计算口径,从 1997 年开始改为全部国有和年销售收入 500 万元及以上的非国有企业数,1996 年以前系乡及乡以上数。

主要指标
National Economy

1980	1985	1990	1995	2000	2001	2002	2003	2004	2005	2006	2007	2008	2009
-	-	583.21	-	687.80	-	-	-	-	750.70	773.10	786.20	796.60	810.00
515.53	543.05	574.78	597.96	621.58	629.14	636.81	642.78	651.68	660.45	666.31	672.35	677.64	683.38
128.88	153.46	169	191.43	226.99	237.77	252.02	263.67	282.58	297.54	309.78	323.75	340.76	354.48
293.98	330.37	363.49	422.55	408.11	413.18	441.14	450.59	455.52	481.1	512.21	533.09	569.16	597.47
40.65	90.49	189.62	762.01	1382.56	1568.01	1781.83	2099.77	2543.18	2943.84	3443.50	4104.01	4788.97	5087.55
8.15	15.97	30.94	69.25	103.96	111.46	114.64	126.59	132.23	148.21	154.86	163.47	179.83	190.51
25.36	52.08	96.17	410	709.32	793.58	901.82	1075.78	1318.23	1494.36	1728.39	2045.88	2372.58	2387.12
7.14	22.44	62.51	282.76	569.28	662.98	765.37	897.4	1092.72	1301.27	1560.25	1894.66	2236.56	2509.92
791	1675	3310	12797	22342	25074	28150	32819	39293	44871	51908	61315	70948	74761
151.74	180	189.56	174.5	153.08	134.78	116.58	100.27	106.8	103.5	107.07	106.93	110.16	107.24
8007	6704	6693	8038	2112	1960	1280	1181	1184	1038	935	912	957	959
46621	51849	60683	61446	80436	78270	62433	61153	65514	70733	67395	69501	78058	80081
18880	22742	26429	19824	24810	24732	25423	24975	25009	25551	26939	28207	29623	30204
6165	7980	11085	13240	9308	10772	11997	12803	14744	16339	18384	20389	18987	17870
190.16	166.1	159	147.58	172.16	179.14	172.49	165.81	164.87	165.28	152.47	151.94	170.43	178.61
9.53	11.16	14.93	19.21	25.24	27.64	29.71	30.06	29.88	30.74	29.25	26.68	29.52	30.92
14080	30400	47588	63294	91626	115087	120613	130174	139540	147800	157300	175944	182098	196520
61.79	128.59	292.26	1020.03	1543.57	1919.51	2400.30	3202.52	4486.58	5441.13	6975.46	8351.4	9379.58	9390.73
13.6	24.81	31.54	63.05	161.61	208.54	274.98	359.54	427.23	450.68	576.51	730.5	802.13	882.62
3905	6724	8119	16620	18607	20342	21089	21348	22833	24124	25810	28026	29084	30116
2070	2488	6522	10347	11459	12443	14347	16815	18895	19909	20924	22569	22550	22372
4.58	14.19	22.92	156.63	376.65	463.49	562.34	895.21	1108.2	1277.8	1373.45	1583.78	1882.29	2195.17
20.54	47.81	98.17	299.35	514.68	579.01	660.65	742.58	855.45	978.43	1119.19	1308.29	1577.59	1804.93

a) Since 1990 the data on passenger traffic and freight traffic included non – transportation system, while data for previous years only included transportation system.

b) Since 1995 the data on foreign tourists included whole municipality, while data for previous years only included urban district.

c) The data on pre – tax profits of industrial enterprises included all state – owned enterprises and non – state – owned industrial enterprises with annual sales income of over 5 million yuan, before 1997, refer to enterprises at township and above level.

1－04　续表

指　　标		Item	
境外旅游者人数	（万人次）	Number of Foreign Tourists	(10000 person－times)
财政总收入	（亿元）	Total Financial Revenue	(100 million yuan)
财政支出合计（预算内）	（亿元）	Total Financial Expenditure	(100 million yuan)
金融机构存款余额	（亿元）	Deposits of Financial Institutions	(100 million yuan)
金融机构贷款余额	（亿元）	Loans of Financial Institutions	(100 million yuan)
城乡居民储蓄余额	（亿元）	Residents´Savings Deposit	(100 million yuan)
城镇以上单位在岗职工工资总额	（亿元）	Total Wages of Fully Employed Staff and Workers in Urban Units	(100 million yuan)
城镇以上单位在岗职工平均工资	（元）	Average Wage of Fully Employed Staff and Workers in Urban Units	(yuan)
市区居民消费价格指数	（以1978年为100）	Consumer Price Index in Urban District	(Year of 1978＝100)
市区商品零售价格指数	（以1978年为100）	Retail Price Index in Urban District	(Year of 1978＝100)
市区居民年人均可支配收入	（元）	Per Capita Annual Disposable Income in Urban District	(yuan)
农村居民年人均纯收入	（元）	Per Capita Annual Net Income in Rural Areas	(yuan)
高等学校在校学生数	（人）	Student Enrollment in Institutions of Higher Education	(person)
中等专业学校在校学生数	（人）	Student Enrollment in Secondary Specialized Schools	(person)
普通中学在校学生数	（人）	Student Enrollment in Secondary Schools	(person)
小学在校学生数	（人）	Student Enrollment in Primary Schools	(person)
卫生机构数	（个）	Number of Health Institutions	(unit)
#医院	（个）	Number of Hospitals	(unit)
卫生技术人员	（人）	Number of Medical Technical Personnel	(person)
#执业（助理）医师	（人）	Number of Certified Doctors(Include Assistant Doctors)	(person)
床位数	（张）	Number of Beds in Health Institutions	(unit)
#医院	（张）	Beds in Hospital	(unit)

注:2002年起医院数据不包括卫生院。

continued

1980	1985	1990	1995	2000	2001	2002	2003	2004	2005	2006	2007	2008	2009
12.5	23.84	38.83	44.13	70.71	81.94	105.63	86.12	123.41	151.36	182.02	208.60	221.33	230.40
11.85	18.65	25.25	55.13	142.85	188.46	257.14	329.71	395.75	520.79	624.49	788.42	910.55	1019.43
2.17	5.77	11.82	24.91	73.43	104.93	141.02	163.59	195.63	238.33	275.48	335.72	419.67	490.40
18.1	48.5	133.77	707.97	2088.47	2621.51	3373.15	4652.73	5707.2	6748.72	7855.55	9310.96	11333.35	14284.21
17.34	58.01	162.27	567.2	1686.64	2087.7	2752.38	3818.7	4800.04	5545.3	6603.86	8430.68	10069.05	13113.30
4.04	15.96	69.75	342.34	788.56	941.84	1183.4	1589.96	1835.17	2191.66	2555.24	2634.83	3476.59	4286.92
6.79	13.01	27.79	89.05	126.75	148.17	161.47	186.78	218.82	297.02	381.17	495.48	641.64	754.91
777	1266	2382	7156	14257	18319	21418	24668	28891	31069	32791	36496	40193	43947
109.24	140.21	246.68	503.06	611.07	608.01	600.71	597.71	612.65	623.07	630.55	652.62	684.60	675.00
110.28	142.61	256.45	476.99	504.42	480.71	470.62	461.68	469.07	470.47	471.41	486.02	515.18	507.97
521	1026	1985	6301	9668	10896	11778	12898	14565	16601	19027	21689	24104	26864
250	624	1171	3012	4894	5330	5708	6250	6950	7655	8515	9549	10692	11822
23545	36996	39866	63124	122386	174894	224048	269798	313599	351918	373563	392770	409559	429774
9453	16527	23564	42784	45238	32763	26255	21735	21262	20344	12540	8927	5514	4016
247734	244399	199940	257071	342533	364835	374586	376940	367594	362257	359704	361191	364758	359956
560244	414839	460514	513988	485679	467982	456535	448969	447971	458942	459529	456152	452143	445132
1381	1582	1738	1712	1599	1496	1817	1901	1985	2196	2570	2607	2544	2687
425	404	440	414	396	391	116	99	114	127	134	138	141	144
21110	25593	30990	34245	35487	36643	37193	39019	39816	42353	45375	49780	52379	56270
8311	11503	14483	16465	16317	16994	16092	16614	16770	17833	18831	20701	21223	22753
16317	19637	24121	26684	27166	27063	27609	29144	31738	33251	33972	36928	38114	40226
13478	15010	18879	21360	23303	23520	22797	22036	24444	25907	27186	29987	31416	33094

a) From 2002, figures of hospitals exclude health centers.

1－05　主要年份全市生产总值及发展指数(1978 年＝100)

Gross Domestic Product and its Indices in Main Years(Year of 1978＝100)

单位:万元　　(10000 yuan)

年份 Year	全市生产总值(当年价格) Gross Domestic Product (Current Price)	第一产业 Primary Industry	第二产业 Secondary Industry	第三产业 Tertiary Industry	人均生产总值(元)(按户籍) Per Capita GDP (yuan)	全市生产总值指数(%) Indices of Gross Domestic product(%) (1978＝100)	第一产业 Primary Industry	第二产业 Secondary Industry	第三产业 Tertiary Industry
1978	284046	63372	169344	51330	565	100.00	100.00	100.00	100.00
1979	335285	83852	194132	57301	659	113.33	114.23	114.00	110.01
1980	406508	81524	253545	71439	791	135.65	105.63	151.06	130.71
1981	468206	90955	287632	89619	904	154.04	108.74	172.17	162.30
1982	501854	108769	294725	98360	957	165.12	129.80	177.73	176.31
1983	558947	101106	334413	123428	1054	183.63	115.62	203.10	219.86
1984	694690	126443	405535	162712	1298	225.25	140.10	245.38	283.68
1985	904897	159684	520853	224360	1675	268.85	139.90	300.80	352.81
1986	1053589	177589	601277	274723	1917	299.88	145.01	335.28	409.85
1987	1260162	204366	718892	336904	2276	338.38	148.69	382.23	471.62
1988	1525427	256838	855305	413284	2717	363.26	145.46	419.82	497.15
1989	1662945	282746	896736	483463	2928	352.06	145.10	396.51	508.97
1990	1896216	309404	961673	625139	3310	372.37	154.40	422.20	528.01
1991	2279545	334024	1131088	814433	3952	439.77	161.12	492.38	669.52
1992	2900690	349033	1487838	1063819	4996	540.48	161.61	637.53	814.80
1993	4247094	419364	2264440	1563290	7263	703.16	171.15	878.66	1004.65
1994	5855239	575131	3143430	2136678	9924	888.09	185.01	1161.59	1225.67
1995	7620055	692510	4100008	2827537	12797	1064.82	198.15	1434.56	1445.06
1996	9066133	839985	4776225	3449923	15095	1203.25	208.85	1644.01	1621.36
1997	10363299	913611	5415017	4034671	17113	1360.88	223.05	1852.80	1861.32
1998	11348899	960558	5879589	4508752	18611	1513.30	244.02	2071.43	2060.48
1999	12252795	975821	6307510	4969464	19961	1667.66	257.44	2280.64	2287.13
2000	13825616	1039641	7093233	5692742	22342	1867.78	272.11	2565.72	2563.87
2001	15680138	1114569	7935809	6629760	25074	2095.65	292.25	2891.60	2884.40
2002	17818302	1146388	9018225	7653689	28150	2372.28	304.23	3276.18	3308.41
2003	20997744	1265890	10757812	8974042	32819	2732.87	322.48	3885.55	3725.27
2004	25431796	1322341	13182254	10927201	39293	3142.80	338.93	4534.44	4257.98
2005	29438430	1482145	14943581	13012704	44871	3551.36	350.45	5037.76	4956.29
2006	34434972	1548594	17283905	15602473	51908	4059.54	364.71	5672.80	5820.31
2007	41040117	1634719	20458811	18946588	61315	4651.74	372.78	6483.45	6761.14
2008	47889748	1798300	23725807	22365641	70948	5165.17	386.73	7062.80	7705.13
2009	50875529	1905093	23871200	25099237	74761	5680.15	398.74	7521.81	8799.61

注:1. 2008 年为经济普查正式数。

2. 2005－2007 已按经济普查数调整。

a) The data of 2008 were numbers of 2008 economic cencus.

b) The data of 2005 to 2008 had been adjusted auording to 2008 economic cencus.

1－06 主要年份市区生产总值及发展指数(1978 年＝100)

Gross Domestic Product and its Indices of Urban District in Main Years(Year of 1978＝100)

单位:万元 (10000 yuan)

年 份 Year	生产总值(当年价格) Gross Domestic Product (Current Price)	第一产业 Primary Industry	第二产业 Secondary Industry	第三产业 Tertiary Industry	人均生产总值(元)(按户籍) Per Capita GDP (yuan)	生产总值指数(%) Indices of Gross Domestic product(%) (1978＝100)	第一产业 Primary Industry	第二产业 Secondary Industry	第三产业 Tertiary Industry
1978	141995	5215	106663	30117	1389	100.00	100.00	100.00	100.00
1979	167206	6527	126517	34162	1555	116.40	109.40	118.10	111.60
1980	208220	5943	159161	43116	1863	145.30	94.00	150.90	133.90
1981	229243	6165	171946	51132	2005	159.90	90.30	163.90	157.20
1982	248297	7327	183284	57686	2125	173.70	107.30	176.00	175.60
1983	282171	5938	200334	75899	2369	197.90	83.10	193.80	229.50
1984	353781	8469	244445	100867	2919	245.40	114.90	235.50	298.40
1985	448574	11233	293579	143762	3633	289.90	120.70	270.10	382.20
1986	513639	12245	324585	176809	4042	317.30	122.60	287.70	445.10
1987	605234	15408	370668	219158	4724	353.20	137.10	313.80	517.40
1988	708474	19602	425319	263553	5441	370.80	136.00	332.70	534.00
1989	772208	23869	435847	312492	5848	347.00	146.70	296.70	545.20
1990	896496	23919	470844	401733	6722	366.50	147.60	314.60	573.60
1991	1096628	25767	547949	522912	8158	426.00	151.40	356.30	691.10
1992	1413278	27611	712697	672969	10420	535.30	153.10	447.40	877.80
1993	2086571	36208	1052187	998176	151196	687.60	157.70	583.70	1117.40
1994	2788314	48257	1395127	1344931	19945	870.90	172.30	779.60	1335.30
1995	3697794	57784	1866784	1773226	25969	10041.70	183.50	945.70	1574.30
1996	4727377	110881	2356408	2260088	28552	1194.90	194.70	1103.60	1769.50
1997	5414265	130062	2630349	2653853	32227	1354.90	214.20	1230.30	2052.60
1998	5905726	134320	2786159	2985247	34620	1482.50	230.70	1337.20	2266.10
1999	6317335	145242	2915614	3256479	36394	1599.30	254.50	1431.10	2467.80
2000	7111586	145715	3278310	3687561	40127	1785.50	255.50	1596.70	2763.90
2001	12260891	582492	6026353	5652046	32607	2017.20	275.70	1805.30	3126.00
2002	14042278	605433	6901224	6535621	36640	2300.80	290.00	2038.60	3607.40
2003	16647332	665083	8343138	7639111	42675	2664.80	302.20	2448.40	4058.30
2004	20362738	664676	10368453	9329609	51241	3077.40	313.10	2873.90	4630.50
2005	23495459	732463	11582930	11180067	57934	3461.24	318.17	3141.49	5406.57
2006	27483121	755663	13254773	13472684	66731	3955.94	320.48	3493.88	6399.62
2007	32738842	773208	15546960	16418675	78541	4525.33	322.73	3948.39	7455.84
2008	38139834	830741	17926048	19383045	90400	5018.47	324.83	4266.45	8505.21
2009	40698687	874987	18120921	21702778	95342	5539.47	332.99	4563.27	9686.26

注:1. 2008 年为经济普查正式数。
2. 2005－2007 已按经济普查数调整。
3. 从 2001 年起市区数据包括萧山区和余杭区。
a) The data of 2008 were numbers of 2008 economic cencus.
b) The data of 2005 to 2008 had been adjusted auording to 2008 economic cencus.
c) Data in this table include Xiaoshan and Yuhang district since 2001.

1-07 主要年份全市生产总值指数(上年=100)

Indices of Gross Domestic Product in Main Years(Preceding Year=100)

年 份 Year	生产总值 Gross Domestic Product	第一产业 Primary Industry	第二产业 Secondary Industry	第三产业 Tertiary Industry	人均生产总值(按户籍) Per Capita GDP (Household)
1978	120.2	119.1	123.7	111.6	119.0
1979	113.3	114.2	114.0	110.0	112.1
1980	119.7	92.5	132.5	118.8	118.4
1981	113.6	102.9	114.0	124.2	112.6
1982	107.2	119.4	103.2	108.6	105.9
1983	111.2	89.1	114.3	124.7	109.9
1984	122.7	121.2	120.8	129.0	121.6
1985	119.4	99.9	122.6	124.4	118.2
1986	111.5	103.7	111.5	116.2	110.3
1987	112.8	102.5	114.0	115.1	111.3
1988	107.4	97.8	109.8	105.4	105.8
1989	96.9	99.8	94.4	102.4	95.8
1990	105.8	106.4	106.5	103.7	104.9
1991	118.1	104.4	116.6	126.8	117.3
1992	122.9	100.3	129.5	121.7	122.1
1993	130.1	105.9	137.8	123.3	129.1
1994	126.3	108.1	132.2	122.0	125.2
1995	119.9	107.1	123.5	117.9	118.8
1996	113.0	105.4	114.6	112.2	112.0
1997	113.1	106.8	112.7	114.8	112.1
1998	111.2	109.4	111.8	110.7	110.5
1999	110.2	105.5	110.1	111.0	109.4
2000	112.0	105.7	112.5	112.1	111.1
2001	112.2	107.4	112.7	112.5	111.1
2002	113.2	104.1	113.3	114.7	111.8
2003	115.2	106.0	118.6	112.6	114.0
2004	115.0	105.1	116.7	114.3	113.7
2005	113.0	103.4	111.1	116.4	111.5
2006	114.3	104.1	112.6	117.4	113.0
2007	114.6	102.2	114.3	116.2	113.6
2008	111.0	103.7	108.9	114.0	110.1
2009	110.0	103.1	106.5	114.2	109.1

注:1. 本表按可比价格计算。

2. 2005-2008 已按经济普查数调整。

a) The indices in this table are calculated at comparable prices.

b) The data of 2005 to 2008 had been adjusted auording to 2008 economic cencus.

1-08 主要年份市区生产总值指数(上年=100)

Indices of Gross Domestic Product of Urban District in Main Years(Preceding Year=100)

年份 Year	生产总值 Gross Domestic Product	第一产业 Primary Industry	第二产业 Secondary Industry	第三产业 Tertiary Industry	人均生产总值(按户籍) Per Capita GDP (Household)
1978	120.1	118.8	122.3	113.6	118.0
1979	116.4	109.4	118.1	111.6	111.4
1980	124.8	85.9	127.8	120.0	119.7
1981	110.1	96.1	108.6	117.4	107.6
1982	108.6	118.8	107.4	111.7	106.3
1983	113.9	77.5	110.1	130.7	111.7
1984	124.0	138.2	121.5	130.0	121.8
1985	118.2	105.0	114.7	128.1	116.0
1986	109.4	101.6	106.5	116.7	107.4
1987	111.3	111.8	109.1	116.0	109.4
1988	105.0	99.2	106.0	103.2	103.3
1989	93.6	107.9	89.2	102.1	92.2
1990	105.6	100.6	106.0	105.2	104.6
1991	116.2	102.6	113.3	120.5	115.3
1992	125.7	101.1	125.6	127.0	124.5
1993	128.5	103.0	130.5	127.3	126.9
1994	126.6	109.3	133.6	119.5	124.4
1995	119.6	106.5	121.3	117.9	117.4
1996	114.7	106.1	116.7	112.4	105.3
1997	113.4	110.0	111.5	116.0	104.7
1998	109.4	107.7	108.7	110.4	107.8
1999	107.9	110.3	107.0	108.9	106.0
2000	111.6	100.4	111.6	112.0	109.3
2001	113.0	107.9	113.1	113.1	111.2
2002	114.1	105.2	112.9	115.4	111.9
2003	115.8	104.2	120.1	112.5	113.8
2004	115.5	103.6	117.4	114.1	113.4
2005	112.5	101.6	109.3	116.8	110.2
2006	114.3	100.7	111.2	118.4	112.5
2007	114.4	100.7	113.0	116.5	113.0
2008	110.9	100.7	108.1	114.1	109.5
2009	110.4	102.5	107.0	113.9	109.1

注:1.本表按可比价格计算。

2.2005-2008已按经济普查数调整。

a)The indices in this table are calculated at comparable prices.

b)The data of 2005 to 2008 had been adjusted auording to 2008 economic cencus.

1－09 全市生产

Composition of

单位：万元

行 业	Sector	全 Whole	
		2009	为上年（%） As Compared with the Preceding Year（%）
全市生产总值	Gross Domestic Product	50875529	110.0
第一产业	Primary Industry	1905093	103.1
第二产业	Secondary Industry	23871200	106.5
工业	Industry	21011393	105.5
建筑业	Construction	2859807	115.3
第三产业	Tertiary Industry	25099237	114.2
交通运输、仓储及邮政业	Transportation, Storage and Post	1486238	100.0
批发和零售业	Wholesale & Retail Trade	4427221	107.7
住宿和餐饮业	Accommodations and Catering	930939	106.7
金融业	Banking and Insurance	5184645	117.1
房地产业	Real Estate	3834454	119.6
科学研究、技术服务和地质勘查业	Scientific Research, Technical Service and Geological Prospecting	970370	116.7
居民服务和其他服务业	Service for the Residents and Other	492195	112.1
教育	Education	1624258	115.0
卫生、社会保障和社会福利业	Health Care, Sports & Social Welfare	811269	118.9
文化、体育和娱乐业	Culture, Sports and Entertainment	364418	113.0
公共管理和社会组织	Public Management and Social Organzations	1809090	120.1

注：1. 本表绝对数按当年价格计算，为上年（%）按可比价格计算。

2. 2008 年相关数据已按经济普查数调整。

3. 从 2001 年起市区数据包括萧山区和余杭区。

总值构成(2009 年)

Gross Domestic Product(2009)

(10000 yuan)

市 Municipality		其 中:市 区 Urban District			
比 重 (%) Proportion(%)		2009	为上年(%) As Compared with the Preceding Year(%)	比 重 (%) Proportion(%)	
2009	2008			2009	2008
100.0	100.0	40698687	110.4	100.0	100.0
3.8	3.8	874987	102.5	2.2	2.2
46.9	49.5	18120921	107.0	44.5	47.0
41.3	44.3	15773546	106.1	38.7	41.5
5.6	5.3	2347375	113.1	5.8	5.5
49.3	46.7	21702778	113.9	53.3	50.8
2.9	3.1	1170905	97.1	2.9	3.2
8.7	8.7	3836046	106.5	9.4	9.6
1.8	1.8	780273	106.6	1.9	1.9
10.2	9.5	4617237	115.9	11.3	10.7
7.5	6.6	3326043	119.4	8.2	7.1
1.9	1.8	934448	116.9	2.3	2.2
1.0	0.9	381687	112.3	0.9	0.9
3.2	3.1	1319663	113.6	3.2	3.2
1.6	1.5	688860	119.2	1.7	1.6
0.7	0.7	331047	113.4	0.8	0.8
3.6	3.3	1452176	121.1	3.6	3.3

a) Absolute figures in this table are calculated at current prices, while indices are calculated at comparable price.

b) The data of 2008 had been adjusted auording to 2008 economic cencus.

c) Data in this table include Xiaoshan and Yuhang district since 2001.

1-10 分县(市)生产总值(2009年)

Gross Domestic Product by Region(2009)

单位:万元 (10000 yuan)

地区	Region	生产总值总计 Gross Domestic Product	第一产业 Primary Industry	第二产业 Secondary Industry			第三产业 Tertiary Industry	人均GDP(按户籍)(元) Per Capita GDP (Household) (yuan)
					工业 Industry	建筑业 Construction		
全市	**Whole Municipality**	**50875529**	**1905093**	**23871200**	**21011393**	**2859807**	**25099237**	**74761**
市区	Urban District	40698687	874987	18120921	15773546	2347375	21702778	95342
萧山区	Xiaoshan	10370744	434100	6376971	5952753	424219	3559673	85986
余杭区	Yuhang	5273262	355552	2818638	2532578	286059	2099072	62563
桐庐县	Tonglu	1672588	144525	1006091	908199	97891	521972	41825
淳安县	Chun'an	1006517	196305	419807	322208	97599	390406	22268
建德市	Jiande	1622480	191383	901608	825643	75966	529489	31610
富阳市	Fuyang	3524948	250004	2114104	1977580	136524	1160840	54646
临安市	Lin'an	2350310	247889	1308668	1204217	104452	793752	44669

注:1. 本表按当年价计算。
2. 从2001年起市区数据包括萧山区和余杭区。
a) Figures in this table are calculated at current prices.
b) Data in this table include Xiaoshan and Yuhang district since 2001.

1－11　主要指标占全省比重(2009 年)
Proportion of Main Indicators in Whole Province(2009)

指　标 Item		全　省 Zhejiang Province	杭州市 Hangzhou Municipality	杭州市占全省(%) Proportion of Hangzhou in Zhejiang(%)
年末常住总人口 Long－term Residents(End of 2009)	(万人) (10000 persons)	5180	810	15.6
年末户籍人口 Household Registration Population(End of 2009)	(万人) (10000 persons)	4716.18	683.38	14.5
#非农业人口 Non－agriculture Population	(万人) (10000 persons)	1433.95	354.48	24.7
年末从业人员数 Total Number of Employed Persons	(万人) (10000 persons)	3591.88	597.47	16.6
生产总值(当年价格) Gross Domestic Product	(亿元) (100 million yuan)	22832.43	5087.55	22.3
第一产业 Primary Industry	(亿元) (100 million yuan)	1161.65	190.51	16.4
第二产业 Secondary Industry	(亿元) (100 million yuan)	11843.3	2387.12	20.2
第三产业 Tertiary Industry	(亿元) (100 million yuan)	9827.48	2509.92	25.5
常住人均生产总值(当年价格) Per Capita GDP of Long－term Residents(Current Price)	(元) (yuan)	44335	63333	－
农林牧渔业总产值(现价) Gross Output Value of Farming,Forestry, Animal Husbandry and Fishery(Current Price)	(亿元) (100 million yuan)	1873.4	289.74	15.5
主要农产品产量 Output of Major Farm Products				
粮食 Grain	(万吨) (10000 tons)	789.15	107.24	13.6
棉花 Cotton	(万吨) (10000 tons)	2.81	0.10	3.4
蚕茧 Silk－worm Cocoons	(万吨) (10000 tons)	6.8296	1.79	26.2
生猪年末存栏 Hogs in Stock at Year End	(万头) (10000 heads)	1225.8	178.61	14.6
猪牛羊肉产量 Output of Pork,Beef & Mutton	(万吨) (10000 tons)	130.95	30.92	23.6
淡水产品总产量 Freshwater Aquatic products	(万吨) (10000 tons)	86.51	19.65	22.7

1－11 续表1 continued 1

指　标 Item	全　省 Zhejiang Province	杭州市 Hangzhou Municipality	杭州市占全省(%) Proportion of Hangzhou in Zhejiang(%)
规模以上工业企业利税总额 (亿元) Total Pre－tax Profits of Industrial Enterprises above Designed Size (100 million yuan)	3634.8	882.62	24.3
主要工业产品产量 Output of Major Industrial Products			
发电量 (亿千瓦时) Electricity (100 million kwh)	2193.27	153.73	7.0
氢氧化钠(烧碱)(折100%) (万吨) Caustic Soda(100% discount) (10000 tons)	98.48	12.4	12.6
碳酸钠(纯碱) (万吨) Soda Ash (10000 tons)	17.57	17.57	100
合成氨 (万吨) Synthetic Ammonia (10000 tons)	64.42	9.73	15.1
水泥 (万吨) Cement (10000 tons)	10796.49	1829.7	16.9
平板玻璃 (万重量箱) Plate Glass (10000 weight cases)	3358.93	423.78	12.6
钢材 (万吨) Steels (10000 tons)	2359.4	805.07	34.1
化学纤维 (万吨) Chemical Fiber (10000 tons)	1207.16	496.56	41.1
纱 (万吨) Yarn (10000 tons)	195.62	52.48	26.8
丝织品 (亿米) Silk Products (100 million meters)	3.28	0.94	28.5
自行车 (万辆) Bicycles (10000 units)	1224.03	525.64	42.9
彩色电视机 (万台) Colour TV Sets (10000 units)	518.35	23.64	4.6
电冰箱 (万台) Household Refrigerator (10000 units)	761.81	93.74	12.3
洗衣机 (万台) Washing Machine (10000 units)	1572.51	281.54	17.9

1－11 续表2 continued 2

指 标 Item		全 省 Zhejiang Province	杭州市 Hangzhou Municipality	杭州市占全省(%) Proportion of Hangzhou in Zhejiang(%)
全社会交通运输客运量 Total Passenger Traffic	(万人次) (10000 person－times)	222130	30116	13.6
全社会交通运输货运量 Total Freight Traffic	(万吨) (10000 tons)	151239	22372	14.8
限额以上固定资产投资 Total Investment in Fixed Assets	(亿元) (100 million yuan)	9906.46	2195.17	22.2
社会消费品零售总额 Total Retail Sales of Consumer Goods	(亿元) (100 million yuan)	8622.26	1804.93	20.9
出口额 Total Exports	(亿美元) (100 million USD)	1330.13	271.80	20.4
实际利用外资 Foreign Capital Actually Used	(亿美元) (100 million USD)	108.58	40.14	37.0
境外旅游者人数 Number of International Tourists	(万人次) (10000 person－times)	570.64	230.40	40.4
财政总收入 Total Financial Revenue	(亿元) (100 million yuan)	4121.89	1019.43	24.7
地方财政预算内收入 Financial Revenue	(亿元) (100 million yuan)	2142.37	520.79	24.3
地方财政预算内支出 Financial Expenditure	(亿元) (100 million yuan)	2653.37	490.40	18.5
金融机构存款余额(本外币) Deposits of Financial Institutions	(亿元) (100 million yuan)	45112.01	14284.21	31.7
金融机构贷款余额(本外币) Loans of Financial Institutions	(亿元) (100 million yuan)	39223.91	13113.30	33.4
城乡居民储蓄存款 Residents´Savings Deposits	(亿元) (100 million yuan)	18169.41	4286.92	23.6
城镇以上单位在岗职工平均工资 Average Wage of Fully Employed Staff and Workers of Urban Units	(元) (yuan)	37395	43947	－
城镇居民人均可支配收入 Per Capita Annual Disposable Income in Urban District	(元) (yuan)	24611	26864	－
农民人均纯收入 Per Capita Annual Net Income in Rural Areas	(元) (yuan)	10007	11822	－
在校学生数 Students Enrollment				
高等学校 Institutions of Higher Education	(万人) (10000 persons)	86.65	39.41	45.5
中等专业学校 Secondary Specialized Schools	(万人) (10000 persons)	9.52	0.40	4.2
普通中学 Secondary Schools	(万人) (10000 persons)	262.27	36.00	13.7
小学 Primary Schools	(万人) (10000 persons)	325.14	44.51	13.7

1－12 国民经济主要指标人均水平(按户籍)

Major Per Capita Indicators of National Economy(Household)

指 标 Item	1995	2000	2001	2002	2003	2004	2005	2006	2007	2008	2009
全市生产总值 (元) Gross Domestic Product (yuan)	12797	22342	25074	28150	32819	39293	44871	51908	61315	70948	74761
规模以上工业总产值 (元) Gross Industrial Output Value above Designatted Size (yuan)	17131	24943	30694	37921	50055	69320	82936	105150	124773	138958	137995
农林牧渔业总产值 (元) Gross Output Value of Farming, Forestry, Animal Husbandry and Fishery (yuan)	1673	2467	2638	2662	3001	3063	3345	3398	3693	4056	4258
社会消费品零售总额 (元) Total Retail Sales of Consumer Goods (yuan)	5027	8317	9259	10437	11606	13217	14869	16768	19368	23087	26523
财政总收入 (元) Financial Revenue (yuan)	926	2308	3014	4062	5153	6115	7938	9414	11780	13490	14980
#地方财政预算内收入 (元) Financial Revenue of Local Government (yuan)	387	1118	1668	1869	2351	3051	3818	4543	5851	6746	7653
#地方财政预算内支出 (元) Financial Expenditure (yuan)	418	1187	1678	2219	2557	3023	3633	4119	5016	6217	7026
城镇居民可支配收入 (元) Annual Disposable Income in Urban District (yuan)	6301	9668	10896	11778	12898	14565	16601	19027	21689	24104	26864
城镇居民消费性支出 (元) Annual Living Expenditure in Urban District (yuan)	5559	7790	8968	9215	9950	11213	13438	14472	14896	16719	18595
农民纯收入 (元) Annual Net Income in Rural Area (yuan)	3012	4894	5330	5708	6250	6950	7655	8515	9546	10692	11822
农民消费性支出 (元) Annual Living Expenditure in Rural Area (yuan)	2373	3393	3909	4404	5142	5608	6004	6674	7568	8446	9065

1－13　企业家信心指数(2009年)
Expectation Indices of Entrepreneurs(2009)

单位:点　(point)

指　标	Item	第一季度 1st. Quarter	第二季度 2nd. Quarter	第三季度 3rd. Quarter	第四季度 4th. Quarter
全市	**Total**	**98.00**	**117.86**	**123.56**	**141.69**
按行业分	**Grouped by Sector**				
工业	Industry	96.74	125.69	131.21	150.14
建筑业	Construction	160.91	118.31	132.64	167.75
交通运输、仓储及邮电通信业	Transportation, Storage and Post	67.63	100	100	100
批发零售贸易业	Wholesale and Retail Trade	81.14	93.28	101.79	122.07
房地产业	Real Estate	76.05	96.77	113.49	137.51
社会服务业	Social Services	100.06	125.61	131.38	109.99
信息传输、计算机服务和软件业	Information Transmission, Computer Service and Software	121.65	134.53	113.99	161.53
住宿和餐饮业	Accommodations and Catering	56.80	120.78	116.33	112.5
按经济类型分	**Grouped by Status of Registration**				
国有企业	State－owned	136.88	104.37	122.71	153.64
集体企业	Collective－owned	108.38	116.87	116.87	108.39
有限责任公司	Limited－liability Companies	70.12	106.24	111.52	122.4
股份有限公司	Share Holding Ltd. Companies	100.05	119.76	134.47	116.64
外商及港澳台投资企业	Funded by Overseas Entrepreneurs	100.58	126.76	128.6	174.41
按企业规模分	**Grouped by Size of Enterprises**				
大型企业	Large	104.09	178.83	182.01	160.52
中型企业	Medium	92.26	106.25	114.49	118.3
小型企业	Small	90.38	110.78	111.38	121.57

1-14 企业景气指数(2009年)

Expectation Indices of Enterprises(2009)

单位:点 (point)

指 标	Item	第一季度 1st. Quarter	第二季度 2nd. Quarter	第三季度 3rd. Quarter	第四季度 4th. Quarter
全市	**Total**	**108.49**	**125.93**	**129.08**	**143.54**
按行业分	**Grouped by Sector**				
工业	Industry	103.14	127.15	132.85	151.38
建筑业	Construction	160.83	137.69	132.46	172.77
交通运输、仓储及邮电通信业	Transportation, Storage and Post	102.63	107.69	103.85	104.45
批发零售贸易业	Wholesale and Retail Trade	93.03	119.16	118.3	114.53
房地产业	Real Estate	117.12	116.82	126.29	138.86
社会服务业	Social Services	106.11	120.48	135.76	116.62
信息传输、计算机服务和软件业	Information Transmission, Computer Service and Software	156.86	144.11	149.22	188.57
住宿和餐饮业	Accommodations and Catering	65.80	136.33	130.25	121.76
按经济类型分	**Grouped by Status of Registration**				
国有企业	State - owned	135.54	119.42	115.18	158.32
集体企业	Collective - owned	108.37	101.72	116.87	102.8
有限责任公司	Limited - liability Companies	96.75	115.85	126.40	129.52
股份有限公司	Share Holding Ltd. Companies	105.73	141.69	134.75	118.08
外商及港澳台投资企业	Funded by Overseas Entrepreneurs	98.77	134.39	122.95	168.7
按企业规模分	**Grouped by Size of Enterprises**				
大型企业	Large	109.68	184.19	185.95	159.44
中型企业	Medium	101.29	116.35	120.19	131.82
小型企业	Small	109.62	113.77	116.17	115.69

1－15 市区分月气象概况(2009 年)

Monthly Meteorological Conditions in Urban District(2009)

月 份 Month	平均气温(度) Average Temperature(℃)	日照时数(小时) Sunshine Hours(hours)	降雨天数(天) Rainfall Days (day)	降水量(毫米) Precipitation(mm.)
全 年 Annual Total	**17.8**	**1709.9**	**142**	**1615.9**
1 月 January	4.4	128.3	10	36.3
2 月 February	9.5	65.2	17	190.7
3 月 March	11.1	109.6	15	117.6
4 月 April	17.6	191.5	9	117.9
5 月 May	22.9	218.8	10	77
6 月 June	26.8	168.4	16	85.6
7 月 July	29.6	204.7	9	227.7
8 月 August	28.4	114.3	18	213
9 月 September	25.5	119	11	113.7
10 月 October	20.6	176.2	3	180
11 月 November	10.8	86.5	14	186.6
12 月 December	6.7	127.4	10	69.8

1－16 气　　象
Meteorological

指标	Item	市区 Urban District	#萧山区 Xiaoshan
一、气　温	**The Atmospheric Temperature**		
全年平均气温（度）	Annual Average Temperature（℃）	17.8	17.7
极端最高气温（度）	The Highest Temperature of the Year（℃）	39.7	40.3
出现日期（日/月）	Date（d/m）	20/7	20/7
极端最低气温（度）	The Lowest Temperature of the Year（℃）	－5.2	－5.5
出现日期（日/月）	Date（d/m）	24/1	24/1
二、降　雨	**Rainfall**		
本年降雨日数（日）	Total Rainy Days（day）	142	149
全年降雨总量（毫米）	Annual Rainfall（millimeters）	1615.9	1500.5
最长连续降雨日数（日）	Longest Consecutive Days of Rain（day）	21	21
最长连续降雨总量（毫米）	Rainfall（millimeters）	219.2	239.2
最长连续降雨起止日期（日/月）	Start/End（d/m）	15/2－7/3	15/2－7/3
日最大降雨量（毫米）	Maximum Daily Rainfall（millimeters）	106.1	111.2
出现日期（日/月）	Date（d/m）	24/7	24/7
三、全年日照总时数（小时）	**Total Sunshine Hours（hours）**	**1709.9**	**1859.9**
四、霜　雪	**Frost & Snow**		
全年降霜日数（日）	Annual Frost Days（day）	31	29
初霜日期（日/月）	Start Date（d/m）	20/11	20/11
终霜日期（日/月）	End Date（d/m）	14/3	31/1

概 况

Conditions by Region

桐庐县 Tonglu	淳安县 Chun'an	建德市 Jiande	富阳市 Fuyang	临安市 Lin'an
17.4	17.6	17.3	17.6	16.6
39.3	38.2	39.3	39.7	39.5
17/7	19/7	19/7	17/7	19/7
-6.2	-4.9	-5.8	-6.5	-8.4
25/1	24/1	25/1	25/1	25/1
143	143	146	148	140
1471.3	1286.3	1300.3	1500.1	1454.1
22	21	22	21	20
266	231.1	207.4	265.2	246.2
15/2 - 8/3	15/2 - 7/3	14/2 - 7/3	15/2 - 7/3	15/2 - 6/3
86.3	63	73.1	166.3	146.8
10/8	19/4	1/7	10/8	10/8
1628	**1835.7**	**1815.9**	**1706.5**	**1825.7**
24	27	32	32	39
20/11	20/11	20/11	20/11	11/11
21/2	1/2	21/2	28/1	30/3

主要统计指标解释

生产总值(GDP) 指一个国家(或地区)所有常住单位在一定时期内生产活动的最终成果。生产总值有三种表现形态,即价值形态、收入形态和产品形态。从价值形态看,它是所有常住单位在一定时期内生产的全部货物和服务价值超过同期中间投入的全部非固定资产货物和服务价值的差额,即所有常住单位的增加值之和;从收入形态看,它是所有常住单位在一定时期内创造并分配给常住单位和非常住单位的初次收入分配之和;从产品形态看,它是所有常住单位在一定时期内最终使用的货物和服务价值与货物和服务净出口价值之和。在实际核算中,生产总值有三种计算方法,即生产法、收入法和支出法。三种方法分别从不同的方面反映生产总值及其构成。

三次产业 是根据社会生产活动历史发展的顺序对产业结构的划分,产品直接取自自然界的部门称为第一产业,对初级产品进行再加工的部门称为第二产业,为生产和消费提供各种服务的部门称为第三产业。它是世界上较为通用的产业结构分类,但各国的划分不尽一致。我国的三次产业划分是:

第一产业:农业(包括种植业、林业、牧业、渔业和农林牧渔服务业)。

第二产业:工业(包括采矿业,制造业,电力、燃气及水的生产和供应业)和建筑业。

第三产业:除第一、第二产业以外的其他各业。由于第三产业包括的行业多、范围广,根据我国的实际情况,第三产业可分为两大部分;一是流通部门,二是服务部门。具体又分为四个层次;

第一层次:流通部门,包括交通运输、仓储及邮电通信业,批发和零售贸易、餐饮业。

第二层次:为生产和生活服务的部门,包括金融、保险业,地质勘查业、水利管理业,房地产业,社会服务业,农、林、牧、渔服务业,交通运输辅助业,综合技术服务业等。

第三层次:为提高科学文化水平和居民素质服务的部门,包括教育、文化艺术及广播电影电视业,卫生、体育和社会福利业,科学研究等。

第四层次:为社会公共需要服务的部门,包括国家机关、政党机关和社会团体以及军队、警察等。

降水量 从天空降落到地面的液态或固态(经融化后)降水,未经蒸发、渗透、流失而在水平面上积聚的深度。降水量以毫米为单位。

空气的温度(简称气温) 表示空气冷热程度的物理量。

日照时数 太阳在一地实际照射地面的时数。

Explanatory Notes on Main Statistical Indicators

Gross Domestic Product (GDP) refers to the final products of all resident units in a country (or a region) during a certain period of time. Gross domestic product is expressed in three different forms, i. e. value, income, and products respectively. The form of value refers to the total value of all products and services produced by all resident units during a certain period of time minus total value of intermediate input of materials and services of the nature of non – fixed assets or the summation of the value – added of all resident units; the form of income includes all the income created by all resident units and distributed primarily to all resident and non – resident units; the form of products refers to the value of all final goods and services for final use by all resident units plus the value of net exports of goods and services during a given period of time. In the practice of national accounting, gross domestic product is calculated with three approached, i. e. production approach, income approach, and expenditure approach, which reflect gross domestic product and its composition from different aspects.

Three Industries Industry structure has been classified according to the historical sequence of development. Primary industry refers to extraction of natural resources; secondary industry involves processing of primary products; and tertiary industry provides services of various kinds for production and consumption. The above classification is universal although it varies to someextent from country to country. Industry in China comprises:

Primary industry: agriculture (including farming, forestry, animal husbandry and fishery and services for agriculture sector)

Secondary industry: industry (including mining and quarrying, manufacturing, production and supply of electricity, water and gas) and construction.

Tertiary industry: all other industries not included in primary of secondary industry.

Due to the fact that tertiary industry involves in a large variety of industries in China, it is divided into two sectors: circulation sector and service sector and further into four levels;

The first level: circulation sector, including transportation, storage, postal and telecommunications, wholesale and retail trade and catering trade.

The second level: service sector providing services for production and consumption, including banking, insurance, geological survey, water conservancy management, real estates, service for residents, service for agriculture, forestry, animal husbandry, fishery, subsidiary services for transportation and communications, comprehensive technical services, etc.

The third level: service sector for upgrading scientific, educational and cultural level of the people, including education, culture and arts, broadcasting, movies, television, public health, sports, social welfare and scientific research, etc.

The fourth level: sector providing services for public needs, including government agencies, political parties, social organizations, military and police service.

Precipitation refers to the depth of rainfall onto the ground (as well as liquefied from solid forms) from above the air prior to its vaporization, seepage, running off.

It is calculated in the unit of millimeter (mm).

Air Temperature refers to the physical quantity reflecting the extent of coldness and hotness of the air.

Duration of sunshine refers to the real time for the ground to receive sunshine at a certain place.

第二篇
CHAPTER-2

人口、劳动力
POPULATION AND LABOR FORCE

人口、劳动力 Population and Labor Force

主要统计指标 Major Statistical Indicators

年末总户数	Total Households(year-end)	215.28	万户	(10000 Subscribers)
为上年	As Compared with the Preceding Year	100.7	%	(%)
年末总人口	Total Population(year-end)	683.38	万人	(10000 persons)
为上年	As Compared with the Preceding Year	100.8	%	(%)
#男性	Male	344.51	万人	(10000 persons)
为上年	As Compared with the Preceding Year	100.6	%	(%)
#非农业人口	Non-agriculture Population	354.48	万人	(10000 persons)
为上年	As Compared with the Preceding Year	104.0	%	(%)
年末市区总人口	Population of Urban District(year-end)	429.44	万人	(10000 persons)
为上年	As Compared with the Preceding Year	101.2	%	(%)
#男性	Male	215.56	万人	(10000 persons)
为上年	As Compared with the Preceding Year	100.9	%	(%)
#非农业人口	Non-agriculture Population	297.83	万人	(10000 persons)
为上年	As Compared with the Preceding Year	104.5	%	(%)
人口自然增长率	Natural Growth Rate	3.42	‰	(‰)
年末从业人员	Number of Employed Persons(year-end)	597.47	万人	(10000 persons)
为上年	As Compared with the Preceding Year	105.0	%	(%)

2－01 历次普查常住人口情况

Long－term Residents in the Past Population Census

单位:万人　　(10000 person)

地　区 Region		第一次人口普查 1953.7.1 the First Population Census (1953.7.1)	第二次人口普查 1964.7.1 the Second Population Census (1964.7.1)	第三次人口普查 1982.7.1 the Third Population Census (1982.7.1)	第四次人口普查 1990.7.1 the Fourth Population Census (1991.7.1)	第五次人口普查 2000.11.1 the Fifth Population Census (2000.11.1)
杭州市	**Hangzhou**	**301.13**	**421.90**	**526.05**	**583.21**	**687.87**
杭州市区	Urban District	172.26	243.65	305.77	346.76	450.23
上城区	Shangcheng	－	－	－	21.10	33.51
下城区	Xiacheng	－	－	－	25.66	41.24
江干区	Jianggan	－	－	－	36.12	56.54
拱墅区	Gongshu	－	－	－	29.34	42.93
西湖区	Xihu	－	－	－	35.40	59.33
高新(滨江)区	Hi－Tech(Binjiang)	－	－	－	－	11.59
萧山区	Xiaoshan	56.32	82.34	106.11	113.06	123.33
余杭区	Yuhang	52.28	64.96	80.50	86.08	81.77
桐庐县	Tonglu	19.73	26.20	34.83	37.66	37.81
淳安县	Chun'an	27.49	38.66	42.03	43.55	38.23
建德市	Jiande	26.42	38.15	43.64	47.63	47.31
富阳市	Fuyang	29.22	39.66	54.13	58.07	62.86
临安市	Lin'an	26.01	35.57	45.65	49.55	51.42

注:2005 年至 2009 年,全市抽样调查年末常住人口分别为 750.7 万人、773.1 万人、786.2 万人、796.6 万人、810 万人。

a) According to the sample survey, the long－term residents reached 7.507 million, 7.731 million, 7.862 million, 7.966 million and 8.10 million from 2005 to 2009 respectively.

2-02 主要年份全市总户数与总人口数
Households and Population in Main Years

年 份 Year	总户数（万户） Total Households (10000 households)	总人口数（万人） Total Population (10000 persons)	#非农业人口(万人) Non-agriculture Population (10000 persons)	按性别分 By Sex 男（万人） Male (10000 persons)	女（万人） Female (10000 persons)
1978	117.89	505.55	116.06	260.74	244.81
1979	116.61	511.83	124.60	263.97	247.86
1980	119.11	515.53	128.88	266.02	249.51
1981	125.96	520.73	134.56	268.69	252.04
1982	131.53	528.06	139.94	272.72	255.34
1983	135.55	533.06	143.34	275.64	257.41
1984	139.24	537.49	147.46	278.04	259.45
1985	145.23	543.05	153.46	281.11	261.94
1986	151.59	549.53	157.19	284.57	264.96
1987	157.66	557.63	161.12	288.70	268.93
1988	164.41	565.04	164.87	292.21	272.83
1989	169.09	570.98	167.28	295.15	275.83
1990	171.94	574.78	169.00	297.02	277.76
1991	174.78	578.73	171.25	298.85	279.88
1992	177.68	582.40	174.03	300.63	281.77
1993	179.17	587.10	179.11	303.03	284.07
1994	180.65	592.93	186.50	306.00	286.93
1995	182.55	597.96	191.43	308.25	289.71
1996	184.33	603.22	196.68	310.76	292.46
1997	186.28	607.96	204.39	313.02	294.94
1998	187.80	611.64	210.52	314.69	296.95
1999	191.60	616.05	219.05	316.63	299.42
2000	193.48	621.58	227.00	319.09	302.49
2001	195.56	629.14	237.77	322.78	306.36
2002	198.27	636.81	252.02	326.62	310.19
2003	201.12	642.78	263.67	329.04	313.74
2004	204.52	651.68	282.58	332.62	319.06
2005	207.42	660.45	297.54	336.12	324.33
2006	209.91	666.31	309.78	338.23	328.08
2007	211.99	672.35	323.75	340.50	331.85
2008	213.74	677.64	340.76	342.45	335.19
2009	215.28	683.38	354.48	344.51	338.87

注:按公安户籍人口统计。

a) Figures in this table are based on the Public Security Bureau.

2-03 主要年份市区总户数与总人口数
Urban District Households and Population in Main Years

年份 Year	总户数(万户) Total Households (10000 households)	总人口数(万人) Total Population (10000 persons)	#非农业人口(万人) Non-agriculture Population (10000 persons)	按性别分 By Sex 男(万人) Male (10000 persons)	女(万人) Female (10000 persons)
1978	25.52	104.53	78.73	53.95	50.58
1979	26.23	110.50	85.05	57.09	53.41
1980	27.23	113.08	87.93	58.56	54.52
1981	29.88	115.59	90.53	59.96	55.63
1982	31.24	118.05	92.72	61.28	56.77
1983	32.69	120.13	94.94	62.43	57.70
1984	34.07	122.29	97.34	63.63	58.66
1985	35.36	124.67	100.01	64.96	59.71
1986	37.02	127.07	102.59	66.29	60.78
1987	38.70	129.16	104.09	67.38	61.78
1988	40.05	131.26	107.30	68.46	62.80
1989	41.19	132.84	108.88	69.28	63.56
1990	42.26	133.89	109.97	69.75	64.14
1991	42.98	134.97	111.20	70.33	64.64
1992	43.63	136.30	112.70	71.08	65.22
1993	44.55	138.33	115.13	72.22	66.11
1994	45.04	141.27	118.48	73.82	67.45
1995	46.06	143.52	121.38	74.91	68.61
1996	52.39	166.73	128.76	87.15	79.58
1997	53.14	169.29	131.76	88.53	80.76
1998	53.92	171.89	134.62	89.86	82.03
1999	54.64	175.27	139.29	91.65	83.62
2000	55.34	179.18	143.69	93.64	85.54
2001	115.81	379.49	193.26	194.59	184.90
2002	117.11	387.01	205.98	198.47	188.54
2003	119.01	393.19	216.13	201.14	192.05
2004	120.56	401.59	233.08	204.43	197.16
2005	122.02	409.52	245.56	207.70	201.82
2006	123.31	414.18	256.42	209.45	204.73
2007	124.40	419.50	269.30	211.59	207.91
2008	125.56	424.30	285.11	213.54	210.76
2009	126.92	429.44	297.83	215.56	213.88

注:从2001年起市区数据包括萧山区和余杭区。

a) Figures in this table include Xiaoshan and Yuhang district since 2001.

2－04 分地区总户数与总人口数(2009年末)

Households and Population by Region(End of 2009)

地 区 Region	总户数 (万户) Total Households (10000 households)	总人口数 (万人) Total Population (10000 persons)	#非农业人口(万人) Non－agriculture Population (10000 persons)	按性别分 By Sex 男(万人) Male (10000 persons)	按性别分 By Sex 女(万人) Female (10000 persons)
全 市 Whole Municipality	**215.28**	**683.38**	**354.48**	**344.51**	**338.87**
市 区 Urban District	126.92	429.44	297.83	215.56	213.88
上城区 Shangcheng	11.52	32.53	32.52	16.40	16.13
下城区 Xiacheng	12.46	39.84	39.84	20.32	19.52
江干区 Jianggan	11.22	44.24	41.54	22.37	21.87
拱墅区 Gongshu	10.37	30.75	30.52	15.70	15.05
西湖区 Xihu	16.16	61.78	54.29	31.87	29.91
高新(滨江)区 Hi－Tech(Binjiang)	3.72	14.47	13.13	7.33	7.14
萧山区 Xiaoshan	37.67	120.99	44.09	59.67	61.32
余杭区 Yuhang	23.82	84.84	41.90	41.90	42.94
桐庐县 Tonglu	15.07	40.08	11.92	20.25	19.83
淳安县 Chun'an	15.06	45.27	7.63	23.21	22.06
建德市 Jiande	17.49	51.34	12.87	26.33	25.01
富阳市 Fuyang	21.88	64.67	13.29	32.79	31.88
临安市 Lin'an	18.86	52.58	10.94	26.37	26.21

2-05 主要年份全市人口自然变动情况

Natural Changes of Population in Main Years

年份 Year	出生 Birth		死亡 Death		自然增长 Natural Growth	
	人数(人) Birth Population (person)	出生率(‰) Birth Rate(‰)	人数(人) Death Population (person)	死亡率(‰) Death Rate(‰)	人数(人) Natural Growth Population (person)	自然增长率(‰) Natural Growth Rate(‰)
1978	73550	14.63	29928	2.95	43622	8.68
1979	71442	14.04	29500	5.80	41942	8.24
1980	52145	10.15	30727	5.98	21418	4.17
1981	73015	14.09	31352	6.05	41663	8.04
1982	82910	15.81	30805	5.87	52105	9.94
1983	69940	13.18	33598	6.33	36342	6.85
1984	60091	11.23	33070	6.18	27021	5.05
1985	66757	12.36	33715	6.24	33042	6.12
1986	84702	15.50	33576	6.15	51126	9.35
1987	94127	17.00	33238	6.00	60889	11.00
1988	85472	15.23	35356	6.30	50116	8.93
1989	81048	14.27	34031	5.99	47017	8.28
1990	76579	13.37	34977	6.11	41602	7.26
1991	66144	11.47	33534	5.81	32610	5.66
1992	61708	10.63	34681	5.97	27027	4.66
1993	62465	10.68	34127	5.84	28338	4.84
1994	63580	10.78	35099	5.95	28481	4.83
1995	62586	10.51	36186	6.08	26400	4.43
1996	63680	10.60	25417	5.90	28263	4.70
1997	58471	9.65	34663	5.72	23808	3.93
1998	53951	8.85	38302	6.28	15649	2.57
1999	59085	9.63	36866	6.01	22219	3.62
2000	62300	10.07	40218	6.50	22082	3.57
2001	52088	8.33	33827	5.41	18261	2.92
2002	53064	8.38	35867	5.67	17197	2.72
2003	51420	8.04	36662	5.73	14758	2.31
2004	59940	9.26	34078	5.27	25862	3.99
2005	57233	8.72	35417	5.39	21816	3.33
2006	57790	8.71	38892	5.86	18898	2.85
2007	60296	9.01	37833	5.65	22463	3.36
2008	61332	9.09	42648	6.32	18684	2.77
2009	62441	9.18	39159	5.76	23282	3.42

注:本表按公安部门统计。

a) Figures in this table are based on the Public Security Bureau.

2-06 主要年份市区人口自然变动情况

Natural Changes of Urban Population in Main Years

年份 Year	出生 Birth		死亡 Death		自然增长 Natural Growth	
	人数(人) Birth Population (person)	出生率(‰) Birth Rate(‰)	人数(人) Death Population (person)	死亡率(‰) Death Rate(‰)	人数(人) Natural Growth Population (person)	自然增长率(‰) Natural Growth Rate(‰)
1978	11923	11.56	6449	6.25	5474	5.31
1979	13184	12.26	5808	5.40	7376	6.86
1980	9708	8.68	6511	5.82	3197	2.86
1981	14938	13.06	6599	5.77	8339	7.29
1982	18092	15.49	6494	5.56	11598	9.93
1983	17107	14.36	6949	5.84	10158	8.52
1984	16257	13.41	6892	5.69	9365	7.72
1985	15824	12.81	7403	6.84	8421	6.82
1986	17120	13.60	6865	5.45	10255	8.15
1987	18701	14.60	7070	5.52	11631	9.08
1988	18503	14.21	7503	5.76	11000	8.45
1989	15868	12.02	6985	5.29	8883	6.73
1990	14085	10.56	7490	5.62	6595	4.94
1991	10195	7.58	7025	5.22	3170	2.36
1992	9994	7.37	7259	5.35	2735	2.02
1993	10099	7.35	7196	5.24	2903	2.11
1994	9918	7.09	7082	5.06	2836	2.03
1995	9806	6.89	7367	5.17	2439	1.72
1996	12098	7.80	8221	5.30	3877	2.50
1997	12304	7.32	8630	5.13	3674	2.19
1998	11714	6.87	9060	5.31	2654	1.56
1999	13694	7.89	8148	4.69	5546	3.20
2000	15058	8.50	10996	6.20	4062	2.30
2001	30902	8.22	19439	5.17	11463	3.05
2002	33156	8.65	19922	5.20	13234	3.45
2003	29019	7.44	21176	5.43	7843	2.01
2004	34858	8.77	19445	4.89	15413	3.88
2005	34056	8.39	21310	5.25	12746	3.14
2006	33260	8.08	21156	5.14	12104	2.94
2007	37029	8.88	20051	4.81	16978	4.07
2008	38703	9.17	21428	5.08	17275	4.09
2009	40293	9.44	22178	5.2	18115	4.24

注:从 2001 年起市区数据包括萧山区和余杭区。

a) Figures in this table include Xiaoshan and Yuhang district since 2001.

2-07 分地区人口自然变动情况(2009年末)
Natural Changes of Population by Region(End of 2009)

地 区 Region	出 生 Birth		死 亡 Death		自然增长 Natural Growth	
	人数(人) Birth Population (person)	出生率(‰) Birth Rate(‰)	人数(人) Death Population (person)	死亡率(‰) Death Rate(‰)	人数(人) Natural Growth Population (person)	自然增长率(‰) Natural Growth Rate(‰)
全 市 Whole Municipality	**62441**	**9.18**	**39159**	**5.76**	**23282**	**3.42**
市 区 Urban District	40293	9.44	22178	5.20	18115	4.24
上城区 Shangcheng	2271	7.00	1718	5.30	553	1.70
下城区 Xiacheng	3356	8.52	1747	4.44	1609	4.08
江干区 Jianggan	4903	11.11	1748	3.96	3155	7.15
拱墅区 Gongshu	2894	9.40	1563	5.08	1331	4.32
西湖区 Xihu	6264	10.28	2367	3.89	3897	6.39
高新(滨江)区 Hi-Tech(Binjiang)	1715	12.03	582	4.08	1133	7.95
萧山区 Xiaoshan	10391	8.62	7227	6.00	3164	2.62
余杭区 Yuhang	8499	10.08	5226	6.20	3273	3.88
桐庐县 Tonglu	3963	9.91	2774	6.94	1189	2.97
淳安县 Chun'an	4066	9.00	3003	6.65	1063	2.35
建德市 Jiande	3889	7.58	3396	6.62	493	0.96
富阳市 Fuyang	5906	9.16	4169	6.47	1737	2.69
临安市 Lin'an	4324	8.22	3639	6.92	685	1.30

2－08 分地区人口机械变动情况(2009 年)
Mechanical Changes of Population by Region(2009)

单位:人 (person)

地 区 Region	本年迁入人数 Number of the Persons Moved in(person)		本年迁出人数 Number of the Persons Moved Out(person)		本年净迁入人数 Net Persons Moved in
	省 内 From Zhejiang Province	省 外 From Other Provinces	省 内 To Zhejiang Province	省 外 To Other Provinces	
全 市 Whole Municipality	**52076**	**56637**	**50179**	**18503**	**40031**
市 区 Urban District	37907	48123	33792	14880	37358
上城区 Shangcheng	2065	2882	539	937	3471
下城区 Xiacheng	4045	5234	2338	1547	5394
江干区 Jianggan	8133	10660	11875	4174	2744
拱墅区 Gongshu	4007	2087	2859	618	2617
西湖区 Xihu	10318	12732	9591	4584	8875
高新(滨江)区 Hi－Tech(Binjiang)	2613	2725	3797	542	999
萧山区 Xiaoshan	2810	4641	1556	1285	4610
余杭区 Yuhang	3916	7162	1237	1193	8648
桐庐县 Tonglu	1138	1301	1362	585	492
淳安县 Chun'an	2542	1420	2933	569	460
建德市 Jiande	3678	1850	4111	744	673
富阳市 Fuyang	3864	2122	3306	819	1861
临安市 Lin'an	2947	1821	4675	906	－813

2－09 计划生育情况(2009 年)

Conditions of Birth Control(2009)

单位:%　　　　(%)

地　区 Region		综合避孕率 Contraception Rate	计划生育率 Rate of Birth Under Control	独生子女领证率 The Only－child Certification Rate
全　市	**Whole Municipality**	**87.45**	**98.36**	**39.84**
市　区	Urban District	85.77	99.25	50.03
上城区	Shangcheng	83.08	99.27	72.17
下城区	Xiacheng	82.97	99.51	60.89
江干区	Jianggan	87.45	99.53	62.68
拱墅区	Gongshu	84	98.90	57.40
西湖区	Xihu	86.1	99.29	44.81
高新(滨江)区	Hi－Tech(Binjiang)	83.47	99.68	36.39
萧山区	Xiaoshan	86.4	99.02	41.63
余杭区	Yuhang	87.16	99.26	49.66
桐庐县	Tonglu	90.64	97.68	18.29
淳安县	Chun'an	91.73	95.68	24.85
建德市	Jiande	90.75	95.96	25.67
富阳市	Fuyang	89.45	96.41	22.52
临安市	Lin'an	88.13	98.20	29.27

2－10 婚姻登记情况

Marriage Registration Conditions

地　区 Region	2009			2008		
	准予登记结婚对数 Marriages Legally Registered(couples)	#再婚人数 Re－married (person)	离婚对数 Divorces (couples)	准予登记结婚对数 Marriages Legally Registered(couples)	#再婚人数 Re－married (person)	离婚对数 Divorces (couples)
全　市 Whole Municipality	**70003**	**20114**	**14512**	**64823**	**16949**	**13155**
市　区 Urban District	49271	12680	9022	44708	10793	8339
萧山区 Xiaoshan	8287	2595	1704	8796	2361	1534
余杭区 Yuhang	8236	2612	1740	7114	2405	1567
桐庐县 Tonglu	3060	1164	997	2968	917	863
淳安县 Chun'an	3991	1237	703	3498	942	628
建德市 Jiande	4058	1378	1004	4073	1292	970
富阳市 Fuyang	5283	1963	1545	5193	1348	1266
临安市 Lin'an	4340	1692	1241	4383	1657	1089

2－11　按三次产业分从业人员人数

Number of Employed Persons by Three Industries

单位：万人　　　　　　　　　　　　　　　　　　　　　　　　　　　　　　　（10000 persons）

指标名称	Item	2009 年	2008 年
全市总计	**Total**	**597.47**	**569.16**
第一产业	Primary Industry	80.21	80.28
第二产业	Secondary Industry	277.98	263.53
第三产业	Tertiary Industry	239.28	225.34
市　　区	**Urban District**	**435.49**	**421.83**
第一产业	Primary Industry	26.97	28.78
第二产业	Secondary Industry	209.76	200.89
第三产业	Tertiary Industry	198.76	192.15

2－12 全市城镇单位
Number of Employed

单位:人

地区、行业	Region Sector	年末单位从业人员 Employed Persons in Urban Units (year－end)	#女性 Female	在岗职工 Fully Employed Staff & Workers
全市总计	**Total**	**2043585**	**731281**	**1734169**
其中:企业	Enterprises	1687547	567586	1407847
事业	Institutions	246661	132708	223624
机关	Agencies & Organizations	92906	23027	88238
民间非营利组织	Non－profit Organizations	6653	3953	5545
其他	Other	9818	4007	8915
市区总计	**Urban District**	**1782354**	**625800**	**1489993**
其中:企业	Enterprises	1500261	493006	1233327
事业	Institutions	198018	108194	177717
机关	Agencies & Organizations	69317	17667	66080
民间非营利组织	Non－profit Organizations	5811	3452	4755
其他	Other	8947	3481	8114
上城区	Shangcheng District	165859	66170	145786
下城区	Xiacheng District	196745	77170	163161
江干区	Jianggan District	129596	33520	115907
拱墅区	Gongshu District	160773	48774	112393
西湖区	Xihu District	277550	82711	196771
高新(滨江)区	Hi－Tech(Binjiang) District	144310	45886	127634
萧山区	Xiaoshan District	403984	143766	375076
余杭区	Yuhang District	152591	64525	143322
桐庐县	Tonglu County	43574	19994	40594
淳安县	Chun'an County	27624	10070	26631
建德市	Jiande City	37606	13554	35874
富阳市	Fuyang City	84414	34888	75289
临安市	Lin'an City	68013	26975	65788

从业人员数(2009年)
Persons in Urban Units(2009)

(person)

其他从业人员 Other Employed Persons	单位平均从业人数 Annual Average Number of Employed Persons in Urban Unit	在岗职工 Fully Employed Staff & Workers	其他从业人员 Other Employed Persons
309416	**2018287**	**1717772**	**300515**
279700	1665432	1393693	271739
23037	243956	221789	22167
4668	92508	87912	4596
1108	6583	5468	1115
903	9808	8910	898
292361	**1759928**	**1476290**	**283638**
266934	1480526	1221553	258973
20301	195789	176134	19655
3237	68926	65813	3113
1056	5758	4689	1069
833	8929	8101	828
20073	160948	140555	20393
33584	197757	163217	34540
13689	129679	115678	14001
48380	156511	111599	44912
80779	273651	193987	79664
16676	142204	126241	15963
28908	399534	371766	27768
9269	151367	142703	8664
2980	43385	40463	2922
993	26987	25998	989
1732	36790	35108	1682
9125	83931	74956	8975
2225	67266	64957	2309

单位:人

2-12 续表

地区、行业	Region Sector	年末单位从业人员 Employed Persons in Urban Units (year-end)	#女性 Female	在岗职工 Fully Employed Staff & Workers
按国民经济行业分组	**Grouped by Sector**			
农、林、牧、渔业	Farming, Forestry, Animal Husbandry & Fishery	1722	486	1687
采矿业	Mining & Quarrying	2332	416	2318
制造业	Manufacturing	715375	305210	649636
电力、煤气及水的生产和供应业	Production & Supply of Electricity, Gas & Water	21903	5381	18716
建筑业	Construction	388583	25548	255417
交通运输、仓储和邮政业	Transportation, Storage, Post & Telecommunications	79176	19206	68614
信息传输、计算机服务和软件业	Information Transmission, Computer Services and Software	55441	21764	47851
批发与零售业	Wholesale & Retail Trade	108290	54458	100436
住宿和餐饮业	Accommodations and Catering	72144	40472	59816
金融业	Banking and Insurance	68331	35773	52064
房地产业	Real Estate	39676	14756	35234
租赁与商务服务业	Renting and Business Service	76612	23350	67122
科学研究、技术服务与地质勘查业	Scientific Research, Technical Service and Geological Prospecting	52357	14395	45225
水利、环境和公共设施管理业	Water Conservancy, Environment and Public Utility	22701	10179	19775
居民服务和其他服务业	Service for the Residents and Other	8343	4372	7012
教育	Education	127813	69698	118205
卫生、社会保障和社会福利业	Health Care, Sports & Social Welfare	67210	43860	61113
文化、体育与娱乐业	Culture, Sports and Entertainment	20705	10646	15344
公共管理与社会组织	Public Management and Social Organzations	114871	31311	108584

continued (person)

其他从业人员 Other Employed Persons	单位平均从业人数 Annual Average Number of Employed Persons in Urban Unit	在岗职工 Fully Employed Staff & Workers	其他从业人员 Other Employed Persons
35	1737	1701	36
14	2297	2283	14
65739	708805	648943	59862
3187	21662	18501	3161
133166	389077	255973	133104
10562	78596	67919	10677
7590	52478	45011	7467
7854	105519	97840	7679
12328	69896	59201	10695
16267	65676	49646	16030
4442	39211	34807	4404
9490	74209	64739	9470
7132	50918	44067	6851
2926	22456	19514	2942
1331	8428	7009	1419
9608	126808	117253	9555
6097	65334	59667	5667
5361	20731	15461	5270
6287	114449	108237	6212

2－13 全市国有单位

Number of Employed Persons

单位：人

地区、行业	Region Sector	年末单位从业人员 Employed Persons in Urban Units (year－end)	#女性 Female	在岗职工 Fully Employed Staff & Workers
总　计	**Total**	**510007**	**201822**	**452977**
按隶属关系分	**Grouped by Subordination**			
中央属	Central	78173	24204	63049
省　属	Provincial	143401	57014	126870
市　属	City	81550	29991	72703
县及县以下	County and Lower Levels	203738	88915	187902
其　他	Others	3145	1698	2453
按企业、事业、机关分	**Grouped by Enterprises, Institutions & Agencies**			
企业	Enterprises	183827	53886	153147
事业	Institutions	232097	124257	210607
机关	Agencies & Organizations	92859	23016	88191
民间非营利组织	Non－profit Organizations	984	543	801
其他	Others	240	120	231
按国民经济行业分组	**Grouped by Sector**			
农、林、牧、渔业	Farming, Forestry, Animal Husbandry & Fishery	872	175	842
采矿业	Mining & Quarrying	－	－	－
制造业	Manufacturing	18487	4540	17953
电力、煤气及水的生产和供应业	Production & Supply of Electricity, Gas & Water	12372	2924	9593
建筑业	Construction	17581	3107	14607
交通运输、仓储和邮政业	Transportation, Storage, Post & Telecommunications	47968	11695	40868
信息传输、计算机服务和软件业	Information Transmission, Computer Services and Software	9410	4438	6010
批发与零售业	Wholesale & Retail Trade	8974	3728	7429
住宿和餐饮业	Accommodations and Catering	10027	5548	9001
金融业	Banking and Insurance	11047	6067	9660
房地产业	Real Estate	3944	1522	3652
租赁与商务服务业	Renting and Business Service	29299	5593	22796
科学研究、技术服务与地质勘查业	Scientific Research, Technical Service and Geological Prospecting	27262	7988	24186
水利、环境和公共设施管理业	Water Conservancy, Environment and Public Utility	14690	7342	12367
居民服务和其他服务业	Service for the Residents and Other	3175	1769	2437
教育	Education	114755	61233	106958
卫生、社会保障和社会福利业	Health Care, Sports & Social Welfare	57536	37746	52424
文化、体育与娱乐业	Culture, Sports and Entertainment	17393	8922	12272
公共管理与社会组织	Public Management and Social Organzations	105215	27485	99922

从业人员数(2009 年)
in State - owned Units(2009)

(person)

其他从业人员 Other Employed Persons	单位平均从业人数 Annual Average Number of Employed Persons in Urban Unit	在岗职工 Fully Employed Staff & Workers	其他从业人员 Other Employed Persons
57030	**506496**	**451411**	**55085**
15124	78606	63406	15200
16531	142326	126187	16139
8847	80046	72385	7661
15836	202411	187040	15371
692	3107	2393	714
30680	183198	153524	29674
21490	229615	208993	20622
4668	92460	87864	4596
183	983	799	184
9	240	231	9
30	882	851	31
–	–	–	–
534	19237	18630	607
2779	12170	9410	2760
2974	18147	16037	2110
7100	47841	40834	7007
3400	9260	5957	3303
1545	8956	7445	1511
1026	10236	9286	950
1387	10664	9344	1320
292	3877	3614	263
6503	28263	21721	6542
3076	26830	23832	2998
2323	14737	12510	2227
738	3266	2476	790
7797	113899	106228	7671
5112	55996	51261	4735
5121	17383	12346	5037
5293	104852	99629	5223

2－14 全市城镇集体

Number of Employed Persons

单位:人

地区、行业	Region Sector	年末单位从业人员 Employed Persons in Urban Units (year－end)	#女性 Female	在岗职工 Fully Employed Staff & Workers
总　　计	**Total**	**52117**	**19446**	**47683**
按企业、事业分	**Grouped by Enterprises, Institutions**			
企业	Enterprises	36894	10748	34047
事业	Institutions	14564	8451	13017
机关	Agencies & Organizations	47	11	47
民间非营利组织	Non－profit Organizations	275	140	236
其他	Others	337	96	336
按国民经济行业分组	**Grouped by Sector**			
农、林、牧、渔业	Farming, Forestry, Animal Husbandry & Fishery	177	67	177
采矿业	Mining & Quarrying	736	117	730
制造业	Manufacturing	6288	2380	6101
电力、煤气及水的生产和供应业	Production & Supply of Electricity, Gas & Water	48	16	48
建筑业	Construction	2413	471	1502
交通运输、仓储和邮政业	Transportation, Storage, Post & Telecommunications	5022	632	4513
信息传输、计算机服务和软件业	Information Transmission, Computer Services and Software	301	159	279
批发与零售业	Wholesale & Retail Trade	2200	907	1926
住宿和餐饮业	Accommodations and Catering	3146	1770	3002
金融业	Banking and Insurance	23	11	23
房地产业	Real Estate	1331	475	1051
租赁与商务服务业	Renting and Business Service	13702	3135	13100
科学研究、技术服务与地质勘查业	Scientific Research, Technical Service and Geological Prospecting	1147	270	1034
水利、环境和公共设施管理业	Water Conservancy, Environment and Public Utility	2329	930	2075
居民服务和其他服务业	Service for the Residents and Other	1002	429	964
教育	Education	4974	3267	4448
卫生、社会保障和社会福利业	Health Care, Sports & Social Welfare	6241	3896	5692
文化、体育与娱乐业	Culture, Sports and Entertainment	132	79	124
公共管理与社会组织	Public Management and Social Organzations	905	435	894

单位从业人员数(2009年)

in Urban Collective - owned Units(2009)

(person)

其他从业人员 Other Employed Persons	单位平均从业人数 Annual Average Number of Employed Persons in Urban Unit	在岗职工 Fully Employed Staff & Workers	其他从业人员 Other Employed Persons
4434	**51156**	**46789**	**4367**
2847	36154	33374	2780
1547	14341	12796	1545
–	48	48	–
39	283	242	41
1	330	329	1
–	178	178	–
6	733	727	6
187	6342	6155	187
–	48	48	–
911	2388	1750	638
509	5324	4756	568
22	306	284	22
274	2220	1897	323
144	3205	3029	176
–	23	23	–
280	1385	1065	320
602	12514	11907	607
113	1109	968	141
254	2334	2087	247
38	1000	961	39
526	4914	4362	552
549	6102	5578	524
8	136	128	8
11	895	886	9

2－15 全市其他单位

Number of Employed Persons

单位：人

地区、行业	Region Sector	年末单位从业人员 Employed Persons in Urban Units (year－end)	#女性 Female	在岗职工 Fully Employed Staff & Workers
总　　计	**Total**	**1481461**	**510013**	**1233509**
按登记注册类型分组	**Grouped by Registration**			
1. 内资	Domestic Funded	975821	272280	797151
2. 港澳台投资经济	Funded by Entrepreneurs from Hong Kong, Macao & Taiwan	211229	102881	192825
3. 外商投资经济	Foreign Funded	294411	134852	243533
按企业、事业分	**Grouped by Enterprises, Institutions**			
企业	Enterprises	1466826	502952	1220653
事业	Institutions	－	－	－
民间非营利组织	Non－profit Organizations	5394	3270	4508
其他	Others	9241	3791	8348
按国民经济行业分组	**Grouped by Sector**			
农、林、牧、渔业	Farming, Forestry, Animal Husbandry & Fishery	673	244	668
采矿业	Mining & Quarrying	1596	299	1588
制造业	Manufacturing	690600	298290	625582
电力、煤气及水的生产和供应业	Production & Supply of Electricity, Gas & Water	9483	2441	9075
建筑业	Construction	368589	21970	239308
交通运输、仓储和邮政业	Transportation, Storage, Post & Telecommunications	26186	6879	23233
信息传输、计算机服务和软件业	Information Transmission, Computer Services and Software	45730	17167	41562
批发与零售业	Wholesale & Retail Trade	97116	49823	91081
住宿和餐饮业	Accommodations and Catering	58971	33154	47813
金融业	Banking and Insurance	57261	29695	42381
房地产业	Real Estate	34401	12759	30531
租赁与商务服务业	Renting and Business Service	33611	14622	31226
科学研究、技术服务与地质勘查业	Scientific Research, Technical Service and Geological Prospecting	23948	6137	20005
水利、环境和公共设施管理业	Water Conservancy, Environment and Public Utility	5682	1907	5333
居民服务和其他服务业	Service for the Residents and Other	4166	2174	3611
教育	Education	8084	5198	6799
卫生、社会保障和社会福利业	Health Care, Sports & Social Welfare	3433	2218	2997
文化、体育与娱乐业	Culture, Sports and Entertainment	3180	1645	2948
公共管理与社会组织	Public Management and Social Organizations	8751	3391	7768

从业人员数(2009 年)

in Units of Other Types of Ownership(2009)

(person)

其他从业人员 Other Employed Persons	单位平均从业人数 Annual Average Number of Employed Persons in Urban Unit	在岗职工 Fully Employed Staff & Workers	其他从业人员 Other Employed Persons
247952	**1460635**	**1219572**	**241063**
178670	964683	786543	178140
18404	208578	190898	17680
50878	287374	242131	45243
246173	1446080	1206795	239285
–	–	–	–
886	5317	4427	890
893	9238	8350	888
5	677	672	5
8	1564	1556	8
65018	683226	624158	59068
408	9444	9043	401
129281	368542	238186	130356
2953	25431	22329	3102
4168	42912	38770	4142
6035	94343	88498	5845
11158	56455	46886	9569
14880	54989	40279	14710
3870	33949	30128	3821
2385	33432	31111	2321
3943	22979	19267	3712
349	5385	4917	468
555	4162	3572	590
1285	7995	6663	1332
436	3236	2828	408
232	3212	2987	225
983	8702	7722	980

主要统计指标解释

人口数 指一定时点、一定地区范围内的有生命的个人的总和。

年度统计的年末人口数是指每年 12 月 31 日 24 时的人口数。

出生率(又称粗出生率) 指一定时期内(通常为一年)平均每千人所出生的人数的比率,一般用千分率表示。计算公式:

$$出生率=\frac{年出生人数}{年平均人数}\times 1000‰$$

出生人数是指活产婴儿,即胎儿脱离母体时(不管怀孕月数),有过呼吸或其他生命现象。

年平均人数是年初、年底人口数的平均数,也可用年中人口数代替。

死亡率(又称粗死亡率) 指一定时期内(通常为一年)一定地区的死亡人数与同期平均人数(或期中人数)之比,一般用千分率表示。计算公式:

$$死亡率=\frac{年死亡人数}{年平均人数}\times 1000‰$$

人口自然增长率 指一定时期内(通常为一年)人口自然增加数(出生人数减死亡人数)与该时期内平均人数(或期中人数)之比,一般用千分率表示。计算公式:

$$人口自然增长率=\frac{本年出生人数-本年死亡人数}{年平均人数}\times 1000‰$$

人口自然增长率=人口出生率-人口死亡率

从业人员 指从事一定社会劳动并取得劳动报酬或经营收入的人员,包括全部职工、再就业的离退休人员、私营业主、个体户主、私营和个体从业人员,乡镇企业从业人员、农村从业人员,其他从业人员(包括民办教师、宗教职业者、现役军人等)。

各单位的从业人员 指在各级国家机关、政党机关、社会团体及企业、事业单位中工作,取得工资或其他形式的劳动报酬的全部人员。包括在岗职工、再就业的离退休人员、民办教师以及在各单位中工作的外方人员和港澳台方人员、兼职人员、借用的外单位人员和第二职业者。不包括离开本单位仍保留劳动关系的职工。各单位的从业人员反映了各单位实际参加生产或工作的全部劳动力。

在岗职工 指在本单位工作并由单位支付工资的人员,以及有工作单位,但由于学习、病伤、产假等原因暂未工作,仍由单位支付工资的人员。

Explanatory Notes on Main Statistical Indicators

Total Population refers to the total number of people alive at a certain point of time within a given area.

The annual statistics on total population is taken at midnight, the 31st of December.

Birth Rate (or Crude Birth Rate) refers to the ratio of the number of births to the average population during a certain period of time (usually a year), which is often expressed in ‰. The following formula is used:

$$\text{Birth Rate} = \frac{\text{Number of Births}}{\text{Average Number of Population}} \times 1000‰$$

Number of births refers to live births, i. e. the births when babies had showed any vital phenomena regardless of the length of pregnancy.

Annual Average Number of Population is the average of the number of population at the beginning of the year and that at the end of the year. Sometimes it is substituted for with the mid - year population.

Death Rate (or Crude Death Rate) refers to the ratio of the number of deaths to the average population (or mid - year population) during a certain period of time (usually a year), which is often expressed in ‰. The following formula is used:

$$\text{Death Rate} = \frac{\text{Number of Deaths}}{\text{Annual Average Number of Population}} \times 1000‰$$

Natural Growth Rate of Population refers to the ratio of natural increase in population (number of births minus number of deaths) in a certain period of time (usually a year) to the average population (or mid - year population) of the same period, which is often expressed in ‰. The following formulas are applied:

$$\text{Natural Growth Rate of Population} = \frac{\text{Number of Births} - \text{Number of Deaths}}{\text{Average Number of Population}} \times 1000‰$$

Natural Growth Rate of Population = Birth Rate - Death Rate

Employed Persons refer to the persons who are engaged in social labour and receive remuneration payment or earn business income, including: total staff and workers, re - employed retirees, employers of private enterprises, self - employed workers, employees in private enterprises and individual economy, employees in the township enterprises, employed persons in the rural areas, other employed persons (including teachers in the schools run by the local people, people engaged in religious profession and the servicemen, etc.).

Persons Employed in Various Units refer to all the persons working in government agencies of various levels, political and party organizations, social organizations, enterprises and institutions, and receiving wages or other forms of payment. They include fully - employed staff and workers, re - employed retirees, teachers in schools run by the local people, foreigners and Chinese compatriots from Hong Kong, Macao, and Taiwan working in various units, part - time employees, employees of other units working temporarily at current posts, and employees holding the second job, but exclude staff and workers who have left their working units while keeping their labour contract (employment relation) unchanged. This indicator reflects the total number of laborers actually engaged in production or other operations in various units.

Fully Employed Staff and Workers refer to persons who work in, and receive wages from their working units, as well as persons who have their work posts, but are temporarily absent from work for reasons of study or on sick, injury or maternal leave and still receive wages from their working units.

第三篇
CHAPTER-3

农业
AGRICULTURE

农　业
Agriculture

主要统计指标
Major Statistical Indicators

农村机械总动力	Total Power of Agricultural Machinery	322.32	万千瓦	(10000 kw)
为上年	As Compared with the Preceding Year	102.2	%	(%)
农村经济总收入	Total Rural Economic Income	11166.55	亿元	(100 million yuan)
为上年	As Compared with the Preceding Year	109.3	%	(%)
乡村劳动力	Rural Laborers	259.32	万人	(10000 persons)
为上年	As Compared with the Preceding Year	99.7	%	(%)
农林牧渔业总产值	Gross Output Value of Farming,Forestry,Animal Husbandry and Fishery	289.74	亿元	(100 million yuan)
为上年	As Compared with the Preceding Year	105.8	%	(%)
粮食总产量	Total Output of Grain Crops	107.24	万吨	(10000 tons)
为上年	As Compared with the Preceding Year	97.4	%	(%)
肉类产量	Total Output of Meat	30.92	万吨	(10000 tons)
为上年	As Compared with the Preceding Year	104.7	%	(%)

3-01 农村基本情况
Basic Conditions of Rural Areas

指标		Item		1995	2000	2005	2006	2007	2008	2009
农村基层组织		**Rural Grassroots Units**								
乡镇政府	(个)	Number of Township & Town Governments	(unit)	230	234	149	141	136	136	130
#镇政府	(个)	Number of Town Governments	(unit)	134	140	110	108	105	105	99
村民委员会	(个)	Number of Villagers' Committees	(unit)	4681	4616	3681	3660	2501	2120	2113
村民小组	(万个)	Villager Group	(10000 units)	3.61	3.53	3.43	3.43	3.4	3.29	3.24
乡村户数、人口、劳动力		**Rural Households, Population & Laborers**								
农村常住户数	(万户)	Resident Households in Rural Areas	(10000 households)	121.23	118.11	139.85	137.01	136.89	131.87	131.46
农村常住人口数	(万人)	Resident Population in Rural Areas	(10000 persons)	402.77	395.00	447.36	444.27	443.49	433.39	429.13
农村从业人员数	(万人)	Practitioners in Rural Areas	(10000 persons)	257.70	247.11	267.05	266.68	266.32	260.16	259.32
按性别分		Grouped by Sex								
男劳动力	(万人)	Male	(10000 persons)	137.57	130.37	141.43	140.75	140.03	137.16	136.86
女劳动力	(万人)	Female	(10000 persons)	120.13	116.74	125.62	125.93	126.29	123	122.46
按行业分		Grouped by Sector								
农林牧渔业	(万人)	Farming, Forestry, Animal Husbandry & Fishery	(10000 persons)	136.65	116.05	88.82	83.99	79.96	78.08	75.79
工业	(万人)	Industry	(10000 persons)	63.40	59.27	85.50	88.65	93.58	89.91	90.75
建筑业	(万人)	Construction	(10000 persons)	12.04	13.02	16.51	16.98	17.66	17.7	18.1
交通运输、仓储业及邮电通讯业	(万人)	Transportation, Storage, Post & Telecommunications	(10000 persons)	8.67	9.29	11.22	11.64	11.66	11.65	11.52
批发、零售贸易、餐饮业	(万人)	Wholesale, Retail Trade & Catering Services	(10000 persons)	7.28	10.62	18.03	18.74	19.57	19.58	20.1
其它非农行业	(万人)	Other Non-agricultural Trades	(10000 persons)	29.66	38.86	46.97	46.68	43.89	43.24	43.06
#外出临时工、合同工	(万人)	Contract or Temporary Workers Going Outside	(10000 persons)	15.40	22.01	23.89	23.55	22.57	24.05	23.08
在乡村劳动力中：外出劳动力	(万人)	Among the Total Rural Laborers: Laborers Going Outside	(10000 persons)	19.14	35.73	43.22	44.12	47.26	-	-
#出省的劳动力	(万人)	Going to Other Provinces	(10000 persons)	2.06	4.47	5.66	5.08	5.62	-	-

注:2002 年起农村住户数、农村人口包括农村居委会户数、人口和农村外来户户数、人口。

a) From 2002, rural households and population in rural areas includes the natives and from the outside.

指　标	Item	全　市 Whole Municipality	市　区 Urban District	#江干区 Jianggan	#拱墅区 Gongshu
农村基层组织	**Rural Grassroots Units**				
乡镇政府 （个）	Number of Township & Town Governments (unit)	130	40	4	2
#镇政府 （个）	Number of Town Governments (unit)	99	39	4	2
农村街道办事处 （个）	Sub－district office in Rural Areas (unit)	36	23	–	1
村民委员会 （个）	Number of Villagers´Committees (unit)	2113	699	14	9
村民小组 （万个）	Villagers´Group (10000 unit)	3.24	1.19	0.01	0.01
乡村户数、人口、劳动力	**Rural Households, Population & Laborers**				
农村常住户数 （万户）	Resident Households in Rural Areas (10000 households)	131.46	64.16	2.51	0.77
农村常住人口数 （万人）	Resident Population in Rural Areas (10000 persons)	429.13	222.7	10.15	2.78
农村从业人员数 （万人）	Practitioners in Rural Areas (10000 persons)	259.32	129.87	5.09	1.42
农村基础设施水平	**Public Facilities in Rural Areas**				
自来水受益村数 （个）	Number of Villages with Access to Tap Water (unit)	2113	699	14	9
通汽车村数 （个）	Number of Villages with Highways (unit)	2111	699	14	9
通电话村数 （个）	Number of Villages with Telephone Communication (unit)	2113	699	14	9

农村基本情况(2009 年)
Rural Areas by Region(2009)

#西湖区 Xihu	#高新(滨江)区 Hi-Tech(Binjiang)	#萧山区 Xiaoshan	#余杭区 Yuhang	桐庐县 Tonglu	淳安县 Chun'an	建德市 Jiande	富阳市 Fuyan	临安市 Lin'an
2	-	17	15	11	23	13	21	22
2	-	17	14	7	11	12	15	15
2	3	11	4	2	-	3	4	4
52	15	411	189	183	425	232	287	287
0.06	0.02	0.72	0.36	0.26	0.4	0.45	0.47	0.47
4.16	3.06	35.4	17.86	10.4	11.83	12.55	16.85	15.67
15.51	9.57	114.55	69.21	31.24	36.91	39.68	53.03	45.57
8.1	5.62	65.44	43.71	20.74	23	24.19	32.8	28.72
52	15	411	189	183	425	232	287	287
52	15	411	189	183	425	232	287	285
52	15	411	189	183	425	232	287	287

单位:万人

指　标	Item	全　市 Whole Municipality	市　区 Urban District	#江干区 Jianggan	#拱墅区 Gongshu
总　计	**Total**	**259.32**	**129.87**	**5.09**	**1.42**
#女	Female	122.46	62.34	2.43	0.64
农、林、牧、渔业	Farming, Forestry, Animal Husbandry & Fishery	75.79	25.81	0.95	0.06
#农业	Farming	57.96	20.9	0.93	0.06
牧业	Animal Husbandry	7.5	1.42	0.01	-
工　业	Industry	90.75	56.04	1.97	0.53
建筑业	Construction	18.1	10.78	0.32	0.05
交通运输、仓储业及邮电通讯业	Transportation, Storage, Post & Telecommunications	11.52	6.32	0.45	0.13
批发、零售贸易、餐饮业	Wholesale, Retail Trade & Catering Services	20.1	11.12	0.73	0.32
其它非农行业	Other Non－agricultural Trades	43.06	19.8	0.67	0.33
#外出临时工、合同工	Contract or Temporary Workers Going Outside	23.08	8.49	0.29	0.09

农村劳动力(2009 年)
by Region(2009)

(10000 persons)

#西湖区 Xihu	#高新(滨江)区 Hi-Tech(Binjiang)	#萧山区 Xiaoshan	#余杭区 Yuhang	桐庐县 Tonglu	淳安县 Chun'an	建德市 Jiande	富阳市 Fuyan	临安市 Lin'an
8.1	**5.62**	**65.44**	**43.71**	**20.74**	**23**	**24.19**	**32.8**	**28.72**
3.86	2.72	31.83	20.61	9.93	10.21	11.35	15	13.63
2.16	0.32	12.7	9.39	7.06	12.25	10.69	10.92	9.06
1.56	0.28	10.35	7.49	5.88	8.31	8.94	8.92	5.01
0.07	0.01	0.85	0.48	0.63	2.44	1.03	0.94	1.04
1.45	2.63	30.6	18.84	6.97	1.5	4.86	11.46	9.92
0.74	0.56	6.24	2.87	1.31	1.13	1.8	1.83	1.25
0.69	0.31	2.8	1.89	0.97	0.36	0.73	1.68	1.46
0.82	0.77	5.06	3.26	1.4	0.88	1.47	2.54	2.69
2.24	1.03	8.04	7.46	3.03	6.88	4.64	4.37	4.34
1.26	0.29	2.7	3.85	1.39	6.54	2.8	2.51	1.35

3－04 主要年份农林牧渔业总产值

Gross Output Value of Farming, Forestry, Animal Husbandry and Fishery in Main Years

单位:万元　　　　(10000 yuan)

年份 Year	农林牧渔业总产值 Gross Output Value	#农业产值 Farming	#种植业产值 Planting	林业产值 Forestry	牧业产值 Animal Husbandry	渔业产值 Fishery
1978	85922	67365	64378	3430	14474	653
1979	115649	84727	81989	4629	25216	1077
1980	112377	79006	76059	7262	25015	1094
1981	120792	87354	81659	8309	23799	1330
1982	150606	107566	103346	8912	31801	2327
1983	148878	103685	96272	9800	32693	2700
1984	177029	122567	115286	14769	35922	3771
1985	212961	136893	126026	19095	50110	6863
1986	238285	150803	138254	19990	58197	9295
1987	281326	173080	155960	26427	70129	11690
1988	358500	208838	187648	31434	101013	17215
1989	386805	225969	201389	27857	113952	19027
1990	421045	260031	233055	26962	113424	20628
1991	463578	284275	254834	37763	117458	24082
1992	497915	300828	256833	35589	133867	27631
1993	600760	365124	300736	47476	154766	33394
1994	812473	496392	415366	58627	217217	40237
1995	996440	620057	526328	81321	244054	51008
1996	1173294	740202	617573	95740	271652	65700
1997	1287650	797812	665172	114510	294153	81175
1998	1367578	845106	701850	121197	289085	112190
1999	1414737	876685	737406	126000	293495	118557
2000	1526530	903322	754311	136848	331563	154797
2001	1649978	965005	816884	149264	362303	173406
2002	1685036	932995	886285	162227	391844	197970
2003	1890129	991556	949138	182595	417798	232599
2004	1982683	1010947	972594	206787	457619	234080
2005	2194799	1136559	1103981	233039	495900	270810
2006	2253822	1224822	1191816	267748	490448	206082
2007	2471427	1308047	1279758	294707	585536	222601
2008	2737605	1408124	1374083	320212	636633	309270
2009	2897371	1497362	1462791	362317	642892	325626

注:本表按当年价格计算;从2003年起农林牧渔总产值包括农林牧渔业服务业产值(下同)。2006年数据已根据农业普查相应调整。

a) Data in this table are calculated at current prices. From 2003, Gross Output Value includes the value of service for the farming, forestry, animal husbandry and fishery sector. The data of 2006 had been adjusted according to 2006 Agriculture Census.

3－05 主要年份农林牧渔业总产值构成

Composition of Gross Output Value of Farming, Forestry, Animal Husbandry and Fishery in Main Years

单位:%　　(%)

年份 Year	农林牧渔业总产值 Gross Output Value	#农业产值 Farming	#种植业产值 Planting	林业产值 Forestry	牧业产值 Animal Husbandry	渔业产值 Fishery
1978	100.0	78.4	74.9	4.0	16.8	0.8
1979	100.0	73.3	70.9	4.0	21.8	0.9
1980	100.0	70.3	67.7	6.5	22.2	1.0
1981	100.0	72.3	67.6	6.9	19.7	1.1
1982	100.0	71.4	68.6	5.9	21.1	1.6
1983	100.0	69.6	64.7	6.6	22.0	1.8
1984	100.0	69.2	65.1	8.3	20.3	2.2
1985	100.0	64.3	59.2	9.0	23.5	3.2
1986	100.0	63.3	58.0	8.4	24.4	3.9
1987	100.0	61.5	55.4	9.4	24.9	4.2
1988	100.0	58.2	52.3	8.8	28.2	4.8
1989	100.0	58.4	52.1	7.2	29.5	4.9
1990	100.0	61.8	55.4	6.4	26.9	4.9
1991	100.0	61.3	55.0	8.2	25.3	5.2
1992	100.0	60.4	51.6	7.2	26.9	5.5
1993	100.0	60.8	50.1	7.9	25.8	5.5
1994	100.0	61.1	51.1	7.2	26.7	5.0
1995	100.0	62.2	52.8	8.2	24.5	5.1
1996	100.0	63.1	52.6	8.2	23.1	5.6
1997	100.0	62.0	51.7	8.9	22.8	6.3
1998	100.0	61.8	51.3	8.9	21.1	8.2
1999	100.0	62.0	52.1	8.9	20.7	8.4
2000	100.0	59.2	49.4	9.0	21.7	10.1
2001	100.0	58.5	52.2	9.0	22.0	10.5
2002	100.0	55.4	52.6	9.6	23.3	11.7
2003	100.0	52.5	50.2	9.7	22.1	12.3
2004	100.0	51.0	49.1	10.4	23.1	11.8
2005	100.0	51.8	50.3	10.6	22.6	12.3
2006	100.0	54.3	52.9	11.9	21.8	9.1
2007	100.0	52.9	51.8	11.9	23.7	9.0
2008	100.0	51.4	50.2	11.7	23.3	11.3
2009	100.0	51.7	50.5	12.5	22.2	11.2

注:本表按当年价格计算。

a) Figures in value terms in this table are calculated at current prices.

3－06　主要年份农林牧渔业分项产值

Gross Output Value of Farming, Forestry, Animal Husbandry and Fishery by Branch in Main Years

单位:万元　(10000 yuan)

指　标	Item	1995	2000	2005	2006	2007	2008	2009
农林牧渔业总产值(现价)	**Gross Output Value (Current Price)**	**996440**	**1526530**	**2194799**	**2253822**	**2471427**	**2737605**	**2897371**
#一、农业产值	**Farming**	**620057**	**903322**	**1136559**	**1224822**	**1308047**	**1408124**	**1497362**
1. 种植业产值	Planting	526328	754311	1103981	1191816	1279758	1374083	1462791
粮食	Grain	262321	208546	178981	187293	194032	217705	217895
油料	Oil－bearing Crops	19675	19583	21608	20111	22987	28809	30796
棉花	Cotton	11829	2205	1146	1012	1058	1126	1155
麻类	Fiber Crops	3863	384	176	115	97	55	30
甘蔗	Sugarcane	14274	23815	19075	17028	18697	18942	20074
烟叶	Tobacco	1	5	7	2	3	1	1
药材类	Crude Drugs	1725	6005	15800	20428	23901	23432	35546
蔬菜	Vegetables	151614	303583	357734	382697	415720	447147	454890
茶、桑、果	Tea, Mulberry & Fruits	48599	106727	254379	285994	306954	330717	360120
其他	Others	12427	83458	255075	277136	296309	306149	342284
2. 其他农业产值	Other Farming	93729	149011	32578	33006	28289	34041	34571
二、林业产值	**Forestry**	**81321**	**136848**	**233039**	**267748**	**294707**	**320212**	**362317**
人造林木生长	Artificial Forestry	11286	18226	23140	22474	22376	24053	26310
林产品	Forest Products	45123	89914	168348	185455	203082	225872	260694
竹木采伐	Lumbering	24912	28708	41551	59819	69249	70287	75313
三、牧业产值	**Animal Husbandry**	**244054**	**331563**	**495900**	**490448**	**585536**	**636633**	**642892**
牲畜	Livestock Raising	143879	175732	292025	283198	366339	390789	387278
家禽饲养	Poultry Raising	35302	65548	68631	50444	61077	72229	72167
活的畜禽产品	Livestock Products	37197	44098	68143	62467	76374	94738	97739
捕猎野兽野禽	Hunting Wild Beast and Wild Fowl	491	2102	2856	3050	3222	3620	4058
其他动物饲养	Other Animals Raising	27185	44083	64245	91289	78524	75257	81650
四、渔业产值	**Fishery**	**51008**	**154797**	**270810**	**206082**	**222601**	**309270**	**325626**

3－07 主要年份农林牧渔业分项产值构成

Composition of Gross Output Value of Farming,Forestry,Animal Husbandry and Fishery by Branch in Main Years

单位:% (%)

指标	Item	1995	2000	2005	2006	2007	2008	2009
农林牧渔业总产值(现价)	**Gross Output Value (Current Price)**	**100**	**100**	**100**	**100**	**100**	**100**	**100**
#一、农业产值	**Farming**	**62.2**	**59.2**	**51.8**	**54.3**	**52.9**	**51.4**	**51.7**
1.种植业产值	Planting	52.8	49.4	50.3	52.9	51.8	50.2	50.5
粮食	Grain	26.3	13.7	8.2	8.3	7.9	8	7.5
油料	Oil Plants	2.0	1.3	1.0	0.9	0.9	1.1	1.1
棉花	Cotton	1.2	0.1	0.1	–	–	–	–
麻类	Fiber Crops	0.4	–	–	–	–	–	–
甘蔗	Sugarcane	1.4	1.6	0.9	0.8	0.8	0.7	0.7
烟叶	Tobacco	–	–	–	–	–	–	–
药材类	Crude Drugs	0.2	0.4	0.7	0.9	1	0.9	1.2
蔬菜	Vegetables	15.2	19.9	16.3	17.0	16.8	16.3	15.7
茶、桑、果	Tea, Mulberry & Fruits	4.9	7.0	11.6	12.7	12.4	12.1	12.4
其他	Others	1.2	5.4	11.5	12.3	12.0	11.1	11.9
2.其他农业产值	Other Farming	9.4	9.8	1.5	1.4	1.1	1.2	1.2
二、林业产值	**Forestry**	**8.2**	**9.0**	**10.6**	**11.9**	**11.9**	**11.7**	**12.5**
人造林木生长	Artificial Forestry	1.2	1.2	1.1	1.0	0.9	0.9	0.9
林产品	Forest Products	4.5	5.9	7.6	8.2	8.2	8.2	9
竹木采伐	Lumbering	2.5	1.9	1.9	2.7	2.8	2.6	2.6
三、牧业产值	**Animal Husbandry**	**24.5**	**21.7**	**22.6**	**21.8**	**23.7**	**23.3**	**22.2**
牲畜	Livestock Raising	14.4	11.5	13.3	12.6	14.8	14.3	13.4
家禽饲养	Poultry Raising	3.6	4.3	3.1	2.2	2.5	2.6	2.5
活的畜禽产品	Livestock Products	3.7	2.9	3.2	2.8	3.1	3.5	3.4
捕猎野兽野禽	Hunting Wild Beast and Wild Fowl	–	0.1	0.1	0.1	0.1	0.1	0.1
其他动物饲养	Other Animals Raising	2.8	2.9	2.9	4.1	3.2	2.8	2.8
四、渔业产值	**Fishery**	**5.1**	**10.1**	**12.3**	**9.1**	**9**	**11.3**	**11.2**

3－08 分地区农林牧

Gross Output Value of Farming, Forestry,

单位:万元

指　　标	Item	全　市 Whole Municipality	市　区 Urban District	#江干区 Jianggan	#拱墅区 Gongshu
合　　计	**Gross Output Value**	**2897371**	**1377081**	**17263**	**5534**
#一、农业产值	**Farming**	**1497362**	**724017**	**13923**	**4752**
(一)种植业产值	Planting	1462791	721797	13923	4752
#副产品产值	By－products	11694	5223	－	4
1. 粮食作物	Grain	217895	103692	1	123
谷　　物	Cereal	160853	82467	－	123
豆　　类	Beans	29216	14159	－	－
薯　　类	Tubers	27826	7066	1	－
2. 油　　料	Oil Plants	30796	8150	－	－
3. 棉　　花	Cotton	1155	814	－	－
4. 麻　　类	Fiber Crops	30	18	－	－
5. 甘　　蔗	Sugarcane	20074	15030	－	－
6. 烟　　叶	Tobacco	1	－	－	－
7. 药 材 类	Crude Drugs	35546	1404	－	－
8. 蔬　　菜	Vegetables	454890	258187	13304	1192
9. 茶、桑、果	Tea, Mulberry & Fruits	360120	100714	45	21
10. 其　　他	Others	342284	233788	573	3416
(二)其他农业产值	Other Farming	34571	2220	－	－
采集野生植物	Wild Plant collected	34571	2220	－	－
二、林业产值	**Forestry**	**362317**	**61937**	**17**	**36**
1. 人造林木生长	Artificial Forestry	26310	6068	17	36
2. 林产品	Forest Products	260694	38883	－	－
3. 村及村以下竹木采伐	Lumbering	75313	16986	－	－
三、牧业产值	**Animal Husbandry**	**642892**	**295282**	**440**	**1**
1. 牲畜	Livestock	387278	211622	248	－
2. 家禽饲养	Poultry Raising	72167	42482	－	1
3. 活的畜禽产品	Livestock Products	97739	27252	－	－
4. 捕猎野兽野禽	Hunting Wild Beast and Wild Fowl	4058	624	－	－
5. 其他动物饲养	Other Animals Raising	81650	13302	192	－
四、渔业产值	**Fishery**	**325626**	**248395**	**2728**	**745**

注:本表按当年价格计算。

渔业总产值(2009 年)

Animal Husbandry and Fishery by Region(2009)

(10000 yuan)

#西湖区 Xihu	#高新(滨江)区 Hi-Tech(Binjiang)	#萧山区 Xiaoshan	#余杭区 Yuhang	桐庐县 Tonglu	淳安县 Chun'an	建德市 Jiande	富阳市 Fuyang	临安市 Lin'an
53614	**26570**	**690588**	**557109**	**216701**	**280070**	**300276**	**363583**	**359660**
21988	**20992**	**392552**	**256072**	**127297**	**166255**	**166879**	**205513**	**107401**
21988	20992	392119	254285	121414	159069	163471	195997	101043
211	14	3042	1941	885	1549	1020	1760	1257
4225	276	49231	49569	19872	21141	18421	30590	24179
2884	250	38919	40024	12898	13574	13324	23123	15467
415	21	9316	4407	3624	3050	2303	3678	2402
926	5	996	5138	3350	4517	2794	3789	6310
49	3	4760	3332	5640	3893	4840	5266	3007
–	1	660	153	–	129	212	–	–
–	–	9	9	–	9	–	–	3
282	277	11457	3014	1561	1038	906	1375	164
–	–	–	–	–	1	–	–	–
–	–	14	1390	4304	16911	7003	3182	2742
6315	6774	151007	73373	29631	42950	37001	64359	22762
5424	1323	20514	66254	41032	66829	77826	45619	28100
5693	12338	154467	57191	19374	6168	17262	45606	20086
–	–	433	1787	5883	7186	3408	9516	6358
–	–	433	1787	5883	7186	3408	9516	6358
530	**15**	**9181**	**52091**	**18982**	**41795**	**14857**	**49735**	**175011**
395	3	1094	4456	173	6208	3292	5334	5235
75	12	6759	32037	14848	27771	5155	36808	137229
60	–	1328	15598	3961	7816	6410	7593	32547
1826	**1611**	**194285**	**89693**	**51366**	**49881**	**95202**	**84708**	**66453**
914	1309	158526	49308	22350	25775	29626	50926	46979
473	143	20273	21383	2100	962	10581	13484	2558
439	80	4395	16438	3591	2307	51767	6490	6332
–	–	320	304	824	93	274	1867	376
–	79	10771	2260	22501	20744	2954	11941	10208
28670	**3952**	**70275**	**136853**	**14974**	**19982**	**16418**	**21027**	**4830**

a) Data in this table are calculated at current prices.

3-09 农林牧渔业

Value-Added and Commodity Output Value of Farming,

单位:万元

指标	Item	全市 Whole Municipality	市区 Urban District	#江干区 Jianggan	#拱墅区 Gongshu
一、总产值	**Gross Output Value**	**2897371**	**1377081**	**17263**	**5534**
#农业产值	Farming	1497362	724017	13923	4752
林业产值	Forestry	362317	61937	17	36
牧业产值	Animal Husbandry	642892	295282	440	1
渔业产值	Fishery	325626	248395	2728	745
二、中间消耗	**Intermediate Consume**	**992278**	**502094**	**6466**	**2036**
1.物质消耗	Material Consume	759433	371825	4798	1390
2.劳务支出	Labor Services Expense	232845	130269	1668	646
#农业中间消耗	Agriculture Consume	431571	203508	5577	1778
林业中间消耗	Forestry Consume	78800	18176	2	13
牧业中间消耗	Animal Husbandry Consume	320904	156159	149	1
渔业中间消耗	Fishery Consume	114937	91966	678	244
三、增加值	**The Value-Added**	**1905093**	**874987**	**10797**	**3498**
1.生产法	1. Production Approach	-	-	-	-
#农业增加值	Farming	1065791	520509	8346	2974
林业增加值	Forestry	283517	43761	15	23
牧业增加值	Husbandry	321988	139123	291	-
渔业增加值	Fishery	210689	156429	2050	501
2.收入法	2. Income Approach	-	-	-	-
#固定资产折旧	Depreciation of Fixed Assets	89031	45152	3244	231
劳动者报酬	Compensation of Laborers	1905338	862782	7553	3267

注:本表按当年价格计算。

商品产值及增加值(2009 年)

Forestry, Animal Husbandry and Fishery (2009)

(10000 yuan)

#西湖区 Xihu	#高新(滨江)区 Hi-Tech(Binjiang)	#萧山区 Xiaoshan	#余杭区 Yuhang	桐庐县 Tonglu	淳安县 Chun'an	建德市 Jiande	富阳市 Fuyang	临安市 Lin'an
53614	**26570**	**690588**	**557109**	**216701**	**280070**	**300276**	**363583**	**359660**
21988	20992	392552	256072	127297	166255	166879	205513	107401
530	15	9181	52091	18982	41795	14857	49735	175011
1826	1611	194285	89693	51366	49881	95202	84708	66453
28670	3952	70275	136853	14974	19982	16418	21027	4830
18134	**9242**	**256488**	**201557**	**72176**	**83765**	**108893**	**113579**	**111771**
14269	5052	185548	154885	47708	67992	90393	89838	91677
3865	4190	70940	46672	24468	15773	18500	23741	20094
7198	6844	109304	69703	38950	40207	50700	59267	38939
74	7	5455	12599	3097	10278	2244	5872	39133
1295	768	97376	53269	22720	25208	46360	42030	28427
9118	1623	28163	50400	4711	7057	4789	4851	1563
35480	**17328**	**434100**	**355552**	**144525**	**196305**	**191383**	**250004**	**247889**
–	–	–	–	–	–	–	–	–
14790	14148	283248	186369	88347	126048	116179	146246	68462
456	8	3726	39492	15885	31517	12613	43863	135878
531	843	96909	36424	28646	24673	48842	42678	38026
19552	2329	42112	86453	10263	12925	11629	16176	3267
–	–	–	–	–	–	–	–	–
2358	1072	21185	15757	7932	3957	12368	5844	13778
33122	16256	419068	366589	143468	195483	218897	244311	240397

a) Data in this table are calculated at current prices.

3－10 主要农作物播种面积及产量
Sown Areas and Yield of Major Farm Crops

指 标	Item	2009			2008		
		播种面积（千公顷）Sown Area（1000 hectares）	总产量（吨）Total Output（ton）	公顷产量（公斤）Yield per Hectare（kg/hectare）	播种面积（千公顷）Sown Area（1000 hectares）	总产量（吨）Total Output（ton）	公顷产量（公斤）Yield per Hectare（kg/hectare）
农作物总计	**Total Farm Crops**	**396.31**	**－**	**－**	**403.59**	**－**	**－**
一、粮食作物合计	**Grain Crops**	**188.99**	**1072434**	**5675**	**192.42**	**1101555**	**5725**
#春粮	#Spring Grain	26.38	96054	3642	21.26	80655	3794
秋粮	Autumn Grain	160.58	963692	6001	169.05	1007970	5963
（一）谷 物	Cereals	127.49	848438	6655	131.2	867153	6610
1.稻谷	Rice	89.01	680616	7646	93.27	704971	7559
①早稻及早中稻	Early Rice & Semi－late Rice	2.04	12688	6220	2.11	12930	6125
②晚稻及迟中稻	Late Rice & Semi－late Rice	86.97	667928	7680	91.16	692041	7591
#单季稻	#Single－crop Rice	84.57	651294	7701	88.86	675685	7604
2.小麦	Wheat	16.38	65545	4001	16.07	65846	4098
3.大麦	Barley	0.69	2476	3588	0.78	2841	3656
4.玉米	Corn	20.06	94625	4718	19.58	87783	4484
5.其他谷物	Other Cereals	1.35	5176	3823	1.5	5712	3785
（二）豆 类	Beans	38.51	101128	2626	38.83	104317	2687
1.大豆	Soybeans	29.68	76412	2574	29.91	79488	2657
2.蚕（豌）豆	Broad Beans	4.47	11865	2657	4.42	11968	2711
3.杂豆	Other Beans	4.36	12851	2948	4.5	12861	2857
（三）蕃 薯	Yam	22.99	122868	5344	22.39	130085	5807

3－10 续表 continued

指 标	Item	2009			2008		
		播种面积（千公顷）Sown Area（1000 hectares）	总产量（吨）Total Output（ton）	公顷产量（公斤）Yield per Hectare（kg/hectare）	播种面积（千公顷）Sown Area（1000 hectares）	总产量（吨）Total Output（ton）	公顷产量（公斤）Yield per Hectare（kg/hectare）
二、油料合计	**Oil Plants**	**42.75**	**90065**	**2107**	**40.7**	**87461**	**2149**
1. 油菜籽	Rapeseeds	38.72	80081	2068	36.79	78058	2122
2. 花生	Peanuts	2.78	8170	2944	2.66	7491	2814
3. 芝麻	Sesame	1.25	1814	1455	1.25	1912	1526
三、棉花（皮棉）	**Cotton**	**0.75**	**959**	**1279**	**0.65**	**957**	**1470**
四、麻类合计	**Fiber Cropers**	**0.03**	**189**	**5906**	**0.04**	**293**	**6659**
五、糖料合计	**Sugar Crops**	**2.61**	**157432**	**60435**	**2.71**	**153268**	**56661**
六、烟叶	**Tobacco**	**－**	**2**	**667**	**－**	**2**	**667**
七、药材类合计	**Crude Drugs**	**3.65**	**26017**	**7122**	**3.52**	**24505**	**6972**
八、蔬菜	**Vegetables**	**98.93**	**3133542**	**31674**	**102.7**	**3236119**	**31511**
九、果用瓜	**Melon as Fruit**	**12.89**	**428884**	**33265**	**13.46**	**430114**	**31962**
#1. 西瓜	Watermelon	10.42	365190	35057	10.63	364732	34302
2. 草莓	Strawberry	0.74	24407	32805	1.22	29389	24109
十、花卉园艺	**Flower Gardening**	**30.78**	**－**	**－**	**31.25**	**－**	**－**
十一、其他作物	**Others**	**14.93**	**－**	**－**	**16.14**	**－**	**－**
#绿肥	Green Manure	2.27	－	－	3.03	－	－

3-11 分地区粮食

Sown Areas and Yield of

指　标		Item		全市 Whole Municipality	市区 Urban District	#江干区 Jianggan	#拱墅区 Gongshu	#西湖区 Xihu	#高新(滨江)区 Hi-Tech (Binjiang)
一、粮食播种面积总计	**(公顷)**	**Sown Area of Grain Crops**	**(hectare)**	**188991**	**83018**	**1**	**71**	**2990**	**288**
春粮	(公顷)	Spring Grain	(hectare)	26376	13825	-	-	147	106
早稻	(公顷)	Early Rice	(hectare)	2040	1159	-	-	1	-
晚稻	(公顷)	Late Rice	(hectare)	86973	44244	-	71	1764	134
薯类	(公顷)	Tubers	(hectare)	22990	3067	1	-	236	15
玉米	(公顷)	Corn	(hectare)	20057	4072	-	-	268	26
大豆	(公顷)	Soybeans	(hectare)	29681	15951	-	-	328	16
杂豆	(公顷)	Other Beans	(hectare)	4359	1353	-	-	191	4
其他谷物	(公顷)	Other Cereals	(hectare)	1354	194	-	-	93	-
二、粮食总产量	**(吨)**	**Yield of Grain Crops**	**(ton)**	**1072434**	**491979**	**8**	**628**	**20384**	**1562**
春粮	(吨)	Spring Grain	(ton)	96054	59137	-	-	384	305
早稻	(吨)	Early Rice	(ton)	12688	7668	-	-	5	-
晚稻	(吨)	Late Rice	(ton)	667928	344293	-	628	13501	1076
薯类	(吨)	Tubers	(ton)	122868	19349	8	-	3151	44
玉米	(吨)	Corn	(ton)	94625	20522	-	-	1585	119
大豆	(吨)	Soybeans	(ton)	76412	38608	-	-	881	37
杂豆	(吨)	Other Beans	(ton)	12851	4349	-	-	420	20
其他谷物	(吨)	Other Cereals	(ton)	5176	916	-	-	552	0
三、粮食平均每公顷产量		**Yield of Grain Crops per Hectare**							
按播种面积计算	(公斤)	Calculated by Sown Area	(kg)	5675	5926	8000	8845	6817	5424
春粮	(公斤)	Spring Grain	(kg)	3642	4278	-	-	2612	2874
早稻	(公斤)	Early Rice	(kg)	6220	6616	-	-	500	-
晚稻	(公斤)	Late Rice	(kg)	7680	7782	-	8845	7654	8030
薯类	(公斤)	Tubers	(kg)	5344	6309	8000	-	13352	2933
玉米	(公斤)	Corn	(kg)	4718	5040	-	-	5914	4577
大豆	(公斤)	Soybeans	(kg)	2574	2420	-	-	2686	2313

备注:春粮包括薯类中的马铃薯。

播种面积及产量(2009 年)
Grain Crops by Region(2009)

#萧山区 Xiaoshan	#余杭区 Yuhang	桐庐县 Tonglu	淳安县 Chun'an	建德市 Jiande	富阳市 Fuyang	临安市 Lin'an
50071	**29335**	**17033**	**26330**	**20204**	**25979**	**16427**
10633	2886	1896	2002	3196	3033	2424
62	1096	–	–	808	73	–
22457	19609	7701	5327	8809	13619	7273
972	1843	3049	6738	3662	3615	2859
2353	1425	1922	7303	1450	2983	2327
13254	2353	2250	5049	2532	2275	1624
489	669	583	450	378	885	710
54	47	257	318	184	308	93
265544	**202515**	**101449**	**112448**	**105867**	**163993**	**96698**
48540	9669	5266	5606	9247	9665	7133
373	7290	–	–	4613	407	0
169497	158492	57950	39238	65588	104385	56474
5240	10906	18795	28286	14514	24197	17727
11075	7743	9513	31417	7350	15070	10753
29602	8088	8623	9805	5891	8512	4973
1633	2276	1966	690	686	3201	1959
214	150	1169	669	644	1479	299
5303	6904	5956	4271	5240	6313	5887
4565	3350	2779	2800	2893	3187	2942
6016	6650	–	–	5705	5575	–
7548	8083	7525	7366	7446	7665	7765
5391	5921	6164	4198	3963	6693	6200
4707	5434	4950	4302	5069	5052	4621
2233	3437	3832	1942	2327	3742	3062

Note: Spring grain includes patato in tubers.

3－12 油、菜、茶、

Statistics on Rapeseeds, Vegetables, Tea,

指标	Item	全市 Whole Municipality	市区 Urban District	#江干区 Jianggan	#拱墅区 Gongshu	#西湖区 Xihu	#高新(滨江)区 Hi－Tech (Binjiang)
一、油菜籽	**Rapeseeds**						
播种面积（公顷）	Sown Area (hectare)	38721	9501	－	－	129	2
每公顷产量（公斤）	Yield per Hectare (kg)	2068	2189	－	－	1713	1500
总产量（吨）	Total Output (ton)	80081	20801	－	－	221	3
二、蔬菜	**Vegetables**						
播种面积（公顷）	Sown Area (hectare)	98930	61663	3510	327	2328	1319
总产量（吨）	Total Output (ton)	3133542	1901188	88694	6971	46505	54145
三、茶叶	**Tea**						
（一）茶园面积（公顷）	Tea Garden Area (hectare)	32644	5905	36	－	640	57
（二）总产量（吨）	Output of Tea (ton)	30204	11197	14	－	580	97
春　茶（吨）	Spring Tea (ton)	20828	6853	14	－	195	39
夏　茶（吨）	Summer Tea (ton)	4826	2157	－	－	129	19
秋　茶（吨）	Autumn Tea (ton)	4550	2187	－	－	256	39
四、桑蚕	**Silkworm Cocoons & Mulberry**						
（一）桑园总面积（公顷）	Mulberry Garden Area (hectare)	17053	2017	2	－	147	－
（二）蚕茧总产量（吨）	Output of Silkworm Cocoons (ton)	17870	912	12	－	－	－
春　茧（吨）	Spring Silkworm Cocoons (ton)	8203	769	11	－	－	－
夏　茧（吨）	Summer Silkworm Cocoons (ton)	1272	20	－	－	－	－
秋　茧（吨）	Autumn Silkworm Cocoons (ton)	8395	123	1	－	－	－

蚕、果生产情况(2009 年)

Silkworm Cocoons and Fruits Production(2009)

#萧山区 Xiaoshan	#余杭区 Yuhang	桐庐县 Tonglu	淳安县 Chun'an	建德市 Jiande	富阳市 Fuyang	临安市 Lin'an
4724	4633	6232	6881	5971	7455	2681
2329	2062	1798	1849	2027	2333	2187
11003	9554	11204	12720	12104	17389	5863
29762	23204	6059	7966	7283	10028	5931
1146211	524094	211648	265122	205889	420923	128772
1295	3534	3795	12388	3601	3379	3576
885	9378	1653	6753	3506	4983	2112
751	5763	1202	5065	2781	3203	1724
23	1945	267	728	469	939	266
111	1670	184	960	256	841	122
98	1770	1932	8403	1405	1139	2157
8	892	3625	7588	928	2080	2737
7	751	1568	3378	476	889	1123
–	20	67	880	15	270	20
1	121	1990	3330	437	921	1594

3－12　续表

指标	Item	全市 Whole Municipality	市区 Urban District	#江干区 Jianggan	#拱墅区 Gongshu	#西湖区 Xihu	#高新(滨江)区 Hi－Tech (Binjiang)
五、水果生产	**Fruits**						
(一)果园面积合计 (公顷)	Area of Orchards (hectare)	28100	6188	2	–	76	93
柑桔园 (公顷)	Citrus (hectare)	9987	123	–	–	11	11
梨　园 (公顷)	Pears (hectare)	4102	1187	–	–	12	29
桃　园 (公顷)	Peaches (hectare)	3005	618	1	–	7	1
杨梅园 (公顷)	Red Bayberry (hectare)	2809	1020	1	–	7	49
枇杷园 (公顷)	Loquat (hectare)	2196	778	–	–	–	–
柿子园 (公顷)	Persimmons (hectare)	898	115	–	–	4	–
葡萄园 (公顷)	Grapes (hectare)	524	172	–	–	32	2
其他果园 (公顷)	Others (hectare)	4579	2175	–	–	3	1
(二)水果总产量 (吨)	Yield of Fruits (ton)	772678	240014	10	120	2577	2870
柑　桔 (吨)	Citrus (ton)	159829	1143	–	–	81	97
梨　头 (吨)	Pears (ton)	55685	13470	–	–	380	1413
桃　子 (吨)	Peaches (ton)	50215	9365	6	–	115	50
杨　梅 (吨)	Red Bayberry (ton)	11885	2851	4	–	10	45
枇　杷 (吨)	Loquat (ton)	12515	5534	–	–	–	–
柿　子 (吨)	Persimmons (ton)	9302	1906	–	–	42	–
葡　萄 (吨)	Grapes (ton)	11000	2664	–	–	867	15
果用瓜 (吨)	Melon as Fruit (ton)	428884	196884	–	120	1033	1250
其他水果 (吨)	Others (ton)	33363	6197	–	–	49	–

注:水果产量包括果用瓜和草莓产量。

continued

#萧山区 Xiaoshan	#余杭区 Yuhang	桐庐县 Tonglu	淳安县 Chun'an	建德市 Jiande	富阳市 Fuyang	临安市 Lin'an
2540	3474	3166	8183	6886	2289	1388
33	67	540	4532	4404	274	114
255	891	1201	556	401	509	248
221	388	462	590	373	661	301
731	232	379	374	467	390	179
1	777	120	628	579	80	11
78	33	45	450	162	90	36
78	58	118	44	24	89	77
1143	1028	301	1009	476	196	422
125740	107343	96584	109419	164757	119954	41950
437	528	8411	58840	85884	4549	1002
2615	9062	16424	3886	5580	13067	3258
2584	6610	8271	5386	4123	17139	5931
1645	1147	1819	1049	929	3772	1465
33	5501	1289	3158	1751	666	117
1384	480	1072	3115	1473	1362	374
1137	595	1576	459	163	5095	1043
111077	82100	53586	23612	61035	71641	22126
4828	1320	4136	9914	3819	2663	6634

a) Yield of fruits including melon as fruit and yield of strawberry.

3－13 分地区畜牧业

Statistics on Animal

指 标		Item		全市 Whole Municipality	市区 Urban District	#江干区 Jianggan	#拱墅区 Gongshu
一、生猪饲养		**Hogs**					
生猪年末存栏头数	（万头）	Being Raised at Year－end	（10000 heads）	178.61	98.04	0.11	－
#能繁殖的母猪	（万头）	#Reproducible	（10000 heads）	15.68	10.47	0.01	－
年内肥猪出栏头数	（万头）	Slaughtered Hogs of the Year	（10000 heads）	310.56	166.43	0.13	－
全年饲养量	（万头）	Number of Hogs Raised in the year	（10000 heads）	489.17	264.47	0.24	－
二、牛		**Cattle & Buffaloes**					
牛年末存栏头数	（头）	Being Raised at Year－end	（head）	23389	8292	－	－
#良种及改良种乳牛	（头）	#Improved Milk Cows	（head）	10527	7301	－	－
牛年内出栏头数	（头）	Slaughtered Cattle & Buffaloes of the Year	（head）	11672	1315	－	－
三、羊		**Sheep & Goats**					
羊年末存栏只数	（万只）	Being Raised at Year－end	（10000 heads）	15.27	7.48	0.44	－
羊年内出栏只数	（万只）	Slaughtered Sheep & Goats of the Year	（10000 heads）	21.25	11.18	0.33	－
四、家禽		**Poultry**					
家禽年末存栏只数	（万只）	Being Raised at Year－end	（10000 heads）	2014.04	816.81	－	0.41
家禽年内出栏只数	（万只）	Slaughtered Poultry of the Year	（10000 heads）	4621.58	2685.7	－	0.63
五、兔		**Rabbits**					
兔年末存栏只数	（万只）	Being Raised at Year－end	（10000 heads）	20.35	9.85	－	－
兔年内出栏只数	（万只）	Slaughtered Rabbits of the Year	（10000 heads）	32.36	16.6	－	－
六、年末养蜂箱数	**（箱）**	**Beehives**	**（case）**	**184841**	**37065**	**3500**	**－**
七、畜禽产品产量		**Output of Livestock Products**					
1.肉类产量	（吨）	Output of Meat	（ton）	309219	164670	179	8
#猪 肉	（吨）	Pork	（ton）	232475	121193	83	－

渔业生产（2009 年）
Husbanday and Fishery by Region（2009）

#西湖区 Xihu	#高新(滨江)区 Hi-Tech(Binjiang)	#萧山区 Xiaoshan	#余杭区 Yuhang	桐庐县 Tonglu	淳安县 Chun'an	建德市 Jiande	富阳市 Fuyang	临安市 Lin'an
1.16	0.54	79.77	15.91	12.8	16.85	16.19	16.55	18.18
0.01	0.04	9.07	1.28	0.78	0.77	1.58	0.91	1.17
1.05	1.31	125.89	37.09	22.39	18.83	23.13	43.3	36.48
2.21	1.85	205.66	53	35.19	35.68	39.32	59.85	54.66
20	–	2015	1057	2867	2213	3022	3357	3638
–	–	1705	396	92	–	366	1441	1327
5	–	95	255	1450	1047	1119	2950	3791
0.11	–	1.75	5.15	1.37	0.27	1.12	3.22	1.81
0.11	–	3.11	7.56	1.6	0.31	0.9	4.1	3.16
17.82	4.55	405.9	384.63	76.9	37.51	806.64	188.4	87.78
34.31	8.91	1293.61	1335.19	130.97	58.93	686.94	898.97	160.07
–	–	1.65	8.2	3.85	0.27	2.09	2.32	1.97
–	–	4.82	11.78	6.94	0.27	1.38	6.06	1.11
–	**–**	**31369**	**2196**	**82900**	**19684**	**8387**	**23653**	**13152**
1078	1074	107735	53534	21069	15648	28830	47264	31738
680	939	88075	30744	17734	14550	18477	32475	28046

3－13　续表

指　标	Item	全市 Whole Municipality	市区 Urban District	#江干区 Jianggan	#拱墅区 Gongshu	#西湖区 Xihu	#高新(滨江)区 Hi－Tech (Binjiang)
牛　肉　（吨）	Beef　（ton）	1838	255	–	–	1	–
羊　肉　（吨）	Mutton　（ton）	4080	2270	96	–	14	–
兔　肉　（吨）	Rabbit Meat　（ton）	622	372	–	–	–	–
禽　肉　（吨）	Poultry Meat　（ton）	69726	40550	–	8	383	135
2. 禽蛋产量　（吨）	Poultry Eggs　（ton）	143146	31596	–	–	600	120
3. 蜂蜜产量　（吨）	Honey　（ton）	22560	2314	240	–	–	15
4. 蜂皇浆产量　（吨）	Honey Tonic　（ton）	661.47	139.79	17	–	–	0.4
5. 牛奶产量　（吨）	Milk　（ton）	39297	27600	–	–	–	–
6. 绵羊毛产量　（吨）		–	–	–	–	–	–
7. 兔毛产量　（吨）	Rabbit Wool　（ton）	16	4	–	–	–	–
八、渔业生产	**Fishery**						
（一）淡水产品产量总计（吨）	Total Output of Freshwater Aquatic Products　（ton）	202802	153428	622	506	32100	2141
其中：养殖产量（吨）	Artificially Cultured　（ton）	180567	137304	537	506	20390	1297
1. 鱼　类　（吨）	Fish　（ton）	113070	77343	314	406	14174	764
#鲫　鱼　（吨）	#Crucians　（ton）	11599	6027	66	77	2287	275
鳊　鱼　（吨）	Breams　（ton）	5925	3023	12	10	849	50
黑　鱼　（吨）	Snake Heads　（ton）	18536	18423	–	21	1157	20
2. 虾蟹类　（吨）	Shrimps, Prawns & Crabs　（ton）	33754	32641	42	21	2276	493
3. 贝　类　（吨）	Shellfish　（ton）	1426	151	–	–	151	–
4. 其　他　（吨）	Others　（ton）	32317	27169	181	79	3789	40
#甲　鱼　（吨）	Turtles　（ton）	29815	25759	101	65	3717	38
（二）淡水养殖面积合计（公顷）	Freshwater Aquiculture Area　（hectare）	61743	12407	151	46	2447	246

continued

#萧山区 Xiaoshan	#余杭区 Yuhang	桐庐县 Tonglu	淳安县 Chun'an	建德市 Jiande	富阳市 Fuyang	临安市 Lin'an
17	55	290	151	156	443	543
587	1561	357	45	170	615	623
71	301	119	4	29	80	18
18985	20843	2459	892	9867	13583	2375
3947	26839	4973	3781	87701	8351	6744
1607	452	10850	2109	465	5549	1273
119.8	2.59	409.43	25.59	18.38	43.15	25.13
6980	1120	440	–	523	5914	4820
–	–	–	–	–	–	–
3	1	2	–	1	–	9
53560	62405	7287	16236	12490	9530	3831
52750	59788	6996	13750	9955	9177	3385
23447	37874	3257	13660	8462	7359	2989
205	3038	738	920	1174	2085	655
–	2074	70	639	1412	708	73
8270	8955	–	–	56	52	5
25140	2997	135	–	227	740	11
–	–	–	–	1055	220	–
4163	18917	3604	90	211	858	385
3744	18094	3210	90	86	358	312
3895	4986	1440	41660	2029	1503	2704

3－14 分地区林业
Statistics on Forestry

指 标	Item	全市 Whole Municipality	市区 Urban District
一、营林情况	**Afforestation**		
1. 当年造林面积 （公顷）	Afforested Areas (hectare)	2158	606
#用材林 （公顷）	#Timber Forest (hectare)	352	－
经济林 （公顷）	Economic Forest (hectare)	313	－
2. 迹地更新面积 （公顷）	Area of Forest Updating (hectare)	2710	59
3. 封山育林面积 （公顷）	Area of Afforestation in Enclosed Mountain (hectare)	51681	1216
4. 零星（四旁）植树 （万株）	Planting Trees (10000 plant)	408.8	254.89
5. 幼林抚育作业面积（公顷）	Area of Seedling Cultivated (hectare)	11080	1209
6. 成林抚育面积 （公顷）	Area of Grown Forest Cultivated (hectare)	25351	15146
二、林产品产量	**Output of Forest Products**		
1. 油桐籽 （吨）	Tung－oil Seeds (ton)	－	－
2. 油茶籽 （吨）	Tea－oil Seeds (ton)	9148	－
3. 竹笋干 （吨）	Dried Bamboo Shoots (ton)	27628	10141
4. 核 桃 （吨）	Walnuts (ton)	20331	30
5. 板 栗 （吨）	Chestnuts (ton)	12552	858
三、竹木采伐量	**Lumbering**		
1. 木 材 （万立方米）	Timber Cut (10000 cu. m)	32.04	2.04
2. 竹 材 （万支）	Bamboo Cut (10000 pieces)	2305	864

生产(2009 年)
by Region(2009)

#萧山区 Xiaoshan	#余杭区 Yuhang	桐庐县 Tonglu	淳安县 Chun'an	建德市 Jiande	富阳市 Fuyang	临安市 Lin'an
54	532	142	346	–	1064	–
–	–	60	60	–	232	–
–	–	79	14	–	220	–
12	47	907	374	451	433	486
142	–	41775	2160	3766	1333	1431
32.5	222.39	30	15.1	66.91	20	21.9
–	1209	1956	3467	4448	–	–
–	15146	–	5533	1554	133	2985
–	–	–	–	–	–	–
–	–	1382	6881	885	–	–
1560	8581	385	3575	585	10795	2147
–	30	1001	5355	27	98	13820
600	258	2605	3613	2283	1644	1549
–	0.83	3.97	9.27	7.53	1.14	8.09
137	725	119	427	218	227	450

3-15 分地区灌溉和水利
Irrigation and Water Conservancy

指标		Item		全市 Whole Municipality
一、乡、村办水电站		**Hydroelectric Station in Rural Areas**		
水电站个数	（个）	Number of Hydroelectric Station	（unit）	349
装机容量	（千瓦）	Installed Capacity	（kw）	367825
发电量	（万千瓦时）	Generating Capacity	（10000 kwh）	82674.51
二、灌溉面积		**Irrigated Area**		
1.有效灌溉面积(农田面积)	（千公顷）	Irrigable Land	（1000 hectares）	172.64
2.旱涝保收面积	（千公顷）	Area of Stable Yields Despite Drought or Excessive Rain	（1000 hectares）	131.07
3.机电排灌面积	（千公顷）	Electrical Irrigation Area	（1000 hectares）	115.98
三、机电井		**Motor - pumped Well**		
已配套机电井	（眼）	Motor - pumped Well System	（unit）	169
装机容量	（千瓦）	Installed Capacity	（kw）	710

设施情况(2009 年)

Facilities by Region(2009)

市 区 Urban District	#江干区 Jianggan	#拱墅区 Gongshu	#西湖区 Xihu	#萧山区 Xiaoshan	#余杭区 Yuhang	桐庐县 Tonglu	淳安县 Chun'an	建德市 Jiande	富阳市 Fuyang	临安市 Lin'an
6	-	-	-	-	6	75	99	49	24	96
2895	-	-	-	-	2895	79450	101940	20995	17825	144720
373.53	-	-	-	-	373.53	15567	21844.01	3369.04	3242.3	38278.63
95.09	1.11	0.2	3.03	56.59	33.4	12.36	10.38	16.03	20.9	17.88
79.75	0.84	-	2.07	44.88	31.22	9	6.33	11.16	13.71	11.12
88.49	1.03	-	3.02	53.08	30.6	5.08	1.8	4.3	13.24	3.07
122	-	-	-	-	122	-	-	-	47	-
480	-	-	-	-	480	-	-	-	230	-

3-16 分地区主要农

Possession of Major Agricultural

指标		Item		全市 Whole Municipality 2009年	为上年(%) As Compared with the Preceding Year(%)
一、农业机械总动力	**(千瓦)**	**Total Power of Agricultural Machinery**	**(kw)**	**3223168**	**102.2**
耕作机械动力	(千瓦)	Cultivation Machinery	(kw)	198160	113.5
收获机械动力	(千瓦)	Harvest Machinery	(kw)	293731	99.1
植保机械动力	(千瓦)	Plant Protection Machinery	(kw)	29144	122.7
排灌机械动力	(千瓦)	Drainage & Irrigation Machinery	(kw)	422034	98.7
农副产品加工机械动力	(千瓦)	Processing Machinery of Agricultural Products	(kw)	181935	100.2
运输机械动力	(千瓦)	Transport Machinery	(kw)	912069	98.9
渔业机械动力	(千瓦)	Fishery Machinery	(kw)	109043	109.9
其他机械动力	(千瓦)	Other Machinery	(kw)	1077052	104.7
二、主要农机具		**Agricultural Machinery and Machinery For Processing Farm Products**			
大中型拖拉机	(台)	Large & Medium Tractors	(unit)	770	113.9
机引农具	(台)	Mechanized Farm Implement	(unit)	1451	112.9
农用小型拖拉机	(台)	Mini - tractors	(unit)	15928	105.7
联合收获机	(台)	Combine Harvesters	(unit)	959	107
机动割晒机	(台)	Motorized Harvesters	(unit)	26	76.5
机动脱粒机	(台)	Motorized Thresher	(unit)	187953	96.5
谷物烘干机	(台)	Cereal Dryer	(unit)	44	146.7
机动喷雾(粉)器	(架)	Motorized Sprayer	(unit)	16018	128
农用水泵	(台)	Water Pump for Agricultural Use	(unit)	144887	94.8
节水喷灌机械	(套)	Saving Water and Sprinkling Machinery	(set)	3797	97.9
粮食加工机械	(台)	Grain Processing Machinery	(unit)	19395	100.2
棉花加工机械	(台)	Cotton Processing Machinery	(unit)	436	121.1
油料加工机械	(台)	Oil Processing Machinery	(unit)	1517	102.2
农用运输机械	(台)	Vehicles for Agricultural Use	(unit)	41809	99.3
淡水机动渔船	(艘)	Motorized Fishing Boats	(unit)	1958	97.9

机具年末拥有量(2009 年)
Machinery at the Year - end by Region(2009)

市　区 Urban District	#萧山区 Xiaoshan	#余杭区 Yuhang	桐庐县 Tonglu	淳安县 Chun'an	建德市 Jiande	富阳市 Fuyang	临安市 Lin'an
1617897	**754470**	**494210**	**245997**	**260253**	**269502**	**405287**	**424232**
99141	48066	46291	15171	13940	16138	26207	27563
142376	45515	90720	38049	7226	31224	55802	19054
5402	3604	1566	697	1502	3883	1518	16142
195626	83250	87871	36374	20036	48457	57025	64516
51719	30138	14830	11573	53412	21979	14168	29084
407652	264611	124966	89601	55442	76454	129501	153419
92315	72384	8749	925	12404	1825	1145	429
623666	206902	119217	53607	96291	69542	119921	114025
683	539	135	12	1	4	68	2
1369	1109	252	13	–	12	56	1
6464	1986	4023	1556	1524	1929	2392	2063
604	435	144	66	4	56	209	20
22	12	10	–	–	1	2	1
93930	25777	63740	25894	3962	19715	32442	12010
32	20	11	2	–	5	3	2
3569	2561	866	260	574	1562	998	9055
42396	15759	22642	15803	4344	23177	15120	44047
472	91	366	47	554	2690	6	28
2476	1380	915	1349	6876	1845	1015	5834
181	164	17	16	162	14	47	16
220	155	44	259	508	271	89	170
17943	11022	5749	4055	2783	3373	7371	6284
271	51	89	9	1373	229	50	26

3－17 农业机械作业和
Agricultural Mechanization and

指　标		Item		全　市 Whole Municipality 2009年	为上年(％) As Compared with the Preceding Year(％)
一、农业机械作业		**Agricultural Mechanization**			
当年机械收割面积	（千公顷）	Harvest Area by Tractors	(1000 hectares)	104.45	101.88
二、农村用电量	**（万千瓦时）**	**Electricity Consumed in Rural Area**	**(10000 kwh)**	**989818**	**101.96**
三、农业化肥用量		**Consumption of Chemical Fertilizer**			
（一）按实物量计算	（吨）	Physical Quantity Consumption	(ton)	625395	99.45
1.氮　肥	（吨）	Nitrogenous Fertilizer	(ton)	295373	97.85
2.磷　肥	（吨）	Phosphate Fertilizer	(ton)	100159	100.82
3.钾　肥	（吨）	Potash Fertilizer	(ton)	46416	98.62
4.复合肥	（吨）	Compound Fertilizer	(ton)	183447	101.58
（二）按折纯法计算	（吨）	Pure Consumption	(ton)	118918	99.68
1.氮　肥	（吨）	Nitrogenous Fertilizer	(ton)	60168	97.42
2.磷　肥	（吨）	Phosphate Fertilizer	(ton)	13845	105.78
3.钾　肥	（吨）	Potash Fertilizer	(ton)	8899	102.01
4.复合肥	（吨）	Compound Fertilizer	(ton)	36006	100.8
四、农用塑料薄膜使用量	**（吨）**	**Use of Plastic Film**	**(ton)**	**7673**	**102.48**
五、农用柴油使用量	**（吨）**	**Consumption of Diesel Oil**	**(ton)**	**27336**	**108.09**
六、农药使用量	**（吨）**	**Consumption of Pesticide**	**(ton)**	**8816**	**96.54**

物资消耗情况(2009 年)
Material Consumption(2009)

市　区 Urban District	#萧山区 Xiaoshan	#余杭区 Yuhang	桐庐县 Tonglu	淳安县 Chun'an	建德市 Jiande	富阳市 Fuyang	临安市 Lin'an
59.7	31.69	24.76	8.15	1.51	11.35	15.67	8.07
482018	**207398**	**176285**	**59997**	**9563**	**18957**	**329944**	**89339**
375543	292790	69688	39896	60708	54351	17686	77211
180557	138000	37394	18449	33676	25185	10981	26525
61952	51341	9039	8783	7459	8070	1919	11976
23724	17078	5697	4343	6605	5243	280	6221
109310	86371	17558	8321	12968	15853	4506	32489
57119	34635	17526	8439	7408	17682	7426	20844
29498	19569	8174	3742	3253	8453	4612	10610
6149	4321	1436	1517	860	2472	691	2156
3662	2135	1251	1053	413	1951	140	1680
17810	8610	6665	2127	2882	4806	1983	6398
3558	**2429**	**551**	**641**	**997**	**1853**	**185**	**439**
10995	**7901**	**2733**	**4464**	**1493**	**3487**	**259**	**6638**
4183	**2725**	**1212**	**827**	**667**	**1014**	**889**	**1236**

3-18 农村经济
Rural Economic Income

单位:万元

指标	Item	全市 Whole Municipality 2009年	全市 Whole Municipality 为上年(%) As Compared with the Preceding Year(%)
一、农村经济总收入	**Total Rural Economic Income**	**111665515**	**109.3**
#出售产品收入	Sales Income	74587476	106.3
1.农、林、牧、渔业收入	Income from Farming, Forestry, Animal Husbandry & Fishery	3021719	114.7
①农业收入	Income from Farming	1643978	112.8
#出售种植业产品收入	Income from Planting	-	-
②林业收入	Income from Forestry	370348	125
③牧业收入	Income from Animal Husbandry	647228	116.2
④渔业收入	Income from Fishery	360165	111.4
2.工业收入	Income from Industry	79060645	105.4
3.建筑业收入	Income from Construction	6973107	123.3
4.运输业收入	Income from Transportation	1394121	120.9
5.商业、饮食业收入	Income from Trade & Catering Services	12039629	121.9
6.服务业收入	Income from Services	7395944	108.4
7.其他收入	Other Income	1780350	175.6
二、农村经济总费用	**Total Rural Economic Expenses**	**99180995**	**109.2**
#生产费用	Production Expenses	91774128	110.1
三、可分配净收入	**Disposable Net Income**	**13295024**	**110.3**
#国家税金	State Taxes	3010421	102.7
农民所得收入	Farmers' Earnings	4900630	112.5
每人平均所得(元)	Per Capita Income(yuan)	12356	-
为上年(%)	As Compared with the Preceding Year(%)	110.6	-
四、村组集体所有年末生产性固定资产原值	**Original Value of Fixed Assets for Production**	**889125**	**101.5**

收入分配(2009 年)
Distribution(2009)

(10000 yuan)

市 区 Urban District	#萧山区 Xiaoshan	#余杭区 Yuhang	桐庐县 Tonglu	淳安县 Chun'an	建德市 Jiande	富阳市 Fuyang	临安市 Lin'an
80724071	**42454791**	**16231778**	**4740656**	**1573831**	**3117769**	**14264248**	**7244940**
51096726	33759162	12933809	4323019	1001064	2458709	9759668	5948290
1275689	662134	459242	267728	367333	265534	544928	300507
716781	394800	213099	133192	213960	141930	312721	125394
–	–	–	–	–	–	–	–
42842	12220	29755	41115	74794	13778	84498	113321
235485	122725	108245	64783	67279	104228	116035	59418
280579	132389	108143	28639	11300	5599	31674	2374
55258773	35709697	13712806	4145186	989464	2399438	10359992	5907792
6098757	2564302	298526	63396	46259	47668	337400	379627
638086	127323	239299	72571	44894	45646	460937	131987
10214343	2289979	809992	79415	66520	42569	1397561	239221
6152052	808287	339010	49308	37938	36114	1026598	93934
1086372	293069	372903	63052	21423	280799	136832	191872
72852544	**38560101**	**13914041**	**4032831**	**1331265**	**2749849**	**12088871**	**6125635**
68575257	37140388	13037468	3684299	1208534	2337232	10515924	5452882
8333681	**4134100**	**2456508**	**753350**	**290750**	**439136**	**2260173**	**1217934**
2234337	1207908	559197	119387	16665	51476	439542	149014
2895865	1438047	935702	301424	239907	313691	669101	480642
–	15201	14164	9898	6511	7992	13156	11383
–	109.4	111.7	109.6	109.1	111.8	112	111.8
788786	**119656**	**68391**	**7800**	**2196**	**12018**	**34435**	**43890**

3－19 乡(镇)
Statistics on Towns

乡镇名称 Town		村民委员会(个) Number of Villagers' Committees (unit)	农村常住户数(户) Resident Households in Rural Areas (household)	农村常住人口数(人) Resident Population in Rural Areas (person)	农村从业人员数(人) Practitioners in Rural Areas (person)
江干区	**Jianggan District**				
丁桥镇	Dingqiao	2	2234	9080	4407
笕桥镇	Jianqiao	8	7464	30050	14651
彭埠镇	Pengbu	–	7984	31908	16026
九堡镇	Jiubao	4	7423	30423	15828
拱墅区	**Gongshu District**				
康桥镇	Kangqiao	9	4187	15829	8032
半山镇	Banshan	–	725	2854	1938
祥符街道	Xiangfu Subdistrict	–	2741	9139	4198
西湖区	**Xihu District**				
留下街道	Liuxia Subdistrict	2	3286	9066	4934
转塘街道	Zhuantang Subdistrict	16	13859	53585	23233
双浦镇	Shuangpu	28	14829	55220	29444
三墩镇	Sandun	6	9626	37258	23226
高新(滨江)区	**Hi－Tech(Bingjiang) District**				
浦沿街道	Puyan Subdistrict	4	9679	35295	20245
长河街道	Changhe Subdistrict	6	14704	38886	23075
西兴街道	Xixing Subdistrict	5	6257	21533	12920
开发区	**Development Zone**				
下沙街道	Xiasha Subdistrict	–	1099	3742	1208
西湖风景名胜区	**The West Lake Scenic Zone**				
西湖街道	West Lake Subdistrict	9	2941	5587	3743

基本情况(2009 年)
and Townships(2009)

粮食播种面积(亩) Sown Area of Grain Crops (mu)	粮食总产量(吨) Yield of Grain Crops (ton)	农业总产值(当年价格)(万元) Gross Output Value of Agriculture (10000 yuan)	财政总收入(万元) Financial Revenue (10000 yuan)	农村经济总收入(万元) Total Income of Rural Economy (10000 yuan)	农民人均年纯收入(元) Per Capita Annual Net Income (yuan)
–	–	701	29471	538731	13885
–	–	6355	118072	2135473	16246
–	–	4777	47440	1564588	15488
–	–	4820	43544	811656	13820
600	332	1019	17358	3052666	15000
470	296	720	42861	1335459	15651
–	–	3799	54537	972899	15009
–	–	–	87613	403417	15342
6166	2552	14653	51141	477385	14760
25087	11045	29535	3286	841188	13798
13568	6787	9426	43098	534606	14623
1181	409	8482	36351	1294176	13916
1230	425	26128	44043	1278994	14768
1904	728	11271	57117	1229925	13875
3920	1339	20517	18838	361507	–
–	–	5886	7080	59887	–

3－19 续表1

乡镇名称 Town		村民委员会(个) Number of Villagers' Committees (unit)	农村常住户数(户) Resident Households in Rural Areas (household)	农村常住人口数(人) Resident Population in Rural Areas (person)	农村从业人员数(人) Practitioners in Rural Areas (person)
萧山区	**Xiaoshan District**				
河上镇	Heshang	15	9270	26570	16877
楼塔镇	Louta	12	9270	26570	13323
浦阳镇	Puyang	18	12308	36167	20061
戴村镇	Daicun	22	10665	36667	23587
临浦镇	Linpu	20	13729	46293	26727
进化镇	Jinhua	25	14699	50611	30495
义桥镇	Yiqiao	21	13561	44208	28339
衙前镇	Yaqian	11	6500	24148	14970
所前镇	Suoqian	19	13252	44946	22930
闻堰镇	Wenyan	6	5905	20855	13316
坎山镇	Kanshan	19	14889	48166	28133
新街镇	Xinjie	15	16741	51614	30503
宁围镇	Ningwei	15	18797	53304	26651
瓜沥镇	Guali	23	17307	52903	31995
义蓬街道	Yipeng Subdistrict	22	16960	56031	33107
南阳街道	Nanyang Subdistrict	13	11502	39151	23933
靖江街道	Jingjiang Subdistrict	10	11195	30709	19974
益农镇	Yinong	19	13650	42482	27768
党山镇	Dangshan	21	14478	43882	27773
新湾街道	Xinwan Subdistrict	12	8144	25295	13498
党湾镇	Dangwan	17	12322	37424	25404
河庄街道	Hezhuang Subdistrict	20	14227	49175	29389
城厢街道	Chengxiang Subdistrict	–	11427	44646	9413
北干街道	Beigan Subdistrict	6	13561	48095	16707
蜀山街道	Shushan Subdistrict	8	14741	43785	27190
新塘街道	Xintang Subdistrict	17	19701	69551	36978
前进街道	Qianjin Subdistrict	3	3894	11556	7893
临江街道	Linjiang Subdistrict	2	1145	3949	2575
余杭区	**Yuhang District**				
运河镇	Yunhe	14	9395	36904	24342

continued 1

粮食播种面积（亩）Sown Area of Grain Crops (mu)	粮食总产量（吨）Yield of Grain Crops (ton)	农业总产值（当年价格）（万元）Gross Output Value of Agriculture (10000 yuan)	财政总收入（万元）Financial Revenue (10000 yuan)	农村经济总收入（万元）Total Income of Rural Economy (10000 yuan)	农民人均年纯收入（元）Per Capita Annual Net Income (yuan)
16726	6771	10247	18319	1043146	11938
14955	5373	8813	14469	399975	10946
23126	10093	21026	30508	491551	12200
20342	7955	12578	23494	691569	12238
14750	5790	22695	44902	1182500	13256
22176	10569	23194	19383	541210	13000
23552	10780	22300	42030	1124601	14485
7100	2702	7650	55622	3928382	17802
24078	10203	20660	25338	1172747	13758
4659	1808	13159	50707	1036380	16066
21751	5661	25099	33895	1182100	15595
15825	4420	66921	72501	2856064	17974
15237	3442	35790	221820	9291034	20518
43847	15269	25131	85780	3416698	15614
71659	22977	47222	30985	929991	15058
39590	15233	24604	33538	1129000	15510
35903	11135	19980	26131	1130260	16717
54677	195449	35463	22055	2523076	15319
63311	23407	29713	36005	2680105	14633
53944	10516	22802	10929	564147	15284
61310	19423	31168	26712	1267171	17282
73468	21921	34769	28451	859838	15758
1816	566	2347	115864	485240	14422
630	138	4332	100406	346253	19323
6690	2571	8921	33219	811956	13427
5622	1791	15652	95683	1739692	14602
19811	6017	9374	10379	41710	–
10300	3179	4903	7804	14778	13963
12793	5589	35821	13185	606364	13878

3－19 续表2

乡 镇 名 称 Town		村民委员会(个) Number of Villagers' Committees (unit)	农村常住户数(户) Resident Households in Rural Areas (household)	农村常住人口数(人) Resident Population in Rural Areas (person)	农村从业人员数(人) Practitioners in Rural Areas (person)
塘栖镇	Tangxi	27	18090	68665	44106
乔司镇	Qiaosi	11	10083	38319	24803
仁和镇	Renhe	18	15942	63375	42860
崇贤镇	Chongxian	11	10374	40850	29600
余杭镇	Yuhang	14	11404	38319	22234
闲林镇	Xianlin	8	5719	22144	13855
仓前镇	Cangqian	9	7932	30075	20570
良渚镇	Liangzhu	24	21201	85198	51637
中泰乡	Zhongtai	10	7196	25291	15994
瓶窑镇	Pingyao	13	10833	38262	25845
径山镇	Jingshan	13	10411	33733	24816
黄湖镇	Huanghu	5	4075	13430	8654
鸬鸟镇	Luniao	6	3731	12254	7736
百丈镇	Baizhang	6	3203	11032	8030
临平街道	Linping Subdistrict	–	2649	11380	6698
南苑街道	Nanyuan Subdistrict	–	7042	28458	13612
五常街道	Wuchang Subdistrict	–	7091	26038	15206
星桥街道	Xingqiao Subdistrict	–	4042	27495	9504
桐庐县	**Tonglu County**				
桐君街道	Tongjun Subdistrict	25	16771	47781	29071
旧县街道	Jiuxian Subdistrict	5	2845	8394	5539
富春江镇	Fuchunjiang	15	6278	19507	12709
江南镇	Jiangnan	20	13662	47123	29854
凤川镇	Fengchuan	8	5656	17517	11259
新合乡	Xinghe	5	1718	5114	3546
横村镇	Hengcun	24	13078	38641	24993
莪山畲族乡	Eshan	7	2731	8738	5649
钟山乡	Zhongshan	11	6091	17898	12644
分水镇	Fenshui	26	16330	45555	30284

continued 2

粮食播种面积（亩）Sown Area of Grain Crops (mu)	粮食总产量（吨）Yield of Grain Crops (ton)	农业总产值（当年价格）（万元）Gross Output Value of Agriculture (10000 yuan)	财政总收入（万元）Financial Revenue (10000 yuan)	农村经济总收入（万元）Total Income of Rural Economy (10000 yuan)	农民人均年纯收入（元）Per Capita Annual Net Income (yuan)
42215	18022	52786	76779	1950100	15537
6306	1567	19528	49319	969000	14690
43528	21056	40317	34189	923563	13571
18053	8247	25160	30847	1262160	14323
53807	26366	34060	71537	1074258	14505
12556	5183	14265	90980	1361853	15131
43915	21324	26210	41439	419322	14500
44673	22363	34947	132909	1739729	13565
15763	7337	19334	23227	373168	14433
36721	17777	44759	37755	1411900	12598
43135	19285	59986	19945	560839	12384
13498	5930	17162	7658	226511	13230
9003	4833	26137	2139	176845	13588
6503	2794	9540	2547	256450	14243
3465	1263	14741	23679	266639	13972
11280	3872	27307	28219	497530	14551
3883	1580	6474	44240	854685	19980
1892	707	12980	26594	364750	15240
27310	11842	34277	43180	1218611	10043
8326	3210	4365	2896	168214	11553
18747	8744	26270	18816	436419	10658
26952	11003	13246	13197	486606	9611
10865	5088	12006	3873	181037	9611
2904	1427	2240	459	38239	8753
37738	15638	24094	13028	900270	11570
8895	3401	4997	1202	89083	8824
19412	6899	11517	5349	154005	9473
34734	13550	40467	11556	667264	9907

3－19 续表3

乡镇名称 Town		村民委员会(个) Number of Villagers' Committees (unit)	农村常住户数(户) Resident Households in Rural Areas (household)	农村常住人口数(人) Resident Population in Rural Areas (person)	农村从业人员数(人) Practitioners in Rural Areas (person)
瑶琳镇	Yaolin	16	10405	31861	23009
百江镇	Baijiang	15	5567	15462	12431
合村乡	Hecun	6	2835	8787	6566
淳安县	**Chun'an County**				
千岛湖镇	Qiandaohu	22	6214	18066	11090
文昌镇	Wenchang	16	4155	12749	7835
石林镇	Shilin	8	1433	4628	2847
临歧镇	Linqi	17	5641	18726	11504
威坪镇	Weiping	44	15559	43554	29208
姜家镇	Jiangjia	28	7462	24068	14775
梓桐镇	Zitong	19	5965	18615	11441
汾口镇	Fenkou	51	15236	50110	30772
中洲镇	Zhongzhou	19	5886	19332	11885
大墅镇	Dashu	17	4339	13944	8584
枫树岭镇	Fengshuling	28	5851	17833	11266
里商乡	Lishang	16	3249	10791	6656
金峰乡	Jinfeng	11	1814	5856	3612
富文乡	Fuwen	10	2498	8221	5050
左口乡	Zuokou	11	3298	10940	6720
屏门乡	Pingmen	15	3942	12385	7616
瑶山乡	Yaoshan	11	2842	9363	6021
王阜乡	Wangfu	18	5968	17584	10814
宋村乡	Songcun	8	2056	5833	3598
鸠坑乡	Jiukeng	9	2763	7916	4890
浪川乡	Langchuan	19	5993	18880	11616

continued 3

粮食播种面积（亩）Sown Area of Grain Crops (mu)	粮食总产量（吨）Yield of Grain Crops (ton)	农业总产值（当年价格）（万元）Gross Output Value of Agriculture (10000 yuan)	财政总收入（万元）Financial Revenue (10000 yuan)	农村经济总收入（万元）Total Income of Rural Economy (10000 yuan)	农民人均年纯收入（元）Per Capita Annual Net Income (yuan)
29023	10396	22206	5033	222786	9620
15722	5051	11845	990	87166	7990
14872	5203	8949	579	32197	7170
11164	3587	14288	7390	211875	7582
15027	4562	10702	3577	106076	7516
5595	1285	5042	1302	29993	7486
19105	5532	15113	4270	43391	7206
36732	10385	28894	4655	140368	6028
27282	8596	16765	3404	94478	6661
32200	8278	14671	1931	101441	6931
52587	17419	26854	7031	240093	6032
16515	5245	9208	2121	43312	5701
12877	4455	8993	2237	142400	7200
16428	5776	16177	2136	79933	6868
12863	2820	10088	1730	34977	7205
7080	2438	5409	1055	12320	6360
8377	2383	6026	1250	24195	6599
13174	3471	8650	1742	17846	6248
20100	4257	9717	1689	38312	6618
12553	3007	9523	1219	28642	6926
15550	3036	10852	1789	31350	5278
4163	719	3849	878	10458	5372
5127	1168	6432	1062	25631	5743
22260	7149	11796	2224	57142	6751

3－19　续表4

乡镇名称 Town		村民委员会(个) Number of Villagers' Committees (unit)	农村常住户数(户) Resident Households in Rural Areas (household)	农村常住人口数(人) Resident Population in Rural Areas (person)	农村从业人员数(人) Practitioners in Rural Areas (person)
界首乡	Jieshou	13	2583	8062	4968
安阳乡	Anyang	15	3540	11645	7184
建德市	**Jiande City**				
新安江街道	Xin'anjiang Subdistrict	8	4691	14357	9142
洋溪街道	Yangxi Subdistrict	6	4297	12373	8297
更楼街道	Genglou Subdistrict	15	7784	23566	13463
莲花镇	Lianhua	6	3134	10362	6623
乾潭镇	Qiantan	24	12409	39183	25344
钦堂乡	Qintang	7	2785	9077	5144
梅城镇	Meicheng	15	8692	26289	15090
杨村桥镇	Yangcunqiao	13	5763	19284	11518
下涯镇	Xiaya	11	7601	25289	16054
大洋镇	Dayang	19	9837	32432	19955
三都镇	Sandu	19	9421	26956	15713
寿昌镇	Shouchang	23	10694	35266	19942
航头镇	Hangtou	18	9746	33315	18563
大慈岩镇	Daciyan	12	5871	14557	11493
大同镇	Datong	34	16128	54018	33644
李家镇	Lijia	10	6662	20522	11992

continued 4

粮食播种面积（亩）Sown Area of Grain Crops (mu)	粮食总产量（吨）Yield of Grain Crops (ton)	农业总产值（当年价格）（万元）Gross Output Value of Agriculture (10000 yuan)	财政总收入（万元）Financial Revenue (10000 yuan)	农村经济总收入（万元）Total Income of Rural Economy (10000 yuan)	农民人均年纯收入（元）Per Capita Annual Net Income (yuan)
9849	2177	10701	1679	23140	6530
16481	4168	11122	1552	36458	6826
3811	1331	15327	24410	431300	9825
3935	1077	4418	4462	186000	8375
17088	7488	9684	3637	165311	8409
9204	2870	20771	2292	89412	10337
36600	13613	19363	12383	716449	10913
9420	3441	3676	1669	48000	9903
19202	6346	23111	11143	411922	7991
19631	6238	27696	3244	207184	10317
18028	6089	34788	1951	120676	7583
22507	7092	27160	4704	228860	7084
13303	6323	33169	1402	164927	6352
28044	12570	11879	11821	367239	7713
29561	11524	17830	2087	94864	7050
16566	8394	12822	1665	104540	6378
38861	16816	24966	5221	127050	6485
17297	6324	10127	3581	74646	7970

3-19 续表5

乡镇名称 Town	村民委员会(个) Number of Villagers' Committees (unit)	农村常住户数(户) Resident Households in Rural Areas (household)	农村常住人口数(人) Resident Population in Rural Areas (person)	农村从业人员数(人) Practitioners in Rural Areas (person)
富阳市 Fuyang City				
万市镇 Wanshi	15	6543	21601	13204
洞桥镇 Dongqiao	11	5982	18069	11147
胥口镇 Xukou	13	5504	17260	10106
永昌镇 Yongchang	5	3328	10433	6183
渌渚镇 Luzhu	13	5173	15961	10130
新登镇 Xindeng	31	17276	53485	33404
上官乡 Shangguan	5	2711	8269	4585
常绿镇 Changlu	8	4593	13849	9303
大源镇 Dayuan	15	10864	35642	21940
灵桥镇 Lingqiao	13	7216	23878	14309
里山镇 Lishan	5	3168	10399	6052
渔山乡 Yushan	4	3534	12571	8192
场口镇 Changkou	24	12250	39996	24493
龙门镇 Longmen	4	2528	6841	4545
环山乡 Huanshan	7	3707	11909	7577
常安镇 Chang'an	16	7378	24045	15761
湖源乡 Huyuan	10	3387	11662	7992
高桥镇 Gaoqiao	16	9724	30551	19770
受降镇 Shouxiang	6	6059	19185	9529
春建乡 Chunjian	6	2931	8733	4876
新桐乡 Xintong	7	4062	12233	8285
鹿山街道 Lushan Subdistrict	9	7212	20792	13431
富春街道 Fuchun Subdistrict	20	13862	36966	23386
春江街道 Chunjiang Subdistrict	9	7780	25650	15062
东洲街道 Dongzhou Subdistrict	15	11723	40299	24686

continued 5

粮食播种面积（亩）Sown Area of Grain Crops (mu)	粮食总产量（吨）Yield of Grain Crops (ton)	农业总产值（当年价格）（万元）Gross Output Value of Agriculture (10000 yuan)	财政总收入（万元）Financial Revenue (10000 yuan)	农村经济总收入（万元）Total Income of Rural Economy (10000 yuan)	农民人均年纯收入（元）Per Capita Annual Net Income (yuan)
30348	11310	34830	5030	273915	10404
22171	8630	44025	5017	218776	10662
16593	7125	22174	4491	120212	10104
9558	4382	13117	4039	79009	12690
17125	7284	17735	5667	97812	12564
42687	17609	60325	26369	900808	12219
3350	1352	4934	2417	57786	12840
5003	1749	4803	3152	86876	10732
11327	4827	14631	9886	1183407	16322
9777	4290	10306	15930	691784	14490
6795	3325	6563	3546	226487	12314
7510	3150	6689	3228	137245	12283
30493	12882	28038	8825	280426	9739
5699	2374	4425	2169	41601	10601
6545	2924	4685	8451	408075	11992
17333	7181	13418	2981	157633	10121
6760	2572	8951	3942	27676	9136
29356	12966	50533	30399	2026858	17473
15162	5594	18179	13847	1039620	17455
10225	4311	19046	2639	107062	12485
11738	5622	6593	3040	57178	10818
14757	7012	21433	30483	369820	14967
21670	9259	16718	63099	2666572	16025
12717	4931	11850	60350	1992340	16938
23232	10502	36176	23504	619140	14822

3－19 续表6

乡镇名称 Town	村民委员会(个) Number of Villagers' Committees (unit)	农村常住户数 (户) Resident Households in Rural Areas (household)	农村常住人口数 (人) Resident Population in Rural Areas (person)	农村从业人员数 (人) Practitioners in Rural Areas (person)
临安市 Lin'an City				
锦城街道 Jincheng Subdistrict	17	17463	45199	26037
玲珑街道 Linlong Subdistrict	16	8992	24883	13698
青山湖街道 Qingshanghu Subdistrict	9	6308	18904	11804
锦南街道 jinnan Subdistrict	9	4220	11496	7619
三口镇 Sankou	6	2775	8304	5206
横畈镇 Hengfan	10	4866	14866	8962
高虹镇 Gaohong	9	6472	20173	16770
太湖源镇 Taihuyuan	20	10798	31661	21238
板桥乡 Banqiao	9	6026	18887	12132
於潜镇 Yuqian	26	14979	43473	23596
藻溪镇 Zaoxi	12	6970	20095	14010
太阳镇 Taiyang	11	5661	17207	10780
潜川镇 Qianchuan	10	4785	12590	8581
西天目乡 Xitianmu	11	4813	13409	7845
千洪乡 Qianhong	4	2021	6305	4244
横路乡 Henglu	7	3072	9127	6361
乐平乡 Leping	6	3351	10218	6577
昌化镇 Changhua	14	7616	24338	11335
龙岗镇 Longgang	8	3647	10665	7118
河桥镇 Heqiao	11	5177	15391	11402
湍口镇 Tuankou	13	3986	13359	8483
清凉峰镇 Qingliangfeng	10	6740	18897	12977
马啸乡 Maxiao	7	3049	9105	5818
岛石镇 Daoshi	10	6734	18674	12303
大峡谷镇 Daxiagu	16	3831	11304	7942
新桥乡 Xinqiao	6	2376	7197	4365

continued 6

粮食播种面积（亩）Sown Area of Grain Crops (mu)	粮食总产量（吨）Yield of Grain Crops (ton)	农业总产值（当年价格）（万元）Gross Output Value of Agriculture (10000 yuan)	财政总收入（万元）Financial Revenue (10000 yuan)	农村经济总收入（万元）Total Income of Rural Economy (10000 yuan)	农民人均年纯收入（元）Per Capita Annual Net Income (yuan)
15065	6049	24154	46408	1084296	11998
10190	4475	16050	14698	923955	12411
5493	2367	6402	43142	933778	15568
4862	1733	5349	3275	68500	10698
4050	1910	10341	1732	91026	11157
8626	4336	14675	2440	116236	12191
9908	4736	16938	6457	328973	12280
18672	6762	37726	5214	802554	12518
13716	5031	19902	6997	231193	11178
13169	5907	31679	5625	694716	11551
13756	6851	16654	2463	162971	10742
10355	5140	13320	2972	398184	11731
6722	2058	17824	1892	142066	9571
6166	2034	23091	2347	126581	11222
1213	327	5127	804	56341	12956
3735	1093	9940	1206	60489	9890
3615	1106	12884	800	140041	12070
12766	4902	12969	7068	231768	12002
11249	4699	9187	2565	136600	11484
13543	5435	11885	3843	65378	7800
11330	3172	10805	2306	41912	9257
15020	4905	14247	1815	67188	10092
7373	2553	5774	779	37430	9865
12485	3339	19495	1729	55417	9418
9118	4171	14137	1227	66746	9207
4191	1609	6560	1318	40028	9198

主要统计指标解释

农林牧渔业总产值 是以货币表现的农、林、牧、渔业全部产品的总量和对农林牧渔生产活动进行的各种支持性服务活动的价值。他反映一定时期内的农林牧渔业生产的总规模和总成果。

农林牧渔业的统计范围是:

(1)农业 包括农作物种植业和其他农业。

农作物种植业 包括谷类、豆类、薯类、棉花、麻类、烟叶、蔬菜、药材、瓜类和其他农作物的种植以及茶园、桑园、果园的生产经营。

其他农业 包括采集野生植物的果实、纤维、树脂、油料以及柴草、野生药材、菌类等。

(2)林业 包括林木的栽培(不包括茶园、桑园和果园的栽培、管理和收获等活动)、林产品的采集和村及村以下合作经济组织和农户的竹木砍伐。

(3)牧业 包括除渔业养殖以外的一切动物饲养和放牧以及野生动物的捕猎和饲养。

(4)渔业 包括水生动物和海藻类植物的养殖和捕捞。

(5)农林牧渔服务业 包括对农林牧渔生产活动进行的各种支持性服务活动。

粮食产量 指全社会的产量,包括国营农场等全民所有制经营、集体统一经营的和农民家庭经营的产量,还包括工矿企业家属办的农场和其他生产单位的产量。粮食除包括稻谷、小麦、大麦、玉米、高粱、谷子及其他杂粮外,还包括薯类和豆类。其产量计算方法,豆类按去豆荚后的干豆计算,薯类按5公斤鲜薯折1公斤粮食计算,其他粮食一律按脱粒后的原粮计算。

猪、牛、羊肉产量 指当年出栏并已屠宰的猪、牛、羊的肉产量,即屠宰后除去头蹄下水后带骨的(即胴体重)重量。

水产品产量 指人工养殖的水产品和天然生长的水产品的捕捞量。包括海水的鱼类、虾蟹类、贝类和藻类以及内陆水域的鱼类、虾蟹类和贝类,不包括淡水生植物。

有效灌溉面积 指具有一定的水源,地块比较平整、灌溉工程或设备已经配套,在一般年景下当年能够进行正常灌溉的耕地面积。

农业机械总动力 指主要用于农、林、牧、渔业的各种动力机械的动力总和。包括耕作机械、排灌机械、收获机械、农用运输机械、植物保护机械、牧业机械、林业机械和其他农业机械[内燃机按引擎马力折成瓦(特)计算,电动机按功率折成瓦(特)计算]。不包括专门用于乡、镇、村、组办工业、基本建设、非农业运输、科学试验和教学等非农业方面的动力机械与作业机械。

农村用电量 指本年度内扣除在农村中的全民所有制工业、交通、基建单位的用电量以后的农村生产上和生活上的全年用电总度数(全年累计数),包括国家电网的供电量,也包括农村自办电站的供电量。

农用化肥施用量 指本年内实际用于农业生产的化肥数量。包括氮肥、磷肥、钾肥及复合肥。化肥施用量要求按折纯量计算数量。折纯量是指氮肥、磷肥、钾肥分别按含氮、含五氧化二磷、含氧化钾的百分之一百成份进行折算后的数量。复合肥按其所含主要成份折算。

Explanatory Notes on Main Statistical Indicators

Gross Output Value of Farming, Forestry, Animal Husbandry and Fishery refers to the total volume of products of farming, forestry, animal husbandry and fishery in value terms and output value of all kinds of service activities that support farming, forestry, animal husbandry and fishery production. It reflects the total scale and total result of agricultural production during a given period of time.

The statistical scopes for Farming, Forestry, Animal Husbandry and Fishery are:

(1) **Farming** include crop cultivation and other farming crop cultivation, include planting of grain, beans, tubers, cotton, oil – bearing crops, sugar crops, fiber crops, tobacco, vegetables, medicinal materials, melons and others, as well as tea, mulberry and fruit plantation.

Other farming include gathering of wild plant fruits, fiber, gum, oil, firewood, wild medicinal materials, fungi and commodity industry run by rural household.

(2) **Forestry** include planting of trees (not including planting, management & harvest of tea, mulberry and fruit plantation), collection of forest products, cutting and felling of bamboo and trees by villages and other cooperative organizations under villages.

(3) **Animal Husbandry** include raising and grazing of any kind of animal and hunting and raising of wild animal, excluding fish breeding.

(4) **Fishery** include cultivation and catches of aquatic animals and seaweed.

(5) **Service Industry for Farming, Forestry, Animal Husbandry and Fishery** refers to all kinds of service activities that support farming, forestry , animal husbandry and fishery production.

Grain Yield refers to the total yield including grains produced by state farms, collective units, industrial enterprises and mines. Grain includes rice, wheat, corn, sorghum, millet and other miscellaneous grains as well as tubers and beans. Output of beans refers to dry beans without pods. The output of tubers was converted into that of grain at the ratio 5:1. Output of all other grains refers to husked grain.

Output of Pork, Beef, and Mutton refers to the meat of slaughtered hogs, cattle, sheep and goats with head, feet and offal taken away.

Output of Aquatic Products refers to catches of both artificially cultured and naturally grown aquatic products, including fish, shrimps, crabs and shellfish in sea and inland water as well as seaweed. Freshwater plants are not included.

Irrigated Area refers to areas that are effectively irrigated, i. e. level land which has water source and complete sets of irrigation facilities to lift and move adequate water for irrigation purpose under normal conditions.

Total Power of Farm Machinery refers to total mechanical power of machinery used in farming, forestry, animal husbandry, and fishery, including ploughing, irrigation and drainage, harvesting, transport, plant protection, stock breeding, forestry and fishery. The power of internal combustion engines is required to convert horsepower into watts and the power of electric motors is required to be converted into watts. Machinery employed for non – agricultural purposes, such as the machines used in township – run and village – run industry, construction, non – agricultural transport, scientific experiments and teaching, is excluded.

Electricity Consumption in Rural Areas refers to the total degree of electricity consumption in rural production and living (annual aggregate) after discounting the ownership by the whole people in the rural areas of industrial, transport and infrastructure unit of electricity consumption, including the national grid power supply, and also including the power supply in rural areas on their own power station.

Consumption of Chemical Fertilizers in Agriculture refers to the quantity of chemical fertilizers applied in agriculture in the year, including nitrogenous fertilizer, phosphate fertilizer, potash fertilizer, and compound fertilizer. The consumption of chemical fertilizers is required in calculation to convert the gross weight into weight into weight containing 100% effective component (e. g. 100% nitrogen content in nitrogenous fertilizer, 100% phosphorous pentoxide contents in phosphate fertilizer, 100% potassium oxide contents in potash fertilizer). Compound fertilizer is converted with its major component.

第四篇
CHAPTER-4

工业、能源
INDUSTRY AND ENERGY

工 业 、 能 源
Industry and Energy

主 要 统 计 指 标
Major Statistical Indicators

规模以上工业企业单位数	Number of Industrial Enterprises above Designated Size	10032	个	(unit)
为上年	As Compared with the Preceding Year	101.3	%	(%)
规模以上工业销售产值	Sales Value of Industrial Enterprises above Designated Size	9261.73	亿元	(100 million yuan)
为上年	As Compared with the Preceding Year	100.6	%	(%)
规模以上工业总产值	Gross Output Value of Industrial Enterprises above Designated Size	9390.73	亿元	(100 million yuan)
为上年	As Compared with the Preceding Year	100.9	%	(%)
轻工业	Light Industry	4011.60	亿元	(100 million yuan)
为上年	As Compared with the Preceding Year	104.0	%	(%)
重工业	Heavy Industry	5379.14	亿元	(100 million yuan)
为上年	As Compared with the Preceding Year	98.6	%	(%)

4－01　主要年份工业企业单位数

Number of Industrial Enterprises in Main Years

单位:个　　　　(unit)

年　份 Year	合　计 Total	国有经济 State－owned Enterprises	集体经济 Collective－owned Enterprises	其他各种经济类型 Enterprises of Other Types of Ownership	合计中:农村工业 of the Total: Rural Industry
全市　Whole Municipality					
1978	2868	680	2188	－	1241
1980	3519	691	－	－	－
1985	5800	823	－	－	－
1990	6183	921	4966	11	3130
1991	6234	933	5219	82	3361
1992	6235	941	5162	132	3274
1995	6744	1086	4722	936	2949
1996	6148	1011	4268	869	2719
1997	4980	760	3250	970	1729
1998	2559	464	815	1280	1366
1999	2474	396	689	1389	1313
2000	2715	282	598	1835	1536
2001	3580	237	252	3091	2051
2002	4015	172	232	3611	2398
2003	4689	144	219	4326	2622
2004	7738	185	192	7361	－
2005	7359	124	169	7066	－
2006	7826	110	162	7554	－
2007	8674	71	131	8472	－
2008	9907	73	101	9733	－
2009	10032	71	84	9877	－
市区　Urban District					
1978	787	313	414	－	59
1980	894	315	579	－	95
1985	1250	345	859	7	184
1990	1360	361	971	28	209
1991	1411	382	990	39	209
1992	1490	395	1024	71	207
1995	1998	440	1102	456	200
1996	2043	458	1109	476	294
1997	1733	372	951	410	200
1998	1019	315	315	389	375
1999	959	255	284	420	349
2000	1005	182	253	570	393
2001	2645	195	200	2250	1369
2002	2838	140	178	2520	1399
2003	3230	115	158	2957	1308
2004	5527	156	122	5249	－
2005	4995	98	104	4793	－
2006	5195	85	91	5019	－
2007	5726	54	77	5595	－
2008	6530	55	64	6411	－
2009	6477	52	49	6376	－

注:1. 本表范围 1998 年开始为全部国有和年销售收入 500 万元及以上的非国有工业,1997 年以前为乡及乡以上工业。

2. 2004 年工业数据根据经济普查已作调整(后同)。

a) Data in this table refer to all state－owned enterprises and non－state－owned industrial enterprises with annual sales income of over 5 million yuan, before 1997, refer to enterprises at township and above level.

b) The data of industry in 2004 have been adjasted auording to the First Economic Cencus. The relative tables in the chapter are the same.

4－02 主要年份

Gross Industrial

单位:万元

年　份 Year	全部工业总产值 All Industrial Output Value	为上年(%) As Compared with the Preceding Year(%)	其中:规模以上工业 Of which:Industry above Designated Size	为上年(%) As Compared with the Preceding Year(%)
全市　Whole Municipality				
1978	–	–	429624	122.4
1980	–	–	617910	124.6
1985	–	–	1285888	127.5
1990	–	–	2922600	106.3
1991	–	–	3524900	119.7
1992	–	–	4527400	126.0
1995	–	–	10200259	114.1
1996	–	–	8831167	111.7
1997	–	–	9114651	122.3
1998	–	–	11099357	112.0
1999	–	–	12000796	110.4
2000	–	–	15435682	131.4
2001	28672833	–	19195133	126.1
2002	34655472	120.9	24002972	125.1
2003	43513526	125.6	32025226	133.4
2004	56941379	130.9	44865779	140.1
2005	65895071	115.7	54411271	121.3
2006	82582990	125.3	69754590	128.2
2007	98464729	119.2	83514029	119.7
2008	110162700	111.9	93795792	112.3
2009	108703234	98.7	93907334	100.9
市区　Urban District				
1978	–	–	304242	126.5
1980	–	–	433623	122.0
1985	–	–	812246	121.7
1990	–	–	1533000	104.1
1991	–	–	1814600	117.3
1992	–	–	2291300	123.8
1995	–	–	4760900	112.9
1996	–	–	4599778	109.3
1997	–	–	4997257	126.8
1998	–	–	6110192	115.1
1999	–	–	6280838	104.6
2000	–	–	7804302	127.2
2001	21008145	–	16156245	125.4
2002	25466884	121.2	20252484	125.4
2003	32010406	125.7	26945006	133.1
2004	42514768	132.8	37564968	139.4
2005	50045260	117.7	44775260	119.2
2006	62823653	125.5	57255453	127.9
2007	73882956	117.6	67565456	118.0
2008	81717903	110.6	74564803	110.4
2009	80383555	98.4	74059755	99.9

注:本表范围1998年开始为全部国有和年销售收入500万元及以上的非国有工业,1997年以前为乡及乡以上工业。
2002年起,市区数据为新口径。

工业总产值
Output Value in Main Years

(10000 yuan)

规模工业中:轻工业 Light Industry	重工业 Heavy Industry	国有经济 State - owned	集体经济 Collective - owned	其他经济 Other Types of Ownership	合计中:农村工业 of the Total: Rural Industry
-	-	334799	94825	-	16201
-	-	451349	166561	-	36215
793766	492122	726172	546642	13074	189353
1848911	1073689	1532900	1300900	88800	634403
2201757	1323143	1779400	1601400	144200	829424
2735168	1792232	2141000	2084000	302400	1178103
5600664	4599595	3585284	3999638	2615337	1940192
4606720	4224447	2905614	3320757	2604796	2475212
4871887	4242764	3185886	2971634	2957131	2494911
5726407	5372950	3422316	2824793	4852248	4377466
6129963	5870833	3164602	2543981	6292213	4785861
7623300	7812382	1860336	2698406	10876940	6548169
9957027	9238106	1788783	1911315	15495035	8440527
12435498	11567474	2147066	2151485	19704421	11088179
15652463	16372763	2484171	2444002	27097053	13132425
19761946	25103833	3419970	558890	40886919	-
24059690	30351581	6054280	603438	47753553	-
29093450	40661140	6776754	667615	62310221	-
35878400	47635629	7688908	517878	75307243	-
38735329	55060463	7440679	386111	85969002	-
40115956	53791378	7576482	354714	85976138	-
-	-	248534	55708	-	1455
-	-	335789	97834	-	3506
512767	301998	536498	267613	8135	19139
1026764	599899	1067400	416500	49100	40537
1140394	674072	1237600	496800	80200	51810
1379154	917085	1497400	601200	192700	76909
2507752	2753196	2252300	908900	1599700	156480
2460319	2139459	2018768	951432	1629578	402627
2889406	2609217	2537740	819984	1639533	435175
3068600	3041592	2989467	1123013	1997712	1354343
3178286	3102552	2668519	979070	2633249	1314897
3635578	4168724	1498595	968509	5337198	1667468
8377563	7778681	1695132	1792228	12668885	6321034
10431428	9821056	2036097	2045450	16170937	8090617
13080771	13864235	2390424	2305431	22249151	8830419
16361706	21203262	3097656	419720	34047592	-
19601053	25174207	5592419	390555	38792286	-
23722868	33532585	6305071	347788	50602594	-
29452269	38113187	7123810	323842	60117804	-
31236743	43328060	6812616	219140	67533047	-
32178951	41880805	6880470	148937	67030348	-

a) Data in this table refer to all state - owned enterprises and non - state - owned industrial enterprises with annual sales income of over 5 million yuan, before 1997, refer to enterprises at township and above level.
b) From 2002, data of urban district belong to new administrative area.

4－03 分县(市)工业

Number of Industrial

单位:个

项 目	Item	全 市 Whole Municipality	为上年(%) As Compared with the Preceding Year(%)	市区 Urban District	#萧山区 Xiaoshan
规模以上工业合计	**Industrial above Designated Size**	**10032**	**101.3**	**6477**	**2419**
一、按轻重工业分	**Grouped by Light & Heavy Industry**				
轻工业	Light Industry	5142	101.3	3275	1400
重工业	Heavy Industry	4890	101.3	3202	1019
二、按所有制分	**Grouped by Ownership**				
国有企业	State－owned Enterprises	71	97.3	52	7
集体企业	Collective－owned Enterprises	84	83.2	49	9
股份合作企业	Cooperative Enterprises	97	78.2	93	3
联营企业	Joint Ownership Enterprises	5	83.3	4	－
股份制企业	Share－holding Corporations	7050	103.4	4637	1710
外商及港澳台投资企业	Enterprises with Investment from Foreign、Hong Kong、Macao and Taiwan	1614	94.2	1235	483
其他企业	Other Enterprises	1111	103.3	407	207
合计中:国有控股企业	Of the Total:Controlling Share Hold Enterprises	206	91.2	163	20
三、按企业规模分	**Grouped by Size of Enterprises**				
大型企业	Large	39	108.3	38	13
中型企业	Medium－sized	715	100	570	279
小型企业	Small	9278	101.3	5869	2127

注:为上年(%)按可比口径计算。

企业单位数(2009 年)
Enterprises by Region(2009)

(unit)

#余杭区 Yuhang	桐庐县 Tonglu	淳安县 Chun'an	建德市 Jiande	富阳市 Fuyang	临安市 Lin'an
2054	**694**	**160**	**714**	**1125**	**862**
1044	472	88	326	565	416
1010	222	72	388	560	446
7	5	2	5	5	2
10	8	6	13	3	5
67	–	–	1	3	–
–	1	–	–	–	–
1621	428	115	478	796	596
258	121	11	30	153	64
91	131	26	187	165	195
21	8	4	10	16	5
4	–	–	–	–	1
94	22	5	15	61	42
1956	672	155	699	1064	819

a) As compared with the precedly year is comparable.

4-04 分县(市)工业
Gross Industrial

单位:万元

项 目	Item	全 市 Whole Municipality	市 区 Urban District	#萧山区 Xiaoshan
规模以上工业合计	**Industrial above Designated Size**	**93907334**	**74059755**	**34358907**
一、按轻重工业分	**Grouped by Light & Heavy Industry**			
轻工业	Light Industry	40115956	32178951	17417956
重工业	Heavy Industry	53791378	41880805	16940951
二、按所有制分	**Grouped by Ownership**			
国有企业	State - owned Enterprises	7576482	6880470	920700
集体企业	Collective - owned Enterprises	354714	148937	29238
股份合作企业	Cooperative Enterprises	269352	263476	13274
联营企业	Joint Ownership Enterprises	8766	5108	-
股份制企业	Share - holding Corporations	56448653	42031948	25167426
外商及港澳台投资企业	Enterprises with Investment from Foreign、Hong Kong、Macao and Taiwan	27068500	23711689	7619315
其他企业	Other Enterprises	2180867	1018128	608953
合计中:国有控股企业	Of the Total: Controlling Share Hold Enterprises	12153953	11165163	1235341
三、按企业规模分	**Grouped by Size of Enterprises**			
大型企业	Large	18780121	18664796	8403179
中型企业	Medium - sized	34114365	27169954	13591223
小型企业	Small	41012848	28225006	12364504

总产值(2009年)

Output Value by Region(2009)

(10000 yuan)

#余杭区 Yuhang	桐庐县 Tonglu	淳安县 Chun'an	建德市 Jiande	富阳市 Fuyang	临安市 Lin'an
10523385	**3028327**	**1244100**	**2698974**	**9055392**	**3820787**
3912974	1554541	919178	893834	2945792	1623661
6610411	1473785	324923	1805140	6109600	2197126
353206	119947	34731	129144	273551	138639
23730	94647	14142	39529	48562	8897
203734	–	–	2102	3774	–
–	3658	–	–	–	–
7495232	1558271	1026353	2162883	7002791	2666408
2260016	1034451	118015	152237	1446719	605390
187469	217352	50859	213079	279995	401453
468719	131174	39632	195285	477484	145216
1301970	–	–	–	–	115325
3157879	943230	186718	725154	3760815	1328495
6063536	2085097	1057382	1973819	5294577	2376967

4-05 分县(市)工业
Indices of Gross Industrial

(上年=100)

项 目	Item	全 市 Whole Municipality	市 区 Urban District	#萧山区 Xiaoshan
规模以上工业合计	**Industrial above Designated Size**	**100.9**	**100.3**	**105.1**
一、按轻重工业分	**Grouped by Light & Heavy Industry**			
轻工业	Light Industry	104.0	103.5	103.2
重工业	Heavy Industry	98.6	97.9	107.1
二、按所有制分	**Grouped by Ownership**			
国有企业	State - owned Enterprises	101.4	100.9	105.8
集体企业	Collective - owned Enterprises	100.8	81.6	91.9
股份合作企业	Cooperative Enterprises	84.5	84.5	105.0
联营企业	Joint Ownership Enterprises	49.0	44.9	31.3
股份制企业	Share - holding Corporations	104.0	104.7	107.7
外商及港澳台投资企业	Enterprises with Investment from Foreign、Hong Kong、Macao and Taiwan	94.6	93.5	97.7
其他企业	Other Enterprises	107.4	100.2	100.8
合计中:国有控股企业	Of the Total: Controlling Share Hold Enterprises	101.4	101.1	102.0
三、按企业规模分	**Grouped by Size of Enterprises**			
大型企业	Large	100.6	101.3	110.2
中型企业	Medium - sized	96.8	95.8	102.0
小型企业	Small	104.8	104.6	105.7

总产值指数(2009 年)

Output by Region(2009)

(preceding year = 100)

#余杭区 Yuhang	桐庐县 Tonglu	淳安县 Chun'an	建德市 Jiande	富阳市 Fuyang	临安市 Lin'an
101.4	**100.5**	**117.5**	**98.3**	**103.2**	**104.7**
97.6	110.1	117.0	113.3	100.3	103.6
103.8	92.0	119.2	92.4	104.7	105.5
115.0	106.2	104.8	102.8	107.6	112.1
126.2	128.7	101.7	122.6	123.9	89.4
84.7	-	-	105.8	76.7	-
-	66.9	-	-	-	-
102.9	96.2	118.3	96.7	103.6	100.0
96.5	104.4	108.1	102.9	101.9	104.4
105.2	101.6	151.0	107.7	95.2	150.5
111.3	107.3	100.5	100.8	105.0	111.4
106.8	-	-	54.6	-	-
100.4	98.5	110.7	86.2	103.3	101.7
100.7	101.3	120.3	109.5	103.2	106.4

4－06 分县(市)工业
Gross Industrial

单位:万元

项　目	Item	全　市 Whole Municipality	市　区 Urban District	#萧山区 Xiaoshan
规模以上工业合计	**Industrial above Designated Size**	**92617331**	**73278661**	**34033102**
一、按轻重工业分	**Grouped by Light & Heavy Industry**			
轻工业	Light Industry	39447763	31691388	17227701
重工业	Heavy Industry	53169569	41587273	16805401
二、按所有制分	**Grouped by Ownership**			
国有企业	State－owned Enterprises	7609771	6916757	913389
集体企业	Collective－owned Enterprises	340584	143522	29210
股份合作企业	Cooperative Enterprises	261134	255398	13073
联营企业	Joint Ownership Enterprises	8802	5234	－
股份制企业	Share－holding Corporations	55483339	41450221	24986509
外商及港澳台投资企业	Enterprises with Investment from Foreign、Hong Kong、Macao and Taiwan	26799881	23509586	7492580
其他企业	Other Enterprises	2113821	997942	598341
合计中:国有控股企业	Of the Total:Controlling Share Hold Enterprises	12289926	11312484	1233122
三、按企业规模分	**Grouped by Size of Enterprises**			
大型企业	Large	18869064	18753739	8392904
中型企业	Medium－sized	33551861	26763191	13476870
小型企业	Small	40196407	27761731	12163327

销售产值(2009 年)
Products Sales by Region(2009)

(10000 yuan)

#余杭区 Yuhang	桐庐县 Tonglu	淳安县 Chun'an	建德市 Jiande	富阳市 Fuyang	临安市 Lin'an
10158058	**2975446**	**1217081**	**2649112**	**8768460**	**3728572**
3789146	1521927	900410	874161	2872717	1587160
6368912	1453519	316671	1774951	5895743	2141411
352708	119677	34731	128847	272587	137170
21942	94560	14085	39192	40365	8861
196480	–	–	2080	3657	–
–	3568	–	–	–	–
7241597	1530390	1001805	2121283	6760964	2618676
2161517	1014595	116172	150188	1420202	589138
183815	212657	50287	207523	270686	374726
466592	130795	39632	192837	470431	143748
1265460	–	–	–	–	115325
3015317	932834	181446	718227	3638032	1318131
5877281	2042611	1035635	1930885	5130428	2295117

4－07 全市规模以上工业

Main Economic Indicators of Industrial

单位：万元

项 目	Item	企业单位数(个) Number of Enterprises (unit)	#亏损企业(个) Loss Making Enterprises (unit)
总 计	**Total**	**10032**	**1577**
按隶属关系分	**Grouped by Subordination**		
中 央 属	Central	27	3
省 属	Provincial	61	11
市 属	Municipal	6401	1023
县(市)属	County and below	3543	540
按所有制分	**Grouped by Ownership**		
国有企业	State－owned Enterprises	71	21
集体企业	Collective－owned Enterprises	84	13
股份合作企业	Cooperative Enterprises	97	18
联营企业	Joint Ownership Enterprises	5	4
股份制企业	Share－holding Corporations	7050	1038
外商及港澳台投资企业	Enterprises with Investment from Foreign、Hong Kong、Macao and Taiwan	1614	387
其他企业	Other Enterprises	1111	96
按企业规模分	**Grouped by Size of Enterprises**		
大型企业	Large	39	1
中型企业	Medium－sized	715	67
小型企业	Small	9278	1509
按轻重工业分	**Grouped by Light & Heavy Industry**		
轻工业	Light Industry	5142	823
重工业	Heavy Industry	4890	754

注：本表范围为年销售收入500万元及以上工业。

企业主要经济指标(一)
Enterprises Above Designated Size(Ⅰ)

(10000 yuan)

工业总产值(当年价格) Gross Industrial Output Value (current price)	工业销售产值 Value of Industrial Products Sales	全部从业人员年平均人数(人) Annual Average Number of Staff and Workers(person)
93907334	**92617331**	**1277379**
5507142	5501405	14291
3368226	3410002	30195
65786788	64967973	933454
19245178	18737952	299439
7576482	7609771	32646
354714	340584	5654
269352	261134	6600
8766	8802	226
56448653	55483339	772939
27068500	26799881	409155
2180867	2113821	50159
18780121	18869064	156131
34114365	33551861	442089
41012848	40196407	679159
40115956	39447763	698209
53791378	53169569	579170

a) Data in this table refer to enterprises with annual sales income of over 5 million yuan.

项　目	Item	企业单位数(个) Number of Enterprises (unit)	#亏损企业(个) Loss Making Enterprises (unit)
按市、县分	**Grouped by County**		
市　区	Urban District	6477	1033
#萧山区	Xiaoshan	2419	234
余杭区	Yuhang	2054	425
桐庐县	Tonglu	694	85
淳安县	Chun'an	160	13
建德市	Jiande	714	71
富阳市	Fuyang	1125	187
临安市	Lin'an	862	188
按国民经济行业分	**Grouped by Economic Sector**		
煤炭开采和洗选业	Coal Mining and Dressing	-	-
黑色金属矿采选业	Ferrous Metals Mining and Dressing	-	-
有色金属矿采选业	Nonferrous Metals Mining and Dressing	8	2
非金属矿采选业	Nonmetal Minerals Mining and Dressing	58	10
农副食品加工业	Agricultural Products Processing	189	25
食品制造业	Food Manufacturing	140	26
饮料制造业	Beverage Manufacturing	77	7
烟草制品业	Tobacco Processing	3	-
纺织业	Textile Industry	1495	210
纺织服装、鞋、帽制造业	Textile Products, Garments, Shoes and Caps Processing	563	136
皮革、毛皮、羽毛(绒)及其制品业	Leather, Furs, Down and Related Products	219	34
木材加工及木、竹、藤、棕、草制品业	Timber Processing, Bamboo, Cane, Palm Fiber and Straw Products	125	20
家具制造业	Furniture Manufacturing	156	22

continued 1　　(10000 yuan)

工业总产值(当年价格) Gross Industrial Output Value (current price)	工业销售产值 Value of Industrial Products Sales	全部从业人员年平均人数(人) Annual Average Number of Staff and Workers(person)
74059755	73278661	974533
34358907	34033102	418973
10523385	10158058	208579
3028327	2975446	53589
1244100	1217081	14735
2698974	2649112	41328
9055392	8768460	111490
3820787	3728572	81704
–	–	–
–	–	–
60270	60445	909
148133	144443	3427
878737	856449	10166
1780755	1744597	28933
1917943	1879574	19022
1609844	1609796	2226
9233034	9034029	191657
2409435	2380471	101572
1487151	1456965	38151
340692	332740	7774
1148136	1117649	27865

项　目	Item	企业单位数(个) Number of Enterprises (unit)	#亏损企业(个) Loss Making Enterprises (unit)
造纸及纸制品业	Paper Making and Paper Products	573	94
印刷业和记录媒介的复制	Printing and Record Media	175	28
文教体育用品制造业	Cultural, Educational and Sports Goods	167	30
石油加工、炼焦及核燃料加工业	Petroleum Processing, Coking and Nudear Fuel Processing	27	4
化学原料及化学制品制造业	Raw Chemical Materials and Chemical Products	581	69
医药制造业	Medical and Pharmaceutical Products	111	16
化学纤维制造业	Chemical Fiber	82	10
橡胶制品业	Rubber Products	87	13
塑料制品业	Plastic Products	486	65
非金属矿物制品业	Nonmetal Minerals Products	431	69
黑色金属冶炼及压延加工业	Smelting and Processing of Ferrous Metals	107	25
有色金属冶炼及压延加工业	Smelting and Processing of Nonferrous Metals	94	20
金属制品业	Metals Products	659	101
通用设备制造业	Ordinary Machinery	951	120
专用设备制造业	For Special Purpose Equipment Manufacturing	384	62
交通运输设备制造业	Transport Equipment Manufacturing	388	62
电气机械及器材制造业	Electric Equipment and Machinery	784	152
通信设备、计算机及其他电子设备制造业	Telecommunications Equipment, Computers and Other Electronic Equipment Manufacturing	366	65
仪器仪表及文化、办公用机械制造业	Instruments, Meters, Cultural and Office Machinery	229	26
工艺品及其他制造业	Craftworks and Other Manufacturing	196	26
废弃资源和废旧材料回收加工业	Waste Resouces and Waste or Old Material Recycled	24	4
电力、热力的生产和供应业	Production and Supply of Electric Power and Hot Water	59	11
燃气生产和供应业	Production and Supply of Gas	13	-
水的生产和供应业	Production and Supply of Tap Water	25	13

continued 2　　(10000 yuan)

工业总产值(当年价格) Gross Industrial Output Value (current price)	工业销售产值 Value of Industrial Products Sales	全部从业人员年平均人数(人) Annual Average Number of Staff and Workers(person)
3537966	3474422	55597
652938	634391	12976
490334	484884	14823
406239	400408	1506
7095937	7068787	52073
1590408	1505126	23801
5272278	5295620	22546
1930689	2042457	29680
2453119	2423698	35134
3316683	3255164	51482
3374067	3360840	22282
1752288	1691768	7083
4452951	4320279	62026
6417538	6361406	105965
1701099	1668949	31987
7196723	7147177	62049
7458846	7309649	109397
5178232	5055588	71564
1976861	1925126	29228
1061266	1030626	22456
232011	224933	1045
4661713	4641723	14271
459852	456907	1812
223169	220245	4894

4－08 全市规模以上工业

Main Economic Indicators of Industrial

单位:万元

项　目	Item	资产总计 Total Assets	#产成品 Finished Products
总　　计	**Total**	**84056230**	**5150912**
按隶属关系分	**Grouped by Subordination**		
中　央　属	Central	4299653	86352
省　　属	Provincial	4129100	98442
市　　属	Municipal	59856852	3881246
县(市)属	County and below	15770625	1084872
按所有制分	**Grouped by Ownership**		
国有企业	State－owned Enterprises	7179036	98712
集体企业	Collective－owned Enterprises	254410	25158
股份合作企业	Cooperative Enterprises	305629	24322
联营企业	Joint Ownership Enterprises	8336	932
股份制企业	Share－holding Corporations	50572946	3269184
外商及港澳台投资企业	Enterprises with Investment from Foreign、Hong Kong、Macao and Taiwan	24360165	1613612
其他企业	Other Enterprises	1375707	118992
按企业规模分	**Grouped by Size of Enterprises**		
大型企业	Large	14642651	716282
中型企业	Medium－sized	31941541	1823404
小型企业	Small	37472038	2611225
按轻重工业分	**Grouped by Light & Heavy Industry**		
轻工业	Light Industry	36503572	2294887
重工业	Heavy Industry	47552657	2856025

企业主要经济指标(二)
Enterprises Above Designated Size(Ⅱ)

(10000 yuan)

流动资产合计 Total Circulating Funds	#本年折旧 Depreciation of the year	固定资产净值 Net Value of Fixed Assets	年末负债合计 Total Liabilities	所有者权益合计 Creditors´Equity
49682101	**2392657**	**21496467**	**49650950**	**34405280**
1674122	273675	1986730	2478362	1821291
1664341	166917	1560529	2155895	1973205
36899434	1585511	13987322	35521222	24335629
9444204	366554	3961886	9495471	6275154
2797675	403987	3076323	3823822	3355214
177176	5850	41353	147141	107270
205607	9626	56693	179410	126219
6085	144	1114	6444	1892
30273609	1256440	11424641	31374154	19198793
15317992	677072	6555634	13222200	11137965
903957	39538	340710	897780	477927
9221186	319173	2747788	7799080	6843570
18607188	945245	8493357	18916544	13024996
21853727	1128239	10255322	22935325	14536713
21797139	999730	9406930	20834483	15669090
27884962	1392927	12089537	28816467	18736190

项　目	Item	资产总计 Total Assets	#产成品 Finished Products
按市、县分	**Grouped by County**		
市　区	Urban District	67914933	4063665
#萧山区	Xiaoshan	28848118	1702033
余杭区	Yuhang	9698402	747917
桐庐县	Tonglu	2182758	154377
淳安县	Chun'an	658416	38565
建德市	Jiande	2171801	127271
富阳市	Fuyang	7794827	550212
临安市	Lin'an	3333495	216822
按国民经济行业分	**Grouped by Economic Sector**		
煤炭开采和洗选业	Coal Mining and Dressing	–	–
黑色金属矿采选业	Ferrous Metals Mining and Dressing	–	–
有色金属矿采选业	Nonferrous Metals Mining and Dressing	54829	1271
非金属矿采选业	Nonmetal Minerals Mining and Dressing	150788	5208
农副食品加工业	Agricultural Products Processing	653197	59280
食品制造业	Food Manufacturing	1188092	82214
饮料制造业	Beverage Manufacturing	1602835	57560
烟草制品业	Tobacco Processing	1618651	64264
纺织业	Textile Industry	8524827	656631
纺织服装、鞋、帽制造业	Textile Products, Garments, Shoes and Caps Processing	2340862	176252
皮革、毛皮、羽毛(绒)及其制品业	Leather, Furs, Down and Related Products	1286212	71458
木材加工及木、竹、藤、棕、草制品业	Timber Processing, Bamboo, Cane, Palm Fiber and Straw Products	262726	25330
家具制造业	Furniture Manufacturing	999762	57802

continued 1

(10000 yuan)

流动资产合计 Total Circulating Funds	#本年折旧 Depreciation of the year	固定资产净值 Net Value of Fixed Assets	年末负债合计 Total Liabilities	所有者权益合计 Creditors´Equity
40181259	1993647	17241864	39935393	27979540
17482848	769320	7267437	17767286	11080832
5819691	338520	2525597	6182461	3515941
1249367	53780	630073	1335488	847270
352718	23514	230217	357326	301090
1164049	55826	610603	1144148	1027653
4796860	176490	1826524	4854016	2940812
1937848	89401	957187	2024580	1308915
–	–	–	–	–
–	–	–	–	–
24855	1179	6568	23207	31622
76037	5132	42106	99170	51618
393966	13356	145371	407964	245233
703477	28844	268937	584406	603686
851187	59789	514177	919594	683241
1247595	20477	145817	170842	1447809
4912526	279499	2497590	5307072	3217756
1498013	47382	547243	1374988	965874
968775	20722	183216	934635	351577
149015	7725	76866	155729	106997
674097	17194	196391	565792	433970

单位:万元　　4－08　续表2

项　目	Item	资产总计 Total Assets	#产成品 Finished Products
造纸及纸制品业	Paper Making and Paper Products	3635485	221346
印刷业和记录媒介的复制	Printing and Record Media	869699	40714
文教体育用品制造业	Cultural, Educational and Sports Goods	371796	23688
石油加工、炼焦及核燃料加工业	Petroleum Processing, Coking and Nudear Fuel Processing	125266	12458
化学原料及化学制品制造业	Raw Chemical Materials and Chemical Products	5389306	317726
医药制造业	Medical and Pharmaceutical Products	1789398	131614
化学纤维制造业	Chemical Fiber	3998743	182649
橡胶制品业	Rubber Products	1349987	147214
塑料制品业	Plastic Products	2034249	140469
非金属矿物制品业	Nonmetal Mineral Products	4042554	297033
黑色金属冶炼及压延加工业	Smelting and Processing of Ferrous Metals	3111198	99041
有色金属冶炼及压延加工业	Smelting and Processing of Nonferrous Metals	702329	90701
金属制品业	Metal Products	3876131	298295
通用设备制造业	Ordinary Machinery	6839539	495428
专用设备制造业	For Special Purpose Equipment Manufacturing	1846275	167832
交通运输设备制造业	Transport Equipment Manufacturing	4946750	252134
电气机械及器材制造业	Electric Equipment and Machinery	6602178	455296
通信设备、计算机及其他电子设备制造业	Telecommunications Equipment, Computers and Other Electronic Equipment Manufacturing	5085412	331822
仪器仪表及文化、办公用机械制造业	Instruments, Meters, Cultural and Office Machinery	1879258	97978
工艺品及其他制造业	Craftworks and Other Manufacturing	708526	66801
废弃资源和废旧材料回收加工业	Waste Resouces and Waste or Old Material Recycled	207562	14015
电力、热力的生产和供应业	Production and Supply of Electric Power and Hot Water	3918523	3115
燃气生产和供应业	Production and Supply of Gas	610087	1479
水的生产和供应业	Production and Supply of Tap Water	1433200	4795

continued 2 (10000 yuan)

流动资产合计 Total Circulating Funds	#本年折旧 Depreciation of the year	固定资产净值 Net Value of Fixed Assets	年末负债合计 Total Liabilities	所有者权益合计 Creditors´Equity
2198872	89609	978053	2227688	1407796
470400	34752	294892	521602	348097
217588	12198	112586	182021	189775
71753	5846	39182	142984	-17719
3235725	129588	1095489	3041199	2348107
1052312	36827	366554	779973	1009424
2022412	118998	1291742	2668986	1329757
680696	60207	505853	840861	509126
1209264	61783	533309	1110303	923947
2390791	141259	1088748	2677785	1364768
1795134	80404	650083	1870445	1240753
514255	10912	112742	468161	234168
2704022	72242	708297	2585395	1290736
4163767	125750	1430314	3891304	2948235
1228440	41923	388432	1051483	794792
3155208	94892	898252	3218606	1728143
4407051	128769	1310174	3722761	2879416
3570274	104802	838588	2637099	2448313
1353349	53820	290656	976146	903112
426046	26381	199333	365554	342972
162498	1977	24298	167576	39986
690137	359101	2805379	2882452	1036071
111555	32776	330037	332594	277493
351013	66545	579193	744572	688628

4－09　全市规模以上工业

Main Economic Indicators of Industrial

单位:万元

项　目	Item	主营业务收　入 Revenues in Main Business	营业费用 Expenses of Business	主营业务税金及附加 Sales Taxes and Extra Charges in Main Business
总　　计	**Total**	**90263232**	**3060491**	**1293045**
按隶属关系分	**Grouped by Subordination**			
中　央　属	Central	3379515	60167	968420
省　　　属	Provincial	3341275	25269	13311
市　　　属	Municipal	65478172	2570022	249005
县(市)属	County and Below	18064269	405034	62308
按所有制分	**Grouped by Ownership**			
国有企业	State－owned Enterprises	5443882	62334	976217
集体企业	Collective－owned Enterprises	338089	8263	1824
股份合作企业	Cooperative Enterprises	253351	3744	1022
联营企业	Joint Ownership Enterprises	9302	350	22
股份制企业	Share－holding Corporations	55590785	1328609	246684
外商及港澳台投资企业	Enterprises with Investment from Foreign、Hong Kong、Macao and Taiwan	26556175	1623445	55349
其他企业	Other Enterprises	2071648	33747	11927
按企业规模分	**Grouped by Size of Enterprises**			
大型企业	Large	18543075	936147	976057
中型企业	Medium－sized	34417375	1297563	156344
小型企业	Small	37302782	826781	160644
按轻重工业分	**Grouped by Light & Heavy Industry**			
轻工业	Light Industry	39670348	1826052	1070099
重工业	Heavy Industry	50592884	1234440	222946

企业主要经济指标(三)
Enterprises Above Designated Size(Ⅲ)

(10000 yuan)

管理费用 Management Expenses	利息支出 Interest Expenditure	利润总额 Total Profits	利税总额 Total Pre - tax Profits	本年应交增值税 Value Added Tax Payable
3926077	**1002668**	**5109669**	**8826155**	**2423441**
111398	8710	273100	1549424	307904
183913	25946	85288	202606	104006
2950968	742258	4034590	5886261	1602666
679798	225754	716691	1187864	408865
239777	10333	267836	1614013	369959
16968	2164	13807	30899	15268
13533	2435	4746	11950	6183
556	9	-493	-291	180
2175444	758361	2665612	4075486	1163190
1402463	213572	2092728	2968767	820690
77336	15793	65434	125332	47972
688263	157357	1402243	2998916	620616
1518381	410760	2109810	3141300	875147
1719432	434551	1597616	2685938	927678
1634759	421005	2492252	4795307	1232956
2291317	581663	2617417	4030848	1190485

项 目	Item	主营业务收入 Revenues in Main Business	营业费用 Expenses of Business	主营业务税金及附加 Sales Taxes and Extra Charges in Main Business
按市、县分	**Grouped by County**			
市 区	Urban District	71612193	2654039	1227989
#萧山区	Xiaoshan	33517206	428403	145165
余杭区	Yuhang	10047139	349911	40834
桐庐县	Tonglu	2850118	50704	8315
淳安县	Chun'an	1161451	64929	6155
建德市	Jiande	2572983	61824	11918
富阳市	Fuyang	8519918	129586	25538
临安市	Lin'an	3546569	99409	13130
按国民经济行业分	**Grouped by Economic Sector**			
煤炭开采和洗选业	Coal Mining and Dressing	–	–	–
黑色金属矿采选业	Ferrous Metals Mining and Dressing	–	–	–
有色金属矿采选业	Nonferrous Metals Mining and Dressing	46394	799	460
非金属矿采选业	Nonmetal Minerals Mining and Dressing	140623	6449	3558
农副食品加工业	Agricultural Products Processing	852875	28209	2665
食品制造业	Food Manufacturing	1625435	286809	3669
饮料制造业	Beverage Manufacturing	2666890	326692	26335
烟草制品业	Tobacco Processing	1607954	45978	913750
纺织业	Textile Industry	8841546	101074	42212
纺织服装、鞋、帽制造业	Textile Products, Garments, Shoes and Caps Processing	2320774	68870	9193
皮革、毛皮、羽毛(绒)及其制品业	Leather, Furs, Down and Related Products	1444382	28925	4218
木材加工及木、竹、藤、棕、草制品业	Timber Processing, Bamboo, Cane, Palm Fiber and Straw Products	323122	7300	2820
家具制造业	Furniture Manufacturing	1101142	34255	3355

continued 1 (10000 yuan)

管理费用 Management Expenses	利息支出 Interest Expenditure	利润总额 Total Profits	利税总额 Total Pre - tax Profits	本年应交增值税 Value Added Tax Payable
3213888	770874	4392445	7612127	1991692
913096	503929	1539956	2256930	571809
500803	115383	402446	679359	236079
111693	20621	107303	180562	64944
29284	7389	47433	80701	27114
122545	22507	136972	214718	65828
258433	136317	285140	491169	180490
190234	44960	140375	246878	93373
–	–	–	–	–
–	–	–	–	–
4154	718	7391	10321	2471
9255	1518	3176	14357	7623
24765	8844	31687	49339	14986
65007	3789	152453	247221	91099
69144	6561	226856	358725	105535
65875	-15242	216968	1335126	204408
274226	119581	313492	519564	163860
145528	25902	109282	186791	68316
56086	18810	40515	76728	31995
13470	5100	12052	23546	8674
45560	11293	89743	111576	18478

单位:万元　　　　4－09　续表2

项　目	Item	主营业务收入 Revenues in Main Business	营业费用 Expenses of Business	主营业务税金及附加 Sales Taxes and Extra Charges in Main Business
造纸及纸制品业	Paper Making and Paper Products	3430634	52904	10973
印刷业和记录媒介的复制	Printing and Record Media	645890	11974	2013
文教体育用品制造业	Cultural, Educational and Sports Goods	471954	12517	1458
石油加工、炼焦及核燃料加工业	Petroleum Processing, Coking and Nudear Fuel Processing	400898	3084	49803
化学原料及化学制品制造业	Raw Chemical Materials and Chemical Products	7044051	338154	19147
医药制造业	Medical and Pharmaceutical Products	1461306	333139	5361
化学纤维制造业	Chemical Fiber	5315044	30913	11435
橡胶制品业	Rubber Products	2017460	68334	6009
塑料制品业	Plastic Products	2396783	47250	7491
非金属矿物制品业	Nonmetal Mineral Products	3201241	129681	14168
黑色金属冶炼及压延加工业	Smelting and Processing of Ferrous Metals	3259837	15388	8884
有色金属冶炼及压延加工业	Smelting and Processing of Nonferrous Metals	1690787	3199	2255
金属制品业	Metal Products	4162204	60958	20666
通用设备制造业	Ordinary Machinery	6469561	181082	21182
专用设备制造业	For Special Purpose Equipment Manufacturing	1648392	46311	7021
交通运输设备制造业	Transport Equipment Manufacturing	7007384	96578	28868
电气机械及器材制造业	Electric Equipment and Machinery	7206321	306826	19531
通信设备、计算机及其他电子设备制造业	Telecommunications Equipment, Computers and Other Electronic Equipment Manufacturing	5091961	232835	17892
仪器仪表及文化、办公用机械制造业	Instruments, Meters, Cultural and Office Machinery	1868220	100256	9100
工艺品及其他制造业	Craftworks and Other Manufacturing	1019205	12187	5659
废弃资源和废旧材料回收加工业	Waste Resouces and Waste or Old Material Recycled	226816	685	508
电力、热力的生产和供应业	Production and Supply of Electric Power and Hot Water	2567835	3478	8093
燃气生产和供应业	Production and Supply of Gas	472531	26655	1829
水的生产和供应业	Production and Supply of Tap Water	215780	10745	1467

continued 2

(10000 yuan)

管理费用 Management Expenses	利息支出 Interest Expenditure	利润总额 Total Profits	利税总额 Total Pre - tax Profits	本年应交增值税 Value Added Tax Payable
112232	62745	129961	228381	87447
39669	7735	34257	55325	19056
24362	2692	12477	24127	10191
7732	4117	-4763	76672	31632
350186	63810	452318	649820	178355
159710	11118	253174	376112	117577
57296	94899	225188	288817	52194
45051	22001	146287	200403	48107
91656	26884	159026	227712	61195
135432	52168	139257	268692	115267
90192	25176	69613	140026	61530
18520	10401	23851	49982	23877
165726	60718	171931	266846	74249
407511	51766	464502	664629	178946
112704	15646	133137	174947	34789
204642	127802	303762	412627	79998
384630	65276	435061	626220	171629
446423	14211	459831	615010	137286
141141	21527	147427	224959	68432
37596	9124	38684	65039	20696
3504	1534	2131	6459	3820
75100	42516	81853	201088	111142
15113	7913	19917	32505	10759
26882	14019	7173	16463	7823

4－10 市区规模以上工业

Main Economic Indicators of Industrial Enterprises

单位:万元

项　目	Item	企业单位数(个) Number of Enterprises (unit)	#亏损企业(个) Loss Making Enterprises (unit)
总　　计	**Total**	**6477**	**1033**
按隶属关系分	**Grouped by Subordination**		
中　央　属	Central	23	3
省　　属	Provincial	53	7
市　　属	Municipal	6401	1023
按所有制分	**Grouped by Ownership**		
国有企业	State－owned Enterprises	52	11
集体企业	Collective－owned Enterprises	49	11
股份合作企业	Cooperative Enterprises	93	17
联营企业	Joint Ownership Enterprises	4	3
股份制企业	Share－holding Corporations	4637	655
外商及港澳台投资企业	Enterprises with Investment from Foreign、Hong Kong、Macao and Taiwan	1235	299
其他企业	Other Enterprises	407	37
按企业规模分	**Grouped by Size of Enterprises**		
大型企业	Large	38	1
中型企业	Medium－sized	570	52
小型企业	Small	5869	980
按轻重工业分	**Grouped by Light & Heavy Industry**		
轻工业	Light Industry	3275	538
重工业	Heavy Industry	3202	495

企业主要经济指标(一)
Above Designated Size in Urban District(Ⅰ)

(10000 yuan)

工业总产值(当年价格) Gross Industrial Output Value (current price)	工业销售产值 Value of Industrial Products Sales	全部从业人员年平均人数(人) Annual Average Number of Staff and Workers(person)
74059755	**73278661**	**974533**
5453268	5447531	13263
2819699	2863157	27816
65786788	64967973	933454
6880470	6916757	27584
148937	143522	3785
263476	255398	6371
5108	5234	196
42031948	41450221	564519
23711689	23509586	349997
1018128	997942	22081
18664796	18753739	152854
27169954	26763191	357017
28225006	27761731	464662
32178951	31691388	528465
41880805	41587273	446068

项　目	Item	企业单位数(个) Number of Enterprises (unit)	#亏损企业(个) Loss Making Enterprises (unit)
按国民经济行业分	**Grouped by Economic Sector**		
煤炭开采和洗选业	Coal Mining and Dressing	–	–
黑色金属矿采选业	Ferrous Metals Mining and Dressing	–	–
有色金属矿采选业	Nonferrous Metals Mining and Dressing	–	–
非金属矿采选业	Nonmetal Minerals Mining and Dressing	19	2
农副食品加工业	Agricultural Products Processing	91	15
食品制造业	Food Manufacturing	94	18
饮料制造业	Beverage Manufacturing	39	6
烟草制品业	Tobacco Processing	3	–
纺织业	Textile Industry	1076	163
纺织服装、鞋、帽制造业	Textile Products, Garments, Shoes and Caps Processing	478	113
皮革、毛皮、羽毛(绒)及其制品业	Leather, Furs, Down and Related Products	134	15
木材加工及木、竹、藤、棕、草制品业	Timber Processing, Bamboo, Cane, Palm Fiber and Straw Products	61	12
家具制造业	Furniture Manufacturing	110	20
造纸及纸制品业	Paper Making and Paper Products	150	22
印刷业和记录媒介的复制	Printing and Record Media	148	23
文教体育用品制造业	Cultural, Educational and Sports Goods	54	17
石油加工、炼焦及核燃料加工业	Petroleum Processing, Coking and Nudear Fuel Processing	21	4

continued 1

(10000 yuan)

工业总产值(当年价格) Gross Industrial Output Value (current price)	工业销售产值 Value of Industrial Products Sales	全部从业人员年平均人数(人) Annual Average Number of Staff and Workers(person)
–	–	–
–	–	–
–	–	–
59329	55759	1319
598045	585315	7096
1590472	1560289	24785
1528354	1503913	15655
1609844	1609796	2226
7554723	7402622	156149
2071577	2052626	91852
1065202	1039849	25917
208280	202944	4453
890939	867492	22109
1083288	1061846	16744
615489	598013	11451
303128	301149	8904
385211	380399	1335

单位:万元　　　　4－10　续表2

项　目	Item	企业单位数(个) Number of Enterprises (unit)	#亏损企业(个) Loss Making Enterprises (unit)
化学原料及化学制品制造业	Raw Chemical Materials and Chemical Products	356	43
医药制造业	Medical and Pharmaceutical Products	77	9
化学纤维制造业	Chemical Fiber	67	7
橡胶制品业	Rubber Products	45	6
塑料制品业	Plastic Products	337	47
非金属矿物制品业	Nonmetal Mineral Products	243	40
黑色金属冶炼及压延加工业	Smelting and Processing of Ferrous Metals	73	12
有色金属冶炼及压延加工业	Smelting and Processing of Nonferrous Metals	31	8
金属制品业	Metal Products	399	58
通用设备制造业	Ordinary Machinery	713	96
专用设备制造业	For Special Purpose Equipment Manufacturing	278	47
交通运输设备制造业	Transport Equipment Manufacturing	304	49
电气机械及器材制造业	Electric Equipment and Machinery	404	76
通信设备、计算机及其他电子设备制造业	Telecommunications Equipment, Computers and Other Electronic Equipment Manufacturing	285	55
仪器仪表及文化、办公用机械制造业	Instruments, Meters, Cultural and Office Machinery	187	23
工艺品及其他制造业	Craftworks and Other Manufacturing	147	17
废弃资源和废旧材料回收加工业	Waste Resouces and Waste or Old Material Recycled	5	1
电力、热力的生产和供应业	Production and Supply of Electric Power and Hot Water	28	5
燃气生产和供应业	Production and Supply of Gas	9	–
水的生产和供应业	Production and Supply of Tap Water	11	4

continued 2 (10000 yuan)

工业总产值(当年价格) Gross Industrial Output Value (current price)	工业销售产值 Value of Industrial Products Sales	全部从业人员年平均人数(人) Annual Average Number of Staff and Workers(person)
5534883	5533195	36765
1460332	1375851	20365
5154187	5179975	21092
1628186	1746800	24233
2049937	2026097	27548
2189674	2144718	34338
2889830	2892236	19633
301403	300047	2750
2995000	2932039	45528
5488268	5457999	88231
1357316	1335088	24636
6969946	6926509	54880
4568077	4490658	62865
4732815	4633527	61577
1872394	1823010	26085
911970	882863	19660
14375	13786	282
3743947	3733328	8561
449521	446963	1622
183814	181962	3887

4-11 市区规模以上工业

Main Economic Indicators of Industrial

单位:万元

项 目	Item	资产总计 Total Assets	#产成品 Finished Products
总 计	**Total**	**67914933**	**4063665**
按隶属关系分	**Grouped by Subordination**		
中 央 属	Central	4223652	86352
省 属	Provincial	3834429	96067
市 属	Municipal	59856852	3881246
按所有制分	**Grouped by Ownership**		
国有企业	State-owned Enterprises	6629679	96182
集体企业	Collective-owned Enterprises	170435	21122
股份合作企业	Cooperative Enterprises	292453	23766
联营企业	Joint Ownership Enterprises	5355	299
股份制企业	Share-holding Corporations	38817047	2451912
外商及港澳台投资企业	Enterprises with Investment from Foreign、Hong Kong、Macao and Taiwan	21291928	1413030
其他企业	Other Enterprises	708037	57352
按企业规模分	**Grouped by Size of Enterprises**		
大型企业	Large	14594501	715650
中型企业	Medium-sized	25693343	1493850
小型企业	Small	27627088	1854165
按轻重工业分	**Grouped by Light & Heavy Industry**		
轻工业	Light Industry	29851034	1858343
重工业	Heavy Industry	38063898	2205322

企业主要经济指标(二)

Enterprises Above Designated Size in Urban District(Ⅱ)

(10000 yuan)

流动资产合计 Total Circulating Funds	#本年折旧 Depreciation of the year	固定资产净值 Net Value of Fixed Assets	年末负债合计 Total Liabilities	所有者权益合计 Creditors' Equity
40181259	**1993647**	**17241864**	**39935393**	**27979540**
1663770	266522	1923576	2411398	1812254
1618056	141615	1330967	2002772	1831657
36899434	1585511	13987322	35521222	24335629
2681476	363032	2696006	3500909	3128770
113606	4302	29833	91998	78437
199551	9506	53352	176202	116251
4570	78	746	5104	251
23345313	990469	8494047	24318624	14498423
13360265	603167	5797317	11386120	9905808
476477	23093	170562	456437	251600
9185926	318113	2737286	7768351	6826150
15054343	785359	6848511	15414096	10279247
15940990	890175	7656067	16752946	10874143
17759733	835673	7712783	16777758	13073277
22421526	1157974	9529081	23157635	14906263

项　目	Item	资产总计 Total Assets	#产成品 Finished Products
按国民经济行业分	**Grouped by Economic Sector**		
煤炭开采和洗选业	Coal Mining and Dressing	–	–
黑色金属矿采选业	Ferrous Metals Mining and Dressing	–	–
有色金属矿采选业	Nonferrous Metals Mining and Dressing	–	–
非金属矿采选业	Nonmetal Minerals Mining and Dressing	45685	2306
农副食品加工业	Agricultural Products Processing	508853	43861
食品制造业	Food Manufacturing	1018947	66622
饮料制造业	Beverage Manufacturing	1309281	42933
烟草制品业	Tobacco Processing	1618651	64264
纺织业	Textile Industry	7574373	587967
纺织服装、鞋、帽制造业	Textile Products, Garments, Shoes and Caps Processing	2020798	155446
皮革、毛皮、羽毛(绒)及其制品业	Leather, Furs, Down and Related Products	1084932	58222
木材加工及木、竹、藤、棕、草制品业	Timber Processing, Bamboo, Cane, Palm Fiber and Straw Products	181244	17917
家具制造业	Furniture Manufacturing	834041	50634
造纸及纸制品业	Paper Making and Paper Products	1156222	52573
印刷业和记录媒介的复制	Printing and Record Media	815777	38486
文教体育用品制造业	Cultural, Educational and Sports Goods	255720	16414
石油加工、炼焦及核燃料加工业	Petroleum Processing, Coking and Nudear Fuel Processing	112796	10120

continued 1 (10000 yuan)

流动资产合计 Total Circulating Funds	#本年折旧 Depreciation of the year	固定资产净值 Net Value of Fixed Assets	年末负债合计 Total Liabilities	所有者权益合计 Creditors´Equity
–	–	–	–	–
–	–	–	–	–
–	–	–	–	–
24518	2148	10765	28151	17533
305382	10541	106662	318016	190837
598557	25362	235150	488535	530412
689828	47021	403788	754335	554946
1247595	20477	145817	170842	1447809
4390530	255533	2243202	4729243	2845130
1295016	41759	492142	1211475	809324
834552	16440	139401	804616	280316
101449	5731	55178	112130	69113
563644	13872	158260	470734	363307
608791	23603	352145	626963	529259
439043	32566	279676	488609	327168
147891	9261	84881	116693	139026
62790	5605	36356	136532	-23736

项 目	Item	资产总计 Total Assets	#产成品 Finished Products
化学原料及化学制品制造业	Raw Chemical Materials and Chemical Products	3911795	241450
医药制造业	Medical and Pharmaceutical Products	1415564	115470
化学纤维制造业	Chemical Fiber	3917449	170295
橡胶制品业	Rubber Products	1184881	133512
塑料制品业	Plastic Products	1657264	111641
非金属矿物制品业	Nonmetal Mineral Products	2843867	230765
黑色金属冶炼及压延加工业	Smelting and Processing of Ferrous Metals	2856050	71773
有色金属冶炼及压延加工业	Smelting and Processing of Nonferrous Metals	246764	13498
金属制品业	Metal Products	2989892	178158
通用设备制造业	Ordinary Machinery	6084328	431157
专用设备制造业	For Special Purpose Equipment Manufacturing	1537362	145738
交通运输设备制造业	Transport Equipment Manufacturing	4734377	240516
电气机械及器材制造业	Electric Equipment and Machinery	3934463	313485
通信设备、计算机及其他电子设备制造业	Telecommunications Equipment, Computers and Other Electronic Equipment Manufacturing	4761783	303329
仪器仪表及文化、办公用机械制造业	Instruments, Meters, Cultural and Office Machinery	1763679	88279
工艺品及其他制造业	Craftworks and Other Manufacturing	594334	59302
废弃资源和废旧材料回收加工业	Waste Resouces and Waste or Old Material Recycled	53360	980
电力、热力的生产和供应业	Production and Supply of Electric Power and Hot Water	3147418	1062
燃气生产和供应业	Production and Supply of Gas	587718	1109
水的生产和供应业	Production and Supply of Tap Water	1155269	4381

continued 2 (10000 yuan)

流动资产合计 Total Circulating Funds	#本年折旧 Depreciation of the year	固定资产净值 Net Value of Fixed Assets	年末负债合计 Total Liabilities	所有者权益合计 Creditors´Equity
2361332	99384	795091	2307811	1603983
903639	32209	276330	593155	822409
1966425	117155	1275084	2613525	1303924
606626	52086	442511	753200	431682
970226	55527	458068	896136	761129
1882064	101941	594941	1898951	944915
1611508	76952	617970	1682249	1173801
174233	5313	52345	162956	83808
2093601	56475	533149	2051068	938824
3699595	110234	1228906	3430946	2653382
1015325	36001	321160	876670	660692
3028643	89183	844441	3088690	1645687
2646840	85291	807944	2104460	1830003
3346441	98341	773734	2434222	2327561
1278787	51823	268330	918272	845406
361496	24051	169146	307127	287207
31059	941	6296	25154	28206
539352	304391	2274551	2425566	721852
101552	32221	319732	326220	261498
252931	54210	438715	582141	573128

4－12 市区规模以上工业

Main Economic Indicators of Industrial

单位:万元

项　目	Item	主营业务收　入 Revenues in Main Business	营业费用 Expenses of Business	主营业务税金及 附 加 Sales Taxes and Extra Charges in Main Business
总　　计	**Total**	**71612193**	**2654039**	**1227989**
按隶属关系分	**Grouped by Subordination**			
中 央 属	Central	3333255	60167	968233
省　　属	Provincial	2800766	23850	10752
市　　属	Municipal	65478172	2570022	249005
按所有制分	**Grouped by Ownership**			
国有企业	State－owned Enterprises	4775185	58490	973639
集体企业	Collective－owned Enterprises	144212	4441	1287
股份合作企业	Cooperative Enterprises	247765	3582	1001
联营企业	Joint Ownership Enterprises	6262	331	21
股份制企业	Share－holding Corporations	42043169	1021289	196228
外商及港澳台投资企业	Enterprises with Investment from Foreign、Hong Kong、Macao and Taiwan	23416501	1552415	49043
其他企业	Other Enterprises	979100	13492	6769
按企业规模分	**Grouped by Size of Enterprises**			
大型企业	Large	18442655	935041	975976
中型企业	Medium－sized	27813407	1163150	132932
小型企业	Small	25356131	555849	119081
按轻重工业分	**Grouped by Light & Heavy Industry**			
轻工业	Light Industry	32160621	1646171	1040874
重工业	Heavy Industry	39451572	1007868	187115

企业主要经济指标(三)
Enterprises Above Designated Size in Urban District(Ⅲ)

(10000 yuan)

管理费用 Management Expenses	利息支出 Interest Expenditure	利润总额 Total Profits	利税总额 Total Pre-tax Profits	本年应交增值税 Value Added Tax Payable
3213888	**770874**	**4392445**	**7612127**	**1991692**
110193	8025	270239	1543638	305167
152727	20592	87617	182228	83860
2950968	742258	4034590	5886261	1602666
190967	2600	271602	1589922	344680
11217	1230	6608	13770	5875
13032	2434	4829	11829	5998
464	9	-389	-208	160
1686692	584411	2120081	3182349	866041
1275334	171360	1959938	2755469	746488
36182	8831	29776	58996	22451
684463	157223	1397749	2991717	617992
1254417	320746	1813302	2676305	730072
1275009	292905	1181395	1944105	643629
1360621	329085	2200845	4285894	1044174
1853267	441790	2191600	3326233	947518

单位:万元　　4-12　续表1

项　目	Item	主营业务收　入 Revenues in Main Business	营业费用 Expenses of Business	主营业务税金及附加 Sales Taxes and Extra Charges in Main Business
按国民经济行业分	**Grouped by Economic Sector**			
煤炭开采和洗选业	Coal Mining and Dressing	-	-	-
黑色金属矿采选业	Ferrous Metals Mining and Dressing	-	-	-
有色金属矿采选业	Nonferrous Metals Mining and Dressing	-	-	-
非金属矿采选业	Nonmetal Minerals Mining and Dressing	55473	2351	1554
农副食品加工业	Agricultural Products Processing	586496	24020	2021
食品制造业	Food Manufacturing	1443568	280882	2488
饮料制造业	Beverage Manufacturing	2349707	263997	21140
烟草制品业	Tobacco Processing	1607954	45978	913750
纺织业	Textile Industry	7237750	82873	37721
纺织服装、鞋、帽制造业	Textile Products, Garments, Shoes and Caps Processing	1990245	62888	6717
皮革、毛皮、羽毛(绒)及其制品业	Leather, Furs, Down and Related Products	1030511	19200	3206
木材加工及木、竹、藤、棕、草制品业	Timber Processing, Bamboo, Cane, Palm Fiber and Straw Products	196670	5030	2263
家具制造业	Furniture Manufacturing	867112	27308	2694
造纸及纸制品业	Paper Making and Paper Products	1079983	29417	3492
印刷业和记录媒介的复制	Printing and Record Media	609731	11508	1810
文教体育用品制造业	Cultural, Educational and Sports Goods	295656	8171	922
石油加工、炼焦及核燃料加工业	Petroleum Processing, Coking and Nudear Fuel Processing	380847	2112	49716

continued 1

(10000 yuan)

管理费用 Management Expenses	利息支出 Interest Expenditure	利润总额 Total Profits	利税总额 Total Pre - tax Profits	本年应交增值税 Value Added Tax Payable
–	–	–	–	–
–	–	–	–	–
–	–	–	–	–
4053	626	3222	7802	3026
17528	6481	25093	38407	11293
56604	1712	144858	233755	86409
57744	3706	201265	313004	90600
65875	-15242	216968	1335126	204408
230586	106779	265025	439501	136755
130622	22510	98798	166952	61438
44665	17046	27740	51696	20750
8989	3484	7287	14778	5228
36552	9117	78124	94922	14104
43886	17351	45334	72174	23347
36867	7372	32490	51936	17637
16114	1574	10002	17029	6105
6255	3904	-5680	75092	31056

项目	Item	主营业务收入 Revenues in Main Business	营业费用 Expenses of Business	主营业务税金及附加 Sales Taxes and Extra Charges in Main Business
化学原料及化学制品制造业	Raw Chemical Materials and Chemical Products	5570279	293873	14296
医药制造业	Medical and Pharmaceutical Products	1331718	326381	4611
化学纤维制造业	Chemical Fiber	5213187	28833	11218
橡胶制品业	Rubber Products	1752012	66011	5427
塑料制品业	Plastic Products	2005652	36647	6314
非金属矿物制品业	Nonmetal Mineral Products	2154698	98658	9484
黑色金属冶炼及压延加工业	Smelting and Processing of Ferrous Metals	2810670	12176	8088
有色金属冶炼及压延加工业	Smelting and Processing of Nonferrous Metals	290241	1290	393
金属制品业	Metal Products	2858685	39872	14612
通用设备制造业	Ordinary Machinery	5596018	160106	18713
专用设备制造业	For Special Purpose Equipment Manufacturing	1335197	34712	5758
交通运输设备制造业	Transport Equipment Manufacturing	6797644	90784	28177
电气机械及器材制造业	Electric Equipment and Machinery	4481018	236901	12846
通信设备、计算机及其他电子设备制造业	Telecommunications Equipment, Computers and Other Electronic Equipment Manufacturing	4697529	220143	16837
仪器仪表及文化、办公用机械制造业	Instruments, Meters, Cultural and Office Machinery	1770391	96917	8621
工艺品及其他制造业	Craftworks and Other Manufacturing	880289	10119	5412
废弃资源和废旧材料回收加工业	Waste Resouces and Waste or Old Material Recycled	14663	250	42
电力、热力的生产和供应业	Production and Supply of Electric Power and Hot Water	1680287	395	4537
燃气生产和供应业	Production and Supply of Gas	462589	25328	1813
水的生产和供应业	Production and Supply of Tap Water	177722	8907	1299

continued 2 (10000 yuan)

管理费用 Management Expenses	利息支出 Interest Expenditure	利润总额 Total Profits	利税总额 Total Pre - tax Profits	本年应交增值税 Value Added Tax Payable
272387	52347	340471	499613	144846
145095	9159	242161	357297	110525
54632	93177	223491	284846	50136
38517	19089	134705	183689	43557
72955	20345	142720	200080	51046
91939	33020	105241	194771	80046
84466	19799	78471	142897	56337
6818	3459	7238	10072	2441
124934	41942	109137	180492	56743
355464	43331	424599	601946	158634
92424	12102	110521	140863	24583
190444	124278	291662	393958	74119
282128	31566	327285	460714	120583
423044	9339	440360	585222	128026
133711	20538	140659	214678	65399
32510	7469	35194	58934	18328
1628	284	2606	3297	649
19768	25695	55004	135372	75830
13970	7998	19014	31494	10667
20714	9520	11378	19720	7043

4－13 全市规模以上工业企业

Main Economic Indicators of Industrial Enterprises

单位:万元

项　目	Item	企业单位数(个) Number of Enterprises (unit)	#亏损企业(个) Loss Making Enterprises (unit)	工业总产值(当年价格) Gross Industrial Output Value (current price)	工业销售产值 Value of Industrial Products Sales
按登记注册类型分组	**Grouped by Status of Registration**				
内资企业	Domestic－funded Enterprises	8418	1190	66838833	65817451
国有企业	State－owned Enterprises	71	21	7576482	7609771
集体企业	Collective－owned Enterprises	84	13	354714	340584
股份合作企业	Cooperative Enterprises	97	18	269352	261134
联营企业	Joint Ownership Enterprises	5	4	8766	8802
国有联营企业	State Joint Ownership Enterprises	－	－	－	－
集体联营企业	Collective Joint Ownership Enterprises	2	1	4373	4373
国有与集体联营企业	Joint State－collective Enterprises	1	1	390	491
其他联营企业	Other Joint Ownership Enterprises	2	2	4004	3938
有限责任公司	Limited Liability Corporations	1068	159	14420784	14268118
国有独资公司	State－funded Corporations	11	2	443650	445621
其他有限责任公司	Other Limited Liability Corporations	1057	157	13977134	13822496
股份有限公司	Share－holding Corporations Ltd.	100	13	6141535	6049875
私营企业	Private Enterprises	6983	958	38030206	37243498
私营独资企业	Private－funded Enterprises	999	79	1905001	1844741
私营合伙企业	Private Partnership Enterprises	102	13	238871	233411
私营有限责任公司	Private Limited Liability Corporations	5802	852	30138639	29445041
私营股份有限公司	Private Share－holding Corporations Ltd.	80	14	5747695	5720306
其他企业	Other Enterprises	10	4	36994	35670
港、澳、台商投资	Enterprises with Investment from Hong Kong, Macao and Taiwan	709	166	10504282	10349055
内地与港澳台合资经营企业	Joint－venture Enterprises with funds from Hong Kong, Macao and Taiwan	448	82	6755471	6645168
内地与港澳台合作经营企业	Cooperative Enterprises with funds from Hong Kong, Macao and Taiwan	12	－	140034	139611
港澳台商独资经营企业	Enterprises with Sole Investment from Hong Kong, Macao and Taiwan	240	80	3218165	3150638
港澳台商投资股份有限公司	Share－holding Corporations Ltd. with Investment from Hong Kong, Macao and Taiwan	9	4	390612	413638
外商投资企业	Enterprises with Foreign Investment	905	221	16564219	16450826
中外合资经营企业	Joint－venture Enterprises	504	104	9275035	9233578
中外合作经营企业	Cooperation Enterprises	18	5	330631	323512
外商独资经营企业	Enterprises with Sole Foreign Investment	372	110	6053650	6012000
外商投资股份有限公司	Share－holding Corporations Ltd. with Foreign Investment	11	2	904903	881736

主要经济指标按登记注册类型分(2009 年)
Above Designated Size by Status of Registration(2009)

(10000 yuan)

全部从业人员年平均人数(人) Annual Average Number of Staff and Workers(person)	资产总计 Total Assets	#产成品 Finished Products	流动资产合计 Total Circulating Funds	#本年折旧 Depreciation of the year
868224	59696064	3537300	34364108	1715585
32646	7179036	98712	2797675	403987
5654	254410	25158	177176	5850
6600	305629	24322	205607	9626
226	8336	932	6085	144
–	–	–	–	–
128	2608	131	1967	61
64	2227	165	2171	12
34	3500	635	1947	71
186488	15601025	854533	8780069	399437
9217	1123391	17729	486677	45311
177271	14477634	836804	8293392	354126
57853	7211694	362784	3966957	176700
577868	29105690	2168287	18411350	718251
42670	1179678	102084	777354	32636
6600	165785	14336	107412	5312
499884	24379710	1890609	15436292	633089
28714	3380517	161257	2090291	47214
889	30244	2572	19191	1590
173679	10554707	709764	6676615	265586
104393	6370697	458964	4179348	163455
2269	156888	12156	117922	2052
63081	3414185	203385	1985839	88403
3936	612938	35258	393507	11675
235476	13805458	903849	8641377	411486
123914	7559474	484004	4869435	209712
6286	241460	11937	118533	7045
92428	5201979	358426	3147018	176429
12848	802546	49482	506391	18300

单位:万元　　4－13　续表

项　目	Item	固定资产净值 Net Value of Fixed Assets	年末负债合计 Total Liabilities	年末所有者权益合计 Creditors´ Equity	主营业务收入 Revenues in Main Business
按登记注册类型分组	**Grouped by Status of Registration**				
内资企业	Domestic－funded Enterprises	14940833	36428750	23267314	63707057
国有企业	State－owned Enterprises	3076323	3823822	3355214	5443882
集体企业	Collective－owned Enterprises	41353	147141	107270	338089
股份合作企业	Cooperative Enterprises	56693	179410	126219	253351
联营企业	Joint Ownership Enterprises	1114	6444	1892	9302
国有联营企业	State Joint Ownership Enterprises	－	－	－	－
集体联营企业	Collective Joint Ownership Enterprises	633	2073	535	4572
国有与集体联营企业	Joint State－collective Enterprises	57	2585	－357	979
其他联营企业	Other Joint Ownership Enterprises	424	1786	1715	3751
有限责任公司	Limited Liability Corporations	3912881	9704766	5896259	14975820
国有独资公司	State－funded Corporations	284420	619498	503893	473305
其他有限责任公司	Other Limited Liability Corporations	3628461	9085268	5392367	14502515
股份有限公司	Share－holding Corporations Ltd.	1365948	3715652	3496042	6171373
私营企业	Private Enterprises	6477754	18832091	10273599	36478566
私营独资企业	Private－funded Enterprises	286317	781431	398246	1804829
私营合伙企业	Private Partnership Enterprises	45624	96923	68862	230145
私营有限责任公司	Private Limited Liability Corporations	5631297	15730826	8648884	28824030
私营股份有限公司	Private Share－holding Corporations Ltd.	514516	2222910	1157607	5619562
其他企业	Other Enterprises	8769	19425	10819	36674
港、澳、台商投资	Enterprises with Investment from Hong Kong,Macao and Taiwan	2824404	5972550	4582157	10150701
内地与港澳台合资经营企业	Joint－venture Enterprises with funds from Hong Kong,Macao and Taiwan	1594099	3843309	2527389	6587989
内地与港澳台合作经营企业	Cooperative Enterprises with funds from Hong Kong,Macao and Taiwan	27053	88448	68440	139210
港澳台商独资经营企业	Enterprises with Sole Investment from Hong Kong,Macao and Taiwan	1042718	1662653	1751531	3003988
港澳台商投资股份有限公司	Share－holding Corporations Ltd. with Investment from Hong Kong,Macao and Taiwan	160534	378140	234797	419514
外商投资企业	Enterprises with Foreign Investment	3731230	7249650	6555808	16405474
中外合资经营企业	Joint－venture Enterprises	1954803	4160070	3399404	9217839
中外合作经营企业	Cooperation Enterprises	88379	143880	97580	307260
外商独资经营企业	Enterprises with Sole Foreign Investment	1530461	2528271	2673708	6028319
外商投资股份有限公司	Share－holding Corporations Ltd. with Foreign Investment	157588	417429	385117	852057

continued

(10000 yuan)

营业费用 Expenses of Business	主营业务税金及附加 Sales Taxes and Extra Charges in Main Business	管理费用 Management Expenses	利息支出 Interest Expenditure	利润总额 Total Profits	利税总额 Total Pre – tax Profits	本年应交增值税 Value Added Tax Payable
1437046	1237696	2523613	789096	3016941	5857388	1602751
62334	976217	239777	10333	267836	1614013	369959
8263	1824	16968	2164	13807	30899	15268
3744	1022	13533	2435	4746	11950	6183
350	22	556	9	-493	-291	180
–	–	–	–	–	–	–
65	15	201	9	-23	79	87
264	5	234	–	-362	-291	66
21	2	121	–	-107	-79	27
476449	53795	725810	202365	950290	1395193	391108
36302	3095	51886	524	32201	52898	17603
440147	50701	673924	201841	918089	1342295	373505
206356	31725	289439	100352	489288	654133	133120
677650	172914	1235053	471375	1290548	2148942	685480
27996	10677	63802	13929	57680	108929	40572
3849	1073	11056	1802	6834	13853	5946
592756	137948	1054873	346179	986552	1713161	588661
53049	23216	105322	109466	239482	312999	50301
1901	176	2478	63	919	2549	1454
531010	14970	467309	104861	638240	943618	290409
259361	8052	228092	83942	389877	558398	160469
1727	280	4936	3249	17898	24887	6708
227610	6271	144582	18113	223573	337898	108054
42312	366	89699	-443	6891	22435	15177
1092435	40380	935155	108711	1454488	2025149	530281
430476	19686	428840	66600	870890	1166293	275717
4441	294	12199	2740	11743	19766	7729
473263	6740	427863	35116	465130	661096	189226
184256	13660	66253	4256	106725	177994	57609

4－14 全市规模以上工业企业

Main Economic Indicators of Industrial

单位:万元

项 目	Item	企业单位数(个) Number of Enterprises (unit)	#亏损企业(个) Loss Making Enterprises (unit)	工业总产值(当年价格) Gross Industrial Output Value (current price)	工业销售产值 Value of Industrial Products Sales
按经济组织类型分组	**Grouped by Type of Ownership**				
独资企业	Solely－owned Enterprises	1766	303	19108012	18957732
国有企业	State－owned	71	21	7576482	7609771
集体企业	Collective－owned	84	13	354714	340584
私营独资企业	Private－owned	999	79	1905001	1844741
港澳台商独资经营企业	Enterprises with Sole Investment from Hong Kong, Macao and Taiwan	240	80	3218165	3150638
外商独资经营企业	Enterprises with Sole Foreign Investment	372	110	6053650	6012000
合作、合伙企业	Cooperation and Partnership Enterprises	244	44	1024649	1002139
股份合作企业	Share－holding Cooperative	97	18	269352	261134
国有联营企业	State Joint Ownership	－	－	－	－
集体联营企业	Collective Joint Ownership	2	1	4373	4373
国有与集体联营企业	Joint State－collective Ownership	1	1	390	491
其他联营企业	Other Joint Ownership	2	2	4004	3938
私营合伙企业	Private Partnership	102	13	238871	233411
内地与港澳台合作经营企业	Cooperative Enterprises with funds from Hong Kong, Macao and Taiwan	12	－	140034	139611
中外合作经营企业	Sino－foreign Cooperation Enterprises	18	5	330631	323512
其他企业	Other Enterprises (Domestic Investment)	10	4	36994	35670
股份有限公司	Share－holding Corporations Ltd.	200	33	13184744	13065555
股份有限公司(内资)	Share－holding Corporations Ltd. (Domestic Investment)	100	13	6141535	6049875
私营股份有限公司	Private Share－holding Corporations Ltd.	80	14	5747695	5720306
港澳台商投资股份有限公司	Share－holding Corporations Ltd. with Investment from Hong Kong, Macao and Taiwan	9	4	390612	413638
外商投资股份有限公司	Share－holding Corporations Ltd. with Foreign Investment	11	2	904903	881736
有限责任公司	Limited Liability Corporations	7822	1197	60589929	59591905
国有独资公司	State－owned	11	2	443650	445621
私营有限责任公司	Private	5802	852	30138639	29445041
内地与港澳台合资经营企业	Joint Venture Enterprises with funds from Hong Kong, Macao and Taiwan	448	82	6755471	6645168
中外合资经营企业	Sino－foreign Joint Venture	504	104	9275035	9233578
其他有限责任公司	Others	1057	157	13977134	13822496

主要经济指标按经济组织类型分(2009年)
Enterprises Above Designated Size by the Type of Ownership(2009)

(10000 yuan)

全部从业人员年平均人数(人) Annual Average Number of Staff and Workers(person)	资产总计 Total Assets	#产成品 Finished Products	流动资产合计 Total Circulating Funds	#本年折旧 Depreciation of the year
236479	17229287	787766	8885062	707306
32646	7179036	98712	2797675	403987
5654	254410	25158	177176	5850
42670	1179678	102084	777354	32636
63081	3414185	203385	1985839	88403
92428	5201979	358426	3147018	176429
22870	908342	66255	574749	25769
6600	305629	24322	205607	9626
–	–	–	–	–
128	2608	131	1967	61
64	2227	165	2171	12
34	3500	635	1947	71
6600	165785	14336	107412	5312
2269	156888	12156	117922	2052
6286	241460	11937	118533	7045
889	30244	2572	19191	1590
103351	12007695	608781	6957146	253889
57853	7211694	362784	3966957	176700
28714	3380517	161257	2090291	47214
3936	612938	35258	393507	11675
12848	802546	49482	506391	18300
914679	53910906	3688111	33265144	1405693
9217	1123391	17729	486677	45311
499884	24379710	1890609	15436292	633089
104393	6370697	458964	4179348	163455
123914	7559474	484004	4869435	209712
177271	14477634	836804	8293392	354126

单位:万元　　4－14　续表

项　目	Item	固定资产净值 Net Value of Fixed Assets	年末负债合计 Total Liabilities	所有者权益合计 Creditors' Equity	主营业务收入 Revenues in Main Business
按经济组织类型分组	**Grouped by Type of Ownership**				
独资企业	Solely－owned Enterprises	5977171	8943319	8285969	16619106
国有企业	State－owned	3076323	3823822	3355214	5443882
集体企业	Collective－owned	41353	147141	107270	338089
私营独资企业	Private－owned	286317	781431	398246	1804829
港澳台商独资经营企业	Enterprises with Sole Investment from Hong Kong, Macao and Taiwan	1042718	1662653	1751531	3003988
外商独资经营企业	Enterprises with Sole Foreign Investment	1530461	2528271	2673708	6028319
合作、合伙企业	Cooperation and Partnership Enterprises	227632	534530	373812	975943
股份合作企业	Share－holding Cooperative	56693	179410	126219	253351
国有联营企业	State Joint Ownership	－	－	－	－
集体联营企业	Collective Joint Ownership	633	2073	535	4572
国有与集体联营企业	Joint State－collective Ownership	57	2585	－357	979
其他联营企业	Other Joint Ownership	424	1786	1715	3751
私营合伙企业	Private Partnership	45624	96923	68862	230145
内地与港澳台合作经营企业	Cooperative Enterprises with funds from Hong Kong, Macao and Taiwan	27053	88448	68440	139210
中外合作经营企业	Sino－foreign Cooperation Enterprises	88379	143880	97580	307260
其他企业	Other Enterprises (Domestic Investment)	8769	19425	10819	36674
股份有限公司	Share－holding Corporations Ltd.	2198585	6734131	5273563	13062505
股份有限公司(内资)	Share－holding Corporations Ltd. (Domestic Investment)	1365948	3715652	3496042	6171373
私营股份有限公司	Private Share－holding Corporations Ltd.	514516	2222910	1157607	5619562
港澳台商投资股份有限公司	Share－holding Corporations Ltd. with Investment from Hong Kong, Macao and Taiwan	160534	378140	234797	419514
外商投资股份有限公司	Share－holding Corporations Ltd. with Foreign Investment	157588	417429	385117	852057
有限责任公司	Limited Liability Corporations	13093079	33438970	20471936	59605678
国有独资公司	State－owned	284420	619498	503893	473305
私营有限责任公司	Private	5631297	15730826	8648884	28824030
内地与港澳台合资经营企业	Joint Venture Enterprises with funds from Hong Kong, Macao and Taiwan	1594099	3843309	2527389	6587989
中外合资经营企业	Sino－foreign Joint Venture	1954803	4160070	3399404	9217839
其他有限责任公司	Others	3628461	9085268	5392367	14502515

continued (10000 yuan)

营业费用 Expenses of Business	主营业务税金及附加 Sales Taxes and Extra Charges in Main Business	管理费用 Management Expenses	利息支出 Interest Expenditure	利润总额 Total Profits	利税总额 Total Pre - tax Profits	本年应交增值税 Value Added Tax Payable
799466	1001730	892992	79655	1028026	2752834	723079
62334	976217	239777	10333	267836	1614013	369959
8263	1824	16968	2164	13807	30899	15268
27996	10677	63802	13929	57680	108929	40572
227610	6271	144582	18113	223573	337898	108054
473263	6740	427863	35116	465130	661096	189226
16012	2867	44757	10297	41647	72714	28200
3744	1022	13533	2435	4746	11950	6183
–	–	–	–	–	–	–
65	15	201	9	-23	79	87
264	5	234	–	-362	-291	66
21	2	121	–	-107	-79	27
3849	1073	11056	1802	6834	13853	5946
1727	280	4936	3249	17898	24887	6708
4441	294	12199	2740	11743	19766	7729
1901	176	2478	63	919	2549	1454
485972	68967	550713	213630	842386	1167560	256207
206356	31725	289439	100352	489288	654133	133120
53049	23216	105322	109466	239482	312999	50301
42312	366	89699	-443	6891	22435	15177
184256	13660	66253	4256	106725	177994	57609
1759041	219481	2437614	699087	3197609	4833046	1415955
36302	3095	51886	524	32201	52898	17603
592756	137948	1054873	346179	986552	1713161	588661
259361	8052	228092	83942	389877	558398	160469
430476	19686	428840	66600	870890	1166293	275717
440147	50701	673924	201841	918089	1342295	373505

4-15 全市1998-2009年规模以上工业企业主要经济效益指标

Main Economic Indicators of Industrial Enterprises Above Designated Size(1998-2009)

单位:亿元 (100 million yuan)

年份 Year	规模以上工业总产值 Output Value of Industrial Enterprises Above Designated Size	规模以上工业增加值 Added Value of Industrial Enterprises Above Designated Size	资产总计 Total Assets	流动资产合计 Total Current Assets	主营业务收入 Revenne from Principal Business	利润总额 Total Profits	利税总额 Total Profits and Tax
1998	1109.94	274.7	1486.02	732.72	1036.09	38.44	101.36
1999	1200.07	298.9	1620.93	800.6	1132.8	54.47	127.89
2000	1543.57	360.97	1828.35	946.32	1465.49	76.2	161.61
2001	1919.51	444.91	2148.96	1122.07	1828.28	107.56	208.54
2002	2400.3	597.01	2514.19	1313.92	2288.21	145.48	274.98
2003	3202.52	783.51	3258.93	1783.5	3117.46	194.16	359.54
2004	4486.58	1019.47	4118.31	2300.84	4363.27	226.74	427.23
2005	5441.13	1126.54	4781.34	2692.73	5282.8	234.99	450.68
2006	6975.46	1363.17	5564.68	3215.19	6807.64	314.49	576.51
2007	8351.4	1717.65	6573.12	3880.23	8057.03	414.55	730.5
2008	9379.58	1743.2	7506.26	4437.5	8976.46	453.92	802.13
2009	9390.73	1792	8405.62	4968.21	9026.32	510.97	882.62

4-15 续表 continued

年份 Year	工业增加值率(%) Rate of Industrial Added Valne (%)	资产负债率(%) Rate of Assets and Liabilites	流动资产周转次数(计量单位为次) the Number of Current Assets Turnover	成本费用利润率(%) Profit Rate of Costs	全员劳动生产率(元/人) All -personnel Labor Productivity (Yuan/Ren)	产品销售率(%) Prodnct Sales Rate(%)
1998	24.75	57.02	1.47	3.86	37976	95.91
1999	24.91	55.69	1.46	5.06	44307	98.07
2000	23.39	58.59	1.62	5.49	52712	97.19
2001	23.18	57.20	1.70	6.26	59517	97.40
2002	24.87	56.82	1.82	6.84	76401	97.76
2003	24.47	58.70	1.87	6.69	91284	97.68
2004	22.72	59.80	2.00	5.50	98809	98.10
2005	20.70	60.12	2.06	4.69	105785	98.25
2006	19.54	59.83	2.23	4.87	120289	98.36
2007	20.57	60.43	2.21	5.44	138016	98.17
2008	18.59	60.42	2.10	5.34	152070	98.14
2009	19.08	59.07	1.86	5.86	151002	98.63

4-16 主要工业产品生产量(2009年)
Output of Major Industrial Products(2009)

产品名称		Item		全市 Whole Municipality		市区 Urban District
				2009年	为上年(%) As Compared with the Preceding Year(%)	
铁矿石原矿量	(万吨)	The volume of iron ore	(10000 tons)			
原油加工量	(万吨)	Crude oil processing volume	(10000 tons)	58.81	94.2	58.81
发电量	(亿千瓦小时)	Electricity	(100 million kwh)	153.73	102.0	99.72
罐头	(万吨)	Canned Food	(10000 tons)	15.80	63.6	10.65
乳制品	(吨)	Dairy Products	(ton)	182470.38	122.7	137262
啤酒	(千升)	Beer	(1000 litres)	996956.00	102.8	828006
软饮料	(万吨)	Soft Drinks	(10000 tons)	537.69	110.6	399.19
精制茶	(吨)	Tea	(ton)	41300.39	136.2	9239
卷烟	(亿支)	Cigarettes	(100 million)	481.47	107.8	481.47
方便面	(吨)	Instant Noodle	(ton)	244277.94	102.9	243946
味精	(吨)	Monosodium Glutamate	(ton)	26089.20	76.3	19043
化学纤维	(吨)	Chemical Fiber	(ton)	4965554.12	118.0	4834843
其中:合成纤维	(吨)	Synthetic Fibre	(ton)	4767606.82	118.7	4636896
纱	(万吨)	Yarn	(10000 tons)	52.48	111.3	40.29
布	(万米)	Cloth	(10000 m)	35.95	105.4	31.32
印染布	(万米)	Printed Fabric	(10000 m)	48.13	108.1	45.71
丝	(吨)	Silk	(ton)	3947.37	107.3	0.08
丝织品	(万米)	Silk Knitwear	(10000 m)	0.94	98.7	0.77
服装	(万件)	Garment	(10000 units)	50577.71	94.1	42596

4-16 续表1 continued 1

产品名称		Item		全市 Whole Municipality 2009年	为上年(%) As Compared with the Preceding Year(%)	市区 Urban District
皮鞋	(万双)	Leather Shoes	(10000 units)	1467.54	119.2	615
家具	(万件)	Furniture	(10000 units)	3495.53	115.6	3156.26
塑料制品	(吨)	Plastic Membrane	(ton)	1666483.76	110.3	1289841
机制纸及纸板	(万吨)	Machine Made Paper and Paperboard	(10000 tons)	750.56	113.5	25.35
焦炭	(万吨)	Coke	(10000 tons)	47.81	94.9	47.81
盐酸(含量31%以上)	(吨)	Mariatic Acid(above 31% percent)	(ton)	110003.00	107.6	82131
氢氧化钠(烧碱)(折100%)	(吨)	Caustic Soda	(ton)	123988.00	93.8	123988
碳酸钠(纯碱)	(吨)	Soda ash	(ton)	175733.00	100.5	162056
初级形态的塑料(塑料树脂及共聚物)	(吨)	Plastics in Primary Form(Plastic Resins and Copolymers)	(ton)	200050.52	100.2	142092
合成氨	(吨)	Synthetic Ammonia	(ton)	97301.00	99.5	78815
农用氮、磷、钾化学肥料总计(折纯)	(吨)	Chemical Fertilizer	(ton)	50085.00	101.3	39853
化学农药原药(折有效成分100%)	(吨)	Chemical Pesticide	(ton)	113544.92	113.1	18899
涂料(油漆)	(吨)	Paint	(ton)	139136.06	107.1	104467
油墨	(吨)	Printing Ink	(ton)	33515.60	104.1	29165
合成洗涤剂	(吨)	Synthetic Detergent	(ton)	109361.30	87.8	96678
化学药品原药(化学原料药)	(吨)	Original Drug Chemicals	(ton)	11496.06	102.1	6084
中成药	(吨)	Traditional Chinese Medicine	(ton)	10242.77	113.4	6294
橡胶轮胎外胎(轮胎外胎)	(万条)	Rubber Tires	(10000 units)	3125.06	125.2	2958.99
水泥	(万吨)	Cement	(10000 tons)	1829.70	105.2	907.27

4-16 续表2 continued 2

产品名称	Item	全市 Whole Municipality 2009年	为上年(%) As Compared with the Preceding Year(%)	市区 Urban District
平板玻璃 (万重量箱)	Plate Glass (10000 weight cases)	423.78	89.5	529.7
钢 (万吨)	Steels (10000 tons)	350.00	96.7	350
生铁 (万吨)	Pig Iron (10000 tons)	261.29	97.8	261.29
铁合金 (万吨)	Iron Alloy (10000 tons)	10.81	99.3	1.72
钢材 (万吨)	Steel Products (10000 tons)	805.07	105.9	740.3
精炼铜(铜) (吨)	Copper (ton)	175194.27	109.9	–
搪瓷制品 (吨)	Enamelware (ton)	29825.90	94.1	29826
工业锅炉 (蒸发量吨)	Industry Boiler (ton)	9001.49	125.6	9001
金属切削机床 (台)	Metal-cutting Machine Tools (unit)	17092.00	82.4	8314
金属成形机床(锻压设备)(台)	Metal Forming Machine(Forge Equipment) (Tai)	13186.00	82.3	13186
泵(液体泵) (万台)	Pump (10000 sets)	46.56	101.3	45.48
滚动轴承(轴承) (万套)	Bearings (10000 units)	2.76	92.1	25934
汽车 (辆)	Motor Vehicles (unit)	13462	99.0	13432
叉车 (台)	Forklift (unit)	34408.00	99.3	14317
两轮自行车(自行车) (万辆)	Bicycles (10000 units)	525.64	98.4	520.27

4－16 续表3 continued 3

产品名称	Item	全市 Whole Municipality 2009 年	为上年(%) As Compared with the Preceding Year(%)	市区 Urban District
交流电动机 (万千瓦)	AC Motor (10000 kw)	42.14	128.0	36.25
钢芯铝绞线 (吨)	Aluminiumt Wisted Wire with Steel Core (ton)	6.03	104.3	55748
通信及电子网络用电缆 (万对千米)	Communication Cable (10000 km)	1417.55	57.4	52.92
光缆(光纤通讯电缆)(万芯千米)	Electric Power Cable (10000 km)	1285.33	145.6	81.68
家用电冰箱 (万台)	Household Refrigerators (10000 units)	93.74	93.6	93.74
家用洗衣机 (万台)	Household Washing Machines (10000 units)	281.54	113.0	281.54
吸排油烟机 (万台)	Smoke Absorbers (10000 units)	101.88	112.3	101.88
移动通信手持机(手机)(万部)	Mobile Telephone Sets (10000 units)	1420.09	101.7	1420.09
电工仪器仪表 (万台)	Electric Instrument and Apparatus (10000 units)	2720.62	105.1	1822.36
自动化仪表及系统(万台)	Automation Apparatus and System (10000 units)	109.37	130.6	109.37
电光源(灯泡) (亿只)	Light Bulbs (100 million units)	19.14	93.2	4.45
彩色电视机 (万部)	Color－Television Sets (10000 units)	23.64	33.4	23.64
微型电子计算机 (万台)	Microcomputer (10000 units)	89.20	84.5	89.2
肥(香)皂 (吨)	Soaps (ton)	30859	131.2	30859

4－17　2009年单位GDP能耗降低情况
Increase or Decrease of Energy Consumption Per Unit of GDP(2009)

地　区	Region	单位GDP能耗（吨标准煤/万元）Energy Consumption Per Unit of GDP (tons of SCE/10000 yuan)		单位GDP电耗（千瓦时/万元）Electricity Consumption Per Unit of GDP (kwh/10000 yuan)		单位工业增加值能耗（吨标准煤/万元）Energy Consumption Per Unit of Industriul Value－Added (tons of SCE/10000 yuan)	
		2009年	降低率 Increase or Decrease Rate (±%)	2009年	降低率 Increase or Decrease Rate (±%)	2009年	降低率 Increase or Decrease Rate (±%)
杭州市	Hangzhou	0.70	5.60	976	2.84	1.02	6.38
#上城区	Shangcheng					0.19	10.78
下城区	Xiacheng					0.18	9.39
江干区	Jianggan					0.32	10.42
拱墅区	Gongshu					2.72	6.12
西湖区	Xihu					0.28	6.5
高新（滨江）区	Hi－Tech(Binjiang)					0.50	10.53
下沙经济技术开发区	HEDA					0.45	5.16
萧山区	Xiaoshan	0.88	5.11	1431	2.51	1.04	5.12
余杭区	Yuhang	0.73	4.63	1122	－3.55	0.91	5.01
桐庐县	Tonglu	0.59	4.61	720	－2.03	0.71	6.85
淳安县	Chun'an	0.41	1.94	671	1.38	0.74	4.26
建德市	Jiande	1.32	6.57	1256	6.93	2.96	6.85
富阳市	Fuyang	1.38	4.81	1598	－1.14	2.29	4.78
临安市	Lin'an	0.70	5.31	1030	0.02	1.23	6.45

注：江干区不含杭州经济技术开发区。

a) HEDA is not included in Jianggan district in this table.

4－18 全市工业企业主要能源

Energy Consumption of Industrial

行 业 Sector	原煤(吨) Raw Coal(Ton)	洗精煤(吨) Washing Coal(Ton)	焦炭(吨) Coke(Ton)	汽油(吨) Gasoline(Ton)	煤油(吨) Kerosene(Ton)
总 计 Total	**14284791**	**688108**	**1389592**	**69054**	**2426**
煤炭开采和洗选业 Coal Mining and Dressing	–	–	–	–	–
黑色金属矿采选业 Ferrous Metals Mining and Dressing	–	–	–	–	–
有色金属矿采选业 Nonferrous Minerals Mining and Dressing	–	–	–	22	–
非金属矿采选业 Nonmetal Minerals Mining and Dressing	35958	–	–	21	–
农副食品加工业 Agricultural Products Processing	34240	–	23	438	–
食品制造业 Food Manufacturing	46008	–	–	933	–
饮料制造业 Beverage Manufacturing	48424	–	–	854	–
烟草加工业 Tobacco Processing	–	–	–	38	–
纺织业 Textile Processing	1291738	13	898	8357	146
纺织服装、鞋、帽制造业 Textile Products, Garments, Shoes and Caps Processing	10655	145	464	3382	–
皮革、毛皮、羽毛(绒)及其制品业 Leather, Furs, Down and Related Products	43268	–	–	1165	–
木材加工及木、竹、藤、棕、草制品业 Timber Processing, Bamboo, Cane, Plam Fiber and Straw Products	1849	–	–	324	6
家具制造业 Furniture Manufacturing	3796	78	884	1091	–
造纸及纸制品业 Paper Making and Paper Products	663435	–	–	1721	–
印刷业和记录媒介的复制 Printing	3748	–	–	1726	7
文教体育用品制造业 Cultural, Educational and Sports Goods	922	–	–	611	–
石油加工、炼焦及核燃料加工业 Petroleum Processing, Coking and Nudear Fuel Processing	2548	–	–	199	–

消费量按行业分(2009 年)
Enterprises by Sector(2009)

柴油(吨) Diesel oil(Ton)	燃料油(吨) Fuel Oil(Ton)	液化石油气(吨) Liquefied Petroleum Gas(Ton)	天然气(万立方米) Natural Gas (10000 cu. m)	其他石油制品(吨) Other Petroleum Products(Ton)	热力(百万千焦) Heat(Million kilo - joule)	电力(万千瓦时) Electricity (10000 kwh)
202446	**120689**	**55619**	**88532**	**319219**	**83320625**	**3036618**
-	-	-	-	-	-	-
-	-	-	-	-	-	-
7	-	-	-	-	-	2444
9323	-	-	-	113	-	11142
1956	-	56	-	43	56957	12403
2694	152	1095	388	-	1385582	17618
5012	527	17	-	-	2088351	57120
5440	-	-	-	-	129009	4627
7624	3426	651	778	251	23121106	485239
4063	-	18	29	-	602357	27314
820	-	2	-	-	107445	13449
348	-	420	-	-	234067	9952
5660	41	-	259	12	70770	11414
3881	-	149	80	2	27264400	297885
1413	-	71	37	17	28870	14749
743	-	89	-	2	121118	8280
554	4875	-	-	193764	4360	5513

4－18　续表

行　业　Sector	原煤(吨) Raw Coal(Ton)	洗精煤(吨) Washing Coal(Ton)	焦炭(吨) Coke(Ton)	汽油(吨) Gasoline(Ton)	煤油(吨) Kerosene(Ton)
化学原料及化学制品制造业 Raw Chemical Materials and Chemical Products	968666	60	100	7738	544
医药制造业 Medical and Pharmaceutical Products	37748	–	–	1093	–
化学纤维制造业 Chemical Fiber	278438	–	–	1087	–
橡胶制品业 Rubber Products	213726	–	157	3381	18
塑料制品业 Plastic Products	40141	–	–	2174	44
非金属矿物制品业 Nonmetal Minerals Products	2879774	80	35	2607	1
黑色金属冶炼及压延加工业 Smelting and Processing of Ferrous Metals	503910	687687	1317690	581	–
有色金属冶炼及压延加工业 Smelting and Processing of Nonferrous Metals	32751	–	16295	358	–
金属制品业 Metal Products	55725	–	50	4505	178
通用设备制造业 Ordinary Machinery	81501	–	30862	5789	934
专用设备制造业 Special Purpose Equipment	9146	44	668	2193	7
交通运输设备制造业 Transportation Equtpment	17493	–	1997	3110	527
电气机械及器材制造业 Electric Equipment and Machinery	11525	–	225	4081	1
通信设备、计算机及其他电子设备制造业 Telecommunications Equipment, Computers and Other Electronic Equipment	4098	–	329	2228	6
仪器仪表及文化、办公用机械制造业 Instruments, Meters, Cultural and Office Machinery	13328	–	27	2685	7
工艺品及其他制造业 Craftworks and Other Manufacturing	2958	–	27	1314	1
废弃资源和废旧材料回收加工业 Waste Resouces and Waste or Old Material Recycled	4391	–	18862	58	–
电力、热力的生产和供应业 Production and Supply of Electric Power and Hot Water	6942884	–	–	2652	–
燃气生产和供应业 Production and Supply of Gas	–	–	–	188	–
水的生产和供应业 Production and Supply of Tap Water	–	–	–	352	–

continued

柴油(吨) Diesel oil(Ton)	燃料油(吨) Fuel Oil(Ton)	液化石油气(吨) Liquefied Petroleum Gas(Ton)	天然气(万立方米) Natural Gas (10000 cu. m)	其他石油制品(吨) Other Petroleum Products(Ton)	热力(百万千焦) Heat(Million kilo - joule)	电力(万千瓦时) Electricity (10000 kwh)
19767	13905	9	627	120324	6970952	219982
2080	–	28	890	–	730825	21458
1486	50637	27	202	1133	6001239	246795
1688	–	–	764	536	2972947	77757
4530	3475	1054	162	766	320844	89645
69331	18680	30181	11677	98	6715881	259288
3838	1047	3557	799	35	2072304	311085
1759	14839	157	161	195	28991	32051
8628	5894	762	1546	113	175883	74144
15189	2184	646	494	860	134195	120967
2371	6	8	107	123	57465	23334
5882	259	1025	34	651	34489	58339
6535	–	15405	389	122	226521	97537
2550	23	86	5	–	285966	55849
2099	–	5	104	10	21988	15223
1577	–	89	49	28	38652	14764
373	719	–	–	–	–	4443
2362	–	–	68898	23	1317090	286350
305	–	6	50	–	–	476
558	–	9	3	–	–	47984

4－19 电力消费量(2009年)
Electricity Consumption(2009)

单位:万千瓦时 (10000 kwh)

项 目	Item	总计 Total 2009年	总计 Total 为上年(%) As Compared with the Preceding Year(%)	杭州市电力局 Hangzhou Electricity Bureau	建德市电力局 Jiande Electricity Bureau	淳安县电力局 Chun'an Electricity Bureau
总 计	**Total**	**4596987**	**106.9**	**4343159**	**190932**	**62896**
#线路损失电量	#Losses in Transmission	175989	101.8	168937	4720	2332
农林牧渔业	Farming, Forestry, Animal Husbandry and Fishery Conservancy	38816	94.5	37313	1033	470
工业	Industry	3225708	105.0	3021244	161582	42882
轻工业	Light Industry	1588169	106.5	1545114	12447	30608
重工业	Heavy Industry	1637539	103.6	1476130	149135	12274
#采矿业	#Mining and Quarrying	35580	100.7	32106	2432	1042
制造业	Manufacturing Industry	2878449	105.0	2691399	148664	38386
建筑业	Construction	74190	126.1	71515	1106	1569
交通运输、仓储及邮政业	Transportation, Storage, Post & Telecommunications	50794	109.8	49419	869	506
信息传输、计算机服务和软件业	Information Transmission, Computer Services and Software	49271	139.2	47413	1054	804
商业、住宿和餐饮业	Commerce, Catering and Accommodations	216774	112.4	209084	3748	3942
金融、房地产、商务及居民服务业	Finance, Real Estate Commerce and Service for the Residents	138673	111.3	135531	1374	1768
公共管理和社会组织	Public Management and Social Organzations	238721	109.3	232511	3705	2505
城乡居民生活用电	Residential Consumption	564041	110.1	539129	16462	8450
#乡村	#Rural Areas	215490	109.0	202751	8060	4679
城市	Cities	348911	110.9	336378	8402	4131

4－20 全市 2001－2009 年水资源量和总用水量

Total Water Resources and Water Consumption(2001－2009)

单位:亿立方米 (100 million Cubic Meters)

		全市 Whole City	市区 Urban District	桐庐 Tonglu	淳安 Chan'an	建德 Jiangde	富阳 Fuyang	临安 Lin'an
2001 年	水资源量 Water Resources	156.37	18.87	14.28	41.14	18.54	14.23	26.76
	用水量 Water Consumption	40.29	28.05	2.01	1.03	2.11	4.17	2.92
2002 年	水资源量 Water Resources	213.0	30.21	24.3	65.46	31.59	23.54	37.9
	用水量 Water Consumption	39.92	27.51	2.01	1.05	2.18	4.35	2.82
2003 年	水资源量 Water Resources	102.65	9.31	10.32	41.43	15.57	8.13	17.9
	用水量 Water Consumption	44.72	29.13	1.98	1.38	2.30	7.12	2.81
2004 年	水资源量 Water Resources	85.28	12.04	10.35	27.82	11.34	9.15	14.58
	用水量 Water Consumption	48.90	32.89	2.21	1.09	2.35	7.17	3.19
2005 年	水资源量 Water Resources	90.65	14.32	9.46	26.66	10.36	10.31	19.54
	用水量 Water Consumption	49.58	32.95	2.25	1.24	2.38	7.16	3.61
2006 年	水资源量 Water Resources	109.8	15.14	11.70	38.42	13.41	10.36	20.75
	用水量 Water Consumption	48.73	31.39	2.39	1.42	2.68	7.13	3.72
2007 年	水资源量 Water Resources	104.13	20.28	10.12	29.88	11.72	11.76	20.36
	用水量 Water Consumption	49.56	32.57	2.53	1.53	3.09	6.45	3.39
2008 年	水资源量 Water Resources	154.28	24.58	14.95	49.22	18.52	14.2	32.92
	用水量 Water Consumption	56.7	39.57	2.9	1.32	2.69	6.49	3.7
2009 年	水资源量 Water Resources	141.5	23.38	16.67	37.46	15.63	16.33	32.03
	用水量 Water Consumption	54.28	39.24	2.52	1.46	2.81	5.18	3.07

主要统计指标解释

工业总产值 是以货币表现的工业企业在报告期内生产的已出售或可供出售工业产品总量，它反映一定时间内工业生产的总规模和总水平，它包括：在本企业内不再进行加工，经检验、包装入库（规定不需包装的产品除外）的成品价值，对外加工费收入，自制半成品，在产品期末初差额价值。工业总产值采用"工厂法"计算，即以工业企业作为一个整体，按企业工业生产活动的最终成果来计算，企业内部不允许重复计算，不能把企业内部各个车间（分厂）生产的成果相加。

工业销售产值 是以货币表现的工业企业在一定时期内销售的本企业生产的工业产品总量。包括已销售的成品、半成品价值，对外提供的工业性作业和对本单位基本建设部门、生活福利部门等提供的产品和工业性作业及自制设备的价值。已销售的成品、半成品不论是本期生产的、还是上期生产的，只要是本期销售出去的均包括在内。对外提供的工业性作业是指企业按合同对外提供的工业性劳务。企业为本单位基本建设部门、生活福利部门等提供的产品和工业性作业及自制设备也应视同销售，这部分也作为销售统计。工业销售产值的计算范围、计算价格和计算方法与工业总产值一致，但两者计算的基础不同；工业销售产值计算的基础是产品销售总量，工业总产值计算的基础是工业产品生产总量。

工业增加值 是指工业行业在报告期内以货币表现的工业生产活动的最终成果。

固定资产原价 固定资产原值指企业在建造、购置、安装、改建、扩建、技术改造某项固定资产时所支出的全部货币总额。它一般包括买价、包装费、运杂费和安装费等。

固定资产净值 是指固定资产原价减去历年已提折旧额后的净额。

利税总额 指企业利润总额、产品销售税金及附加和应交增值税之和。

产品销售收入 指企业销售产品的销售收入和提供劳务等主要经营业务取得的收入总额。

产品销售成本 指企业销售产品和提供劳务等主要经营业务的实际成本。

产品销售税金及附加 指企业销售产品和提供工业性劳务等主要经营业务应负担的城市维护建设税、消费税、资源税和教育费附加。

产品销售利润 指企业销售产品和提供工业性劳务等主要经营业务收入和除其成本、费用、税金后的利润。

利润总额 指企业实现的利润。

应交增值税 指企业在报告期内应交纳的增值税额。

总资产 指企业拥有或控制的全部资产。包括流动资产、长期投资、固定资产、无形及递延资产、其他长期资产、递延税项等，即为企业资产负债表的资产总计项。

（1）流动资产指企业可以在一年内或者超过一年的一个生产周期内变现或耗用的资产合计。包括现金及各种存款、短期投资、应收及预付款项、存货等。

（2）固定资产指企业固定资产净值、固定资产清理、在建工程、待处理固定资产损失所占用的资金合计。

（3）无形资产指企业长期使用而没有实物形态的资产。包括专利权、非专利技术、商标权、著作权、土地使用权、商誉等。

总负债 指企业承担并需要偿还的全部债务。包括流动负债和长期负债、递延税项等，即为企业资产负债表的负债合计项。

（1）流动负债指企业在一年内或者超过一年的一个营业周期内需要偿还的债务合计，其中包括短期借款、应付及预收款项、应付工资、应交税金和应交利润等。

（2）长期负债指企业在一年以上或者超过一年的一个生产周期以上需要偿还的债务合计，其中包括长期借款、应付债务、长期应付款项等。

所有者权益 指企业投资人对企业净资产的所有权。企业净资产等于企业全部资产减去全部负债后的余额。其中包括投资者对企业的最初投入，以及资本公积金、盈余公积金和未分配利润，对股份制企业即为股东权益。

Explanatory Notes on Main Statistical Indicators

Gross Industrial Output Value is the total volume of industrial products sold or available for sale in value terms which reflects the total achievements and overall scale of industrial production during a given period. It includes the value of the finished products, which are not to be further processed in the enterprises and have been inspected, packed and put in storage, the value of industrial services rendered to other units, and the changes in the value of the semi – finished products and products in process between the beginning and closing of the period. The gross industrial output value is calculated with "factory method". No double calculations are to be made within the same enterprise. However, double counting does occur among different enterprises.

Industrial Sales Output Value is the total volume of industrial products sold in value term of an industrial enterprise during a given period. It includes the value of finished products, semi – finished products, industrial operations rendered to other units, products industrial operations & self – made equipment provided to the basic construction department, welfare department, etc. of the enterprise. For finished products & semi – finished products, whether produced in this calculation period or the previous one, if they are sold in this calculation period, they should be included. Industrial operations are industrial services rendered to other units according to contracts. Products, industrial operations & self – made equipment provided to basic construction department, welfare department, etc. of the enterprise should be regarded as act of sale, and included in sales statistics.

The scope , price and method of calculation of industrial sales output value are the same as those for gross industrial output value. But the calculation bases are different: the base for sales output value is the total volume of products sold; the base for gross industrial output value is total volume of production of industrial products.

Value – added of Industry refers to the final results of industrial production of the industrial trade in money terms during the reference period.

Original Value of Fixed Assets refers to the original value of all assets owned by industrial enterprises, calculated at the cost paid at the time of purchase, installation, reconstruction, expansion, and technical innovation and transformation of the said assets, which includes expenses on purchase, package, transportation, and installation, etc.

Net Value of Fixed Assets is obtained by deducting depreciation over years from the original value of fixed assets.

Total Pre – tax Profits refers to the sum of sales tax and extra charges adding total profits.

Sales Revenue of Industrial Products refers to the revenue from the sales of products by industrial enterprises and the revenue from services provided and etc.

Sales Cost of Industrial Products refers to the actual cost of products of industrial enterprises and industrial services provided, etc. .

Tax and Extra Charges on Sales of Products refer to the tax on city maintenance and construction, consumption tax, resources tax and extra charges for education , which should be borne by the enterprises in selling products and providing industrial services.

Sales Profit of Products refers to the profit gained by the enterprises by deducting cost, charges and taxes from the business income of the enterprises obtained in selling products and providing industrial services.

Total Profits refer to the profits gained by the enterprises.

Value – added Tax Payable refers to the amount of the value added tax which should be paid by the enterprises in the reporting period.

Total Assets refer to all assets which are owned or controlled by enterprises, including circulating assets, long term investment, fixed assets, intangible assets and deferred assets, other long term assets, and deferred taxes, etc. The summation of above items is equal to total assets shown in the balance sheets of the enterprises.

(1) Circulating assets (working capital) refer to assets which can be cashed in or spent or consumed in an operating cycle of one year or over one year, including cash, all kinds of deposits, short term investment, receivables, advance payment, stock, etc.

(2) Fixed assets refer to the net value of fixed assets, clearance of fixed assets, project under construction, fixed assets losses in suspense. These are corporations' fund holdings.

(3) Intangible assets refer to assets without material form used by enterprises over a lone time, such as patents, non – patent technologies, trade marks, copyright, land use right, business reputation, etc.

Total Liabilities refer to the debts that enterprises are responsible for repayment, including liquid liabilities, long – term liabilities and deferred taxes, etc. Total liabilities correspond to the summation item of liabilities shown in the balance sheets of the enterprises.

(1) Liquid liabilities (also called quick liabilities or immediate liabilities) refer to enterprises' total debt payable within an operating cycle of one year or over one year, including short term loans, payables and advance payments, wages payable, taxes payable and profit payable, etc.

(2) Long term liabilities refers to total debt payable within an operating cycle of one year or over one year, including long – term loans, payable liabilities, long – term payables, etc.

Creditors' Equity refers to investors' ownership of net assets of the enterprise. It is equal to the total assets of the enterprise minus its total liabilities, including the primary input from investors, capital accumulation fund, surplus accumulation fund and undistributed profit. It is the shareholder's equity in share – holding companies.

第五篇
CHAPTER-5

建筑业
CONSTRUCTION

建筑业
Construction

主要统计指标
Major Statistical Indicators

建筑业总产值	Gross Output Value of Construction	2110.17	亿元	(100 million yuan)
为上年	As Compared with the Preceding Year	117.2	%	(%)
房屋建筑施工面积	Floor Space of Buildings Under Construction	19434	万平方米	(10000 sq.m)
为上年	As Compared with the Preceding Year	121.0	%	(%)
房屋建筑竣工面积	Floor Space of Buildings Completed	6610	万平方米	(10000 sq.m)
为上年	As Compared with the Preceding Year	114.0	%	(%)

5-01 建筑业总产值

Gross Output Value of Construction

单位:万元 (10000 yuan)

地 区	Region	建筑企业单位数(个) Number of Construction Enterprises (unit)	建筑企业年末从业人员数(人) Number of Employed Persons at the end of the Year (Person)	建筑业总产值 Gross Output Value of Construction	其中: 建筑工程产值 Output Value of Construction Projects	安装工程产值 Output value of Installation Projects	其他产值 Other Output Values
全 市	**Total**	**1230**	**923046**	**21101673**	**18280567**	**2193971**	**627135**
市 区	Urban District	1009	828049	19462816	16868048	2013792	580976
上城区	Shangcheng	84	52599	1602668	1103027	455656	43985
下城区	Xiacheng	101	40443	1160245	996436	156392	7417
江干区	Jianggan	135	78784	1775133	1560856	203479	10798
拱墅区	Gongshu	141	69579	1498743	1111926	308631	78187
西湖区	Xihu	159	220845	4566492	4053703	325955	186834
高新(滨江)区	Hi-Tech (Binjiang)	40	47640	1640350	1529611	54654	56084
萧山区	Xiaoshan	208	254289	5933185	5376036	383225	173924
余杭区	Yuhang	130	55713	1085935	957516	104863	23556
桐庐县	Tonglu	43	15628	227425	206689	16253	4483
淳安县	Chun'an	36	9044	135719	98448	30185	7086
建德市	Jiande	31	11160	132421	104935	27115	371
富阳市	Fuyang	67	27872	635161	535219	67858	32084
临安市	Lin'an	44	31293	508131	467228	38768	2135

5-02 各种分组总专包

Financial Condition

单位:万元

指标名称	Item	二、年末资产 Asset and Liabilities 流动资产合计 Circulating Funds	固定资产合计 Fixed Assets	资产合计 Total Assets
总 计	**Total**	**10148822**	**1392917**	**12847637**
其中:特、一、二级企业	of Which: Special Grade, First Grade, Second Grade	8272833	1044332	10515312
其中:国有及国有控股企业	of Which: State - owned and State Holding Enterprises	1120501	157111	1470536
一、按登记注册类型分组	**Grouped by Registration Status**			
内资企业	Domestic Funded	10129383	1390639	12824648
国有企业	State - owned	414032	78066	506953
集体企业	Collective - owned	71306	2733	74422
股份合作企业	Share - holding Cooperative Enterprises	38	99	137
联营企业	Joint Venture	6856	4344	12265
有限责任公司	Limited Liability Corporations	5285972	558655	6653635
股份有限公司	Share - holding Corporations Ltd.	375947	54021	486053
私营企业	Private Enterprises	3975232	692721	5091184
港、澳、台商投资企业	Funded from Hong Kong, Macao and Taiwan	9200	2068	12170
外商投资企业	Foreign Funded	10239	210	10819
二、按国民经济行业分组	**Grouped by Sector**			
房屋和土木工程建筑业	Housing and Civil Engineering Construction	8966810	1203475	11394089
建筑安装业	Installation of Lines, Pipelines and Equipment	594695	92612	734365
建筑装饰业	Fitting and Decoration of Buildings	433258	60077	518243
其他建筑业	Others Construction	154059	36754	200940

企业财务汇总表
of Construction

(10000 yuan)

负债 at Year - end				
流动负债合计 Liquid Liabilities	负债合计 Total Liabilities	所有者权益合计 Owners´Equity	其中:实收资本 of Which: Paid - in Capitals	其中:国家资本 of Which: State Capital
8161089	**8420381**	**4427256**	**2674474**	**215162**
6849108	7083952	3431360	1897562	201631
1051590	1149882	320655	214677	199708
8144608	8403810	4420838	2668227	215162
375711	378067	128886	71325	71325
57746	57805	16617	7570	-
51	51	86	116	-
7058	7058	5207	3010	3010
4642144	4803545	1850090	1022340	138647
248000	282033	204020	61435	2180
2813898	2875252	2215933	1502430	-
8550	8550	3620	3148	-
7932	8021	2798	3100	-
7264517	7496589	3897500	2278659	192865
477614	499176	235189	176322	11402
303187	306877	211366	160482	7405
115772	117739	83201	59011	3490

指标名称	Item	三、损益 Expenditure, Income 工程结算收入 Revenue of Project Settlement Accounts	工程结算成本 Costs of Project Settlement Accounts
总　计	**Total**	**19159766**	**17454560**
其中:特、一、二级企业	of Which: Special Grade, First Grade, Second Grade	16447229	15110955
其中:国有及国有控股企业	of Which: State－owned and State Holding Enterprises	1787706	1602743
一、按登记注册类型分组	**Grouped by Registration Status**		
内资企业	Domestic Funded	19114125	17413045
国有企业	State－owned	822939	721343
集体企业	Collective－owned	43627	35409
股份合作企业	Share－holding Cooperative Enterprises	17	10
联营企业	Joint Venture	20818	18610
有限责任公司	Limited Liability Corporations	9606111	8852149
股份有限公司	Share－holding Corporations Ltd.	883415	795358
私营企业	Private Enterprises	7737198	6990165
港、澳、台商投资企业	Funded from Hong Kong, Macao and Taiwan	10478	8359
外商投资企业	Foreign Funded	35162	33156
二、按国民经济行业分组	**Grouped by Sector**		
房屋和土木工程建筑业	Housing and Civil Engineering Construction	17220740	15746425
建筑安装业	Installation of Lines, Pipelines and Equipment	921627	804764
建筑装饰业	Fitting and Decoration of Buildings	750997	663055
其他建筑业	Others Construction	266402	240316

continued (10000 yuan)

及分配 and Distribution						六、全部从业人员年平均人数（人） Annual Average Number of Employed Persons (person)
工程结算税金及附加 Taxes and Extra Charges Project Settlement Accounts	经营费用 Operating Cost	管理费用 Management Expenditure	财务费用 Financial Expenditure	利润总额 Total Profits	应交所得税 Income Taxes Payable	
646066	**41833**	**475413**	**110874**	**509497**	**114192**	**985452**
557358	23575	336202	96695	386579	87241	831185
56399	3940	95395	4845	31247	7365	59465
644625	41824	473105	110736	508927	113959	983527
24554	3667	61036	814	16573	4052	25007
1332	105	4325	-125	2534	609	2228
0.7	-	23	-	-16	0.3	12
696	0.1	1426	4	113	26	2053
326198	7212	197174	61452	216890	44704	478900
28626	6118	21490	2436	35282	8771	38326
263218	24722	187631	46156	237551	55797	473001
326	2	1040	68	1031	166	546
1115	8	1269	69	-460	67	1379
585915	32562	375526	101336	450267	99942	892095
26134	6373	57910	3556	26688	6215	39037
25600	2434	31946	4059	25381	6202	42117
8416	464	10031	1923	7161	1833	12203

5－03 建筑业企业生产情况
Statistics on Construction

指标名称	Item	2006	2007	2008	2009
建筑业合同情况	Contract of Construction				
签订的合同额 （万元）	Total Value of Contracts （10000 yuan）	20010853	24696898	30088537	36623552
上年结转合同额 （万元）	Value from Contracts Signed in 2008 （10000 yuan）	7548539	9290912	11210961	14824477
本年新签合同额 （万元）	Value from New Contracts Signed in 2009 （10000 yuan）	12462314	15405986	18877576	21799075
承包工程完成情况 （万元）	Completion of Contracted Projects （10000 yuan）				
直接从建设单位承揽工程完成的产值 （万元）	Complete Output Value of Projects Contacted Directly from Investors （10000 yuan）	12662433	14853868	17871119	20791153
自行完成施工产值 （万元）	Own－completed Output Value （10000 yuan）	12326935	14495495	17427692	20424041
分包出去工程的产值 （万元）	Output Value of Out－sourced Projects （10000 yuan）	335498	358373	443427	367112
从建设单位以外承揽工程完成的产值 （万元）	Completed Output Value of Projects Contacted from Non－investors （10000 yuan）	345587	349254	576832	677632
建筑业总产值 （万元）	Gross Output Value （10000 yuan）	12672522	14844749	18004524	21101673
其中:装饰装修产值 （万元）	of Which：Output Value of Fitting and Decoration of Buildings （10000 yuan）	882969	1149597	1404589	1641467
其中:在外省完成的产值 （万元）	of Which：Completed Output Value outside of Zhejiang Province （10000 yuan）	2686936	3489987	4971040	5828938
按构成分	by Structure				
建筑工程产值 （万元）	Output Value of Construction Projects （10000 yuan）	10749915	12768968	15351303	18280567
安装工程产值 （万元）	Output value of Installation Projects （10000 yuan）	1497416	1729043	2083405	2193971
其他产值 （万元）	Other Output Values （10000 yuan）	425191	346738	569816	627135
竣工产值 （万元）	Output Value of Buildings Completed （10000 yuan）	8828029	9344723	10976179	12919145
房屋建筑施工面积 （平方米）	Floor Space of Buildings Under Construction （sq. m）	136123500	151089346	160591516	194338183
其中:本年新开工面积 （平方米）	of Which：Beginning Projects in this Year （sq. m）	71652045	75166956	72814916	78393242
其中:实行投标承包面积 （平方米）	of Which：Floor Space of Biding System （sq. m）	124219345	138652667	147255606	181334022
其中:本年新开工 （平方米）	of Which：Beginning Projects in this Year （sq. m）	66958170	70647024	66460877	73903950
年末自有施工机械设备	Machinery and Equipment Owned （year－end）				
年末自有施工机械设备净值 （万元）	Net Value of Machinery and Equipment Owned （10000 yuan）	439174	462157	559442	683528
年末自有施工机械设备总台数 （台）	Number of Machinery and Equipment Owned （set）	144384	148722	157385	178586
年末自有施工机械设备总功率（千瓦）	Total Power of Machinery and Equipment Owned （10000 kw）	1845585	1958612	2435575	2748357
从业人员情况	Number of Employed Persons				
计算劳动生产率的平均人数 （人）	Average Employed Persons Overall Labor Productivity （person）	695674	775498	863862	966098
年末从业人员数 （人）	Employed Persons （year－end） （person）	671610	758171	801246	923046

主要统计指标解释

建筑业总产值　建筑业总产值是以货币表现的建筑业企业在一定时期内生产的建筑业产品和服务的总和。建筑业总产值包括建筑工程产值、安装工程产值和其他产值三部分内容。

房屋建筑施工面积　指报告期内施过工的全部房屋建筑面积，它包括本期新开工的面积、上期跨入本期继续施工的房屋面积、上期停缓建在本期恢复施工的房屋面积、本期竣工的房屋面积以及本期施工后又停缓建的房屋面积。

房屋建筑竣工面积　指在报告期内房屋建筑按照设计要求已全部完工，达到了使用条件，经检查验收鉴定合格的房屋建筑面积。

工程结算收入（主营业务收入）　指本企业承包工程实现的工程价款结算收入以及向发包单位收取的除工程价款以外按规定列作营业收入的各种款项，如临时设施费、劳动保险费、施工机构调迁费等以及向发包单位收取的各种索赔款。

工程结算成本（主营业务成本）　指在报告期内与发包单位办理工程价款结算的已完工程实际成本。

Explanatory Notes on Main Statistical Indicators

Gross Output Value of Construction refers to total of construction products and services, expressed in money terms, produced or rendered by construction and installation enterprises during a given period of time. It includes: output value of construction projects, output value of installation projects and other output values.

Floor Space of Buildings Under Construction refers to floor space of buildings under construction during the reference period, including the floor space of buildings for which construction has newly started; buildings for which construction has started earlier and is continuing during the reference period; and buildings for which construction has been suspended earlier but has restarted during the reference period; buildings completed during the reference period; and buildings under construction but construction has subsequently been during the reference period.

Floor Space of Buildings Completed refers to the floor space of buildings that are completed in the reference period in accordance with the requirements of the design, up to the standard for being put into use, and having been checked and accepted by departments concerned as qualified ones.

Income from Settlement of Projects refers to the income received by the construction enterprise from the contracted project through settlement procedures, and other charges to the contractor as operational costs in addition to the value of the project, such as temporary facility fee, labor insurance premium, moving cost of construction equipment, as well as various types of claims to the contractor.

Project Settlement Costs refers to the contracting process works price of the actual settlement costs of projects have been completed during the reporting period.

第六篇
CHAPTER-6

交通运输、邮电
TRANSPORTATION, POST AND TELECOMMUNICATIONS

交通运输、邮电
Transportation, Post and Telecommunications

主要统计指标
Major Statistical Indicators

客运量	Passenger Traffic	30116	万人次	(10000 person-times)
为上年	As Compared with the Preceding Year	103.5	%	(%)
货运量	Freight Traffic	22372	万吨	(10000 tons)
为上年	As Compared with the Preceding Year	99.2	%	(%)
邮电业务收入	Business Income of Post & Telecommunication Service	135.54	亿元	(100 million yuan)
为上年	As Compared with the Preceding Year	108.6	%	(%)
年末固定电话用户数	Number of Local Telephone Subscribers(year-end)	390.38	万户	(10000 subscribers)
为上年	As Compared with the Preceding Year	93.8	%	(%)
年末移动电话用户数	Number of Mobile Telephone Subscribers(year-end)	1011.93	万户	(10000 subscribers)
为上年	As Compared with the Preceding Year	116.7	%	(%)

6-01 全市主要年份客运量
Total Passenger Traffic in Main Years

单位:万人次 (10000 person - times)

年 份 Year	合 计 Total	铁 路 Railways	公 路 Highways	水 路 Waterways	民 航 Civil Aviation
1978	2878	485	-	-	3
1979	3122	560	1829	729	4
1980	3905	672	2358	870	5
1981	4484	769	2857	850	8
1982	5263	813	3377	1064	9
1983	5451	878	3530	1035	8
1984	6056	983	3912	1151	10
1985	6724	1004	4595	1111	14
1986	6765	1034	4768	941	22
1987	6905	1127	4852	896	30
1988	6593	1237	4445	877	34
1989	7493	1182	5488	801	22
1990	8119	1056	6350	691	22
1991	10701	1062	8876	710	53
1992	13358	1083	11538	670	67
1993	13070	1139	11403	454	74
1994	13373	1230	11669	390	84
1995	16620	1242	14921	339	118
1996	16714	1112	15184	273	145
1997	17034	1040	15623	260	111
1998	17395	1120	15925	235	115
1999	17882	1168	16369	235	110
2000	18607	1202	17102	179	124
2001	20342	1342	18707	148	145
2002	21089	1574	19213	108	194
2003	21348	1534	19510	89	215
2004	22833	1908	20372	237	316
2005	24124	2011	21431	304	378
2006	25810	2124	22961	267	458
2007	28026	2255	24836	306	629
2008	29084	2498	25630	277	679
2009	30116	2494	26454	372	796

注:客运量全市数自1990年起为全社会数,1990年以前为交通系统数。

a) Since 1990 the data in this table inclued non - transportation system, while data for previous years only included transportation system.

6－02 全市主要年份货运量
Total Freight Traffic in Main Years

单位:万吨 (10000 tons)

年 份 Year	合 计 Total	铁 路 Railways	公 路 Highways	水 路 Waterways	民 航 Civil Aviation
1978	1706	418	633	655	－
1979	1983	440	771	772	－
1980	2070	444	762	864	－
1981	1972	449	886	637	－
1982	2261	485	795	981	－
1983	2299	488	838	973	－
1984	2385	510	888	987	－
1985	2488	524	890	1074	－
1986	2558	551	874	1133	－
1987	2515	574	899	1041	1
1988	2416	555	823	1037	1
1989	7377	539	5095	1743	－
1990	6522	449	4479	1594	－
1991	7017	451	4891	1675	－
1992	8434	534	6063	1836	1
1993	9082	580	6353	2148	1
1994	8962	491	6563	1907	1
1995	10347	482	7021	2842	2
1996	10962	445	7735	2780	2
1997	11015	406	7932	2676	1
1998	11329	418	8196	2713	2
1999	11684	403	8037	3241	3
2000	11459	417	7865	3173	4
2001	12443	452	8588	3398	5
2002	14347	446	10391	3504	6
2003	16815	438	12118	4253	6
2004	18895	480	13117	5289	9
2005	19909	525	13539	5833	12
2006	20924	569	14588	5754	13
2007	22569	573	16484	5500	12
2008	22550	483	16822	5232	13
2009	22372	427	16536	5396	13

注:货运量全市数自1990年起为全社会数,1990年以前为交通系统数。

a) Since 1990 the data in this table inclued non－transportation system, while data for previous years only included transportation system.

6－03 全社会客货运输量(2009年)
Total Passenger and Freight Traffic(2009)

项 目	Item	全市 Whole Municipality	为上年(%) As Compared with the Preceding Year(%)
一、客运量合计(万人次)	**Passenger Traffic(10000 person－times)**	**30116**	**103.5**
铁路客运量	Passenger Railways	2494	99.8
民航客运量	Passenger Civil Aviation	796	117.2
公路客运量	Passenger Highways	26454	103.2
水路客运量	Passenger Waterways	372	134.4
二、旅客周转量合计(万人公里)	**Total Passenger－kilometers(10000 passenger－km)**	**1321519**	**104.7**
公路旅客周转量	Passenger－kilometers Highways	1316143	104.7
水路旅客周转量	Passenger－kilometers Waterways	5376	112.1
三、货运量合计(万吨)	**Total Freight Traffic(10000 tons)**	**22372**	**99.2**
铁路货运量	Freight Railways	427	88.4
民航货运量	Freight Civil Aviation	13.49	103.8
公路货运量	Freight Highways	16536	98.3
水路货运量	Freight Waterways	5396	103.1
四、货运周转量合计(万吨公里)	**Total Freight Ton－kilometers(10000 ton－km)**	**2453539**	**144.9**
公路货物周转量	Freight Ton－kilometers Highways	1389556	187.6
水路货物周转量	Freight Ton－kilometers Waterways	1063983	111.7

6-04 社会机动车辆年末拥有量(2009年)

Total Number of Motor Vehicles End of the Year(2009)

单位:辆 (unit)

项目	Item	全市 Whole Municipality	为上年(%) As Compared with the Preceding Year(%)	市区 Urban District
总计	**Total**	**1578881**	**113.1**	**1166964**
民用汽车拥有量	**Possession of Civilian Vehicles**	**993019**	**120.7**	**842776**
#私人汽车	Private Vehicles	718675	127.2	601204
载客汽车	**Passenger Vehicles**	**842384**	**123.4**	**718713**
大型载客汽车	Large	13172	105.9	11392
中型载客汽车	Medium	20051	94	15395
小型载客汽车	Small	775326	126.3	666421
微型载客汽车	Minicar	33835	96.9	25505
载货汽车	**Trucks**	**140624**	**110.8**	**116919**
重型载货汽车	Heavy	17101	171.2	14637
中型载货汽车	Light - heavy	29094	93.8	25167
轻型载货汽车	Light	92625	111.2	75765
微型载货汽车	Mini	1804	69	1350
其他汽车	**Else**	**10011**	**77.1**	**7144**
摩托车	**Motorcycles**	**581611**	**102.2**	**320502**
普通摩托车	Genera Motorcycles	517981	102.5	278547
轻便摩托车	Light Motorcycles	63630	100.1	41955

6－05 邮政、电信主要指标(2009年)
Post and Telecommunications(2009)

项 目		Item		全市 Whole Municipality	为上年(%) As Compared with the Preceding Year(%)	市区 Urban District
邮电业务总收入	(万元)	Total Business Income of Post & Telecommunications Service	(10000 yuan)	1355414	108.6	1147261
函件	(万件)	Number of Letters	(10000 pcs)	10366	101.1	9864
包件	(万件)	Number of Parcels	(10000 pcs)	133	100	93
汇票	(万张)	Number of Bill of Exchange	(10000 pcs)	346	77.6	290
订销报刊累计量	(万份)	Number of Newspapers & Magazines Circulation	(10000 copies)	27136	100.7	21673
集邮	(万枚)	Philutely	(10000 pcs)	938	78.0	735
邮储期末余额	(万元)	Balance of Postal Deposits	(10000 yuan)	1681474	121.4	1247250
年末固定电话用户数	(万户)	Number of Local Telephone Subscribers (year－end)	(10000 subscribers)	390.38	93.8	307.09
年末移动电话用户数	(万户)	Number of Subscribers of Mobile Telephone(year－end)	(10000 subscribers)	1011.93	116.7	805.47
年末国际互联网用户数	(万户)	Number of Internet Subscribers(year－end)	(10000 subscribers)	178.33	109.0	146.64
#宽带业务户数	(万户)	Number of Wide Band Subscribers	(10000 subscribers)	162.40	122.9	132.96

主要统计指标解释

货(客)运量　指在一定时期内,各种运输工具实际运送的货物(旅客)数量。是反映运输业为国民经济和人民生活服务的数量指标,也是制定和检查运输生产计划、研究运输发展规模和速度的重要指标。货运按吨计算,客运按人计算。货物不论运输距离长短、货物类别,均按实际重量统计。旅客不论行程远近或票价多少,均按一人一次作为客运量统计;半价票、小孩票也按一人统计。

货物(旅客)周转量　指在一定时期内,由各种运输工具运送的货物(旅客)数量与其相应运输距离的乘积之总和。是反映运输业生产总成果的重要指标,也是编制和检查运输生产计划,计算运输效率、劳动生产率以及核算运输单位成本的主要基础资料。通常以吨公里和人公里为计算单位。计算货物周转量通常按发出站与到达站之间的最短距离,也就是计费距离计算。

移动电话用户　指在邮电部门登记,通过移动电话交换机进入移动电话网,占有移动电话号码的电话用户。用户数量以实际办理登记手续进入邮电部门移动电话网的户数进行计算,一部或一台移动电话统计为一户。

Explanatory Notes on Main Statistical Indicators

Freight(passenger) Traffic refers to the volume of freight (passenger) transported with various means. Freight transport is calculated in tons and passenger traffic is calculated in the number of persons. Despite the type of freight and traveling distance, the freight transport is calculated in the actual weight of the goods; and despite the traveling distance and ticket price, the passenger traffic is calculated by the principle that one person can be counted only once in one travel. The passenger who travel with a half – price ticket or a child ticket is also calculated as one person. The freight (passenger) traffic provides a quantitative measure to show how the transport industry serves the national economy and people, and is also an important indicator for plan the transport industry and for studying the development scale and speed of the transport industry.

Freight Ton – kilometers(Passenger – kilometers) refer to the sum of the products of the volume of transported cargo (passengers) multiplying by the transport distance, usually using ton – kilometer and passenger – kilometer as units for measurement . Normally, the shortest distance between the departure station and the destination station (i. e. , the payable distance) is the basis to calculate the freight ton – kilometers. This is an important indicator to show the total results of the transport industry, to prepare and examine the transport plan and to measure the efficiency, the labour productivity and the unit cost of transport.

Mobile Telephone Subscribers refer to the persons who own mobile telephone number connected with the mobile telephone communication network and registered by post and telecommunications organization. The number of subscribers is calculated only when the subscribers who have gone through all the register formalities and entered into the mobile telephone network. One mobile telephone is treated as a subscriber.

第七篇
CHAPTER-7

固定资产投资
INVESTMENT IN FIXED ASSETS

固定资产投资
Investment in Fixed Assets

主要统计指标
Major Statistical Indicators

全市限额以上固定资产投资	Investment of Super-scale projects	2195.17	亿元	(100 million yuan)
为上年	As Compared with the Preceding Year	116.6	%	(%)
第一产业	Primary Industry	3.13	亿元	(100 million yuan)
为上年	As Compared with the Preceding Year	101.7	%	(%)
第二产业	Secondary Industry	611.55	亿元	(100 million yuan)
为上年	As Compared with the Preceding Year	107.2	%	(%)
第三产业	Tertiary Industry	1580.49	亿元	(100 million yuan)
为上年	As Compared with the Preceding Year	120.8	%	(%)

7-01 主要年份全市全社会固定资产投资总额
Total Investment in Fixed Assets in Main Years

单位:万元 (10000 yuan)

年份 Year	合计 Total	基本建设 Capital Construction	更新改造 Innovation	房地产开发 Real Estate Development	其他投资 Others	农村集体 Rural collective-owned Units	农村私人投资 Rural Individuals
1978	48307	23941	5316	-	765	10242	8043
1979	55828	25008	8327	-	1072	11380	10041
1980	70936	33257	9190	-	3305	12645	12539
1981	79791	23772	21423	-	6343	14050	14203
1982	97895	32518	25596	-	8009	15611	16161
1983	102413	35269	22181	-	1056	13350	20757
1984	148601	52313	27269	-	13662	25922	2945
1985	229746	85718	33219	-	22952	48611	39246
1986	284936	95102	52701	-	34595	48352	54223
1987	350033	93113	70399	-	34304	61848	87669
1988	370954	80939	77481	-	47547	55456	109531
1989	345548	87320	72994	-	41817	42340	101077
1990	366296	99805	73933	20409	35067	38442	98640
1991	418845	96589	92103	25247	41757	64433	98716
1992	654537	119216	136850	41886	86204	140783	129618
1993	1310914	273991	204412	218006	128973	342267	143265
1994	1620301	397651	205109	320532	136145	358581	202283
1995	2323355	541890	279388	527985	217017	453746	303329
1996	2611772	688794	254507	572749	302283	453720	339719
1997	3033904	906554	323091	572686	335681	538980	355912
1998	3636607	1240740	492814	666244	281942	590911	363956
1999	4354770	1535925	625617	848441	223626	711076	410085
2000	5154923	1704012	770229	1015347	276885	997463	390987
2001	6309723	1938875	996305	1409132	290617	1308500	366294
2002	7697578	2424601	1011054	1982517	205194	1758436	315776
2003	10067440	3260181	945777	2588452	375214	2577280	320536
2004	12022243	-	-	3285409	-	-	-
2005	13866833	-	-	4105706	-	-	-
2006	14607422	-	-	4426534	-	-	-
2007	16841298	-	-	5187904	-	-	-
2008	19805018	-	-	6154060	-	-	-
2009	22916543	-	-	7046752	-	-	-

注:2006 年起全市固定资产投资口径不含 50 万元以下农村非农户投资(下同)。

a) From 2006, the data of investment of non-farmers in village bellow 500000 yuan are excluded in the total investment in fixed assets. The same as in the following tables.

7－02 主要年份市区全社会固定资产投资总额

Total Investment in Fixed Assets of Urban District in Main Years

单位:万元 (10000 yuan)

年份 Year	合计 Total	基本建设 Capital Construction	更新改造 Innovation	房地产开发 Real Estate Development	其他投资 Others	农村集体 Rural collective－owned Units	农村私人投资 Rural Individuals
1978	22468	16451	3403	－	557	1087	970
1979	26793	18085	5499	－	820	1207	1182
1980	35925	24385	6904	－	1850	1342	1444
1981	41729	19478	15248	－	3744	1491	1768
1982	52541	26703	17174	－	4878	1657	2129
1983	57191	29654	15431	－	4616	3220	4270
1984	88074	45993	20494	－	6133	8242	7212
1985	125927	70527	22495	－	10579	14776	7550
1986	154417	81678	36880	－	17252	6788	11819
1987	163067	80067	46885	－	13163	8636	14316
1988	159599	63482	46636	－	22657	9633	17191
1989	150113	65322	44310	－	20422	7972	12087
1990	170878	79792	48131	12750	12470	6045	11690
1991	176914	66724	56497	16509	14664	12096	10424
1992	231616	62271	84548	29784	22568	20070	12375
1993	499373	140113	119235	115116	37049	70355	17505
1994	717285	227983	129824	189357	46645	100385	23091
1995	1148688	339016	162799	375816	129480	105247	36330
1996	1485008	523573	165631	439245	140633	148576	67350
1997	1821969	731925	245759	445316	176948	147506	74515
1998	2260918	939373	407351	538499	124538	166389	84768
1999	2672757	1195699	466289	636705	98869	193173	82022
2000	3009630	1233350	515716	737950	214280	216928	91406
2001	5381284	1768151	868561	1255605	25330	996347	237290
2002	6388204	2168121	811362	1724128	196471	1301262	186860
2003	7971044	2814796	725643	2176433	334528	1746610	173034
2004	9648206	－	－	3088508	－	－	－
2005	10787387	－	－	3485810	－	－	－
2006	11169155	－	－	3653393	－	－	－
2007	13150724	－	－	4298687	－	－	－
2008	15634404	－	－	5269947	－	－	－
2009	18172403	－	－	6261562	－	－	－

注:2001 年起市区数据含萧山、余杭区。

a) Date of 2001 inculude Xiaoshan district and Yuhang district.

7-03 主要年份全市固定资产投资按三次产业分

Investment in Fixed Assets Grouped by Three Industries in Main Years

单位:万元 (10000 yuan)

年份 Year	绝对数(万元) Absolute Figure(10000 yuan)				比重(以投资总额为100) Proportion(%)		
	合计 Total	第一产业 Primary Industry	第二产业 Secondary Industry	第三产业 Tertiary Industry	第一产业 Primary Industry	第二产业 Secondary Industry	第三产业 Tertiary Industry
1978	23941	2174	14455	7312	9.1	60.4	30.5
1979	34407	2454	19927	12026	7.1	57.9	35.0
1980	45752	1608	26211	17933	3.5	57.3	39.2
1981	51538	850	29176	21512	1.6	56.6	41.8
1982	66123	1352	37648	27123	2.0	57.0	41.0
1983	68306	1297	37823	29186	1.9	55.4	42.7
1984	93244	2831	46619	43794	3.0	50.0	47.0
1985	141889	3207	71608	67074	2.3	50.5	47.2
1986	182398	2265	94394	85739	1.2	51.8	47.0
1987	200516	2994	106600	90922	1.5	53.2	45.3
1988	205967	4746	118736	82485	2.3	57.6	40.1
1989	202131	3038	117651	81442	1.5	58.2	40.3
1990	229214	2181	126263	100770	1.0	55.1	43.9
1991	255696	3204	132303	120189	1.3	51.7	47.0
1992	384136	4424	206659	173053	1.2	53.8	45.0
1993	825382	5650	346416	473316	0.7	42.0	57.3
1994	1059437	3905	354672	700860	0.4	33.5	66.1
1995	1566280	5821	534687	1025772	0.4	34.1	65.5
1996	1819333	3100	640273	1175960	0.2	35.2	64.6
1997	2139012	1712	595966	1541334	–	27.9	72.1
1998	2681740	4053	706948	1970739	0.2	26.4	73.4
1999	3233609	23546	764309	2445754	0.7	23.6	75.7
2000	3766473	774	844334	2921365	0.2	22.4	77.4
2001	4634929	595	953494	3680840	–	20.6	79.4
2002	5623366	6514	1104212	4512640	0.1	19.6	80.3
2003	8952090	10489	3208885	5732716	0.1	35.9	64.0
2004	11081993	15992	4369015	6696986	0.1	39.4	60.5
2005	12777972	13982	4451936	8312054	0.1	34.8	65.1
2006	13734482	17892	4651420	9065170	0.1	33.9	66.0
2007	15837775	23278	5286340	10528157	0.1	33.4	66.5
2008	18822936	30810	5705736	13086390	0.2	30.3	69.5
2009	21951706	31335	6115482	15804889	0.1	27.9	72.0

注:2002年以前为全部城镇及以上投资,不包括农村集体及私人投资。从2003年开始为全部限额以上投资口径。

a) Before year 2002, data in this table refer to urban investments and the rural investments are excluded. From 2003, refer to investment of super-scale projects.

7-04 主要年份全市固定资产投资房屋建筑面积及造价

Floor Space of Buildings and Their Cost in Main Years

年份 Year	施工面积（万平方米）Floor Space of Buildings Under Construction (10000sq. m)	#住宅 Residential Buildings	竣工面积（万平方米）Floor Space of Buildings Completed (10000 sq. m)	#住宅 Residential Buildings	竣工房屋价值（万元）Value of Buildings Completed (10000 yuan)	#住宅 Residential Buildings	每平方米造价（元）Cost Per Square (yuan)	#住宅 Residential Buildings
1978	-	-	101.95	39.58	8869	2810	87	71
1979	-	-	150.26	68.01	13223	4965	88	73
1980	456.54	-	202.58	104.44	19448	8564	96	82
1981	507.94	-	232.25	120.35	26709	12396	115	103
1982	554.89	258.09	281.63	148.66	34095	16470	121	111
1983	531.79	244.36	247.07	125.86	33938	15494	137	123
1984	620.71	293.21	267.85	138.71	42740	18398	160	133
1985	741.47	333.72	327.75	157.85	56561	22825	173	145
1986	674.58	278.19	338.19	160.19	50561	27338	238	170
1987	544.64	149.07	254.73	73.16	68801	14944	270	204
1988	526.70	156.92	230.21	75.44	68407	17820	297	236
1989	420.81	116.12	202.15	64.15	69750	18200	345	284
1990	472.59	209.50	236.44	112.77	93557	34266	396	304
1991	459.00	205.41	226.84	92.72	93158	28599	411	308
1992	604.85	301.21	262.11	114.97	116169	39834	452	350
1993	958.91	533.01	380.29	199.96	224251	105107	589	525
1994	1069.68	613.62	460.20	274.19	375211	212705	815	776
1995	1320.68	737.79	524.58	319.41	491705	274314	937	859
1996	1399.70	758.00	582.70	354.50	688569	370485	1182	1045
1997	1363.80	660.70	642.10	338.00	871361	449235	1357	1329
1998	1456.02	743.59	515.16	271.91	709730	390624	1378	1437
1999	1681.71	956.15	709.10	411.44	1119141	641717	1578	1560
2000	1721.58	949.32	744.42	419.80	1207767	709044	1622	1689
2001	2318.95	1251.92	830.05	402.46	1310380	679449	1579	1688
2002	2713.02	1586.28	890.05	492.95	1623662	956643	1820	1941
2003	4392.79	2083.58	1618.01	651.58	2732763	1353422	1689	2077
2004	5731.48	2909.03	1865.83	717.46	2791115	1313596	1496	1831
2005	6671.39	3628.34	1856.34	801.34	3265491	1865538	1759	2328
2006	7260.08	3747.6	1737.51	706.13	2900836	1580689	1670	2239
2007	7942.07	4040.54	1849.24	858.99	3750264	2329184	2028	2712
2008	9471.42	4160.27	2057.86	846.34	4113211	2171525	1999	2566
2009	10308.45	4441.84	2009.90	700.63	3626421	1684092	1804	2404

注:2002 年以前为全部城镇及以上投资,不包括农村集体及私人投资。从 2003 年开始为全部限额以上投资口径。

a) Before year 2002, data in this table refer to urban investments and the rural investments are excluded. From 2003, refer to investment of super-scale projects.

7-05 主要年份市区固定资产投资房屋建筑面积及造价

Urban District Floor Space of Buildings and Their Cost in Main Years

年份 Year	施工面积(万平方米) Floor Space of Buildings Under Construction (10000 sq. m)	#住宅 Residential Buildings	竣工面积(万平方米) Floor Space of Buildings Completed (10000sq. m)	#住宅 Residential Buildings	竣工房屋价值(万元) Value of Buildings Completed (10000 yuan)	#住宅 Residential Buildings	每平方米造价(元) Cost Per Square (yuan)	#住宅 Residential Buildings
1978	-	-	71.56	29.06	6941	2237	97	77
1979	-	-	109.23	53.37	10267	4056	94	76
1980	-	-	137.11	76.73	14396	6752	105	88
1981	-	-	163.36	90.12	20093	9643	123	107
1982	378.88	172.11	189.92	100.07	25200	11980	133	120
1983	376.32	169.17	157.14	81.68	24029	11045	153	135
1984	465.27	221.72	191.13	104.55	33863	14658	177	140
1985	532.66	258.19	219.79	114.26	40344	17489	184	153
1986	465.75	203.22	219.33	116.70	58619	21149	267	181
1987	336.85	86.05	150.59	41.72	46530	9513	309	228
1988	315.80	90.98	117.71	37.63	38501	10117	330	269
1989	253.41	56.39	99.86	28.89	38680	9087	387	315
1990	301.82	128.50	137.88	62.47	60551	20361	439	326
1991	265.61	118.99	114.19	42.31	53819	12892	471	305
1992	329.16	190.55	115.59	57.36	55758	19706	483	344
1993	500.08	266.80	175.22	104.83	101528	53540	579	511
1994	618.91	352.16	212.06	123.74	182730	102924	862	832
1995	821.03	463.98	244.94	152.10	250073	139666	1021	918
1996	969.10	538.50	350.10	229.00	437239	274244	1249	1196
1997	1017.30	485.20	442.00	232.70	675762	357624	1529	1537
1998	1055.24	541.41	321.17	184.18	516400	317402	1608	1723
1999	1204.30	656.07	489.23	294.85	908844	533675	1858	1810
2000	1176.29	617.80	497.64	269.94	916212	528385	1841	1957
2001	2053.02	1085.30	698.29	325.64	1193818	615802	1710	1891
2002	2330.97	1335.78	744.48	404.35	1483862	869969	1993	2152
2003	3637.82	1699.61	1325.48	516.33	2395039	1174735	1807	2275
2004	4740.42	2453.87	1389.30	528.26	2257386	1068708	1625	2023
2005	5533.58	3039.08	1478.07	661.56	2804402	1626514	1897	2459
2006	5898.15	3114.45	1327.37	580.22	2365342	1357671	1782	2340
2007	6496.01	3357.18	1355.43	674.97	3063585	1992874	2260	2953
2008	7812.71	3466.88	1537.69	668.13	3372465	1827426	2193	2735
2009	8558.17	3807.67	1398.49	537.39	2725150	1321357	1949	2459

注:2002 年以前为全部城镇及以上投资,不包括农村集体及私人投资。从 2003 年开始为全部限额以上投资口径。

a) Before year 2002, data in this table refer to urban investments and the rural investments are excluded. From 2003, refer to investment of super - scale projects.

7－06 分县(市)固定资产

Investment in Fixed Assets

单位:万元

指标	Item	全市 Total 2009年	全市 Total 上年 Preceding Year	全市 Total 为上年(%) As Compared with the Preceding Year(%)	市区 Urban District 2009年
全社会固定资产投资	**Total Investment in Fixed Assets**	**22916543**	**19805018**	**15.7**	**18172403**
限额以上固定资产投资额	**Investment of Super－scale Projects**	**21951706**	**18822936**	**16.6**	**17797778**
#住宅	#Residential Buildings	5795988	5044239	14.9	5113183
#工业投资	Industrial Investment	6091653	5693385	7.0	3821313
#基础设施投资	Infrastructural Investment	6018416	5410313	11.2	5070500
一、按投资、房地产分	**Grouped by Sector**				
投资项目完成额	Investment Projects	14904954	12668876	17.7	11536216
房地产开发完成额	Real Estate	7046752	6154060	14.5	6261562
二、按登记注册类型分	**Grouped by Status of Registration**				
内资	Domestic－funded	19729856	16760528	17.7	16124285
国有	State－owned	6772964	5781452	17.1	5844629
集体	Collective－owned	504752	347089	45.4	414631
股份合作	Cooperative	72460	45610	58.9	72460
国有联营	Joint State Ownership	4707	2500	88.3	－
集体联营	Collective Joint Ownership	4850	6581	－26.3	4850
国有与集体联营	Joint State－collective Ownership	379	10254	－96.3	－
其他联营	Other Joint Ownership	－	－	－	－
国有独资公司	State－owned Corporations	528685	278898	89.6	419912
其他有限责任公司	Other Limited Liability Corporations	7475964	6593178	13.4	6544114
股份有限公司	Share－holding Corporations Ltd.	947213	860960	10.0	755601
私营	Private	3188840	2596650	22.8	1932782
其他	Other	229042	237356	－3.5	135306
港、澳、台商投资	Investment from Hong Kong, Macao and Taiwan	1139267	930533	22.4	913309
外商投资	Foreign Investment	1059272	1124230	－5.8	895104

投资完成额(2009 年)
by Region(2009)

(10000 yuan)

上　年 Preceding Year	为上年(%) As Compared with the Preceding Year(%)	#萧山区 Xiaoshan	#余杭区 Yuhang	桐庐县 Tonglu	淳安县 Chun'an	建德市 Jiande	富阳市 Fuyang	临安市 Lin'an
15634404	**16.2**	**3997153**	**2961331**	**881955**	**608820**	**669223**	**1680740**	**903402**
15184281	**17.2**	**3769557**	**2823192**	**738391**	**542037**	**575374**	**1534401**	**763725**
4295953	19.0	4956800	825824	121076	157838	43809	246170	113912
3676567	3.9	1833491	807277	407697	180540	342457	874810	464836
4726734	7.3	1127042	786218	99187	177094	160784	373985	136866
9914334	16.4	3156576	1859901	596312	370646	509428	1271087	621265
5269947	18.8	612981	963291	142079	171391	65946	263314	142460
13506807	19.4	3330347	2525236	595443	494337	570111	1335383	610297
5088601	14.9	998158	856157	66206	176605	210428	253821	221275
299632	38.4	77354	17288	5980	2850	7768	44986	28537
42900	68.9	4000	10739	–	–	–	–	–
–	–	–	–	–	4707	–	–	–
6581	-26.3	–	–	–	–	–	–	–
9167	-100.0	–	–	–	–	–	379	–
–	–	–	–	–	–	–	–	–
201952	107.9	147451	91151	39218	5368	1350	62837	–
5608808	16.7	1373947	872997	178709	215829	136409	186818	214085
662034	14.1	262453	29366	35241	7705	83167	36420	29079
1405998	37.5	465284	627986	266228	23891	111048	738120	116771
181134	-25.3	1700	19552	3861	57382	19941	12002	550
709386	28.7	212971	165068	86181	12258	1150	123371	2998
967438	-7.5	218699	–	52609	35442	–	68667	7450

单位:万元 7-06 续表

指 标	Item	全 市 Total 2009年	上 年 Preceding Year	为上年(%) As Compared with the Preceding Year(%)	市 区 Urban District 2009年
三、按行业分	**Grouped by Sector**				
农林牧渔业	Farming, Forestry, Animal Husbandry and Fishery	31335	30810	1.7	6714
采矿业	Mining & Quarrying	35088	30140	16.4	-
制造业	Manufacturing	5319748	5090185	4.5	3254453
电力、燃气及水的生产和供应业	Production and Supply of Electricity, Gas and Hot Water	736817	573060	28.6	566860
建筑业	Construction	22936	12351	85.7	21469
交通运输、仓储及邮政业	Transportation, Storage, Post & Telecommunications	1726152	1385250	24.6	1455671
信息传输、计算机服务和软件业	Information Transmission, Computer Services and Software	362142	231080	56.7	361842
批发和零售业	Wholesale & Retail Trade	616104	518139	18.9	558287
住宿和餐饮业	Accommodations and Catering	316649	163574	93.6	237451
金融业	Banking and Insurance	41245	52650	-21.7	41245
房地产业	Real Estate	8746206	6851075	27.7	7878044
租赁和商务服务业	Renting and Business Service	416630	285482	45.9	370317
科学研究、技术服务和地质勘查业	Scientific Research, Technical Service and Geological Prospecting	66362	81909	-19.0	65447
水利、环境和公共设施管理业	Water Conservancy, Environment and Public Utility	2639993	2742540	-3.7	2244755
居民服务和其他服务业	Service for the Residents and Other	9991	9348	6.9	8656
教育	Education	335848	322850	4.0	244516
卫生、社会保障和社会福利业	Health Care, Sports & Social Welfare	187735	162219	15.7	168873
文化、体育和娱乐业	Culture, Sports and Entertainment	269450	99601	170.5	257059
公共管理和社会组织	Public Management and Social Organzations	71275	180673	-60.6	56119
国际组织	International Organzations	-	-	-	-

continued (10000 yuan)

上 年 Preceding Year	为上年(%) As Compared with the Preceding Year(%)	#萧山区 Xiaoshan	#余杭区 Yuhang	桐庐县 Tonglu	淳安县 Chun'an	建德市 Jiande	富阳市 Fuyang	临安市 Lin'an
19264	-65.1	3231	3483	2933	1890	7239	6174	6385
637	-100.0	–	–	3924	3688	2850	22286	2340
3219014	1.1	1719886	744953	374650	154787	297376	799484	438998
456916	24.1	113605	62324	29123	22065	42231	53040	23498
10497	104.5	680	–	–	–	–	–	1467
1176298	23.8	491846	300006	13298	46174	25493	138870	46646
230777	56.8	–	–	–	–	–	300	–
466730	19.6	47082	164338	25649	3175	2658	16245	10090
134519	76.5	51322	10152	35606	11365	2544	14110	15573
52650	-21.7	2900	–	–	–	–	–	–
5929941	32.9	767701	1094972	149574	180675	95426	298427	144060
261106	41.8	6066	9656	42463	2500	1350	–	–
80087	-18.3	20627	945	–	–	–	–	915
2466261	-9.0	432658	346108	48802	96188	76614	131252	42382
9348	-7.4	4540	2490	1335	–	–	–	–
253253	-3.4	35527	57971	6568	2659	14293	48152	19660
150733	12.0	16617	17783	270	11156	2485	2371	2580
95140	170.2	47753	2026	1752	1731	–	1908	7000
171110	-67.2	7515	5985	2444	3984	4815	1782	2131
–	–	–	–	–	–	–	–	–

7-07 分县(市)限额以上工业
Super-Scale Investment

单位:万元

指　　标	Item	全市 Total 2009年	全市 Total 上年 Preceding Year	全市 Total 为上年(%) As Compared with the Preceding Year(%)	市区 Urban District 2009年
总计	**Total**	**6091653**	**5693385**	**7.0**	**3821313**
一、按登记注册类型分	**Total Investment**				
内资	Domestic-funded	4904821	4428674	10.8	2917862
国有	State-owned	779694	616997	26.4	557170
集体	Collective-owned	63203	66589	-5.1	16447
股份合作	Cooperative	14242	7050	102.0	14242
集体联营	Collective Joint Ownership	-	1631	-100.0	-
国有独资公司	State-funded Corporations	112461	112839	-0.3	109716
其他有限责任公司	Other Limited Liability Corporations	1861383	1860208	0.1	1209280
股份有限公司	Share-holding Corporations Ltd.	435855	400043	9.0	257703
私营	Private	1616682	1324381	22.1	753304
其他	Other	21301	38936	-45.3	-
港、澳、台商投资	Investment from Hong Kong, Macao and Taiwan	493640	567724	-13.0	327173
外商投资	Foreign Investment	676050	691890	-2.3	569738
二、按行业分	**Grouped by Sector**				
农林牧渔业		-	-	-	-
采矿业	Mining & Quarrying	35088	30140	16.4	-
制造业	Manufacturing	5319748	5090185	4.5	3254453
农副食品加工业	Agricultural Products Processing	98252	29545	232.6	58536
食品制造业	Food Manufacturing	103558	112150	-7.7	72052
饮料制造业	Beverage Manufacturing	85002	154174	-44.9	31777
烟草制品业	Tobacco Processing	31983	1215	2532.3	31983
纺织业	Textile Processing	544187	449589	21.0	408696
纺织服装、鞋、帽制造业	Textile Products, Garments, Shoes and Caps Processing	133380	191763	-30.4	95258

投资完成额(2009年)

in Industrial Sector by Region(2009)

(10000 yuan)

上 年 Preceding Year	为上年(%) As Compared with the Preceding Year(%)	#萧山区 Xiaoshan	#余杭区 Yuhang	桐庐县 Tonglu	淳安县 Chun'an	建德市 Jiande	富阳市 Fuyang	临安市 Lin'an
3676567	**3.9**	**1833491**	**807277**	**407697**	**180540**	**342457**	**874810**	**464836**
2713945	7.5	1430453	645969	336289	167543	340557	688702	453868
473684	17.6	37764	66038	13081	13862	51543	10225	133813
39635	-58.5	5630	3424	2723	-	7768	18820	17445
4340	228.2	1500	10354	-	-	-	-	-
1631	-100.0	-	-	-	-	-	-	-
108526	1.1	31380	8300	-	2745	-	-	-
1246721	-3.0	826473	208653	95599	130980	122790	119522	183212
218013	18.2	222779	15286	31572	7705	83167	26629	29079
616793	22.1	304927	333914	192504	12251	55348	513506	89769
4602	-100.0	-	-	810	-	19941	-	550
376561	-13.1	183170	48781	41992	8658	1150	111669	2998
585411	-2.7	213328	112527	25856	4339	-	68667	7450
-	-	-	-	-	-	-	-	-
637	-100.0	-	-	3924	3688	2850	22286	2340
3219014	1.1	1719886	744953	374650	154787	297376	799484	438998
21683	170.0	20154	35649	3561	10195	8839	8550	8571
73354	-1.8	7846	25234	7897	3398	510	12631	7070
84185	-62.3	21600	400	7520	25224	19356	1125	-
1215	2532.3	-	-	-	-	-	-	-
349255	17.0	345519	51093	40424	50813	10965	22165	11124
151418	-37.1	34250	43123	17211	13565	3330	1400	2616

指标	Item	全市 Total 2009年	上年 Preceding Year	为上年(%) As Compared with the Preceding Year(%)	市区 Urban District 2009年
皮革、毛皮、羽毛(绒)及其制造业	Leather, Furs, Down and Related Products	37821	41322	-8.5	21050
木材加工及木、竹、藤、棕、草制品	Timber Processing, Bamboo, Cane, Palm Fiber and Straw Products	25988	20667	25.7	19009
家具制造业	Furniture Manufacturing	47022	78536	-40.1	32654
造纸及纸制品业	Paper Making and Paper Products	238202	255756	-6.9	61858
印刷业和记录媒介的复制	Printing and Record Media	52862	66850	-20.9	37606
文教体育用品制造业	Cultural, Educational and Sports Goods	66786	54511	22.5	28302
石油加工、炼焦及核燃料加工业	Petroleum and Nuclear Fuel Processing	1458	1761	-17.2	358
化学原料及化学制品制造业	Raw Chemical Material and Chemical Products	427115	437584	-2.4	277943
医药制造业	Medical and Pharmaceutical Products	120027	110729	8.4	47778
化学纤维制造业	Chemical Fiber	64385	226979	-71.6	57736
橡胶制造业	Rubber Products	89963	75883	18.6	51247
塑料制品业	Plastic Products	133386	113128	17.9	82971
非金属矿物制品业	Nonmetal Mineral Products	286732	311392	-7.9	128928
黑色金属冶炼及压延加工业	Smelting and Pressing of Ferrous Metals	77720	53289	45.8	37804
有色金属冶炼及压延加工业	Smelting and Pressing of Nonferrous Metal	70865	74491	-4.9	14203
金属制品业	Metal Products	360505	327130	10.2	198750
通用设备制造业	Ordinary Machinery	601509	558298	7.7	305138
专业设备制造业	Special Purpose Equipment	272257	237214	14.8	222441
交通运输设备制造业	Transportation Equipment	351460	268459	30.9	305703
电气机械及器材制造业	Electric Equipment and Machinery	600350	410414	46.3	353295
通信设备、计算机及其他电子设备制造业	Telecommunications Equipment, Computers and Other Electornic Equipment	256233	264718	-3.2	187821
仪器仪表及文化、办公用机械制造业	Instruments, Meters, Cultural and Office Machinery	58856	48095	22.4	40024
工艺品及其他制造业	Craftworks and Other Manufacturing	73201	108486	-32.5	42832
废弃资源和废旧材料回收加工业	Scrap Recycle and Processing	8683	6057	43.4	700
电力、燃气及水的生产和供应业	Production and Supply of Electricity, Gas and Water	736817	573060	28.6	566860

continued (10000 yuan)

上 年 Preceding Year	为上年(%) As Compared with the Preceding Year(%)	#萧山区 Xiaoshan	#余杭区 Yuhang	桐庐县 Tonglu	淳安县 Chun'an	建德市 Jiande	富阳市 Fuyang	临安市 Lin'an
17132	22.9	20640	410	1792	–	840	13316	823
16350	16.3	9717	7888	1178	450	–	2946	2405
58608	-44.3	19648	12720	3060	1120	3860	5528	800
61610	0.4	27698	9461	15671	–	3450	129199	28024
49324	-23.8	5023	9544	3756	–	1570	9930	–
29413	-3.8	12818	1531	19811	–	–	15723	2950
1261	-71.6	–	–	–	–	–	–	1100
315717	-12.0	233036	26069	7629	2120	82578	37739	19106
59719	-20.0	12226	11934	1210	7817	6420	55743	1059
222728	-74.1	55515	619	580	–	–	6069	–
49537	3.5	645	2082	–	–	10727	26539	1450
61761	34.3	40223	37293	6201	2281	5130	22618	14185
147775	-12.8	55010	57078	34382	10282	62377	42724	8039
29249	29.2	20276	11896	4796	–	1090	22815	11215
11388	24.7	10238	3965	16502	–	10432	26828	2900
175384	13.3	109020	75770	20450	500	26830	99131	14844
312439	-2.3	188859	57765	84208	698	19232	53230	139003
157775	41.0	62550	119240	15752	3501	1660	19916	8987
230187	32.8	263214	27220	15227	3589	1215	24026	1700
193042	83.0	103544	63270	34275	7614	12793	85356	107017
211359	-11.1	18837	27221	4626	5090	–	31892	26804
40558	-1.3	2800	12316	–	6100	–	12732	–
85288	-49.8	18980	13462	6931	430	4172	1630	17206
300	133.3	–	700	–	–	–	7983	–
456916	24.1	113605	62324	29123	22065	42231	53040	23498

7－08 分县(市)房地产开发
Real Estate Development

指　　标	Item	全　　市 Total 2009 年	上　年 Preceding Year	为上年(%) As Compared with the Preceding Year(%)	市　　区 Urban District 2009 年
房地产开发投资额　（万元）	**Investment in Real Estate Development (10000 yuan)**	**7046752**	**6154060**	**14.5**	**6261562**
住宅　（万元）	Residential Buildings (10000 yuan)	5096425	4562170	11.7	4458247
办公楼　（万元）	Office Buildings (10000 yuan)	722468	541986	33.3	716222
商业营业用房　（万元）	Buildings for Commercial Business (10000 yuan)	499939	400707	24.8	429310
其他　（万元）	Others (10000 yuan)	727920	649197	12.1	657783
房屋建筑面积	**Floor space of Buildings**				
施工面积　（万平方米）	Under Construction (10000 sq. m)	5151.62	4987.39	3.3	4445.05
其中:住宅　（万平方米）	#Residential Buildings (10000 sq. m)	3676.04	3623.41	1.5	3134.50
新开工面积(万平方米)	Beginning to Construction Floor Space (10000 sq. m)	1092.00	1312.51	－16.8	948.59
其中:住宅　（万平方米）	#Residential Buildings (10000 sq. m)	769.95	963.94	－20.1	653.53
竣工面积　（万平方米）	Construction Completed (10000 sq. m)	836.95	1030.63	－18.8	634.33
其中:住宅　（万平方米）	#Residential Buildings (10000 sq. m)	626.64	772.68	－18.9	474.13
商品房销售情况	**Selling of Buildings**				
销售金额　（万元）	Total Sales of Buildings (10000 yuan)	15372226	6517463	135.9	13814248
其中:住宅　（万元）	#Residential Buildings (10000 yuan)	13949554	5559079	150.9	12539126
现房销售额(万元)	Selling of Completed Buildings (10000 yuan)	1383771	767615	80.3	1116894
其中:住宅　（万元）	#Residential Buildings (10000 yuan)	959299	524516	82.9	747121
期房销售金额(万元)	Selling of Futures Buildings (10000 yuan)	13988455	5749848	143.3	12697354
其中:住宅　（万元）	#Residential Buildings (10000 yuan)	12990255	5034563	158	11792005
销售面积　（万平方米）	Floor Space of Buildings Sold (10000 sq. m)	1456.38	775.02	87.9	1207.09
其中:住宅　（万平方米）	#Residential Buildings (10000 sq. m)	1314.38	676.99	94.2	1088.94
现房销售面积(万平方米)	Floor Space of Completed Buildings Sold (10000 sq. m)	166.02	118	40.7	104.96
其中:住宅　（万平方米）	#Residential Buildings (10000 sq. m)	121.05	82.6	46.6	69.52
期房销售面积(万平方米)	Floor Space of Futures Buildings Sold (10000 sq. m)	1290.37	657.02	96.4	1102.13
其中:住宅　（万平方米）	#Residential Buildings (10000 sq. m)	1193.33	594.39	100.8	1019.43

投资情况(2009年)
by Region(2009)

上年 Preceding Year	为上年(%) As Compared with the Preceding Year(%)	#萧山区 Xiaoshan	#余杭区 Yuhang	桐庐县 Tonglu	淳安县 Chun'an	建德市 Jiande	富阳市 Fuyang	临安市 Lin'an
5269947	**18.8**	**612981**	**963291**	**142079**	**171391**	**65946**	**263314**	**142460**
3834284	16.3	507043	821742	119456	147701	43809	213300	113912
534087	34.1	31775	22070	422	141	242	4170	1271
336252	27.7	39357	52009	19208	6323	12305	24052	8741
565324	16.4	34806	67470	2993	17226	9590	21792	18536
4166.06	6.7	682.18	944.36	158.55	113.32	77.79	225.66	131.25
2970.69	5.5	493.61	793.77	126.66	76.90	53.20	179.10	105.69
1077.19	-11.9	165.13	247.65	42.84	24.00	7.72	41.74	27.12
771.14	-15.3	130.99	208.11	33.61	20.70	6.71	32.84	22.57
832.31	-23.8	105.44	89.82	55.21	28.02	16.14	69.73	33.51
608.05	-22.0	80.64	69.22	46.28	20.04	11.05	51.59	23.55
5812439	137.7	1415166	2550657	248654	249599	133384	614816	311525
4915739	155.1	1317524	2462658	219613	233342	108974	561180	287319
627616	78.0	173482	92074	65629	1933	28919	49456	120940
414578	80.2	150560	68683	51045	510	20082	36436	104105
5184823	144.9	1241684	2458583	183025	247666	104465	565360	190585
4501161	162.0	1166964	2393975	168568	232832	88892	524744	183214
625.41	93.0	165.69	283.89	58.36	25.05	28.25	80.02	57.61
541.02	101.3	150.48	272.56	53.05	22.18	24.91	73.05	52.25
81.15	29.3	27.71	12.11	16.43	0.65	4.66	9.26	30.06
53.02	31.1	23.41	9.49	13.97	0.31	4.06	7.13	26.06
544.26	102.5	137.98	271.78	41.94	24.40	23.59	70.75	27.55
488	108.9	127.07	263.07	39.08	21.87	20.85	65.92	26.19

7－09 分县(市)限额以上农村

Super－Scale Rural Investment

单位:万元

指 标	Item	全 市 Total 2009年	上 年 Preceding Year	为上年(%) As Compared with the Preceding Year(%)	市 区 Urban District 2009年
本年完成投资额	**Total Investment of the Year**	**3870719**	**3050476**	**26.9**	**2329787**
按行业分	**Grouped by Sector**				
农林牧渔业	Farming, Forestry, Animal Husbandry and Fishery	29346	30810	－4.8	6714
采矿业	Mining & Quarrying	32838	28580	14.9	－
制造业	Manufacturing	2822284	2350889	20.1	1650134
电力、燃气及水的生产和供应业	Production and Supply of Electricity, Gas and Hot Water	166768	97230	71.5	93675
建筑业	Construction	680	6400	－89.4	680
交通运输、仓储及邮政业	Transportation, Storage, Post & Telecommunications	134185	93863	43.0	76675
信息传输、计算机服务和软件业	Information Transmission, Computer Services and Software	－	－	－	－
批发和零售业	Wholesale & Retail Trade	42628	26056	63.6	33083
住宿和餐饮业	Accommodations and Catering	69525	33701	106.3	55318
金融业	Banking and Insurance	200	－	－	200
房地产业	Real Estate	205587	128132	60.4	174700
租赁和商务服务业	Renting and Busyness Service	8962	1500	497.5	5411
科学研究、技术服务和地质勘查业	Scientific Research, Technical Service and Geological Prospecting	5839	3956	47.6	5204
水利、环境和公共设施管理业	Water Conservancy, Environment and Public Utility	283267	208966	35.6	188543
居民服务和其他服务业	Service for the Residents and Other Service Sector	6931	7020	－1.3	6030
教育	Education	35986	22712	58.4	23116
卫生、社会保障和社会福利业	Health Care, Sports & Social Welfare	5821	1236	371.0	2495
文化、体育和娱乐业	Culture, Sports and Entertainment	10786	5222	106.5	2605
公共管理和社会组织	Public Management and Social Organzations	9086	4203	116.2	6410
国际组织	International Organzations	－	－	－	－
房屋建筑施工面积(万平方米)	**Floor Space of Buildings Under Construction (10000sq. m)**	**1470.99**	**1274.88**	**15.4**	**965.2**
其中:住宅	Residential Buildings	163.97	141.1	16.2	89.55
房屋建筑竣工面积(万平方米)	**Floor Space of Buildings Completed (10000sq. m)**	**519.39**	**473.36**	**9.7**	**281.08**
其中:住宅	Residential Buildings	12.17	23.5	－48.2	1.44

固定资产投资完成额(2009 年)
by Region(2009)

(10000 yuan)

上 年 Preceding Year	为上年(%) As Compared with the Preceding Year(%)	#萧山区 Xiaoshan	#余杭区 Yuhang	桐庐县 Tonglu	淳安县 Chun'an	建德市 Jiande	富阳市 Fuyang	临安市 Lin'an
1884354	**23.6**	**1697292**	**531832**	**282064**	**107667**	**237490**	**661252**	**252459**
19264	-65.1	3231	3483	2933	540	6600	6174	6385
637	-100.0	-	-	3924	3688	600	22286	2340
1420424	16.2	1251514	387159	227199	32478	194661	536795	181017
53767	74.2	62289	9821	21447	12535	16285	9622	13204
6400	-89.4	680	-	-	-	-	-	-
53336	43.8	68475	8200	5599	32952	8764	-	10195
-	-	-	-	-	-	-	-	-
25356	30.5	18500	2012	850	-	-	4445	4250
27183	103.5	48722	-	598	-	-	3006	10603
-	-	200	-	-	-	-	-	-
115948	50.7	97075	27949	-	-	-	30287	600
1500	260.7	-	5411	2201	-	1350	-	-
3956	31.5	5204	-	-	-	-	-	635
131282	43.6	121570	66973	15733	18648	3356	46848	10139
7020	-14.1	3540	2490	901	-	-	-	-
12312	87.8	6282	16834	679	-	5874	1307	5010
825	202.4	995	1500	-	3326	-	-	-
3237	-19.5	2605	-	-	1181	-	-	7000
1907	236.1	6410	-	-	1113	-	482	1081
-	-	-	-	-	-	-	-	-
917.79	**5.2**	**600.86**	**316.57**	**106.11**	**14.45**	**68.2**	**245.62**	**71.41**
137.58	-34.9	44.54	-	1.38	2.27	-	70.77	-
274.81	**2.3**	**204.03**	**76.47**	**75.39**	**8.12**	**33.67**	**92.25**	**28.88**
22.56	-93.6	1.44	-	1.38	1.91	-	7.44	-

7-10 房屋建筑面积及造价(2009 年)

Floor Space of Buildings and Their Cost(2009)

指　　标	Item	施工面积(万平方米) Floor Space of Buildings Under Construction (10000 sq. m)	竣工面积(万平方米) Floor Space of Buildings Completed (10000 sq. m)	竣工房屋的价值(万元) Value of Buildings Completed (10000 yuan)	每平方米造价(元) Cost Per Square Meter (yuan)
全　市	**Total**				
房屋建筑面积合计	**Floor Space of Buildings**	**10308.45**	**2009.90**	**3626421**	**1804**
#住宅	#Residential Buildings	4441.84	700.63	1684092	2404
房地产开发	Real Estate Development	5151.62	836.95	2076590	2481
#住宅	#Residential Buildings	3676.04	626.64	1550213	2474
市　区	**Urban District**				
房屋建筑面积合计	**Floor Space of Buildings**	**8558.17**	**1374.61**	**2715812**	**1976**
#住宅	#Residential Buildings	3807.67	537.39	1321357	2459
房地产开发	Real Estate Development	4445.05	634.33	1619059	2552
#住宅	#Residential Buildings	3134.50	474.13	1199403	2530
#萧 山 区	**Xiaoshan**				
房屋建筑面积合计	**Total Floor Space of Buildings**	**1713.83**	**366.77**	**550905**	**1502**
#住宅	#Residential Buildings	540.36	82.78	205742	2485
房地产开发	Real Estate Development	682.18	105.44	267039	2533
#住宅	#Residential Buildings	493.61	80.64	203642	2525
余 杭 区	**Yuhang**				
房屋建筑面积合计	**Total Floor Space of Buildings**	**1773.45**	**262.18**	**408223**	**1557**
#住宅	#Residential Buildings	798.01	69.22	163263	2359
房地产开发	Real Estate Development	944.36	89.82	214290	2386
#住宅	#Residential Buildings	793.77	69.22	163263	2359

注:本表为限额以上口径。

a) Data in this table refer to super-scale investments.

7－10 续表 continued

指 标	Item	施工面积（万平方米）Floor Space of Buildings Under Construction（10000 sq. m）	竣工面积（万平方米）Floor Space of Buildings Completed（10000 sq. m）	竣工房屋的价值（万元）Value of Buildings Completed（10000 yuan）	每平方米造价（元）Cost Per Square Meter（yuan）
桐 庐 县	**Tonglu**				
房屋建筑面积合计	**Total Floor Space of Buildings**	**413.40**	**178.14**	**282981**	**1589**
#住宅	#Residential Buildings	128.04	47.66	137413	2883
房地产开发	Real Estate Development	158.55	55.21	155916	2824
#住宅	#Residential Buildings	126.66	46.28	135873	2936
淳 安 县	**Chun'an**				
房屋建筑面积合计	**Total Floor Space of Buildings**	**175.56**	**53.26**	**82471**	**1548**
#住宅	#Residential Buildings	89.12	40.08	42847	1069
房地产开发	Real Estate Development	113.32	28.02	58664	2094
#住宅	#Residential Buildings	76.90	20.04	41360	2064
建 德 市	**Jiande**				
房屋建筑面积合计	**Total Floor Space of Buildings**	**182.81**	**56.02**	**72019**	**1286**
#住宅	#Residential Buildings	53.20	11.05	21694	1964
房地产开发	Real Estate Development	77.79	16.14	36231	2245
#住宅	#Residential Buildings	53.20	11.05	21694	1964
富 阳 市	**Fuyang**				
房屋建筑面积合计	**Total Floor Space of Buildings**	**689.65**	**241.87**	**325172**	**1344**
#住宅	#Residential Buildings	258.13	59.03	107275	1817
房地产开发	Real Estate Development	225.66	69.73	132964	1907
#住宅	#Residential Buildings	179.10	51.59	98377	1907
临 安 市	**Lin'an**				
房屋建筑面积合计	**Total Floor Space of Buildings**	**288.87**	**82.11**	**138628**	**1688**
#住宅	#Residential Buildings	105.69	23.55	53506	2272
房地产开发	Real Estate Development	131.25	33.51	73756	2201
#住宅	#Residential Buildings	105.69	23.55	53506	2272

7－11　固定资产投资新增生产能力(或效益)(2009 年)

The New Productive Capacity or Facilities Created by Investment in Fixed Assets(2009)

指　　标	Item	全　市 Total	市　区 Urban District
化学农药原药　(吨/年)	Chemical Pesticide(TC)　(tons/year)	10160	160
塑料树脂及共聚物　(吨/年)	Plastic Resins and Copolymers (tons/year)	38100	38100
化学纤维　(万吨/年)	Chemical Fiber　(10000tons/year)	25.64	25.64
其中:合成纤维　(万吨/年)	Of Which:Synthetic fiber (10000tons/year)	12.82	12.82
棉纺锭　(锭)	Cotton Spindles　(spindles)	26000	26000
水力发电　(万千瓦)	Waterpower and Eletricity (10000kilowatt)	0.78	–
其他发电　(万千瓦)	Else　(10000kilowatt)	4.8	–
输电线路长度(11 万伏及以上)　(千米)	Length of Electricity Transmission Line (110000volts and above)　(km)	242.32	242.32
新建公路　(公里)	New Highway　(km)	100.72	52.82
改建公路　(公里)	Revamped Highway　(km)	153.7	101.08
城市污水处理能力　(万吨/每日)	Urban Sewage Treatment Capacity (10000tons/day)	17.3	13.5

注:本表为城镇 50 万元以上固定资产投资项目和农村非农户 50 万元以上建设项目。

a) Data in this table refer to cities and towns more than 500,000 yuan in fixed assets investment projects and rural non－farm households more than 500,000 yuan construcion projects.

主要统计指标解释

固定资产投资完成额 固定资产投资完成额是以货币表现的建造和购置固定资产的工作量以及与此有关的费用的总称。它是反映固定资产投资规模、速度、比例关系和使用方向的综合性指标。

房地产开发投资 包括各种经济类型的房地产开发公司、商品房建设公司及其他房地产开发单位统一开发的包括统代建、拆迁还建的住宅、厂房、仓库、饭店、宾馆、度假村、写字楼、办公楼等房屋建筑物和配套的服务设施、土地开发工程，如道路、给水、排水、供电、供热、通讯、平整场地等基础设施工程的投资。包括非房地产企业实际从事房地产开发或经济活动，不包括单纯的土地交易活动。

施工和竣工房屋建筑面积 房屋建筑面积是从房屋外墙线算起的各层平面面积的总和，包括房屋结构（如柱、墙）占用的面积和地下室面积。多层建筑按各自然层面积总和计算，包括房屋内的楼隔层，突出墙面的眺望间、门斗、有柱雨罩的面积。不包括突出墙面结构的构件、艺术装饰等所占的面积，如台阶等。凹阳台、挑阳台按其水平投影面积一半计算建筑面积。

房屋新开工面积 指在报告期内新开工建设的房屋面积。不包括上期跨入报告期继续施工的房屋面积和上期停缓建而在本期恢复施工的房屋面积。房屋的开工应以房屋正式开始破土刨槽（地基处理或打永久桩）的日期为准。

商品房销售面积 指报告期内出售商品房屋的合同总面积（即双方签署的正式买卖合同中所确定的建筑面积）。由现房销售建筑面积和期房销售建筑面积两部分组成。

(1)现房销售面积：是指在报告期内正式签订买卖合同、已经竣工达到入住条件的商品房屋建筑面积。包括以一次性付款方式和分期付款方式销售的现房建筑面积。

(2)期房销售面积：是指在报告期内正式签订买卖合同、正在建设尚未竣工交付使用的商品房屋建筑面积。包括以一次性付款方式和分期付款方式销售的商品房屋建筑面积。期房销售建筑面积竣工后不再转为现房销售建筑面积。

新增固定资产 指通过投资活动所形成的新的固定资产价值。包括已经建成投入生产或交付使用的工程价值和达到固定资产标准的设备、工具、器具的价值及有关应摊入的费用。它是以价值形式表示的固定资产投资成果的综合性指标，可以综合反映不同时期、不同部门、不同地区的固定资产投资成果。

Explanatory Notes on Main Statistical Indicators

Total Investment in Fixed Assets refer to the volume of activities in construction and purchases of fixed assets in monetary terms and other relative expenses. It is a comprehensive indicator which shows the size, pace, proportional relations and use orientation of investment in fixed assets.

Investment in Real Estate Development include the investment by the real estate development companies, commercial buildings construction companies and other real estate development units of various types of ownership in the construction of house buildings, such as residential buildings, factory buildings, warehouses, hotels, guesthouses, holiday supply, water drainage, power supply, heating, telecommunications, land leveling and other projects of infrastructure, it excludes the activities in simple land transaction.

Floor space of Building Under Construction and Completed refer to total floor space in each story of buildings calculate from the outside line of building walls, including the space occupied by construction like pillars or walls and basements. The floor space of multi – story building includes the total floor space of each story, including area occupied by separating walls, watching rooms, door – ways, and pillars, but excluding protruding wall structures, artistic decoration, etc. (for example, flight of steps). The space of balcony is counted by half of the projection area.

Beginning to Construction Floor Space of Building refer to the area space which constructed in report period, not including the floor whose construction lasted to report period and which stopped in the last period to continue construction in the report period. And the beginning of construction of floor space should base on the date of breaking the earth(disposal the basement or piling).

Selling of the Commercial Building refer to the total area that sold by contract(which reflected in the contract), which include completed and future buildings.

(1) Floor Space of Completed Building: refer to the area which formal contract has been signed and which has been completed and reached the condition of living, including payment in one time and installment payment.

(2) Floor Space of Future Building: refer to the area which signed by formal contract and under constructing, including payment in one time and installment payment. Which can not be turned into completed building' s sale when they completed.

Newly Increased Fixed Assets refer to the newly increased value of fixed assets through investment, including the value of projects completed and put into production, the value of equipment, tools, and vessels considered as fixed assets, as well as the relevant expenses as investment in fixed assets. This is a comprehensive indicator of investment in fixed assets, reflecting the achievements of investment in fixed assets in different periods, different sectors, and different regions.

第八篇
CHAPTER-8

国内商业
DOMESTIC TRADE

国 内 商 业
Domestic Trade

主 要 统 计 指 标
Major Statistical Indicators

社会消费品零售总额	Total Retail Sales of Consumer Goods	1804.93	亿元	(100 million yuan)
为上年	As Compared with the Preceding Year	114.4	%	(%)
批发和零售贸易业	Wholesale and Retail Trade	1597.26	亿元	(100 million yuan)
为上年	As Compared with the Preceding Year	114.5	%	(%)
住宿和餐饮业	Accommodations and Catering	203.28	亿元	(100 million yuan)
为上年	As Compared with the Preceding Year	113.8	%	(%)
其他	Others	4.39	亿元	(100 million yuan)
为上年	As Compared with the Preceding Year	103.5	%	(%)

8－01 主要年份社会消费品零售总额
Total Retail Sale of Consumer Goods in Main Years

单位:万元　　(10000 yuan)

年份 Year	全市 Total	市区 Urban District	县(市)合计 All Counties
1978	119509	73653	45856
1979	150462	93342	57120
1980	205381	128440	76941
1981	236188	148152	88036
1982	251068	154582	96486
1983	273664	169508	104156
1984	343722	215901	127821
1985	478117	308901	169216
1986	557963	360479	197484
1987	657838	426745	231093
1988	866373	557374	308999
1989	927019	600816	326203
1990	981713	650278	331435
1991	1155476	777559	377917
1992	1408525	928586	479939
1993	1901509	1300037	601472
1994	2616477	1733572	882905
1995	2993250	1930140	1063110
1996	3478156	2310619	1167537
1997	3815537	2537537	1278000
1998	4178013	2794171	1383842
1999	4574924	3053983	1520941
2000	5146789	3436536	1710253
2001	5790138	4993078	797060
2002	6606548	5701707	904841
2003	7425760	6401970	1023790
2004	8554476	7385662	1168814
2005	9784275	8440559	1343716
2006	11191900	9630210	1561690
2007	13082930	11247539	1835391
2008	15775872	13542665	2233207
2009	18049303	15498990	2550313

注:1. 根据国家统一规定,2008 年经济普查后对 2005－2008 年度数据作了相应调整。
2. 从 2001 年起市区数据包括萧山区和余杭区。

a) According to national unification stipulation, the 2005－2008 year data has been made the corresponding adjustment after the 2008 economic census.

b) Data of urban district include Xiaoshan and Yuhang district since 2001.

8－02　主要年份分县(市)

Total Retail Sale of Consumer Goods

单位:万元

年　份 Year	全　市 Whole Municipality		市　区 Urban District		
	合　计 Total	为上年(%) As Compared with the Preceding Year(%)	合　计 Total	为上年(%) As Compared with the Preceding Year(%)	#萧山区 Xiaoshan
1978	119509	112.5	73653	115.8	12985
1979	150462	125.9	93342	127.2	16270
1980	205381	136.5	128440	138.1	22292
1981	236188	115.0	148152	115.6	25297
1982	251068	106.3	154582	103.3	29007
1983	273664	109.0	169508	110.1	32136
1984	343722	125.6	215901	128.4	41210
1985	478117	139.1	308901	145.2	51879
1986	557963	116.7	360479	116.8	61421
1987	657838	117.9	426745	118.6	73159
1988	866373	131.7	557374	130.1	101227
1989	927019	107.0	600816	108.3	103419
1990	981713	105.9	650278	109.5	111757
1991	1155476	117.7	777559	120.4	123753
1992	1408525	121.9	928586	118.3	153254
1993	1901509	135.0	1300037	134.4	195472
1994	2616477	137.6	1733572	132.2	299072
1995	2993250	114.4	1930140	118.2	339447
1996	3478156	116.2	2310619	120.9	390364
1997	3815537	109.7	2537537	109.9	431742
1998	4178013	109.5	2794171	110.5	470599
1999	4574924	109.5	3053983	109.3	520482
2000	5146789	112.5	3436536	112.8	602198
2001	5790138	113.6	4993078	113.9	690721
2002	6606548	114.1	5701707	114.2	795711
2003	7425760	112.4	6401970	112.3	929390
2004	8554476	115.2	7385662	115.4	1069728
2005	9784275	114.4	8440559	114.3	1234568
2006	11191900	114.4	9630210	114.1	1462157
2007	13082930	116.9	11247539	116.8	1721511
2008	15775872	120.6	13542665	120.4	2059811
2009	18049303	114.4	15498990	114.4	2376949

注:1. 2008 年经济普查后,对 2005－2008 年度数据作了相应调整。
　2. 从 2001 年起市区数据包括萧山区和余杭区。

社会消费品零售总额

by Region in Main Years

(10000 yuan)

#余杭区 Yuhang	桐庐县 Tonglu	淳安县 Chun'an	建德市 Jiande	富阳市 Fuyang	临安市 Lin'an
11472	3536	3507	4390	5209	4757
14439	4283	4274	5300	6435	6119
19917	5501	5225	7119	8661	8226
22172	6456	6201	7970	10226	9714
23435	7101	6663	8562	11016	10702
23496	7694	7168	9380	12307	11975
29292	9235	8331	10770	14972	14011
39798	11826	11081	14687	21013	18932
47499	13217	12525	15832	23400	23590
53005	17394	14449	18076	27939	27071
64653	24390	18944	23545	42601	33639
74044	23029	19014	23138	48836	34723
69360	23141	18764	23820	45364	39229
84399	26350	20950	25107	52807	44551
110075	34110	23983	30770	74865	52882
149128	44909	28038	40237	76162	67526
212955	69025	34179	54562	101829	111283
255972	93736	42143	70570	127592	133650
266467	104234	51794	77620	146348	130710
294446	114032	58994	83837	163324	131625
321241	123154	67136	93169	171654	136889
352723	135223	74293	103417	185730	149073
397166	148745	81054	115062	198917	167111
446812	166892	90133	128754	223782	187499
508919	188087	101581	144849	254887	215437
584748	209153	114990	163244	289297	247106
674799	237598	130974	185772	331534	282936
778848	272394	149456	212138	382960	326768
906960	317484	173272	247425	450365	373144
1064956	371057	201769	288873	526750	446942
1302135	451356	244069	350854	643169	543759
1499377	516037	278356	400157	734925	620838

a) The 2005 - 2008 year data has been made the corresponding adjustment after the 2008 economic census.

b) Data of urban district include Xiaoshan and Yuhang district since 2001.

单位:万元

地 区	Region	合 计 Total	按销售分	
			市的零售额 City	县的零售额 County
全 市	**Total**	**18049303**	**16678390**	**486519**
市 区	Urban District	15498990	15498990	－
上城区	Shangcheng	1651009	1651009	－
下城区	Xiacheng	3977317	3977317	－
江干区	Jianggan	1574924	1574924	－
拱墅区	Gongshu	1956811	1956811	－
西湖区	Xihu	1787421	1787421	－
高新(滨江)区	Hi－Tech(Binjiang)	253334	253334	－
萧山区	Xiaoshan	2376949	2376949	－
余杭区	Yuhang	1499377	1499377	－
桐庐县	Tonglu	516037	－	321109
淳安县	Chun'an	278356	－	165410
建德市	Jiande	400157	244134	－
富阳市	Fuyang	734925	578617	－
临安市	Lin'an	620838	356649	－

零售总额(2009 年)
Consumer Goods(2009)

(10000 yuan)

By Location	按行业分 By sector		
县以下的零售额 Under County Level	批发和零售贸易业 Wholesale and Retail Trades	住宿和餐饮业 Hotels and Catering Services	其 他 Others
884394	**15972608**	**2032831**	**43864**
–	13779950	1676351	42689
–	1341282	289182	20545
–	3743108	217836	16373
–	1436659	136411	1854
–	1861405	95407	–
–	1463692	323729	–
–	218347	34987	–
–	2170341	202691	3917
–	1268165	231212	–
194928	451541	64496	–
112946	236817	41539	–
156023	349765	49217	1175
156308	634050	100875	–
264189	520485	100353	–

8-04 全市限额以上批发零售贸易企业商品销售总额按登记注册类型分(2009年)

Sales of Wholesale and Retail Trade Above Designated Size by Status of Registration(2009)

单位:万元 (10000 yuan)

项目	Item	法人企业(个) Number of Enterprises (unit)	销售总额 Total Sales	批发额 Wholesale	零售额 Retail
总计	**Total**	**3080**	**79069122**	**67799589**	**11269534**
1. 内资企业	**Domestic-funded Enterprises**	**3025**	**77084148**	**67158196**	**9925952**
国有企业	State-owned Enterprises	86	6397454	6065896	331558
集体企业	Collective-owned Enterprises	27	587234	538738	48496
股份合作企业	Cooperative Enterprises	12	145801	139958	5843
联营企业	Joint Ownership Enterprises	15	183332	128559	54773
国有联营企业	State Joint Ownership Enterprises	2	27804	10212	17592
集体联营企业	Collective Joint Ownership Enterprises	2	27139	23758	3381
国有与集体联营企业	Joint State-collective Enterprises	8	44991	11191	33800
其他联营企业	Other Joint Ownership Enterprises	3	83399	83399	-
有限责任公司	Limited Liability Corporations	874	34792766	29692663	5100103
国有独资公司	State-funded Corporations	8	210506	198283	12223
其他有限责任公司	Other Limited Liability Corporations	866	34582261	29494380	5087881
股份有限公司	Share-holding Corporations Ltd.	102	8399882	5691320	2708562
私营企业	Private Enterprises	1900	25955817	24279200	1676617
私营独资企业	Private-funded Enterprises	50	378669	328547	50123
私营合伙企业	Private Partnership Enterprises	11	94021	63876	30145
私营有限责任公司	Private Limited Liability Corporations	1789	24836303	23281868	1554436
私营股份有限公司	Private Share-holding Corporations Ltd.	50	646823	604910	41914
其他企业	Other Enterprises	9	621862	621862	-
2. 港、澳、台商投资企业	**Enterprises With Investment from Hong Kong, Macao and Taiwan**	**15**	**438012**	**241054**	**196959**
合资经营企业(港或澳、台资)	Joint-venture Enterprises (With Funds from Hong Kong, Macao and Taiwan)	6	93726	60931	32796
合作经营企业(港或澳、台资)	Coorperative Enterprises (With Funds from Hong Kong, Macao and Taiwan)	1	62564	-	62564
港、澳、台商独资经营企业	Enterprises With Sole Investment from Hong Kong, Macao and Taiwan	7	276690	180123	96567
港、澳、台商投资股份有限公司	Share-holding Corporations Ltd. With Investment from Hong Kong, Macao and Taiwan	1	5031	-	5031
3. 外商投资企业	**Enterprises With Foreign Investment**	**40**	**1546963**	**400339**	**1146623**
中外合资经营企业	Joint-venture Enterprises	12	593666	224317	369349
中外合作经营企业	Cooperation Enterprises	2	20814	-	20814
外资企业	Enterprises With Sole Foreign Investment	25	923131	166671	756461
外商投资股份有限公司	Share-holding Corporations Ltd. With Foreign Investment	1	9352	9352	-

8－05 全市限额以上批发零售贸易企业商品销售总额按国民经济行业分(2009年)
Sales of Wholesale and Retail Trade Above Designated Size by Sector(2009)

单位:万元 (10000 yuan)

项目	Item	法人企业(个) Number of Enterprises (unit)	销售总额 Total Sales	批发额 Wholesale	零售额 Retail
总计	**Total**	**3080**	**79069122**	**67799589**	**11269534**
一、批发业	**Wholesale**	**2511**	**69725322**	**66694071**	**3031251**
农畜产品批发业	Wholesale of Farm and Animal Products	33	549778	547091	2687
食品、饮料及烟草制品批发	Wholesale of Food, Beverages and Tobaccos	124	5998913	5975344	23569
纺织品、服装和鞋、帽批发业	Wholesale of Textile Products, Garments, Shoes and Caps	506	7657576	7590899	66677
文化、体育用品及器材批发	Wholesale of Cultural and Sports Goods	65	1095368	1079584	15784
医药及医疗器材批发	Wholesale of Medicines and Medical Appliances	84	3262875	1950272	1312603
矿产品、建材及化工产品批发	Wholesale of Mineral Products, Building and Chemical Materials	1180	40891056	39542185	1348871
机械设备、五金交电及电子产品批发	Wholesale of Machinery, Hardware and Electronic Products	467	9062401	8801341	261060
其中:汽车、摩托车及零配件批发	Wholesale of Automobiles, Motorcycle and Parts	63	2102786	1953526	149260
其他批发	Other	51	1207355	1207355	-
二、零售业	**Retail Trade**	**569**	**9343800**	**1105518**	**8238283**
综合零售	Comprehensive Retail Trade	83	2662418	361252	2301166
食品、饮料及烟草制品专门零售	Specialism Retail of Food, Beverages and Tobaccos	19	98224	11512	86712
纺织品、服装和鞋、帽专门零售	Specialism Retail of Textile Products, Garments, Shoes and Caps	28	145957	28404	117553
文化、体育用品及器材专门零售	Specialism Retail of Cultural and Sports Goods	33	233066	30713	202353
医药及医疗器材专门零售	Specialism Retail of Medicines and Medical Appliances	37	208556	7560	200996
汽车、摩托车、燃料及零配件专门零售	Specialism Retail of Automobiles, Motorcycle, Fuels and Parts	283	4942602	521568	4421034
其中:汽车零售	Specialism Retail of Automobiles	172	4097978	378123	3719855
家用电器及电子产品专门零售	Specialism Retail of Household Electric Applianes, and Electronic Products	66	934481	125768	808712
五金家具及室内装修材料专门零售	Specialism Retail of Hardware and Upholstery Materials	10	33692	-	33692
无店铺及其他零售	Other Retail Trade	10	84806	18741	66065

8－06 全市限额以上批发零售贸易企业

Main Financial Indicators of Enterprises Above Designated Size in

单位:万元

项目	Item	企业数(个) Number of Enterprises (unit)	年末资产负债 Assets and Liabilities 流动资产合计 Circulating Funds	# 存货 Inventory	固定资产原价 Orginal Value of Fixed Assets
批发、零售贸易企业总计	**Total**	**3080**	**27521206**	**3845886**	**2675172**
1. 内资企业	**Domestic－funded Enterprises**	**3025**	**26842623**	**3748551**	**2469371**
国有企业	State－owned Enterprises	86	2036918	361930	300625
集体企业	Collective－owned Enterprises	27	321225	68677	25037
股份合作企业	Cooperative Enterprises	12	40938	2990	2689
联营企业	Joint Ownership Enterprises	15	46116	3662	4599
国有联营企业	State Joint Ownership Enterprises	2	5932	202	688
集体联营企业	Collective Joint Enterprises	2	18286	389	328
国有与集体联营企业	Joint State－collective Enterprises	8	2896	610	1442
其他联营企业	Other Joint Ownership Enterprises	3	19002	2461	2142
有限责任公司	Limited Liability Corporations	874	11938412	1777669	955975
国有独资公司	State－funded Corporations	8	182894	82605	17612
其他有限责任公司	Other Limited Liability Corporations	866	11755518	1695064	938363
股份有限公司	Share－holding Corporations Ltd.	102	2189780	437458	563840
私营企业	Private Enterprises	1900	10117340	1069299	612165
私营独资企业	Private－funded Enterprises	50	140195	18239	9203
私营合伙企业	Private Partnership Enterprises	11	29056	4799	3094
私营有限责任公司	Private Limited Liability Corporations	1789	9471220	1023447	569978
私营股份有限公司	Private Share－holding Corporations Ltd.	50	476869	22813	29890
其他企业	Other Enterprises	9	151895	26866	4441
2. 港、澳、台商投资企业	**Enterprises With Investment from Hong Kong, Macao and Taiwan**	**15**	**113465**	**21515**	**42034**
合资经营企业(港或澳、台资)	Joint－venture Enterprises (With Funds from Hong Kong, Macao and Taiwan)	6	55970	4333	7409
合作经营企业(港或澳、台资)	Coorperative Enterprises (With Funds from Hong Kong, Macao and Taiwan)	1	10899	445	11901
港、澳、台商独资经营企业	Enterprises With Sole Investment from Hong Kong, Macao and Taiwan	7	45584	16297	21705
港、澳、台商投资股份有限公司	Share－holding Corporations Ltd. With Investment from Hong Kong, Macao and Taiwan	1	1011	440	1019
3. 外商投资企业	**Enterprises With Foreign Investment**	**40**	**565118**	**75821**	**163767**
中外合资经营企业	Joint－venture Enterprises	12	115155	29224	66219
中外合作经营企业	Cooperation Enterprises	2	2889	814	12169
外资企业	Enterprises With Sole Foreign Investment	25	445759	45783	85265
外商投资股份有限公司	Share－holding Corporations Ltd. With Foreign Investment	1	1315	－	114

财务状况按登记注册类型分(2009 年)
Wholesale and Retail Sale Trade by Status of Registration(2009)

(10000 yuan)

累计折旧 Accumulated Depreciation	#本年折旧 Depreciation	资产合计 Total Assets	负债合计 Total Liabilities	所有者权益 Creditors' Equity	实收资本 Capital Hold	#国家资本 State Capital
820324	**154318**	**36728389**	**27270842**	**9457546**	**5483277**	**1063481**
754740	**143418**	**35755901**	**26608936**	**9146966**	**5253275**	**1053414**
93044	12427	2900997	1533192	1367805	365569	345319
10909	985	470616	307204	163413	65964	–
1163	199	44030	36998	7032	3729	500
1499	277	53192	30494	22698	10086	1727
299	28	6709	2551	4159	1217	1217
92	27	21956	17418	4539	3500	–
727	111	3751	1413	2338	1359	511
381	111	20776	9112	11663	4010	–
291260	54536	15833776	12354614	3479163	1858049	286903
4750	1083	248983	174731	74252	17405	16405
286510	53453	15584793	12179883	3404910	1840644	270498
179735	27917	4004651	2511187	1493464	972273	411965
175187	46587	12282657	9715165	2567492	1961305	–
3820	1192	152473	134401	18073	20874	–
843	266	32992	28381	4610	4420	–
164603	43200	11500489	9065659	2434830	1855902	–
5922	1930	596703	486724	109979	80109	–
1943	490	165982	120083	45899	16300	7000
14349	**2342**	**185854**	**89513**	**96341**	**52416**	**4250**
3740	359	88539	32960	55579	13221	4250
8016	787	22465	2237	20228	18975	–
2245	849	73160	53539	19621	19282	–
348	348	1690	778	913	937	–
51235	**8557**	**786633**	**572394**	**214240**	**177586**	**5817**
20179	1449	183028	167852	15176	36101	5817
3161	868	13009	3933	9077	13232	–
27852	6221	589202	399608	189594	128083	–
43	19	1394	1001	393	170	–

项　目	Item	营业收入 Revenue of Business	其中:主营业务收入 Main Revenue of Business	主营业务成本 Main Cost of Business	主营业务税金及附加 Main Sales Tax and Extra Charges
总　计	**Total**	**70133588**	**69269172**	**65603723**	**128898**
1.内资企业	**Domestic－funded Enterprises**	**68343546**	**67522855**	**64060367**	**125087**
国有企业	State－owned Enterprises	5617642	5580337	5155102	41094
集体企业	Collective－owned Enterprises	532494	529982	527706	1881
股份合作企业	Cooperative Enterprises	134031	133949	127294	529
联营企业	Joint Ownership Enterprises	171269	171269	156997	199
国有联营企业	State Joint Ownership Enterprises	24073	24073	20997	49
集体联营企业	Collective Joint Enterprises	26648	26648	25807	－
国有与集体联营企业	Joint State－collective Enterprises	38454	38454	35798	48
其他联营企业	Other Joint Ownership Enterprises	82094	82094	74395	102
有限责任公司	Limited Liability Corporations	31676462	31058963	29590121	39431
国有独资公司	State－funded Corporations	202325	201727	184565	712
其他有限责任公司	Other Limited Liability Corporations	31474137	30857236	29405556	38719
股份有限公司	Share－holding Corporations Ltd.	6930573	6834144	6253472	12673
私营企业	Private Enterprises	22744561	22678511	21725328	29050
私营独资企业	Private－funded Enterprises	339268	332479	313006	513
私营合伙企业	Private Partnership Enterprises	86847	86687	82023	136
私营有限责任公司	Private Limited Liability Corporations	21752282	21695548	20794132	27858
私营股份有限公司	Private Share－holding Corporations Ltd.	566164	563798	536167	544
其他企业	Other Enterprises	536515	535700	524348	230
2.港、澳、台商投资企业	**Enterprises With Investment from Hong Kong,Macao and Taiwan**	**384457**	**380180**	**339383**	**633**
合资经营企业(港或澳、台资)	Joint－venture Enterprises(With Funds from Hong Kong,Macao and Taiwan)	85841	84975	70641	382
合作经营企业(港或澳、台资)	Coorperative Enterprises (With Funds from Hong Kong,Macao and Taiwan)	55821	53474	47176	－
港、澳、台商独资经营企业	Enterprises With Sole Investment from Hong Kong,Macao and Taiwan	238489	237431	218860	246
港、澳、台商投资股份有限公司	Share－holding Corporations Ltd. With Investment from Hong Kong,Macao and Taiwan	4306	4300	2707	5
3.外商投资企业	**Enterprises With Foreign Investment**	**1405585**	**1366137**	**1203973**	**3178**
中外合资经营企业	Joint－venture Enterprises	551857	534712	492558	1001
中外合作经营企业	Cooperation Enterprises	19085	17955	12681	33
外资企业	Enterprises With Sole Foreign Investment	825262	804118	690168	2144
外商投资股份有限公司	Share－holding Corporations Ltd. With Foreign Investment	9380	9352	8566	－

continued (10000 yuan)

主营业务利润 Main Profits of Business	营业费用 Expenses of Business	管理费用 Administration Cost	财务费用 Financil Cost	营业利润 Management Profits	利润总额 Total Profits	本年应付工资总额 Total Wages Payable	本年应付福利费总额 Total Welfare Expenses Payable	本年应交所得税 Income Tax
3536551	**1804698**	**970159**	**284742**	**706755**	**1181327**	**555609**	**31947**	**307659**
3337401	**1693182**	**906513**	**272774**	**656348**	**1123366**	**517369**	**29227**	**291765**
384142	58852	92345	343	263958	273694	45235	4502	99191
395	7193	7277	5712	-16967	22757	4430	214	1745
6127	2599	1425	395	2954	2672	1058	3	460
14072	2906	1809	612	9888	9914	896	15	2181
3027	247	151	-124	2753	2756	73	-	688
841	126	50	164	1642	1654	81	3	127
2608	922	192	-7	1501	1492	384	10	362
7596	1611	1416	578	3992	4013	358	2	1003
1429411	849744	348848	96891	331893	504910	282810	14312	113445
16450	7151	8464	1500	-75	4450	2805	331	933
1412961	842593	340384	95391	331968	500460	280004	13981	112512
567999	280377	144317	69930	225	90215	64293	4625	37290
924133	488160	307558	97315	60091	215077	116974	5472	36405
18960	13764	9358	794	435	357	3169	116	609
4528	2447	1632	327	224	310	570	21	82
873558	455701	286879	92615	59432	205545	109303	4994	35056
27088	16248	9689	3579	-	8866	3932	340	659
11122	3352	2935	1577	4305	4127	1674	84	1048
40164	**16652**	**18128**	**1061**	**8808**	**10281**	**10742**	**433**	**1933**
13952	5910	4981	-159	4325	4997	5041	92	908
6298	1812	4407	131	2296	2306	1566	185	641
18325	8560	7568	1060	2167	2951	3993	107	382
1589	371	1173	29	21	28	142	49	2
158986	**94863**	**45518**	**10907**	**41599**	**47681**	**27498**	**2287**	**13961**
41153	45216	8337	1021	2203	3047	10169	951	1196
5241	5071	416	1	643	211	1282	39	107
111807	44225	36398	9885	38658	44320	15828	1288	12634
786	351	367	-	95	102	219	9	24

8－07 全市限额以上批发零售贸易企业

Main Financial Indicators of Enterprises Above Designated

单位:万元

项目	Item	企业数(个) Number of Enterprises (unit)	年末资产负债 Assets and Liabilities		
			流动资产合计 Circulating Funds	# 存货 Inventory	固定资产原价 Orginal Value of Fixed Assets
总计	**Total**	**3080**	**27521206**	**3845886**	**2675172**
一、批发业	**Wholesale**	**2511**	**24458853**	**3265426**	**1836236**
农畜产品批发业	Wholesale of Farm and Animal Products	33	395632	31375	30377
食品、饮料、烟草制品批发	Wholesale of Food, Beverages and Tobaccos	124	1935814	262090	303469
纺织品、服装和鞋、帽批发业	Wholesale of Textile Products, Garments, Shoes and Caps	506	2935509	320152	228235
文化、体育用品及器材批发	Wholesale of Cultural and Sports Goods	65	530324	158317	88917
医药及医疗器材批发	Wholesale of Medicines and Medical Appliances	84	999140	209346	73128
矿产品、建材及化工产品批发	Wholesale of Mineral Products, Building and Chemical Materials	1180	13766403	1752697	833139
机械设备、五金交电及电子产品批发	Wholesale of Machinery, Hardware and Electronic Products	467	3624581	515435	269290
其中:汽车、摩托车及零配件批发	Wholesale of Automobiles, Motorcycle and Parts	63	847557	83319	31065
其他批发	Other	51	255426	16015	9601
二、零售业	**Retail Trade**	**569**	**3062353**	**580460**	**838936**
综合零售	Comprehensive Retail Trade	83	1226159	116249	471337
食品、饮料及烟草制品专门零售	Specialism Retail of Food, Beverages and Tobaccos	19	36817	10733	6140
纺织品、服装和鞋、帽专门零售	Specialism Retail of Textile Products, Garments, Shoes and Caps	28	65303	43072	8787
文化、体育用品及器材专门零售	Specialism Retail of Cultural and Sports Goods	33	127071	48731	63794
医药及医疗器材专门零售	Specialism Retail of Medicines and Medical Appliances	37	80902	30546	11341
汽车、摩托车、燃料及零配件专门零售	Specialism Retail of Automobiles, Motorcycle, Fuels and Parts	283	1059884	248919	211239
其中:汽车零售	Specialism Retail of Automobiles	172	972254	232335	156415
家用电器及电子产品专门零售	Specialism Retail of Household Electric Applianes, and Electronic Products	66	426183	76789	31659
五金家具及室内装修材料专门零售	Specialism Retail of Hardware and Upholstery Materials	10	14067	3986	12775
无店铺及其他零售	Other Retail Trade	10	25969	1436	21865

财务状况按国民经济行业分(2009 年)

Size in Wholesale and Retail Sale Trade by Sector(2009)

(10000 yuan)

累计折旧 Accumulated Depreciation	#本年折旧 Depreciation	资产合计 Total Assets	负债合计 Total Liabilities	所有者权益 Creditors' Equity	实收资本 Capital Hold	#国家资本 State Capital
820324	**154318**	**36728389**	**27270842**	**9457546**	**5483277**	**1063481**
573716	**110978**	**32390510**	**24045045**	**8345465**	**4718380**	**975138**
9391	1379	579649	367344	212306	140784	102305
94246	16474	3135873	2122394	1013479	368279	79958
78014	17581	3629373	2756073	873300	509381	27104
29137	3236	903860	479045	424815	134710	76540
30642	4677	1146428	885557	260871	166018	25052
244259	48122	18176387	13904513	4271874	2731397	624538
84732	18793	4514655	3276803	1237852	626345	34741
10287	2539	1061786	576804	484982	132520	1875
3248	702	288173	242895	45277	40466	4900
246608	**43340**	**4337879**	**3225797**	**1112082**	**764898**	**88342**
139092	19257	1868360	1424835	443525	296082	13291
2523	600	47579	27263	20316	17059	571
5065	1017	171414	157767	13647	26882	–
13771	2412	200662	116759	83902	40096	25932
4740	815	95359	76680	18679	16221	2246
62403	14615	1378142	1007499	370643	244617	38419
42175	11817	1224312	929192	295120	189196	15127
8392	2091	505271	374882	130389	85084	–
3353	1205	24621	14271	10350	17111	–
7270	1328	46473	25841	20632	21746	7883

项　　目	Item	营业收入 Revenue of Business	其中:主营业务收入 Main Revenue of Business	主营业务成本 Main Cost of Business	主营业务税金及附加 Main Sales Tax and Extra Charges
总　　计	**Total**	**70133588**	**69269172**	**65603723**	**128898**
一、批发业	**Wholesale**	**61732731**	**61089515**	**58198103**	**103249**
农畜产品批发业	Wholesale of Farm and Animal Products	516106	496992	471750	212
食品、饮料、烟草制品批发	Wholesale of Food, Beverages and Tobaccos	5617786	5553405	4758990	47474
纺织品、服装和鞋、帽批发业	Wholesale of Textile Products, Garments, Shoes and Caps	7139651	7119720	6659284	4383
文化、体育用品及器材批发	Wholesale of Cultural and Sports Goods	981888	975014	918315	1647
医药及医疗器材批发	Wholesale of Medicines and Medical Appliances	2879126	2862822	2664316	4118
矿产品、建材及化工产品批发	Wholesale of Mineral Products, Building and Chemical Materials	35266477	34800890	33872719	22075
机械设备、五金交电及电子产品批发	Wholesale of Machinery, Hardware and Electronic Products	8215323	8165863	7705171	10508
其中:汽车、摩托车及零配件批发	Wholesale of Automobiles, Motorcycle and Parts	1978302	1975518	1890020	1791
其他批发	Other	1110894	1109838	1147559	12519
二、零售业	**Retail Trade**	**8400858**	**8179657**	**7405620**	**25649**
综合零售	Comprehensive Retail Trade	2460865	2317315	2005450	11568
食品、饮料及烟草制品专门零售	Specialism Retail of Food, Beverages and Tobaccos	87505	86130	64546	459
纺织品、服装和鞋、帽专门零售	Specialism Retail of Textile Products, Garments, Shoes and Caps	134307	126408	99946	490
文化、体育用品及器材专门零售	Specialism Retail of Cultural and Sports Goods	204435	200009	159104	3908
医药及医疗器材专门零售	Specialism Retail of Medicines and Medical Appliances	183063	180641	138391	856
汽车、摩托车、燃料及零配件专门零售	Specialism Retail of Automobiles, Motorcycle, Fuels and Parts	4383318	4361124	4113114	5782
其中:汽车零售	Specialism Retail of Automobiles	3654080	3635027	3431451	5101
家用电器及电子产品专门零售	Specialism Retail of Household Electric Appliances, and Electronic Products	839980	802240	738709	2260
五金家具及室内装修材料专门零售	Specialism Retail of Hardware and Upholstery Materials	30111	28872	22544	70
无店铺及其他零售	Other Retail Trade	77273	76917	63816	258

continued (10000 yuan)

主营业务利润 Main Profits of Business	营业费用 Expenses of Business	管理费用 Administration Cost	财务费用 Financil Cost	营业利润 Management Profits	利润总额 Total Profits	本年应付工资总额 Total Wages Payable	本年应付福利费总额 Total Welfare Expenses Payable	本年应交所得税 Income Tax
3536551	**1804698**	**970159**	**284742**	**706755**	**1181327**	**555609**	**31947**	**307659**
2788163	**1327103**	**745381**	**249266**	**515203**	**965381**	**382192**	**21769**	**249796**
25031	7286	12883	9717	16469	18988	4638	198	4456
746942	305870	109317	5782	250775	279473	73873	4037	109196
456053	205275	144110	35408	88477	137836	81785	3252	24934
55052	22631	19795	-1100	17287	13005	8787	789	1838
194389	100029	49092	12520	42660	58766	28953	1796	11994
906096	464047	264118	157592	64930	335427	101992	6888	66100
450184	217634	138964	24340	94603	125991	80218	4603	30082
83707	63085	16129	-1	9012	9537	10030	395	2249
-50241	3887	5388	5010	-63008	-7179	1827	188	1197
748388	**477594**	**224779**	**35476**	**191552**	**215946**	**173417**	**10178**	**57863**
300298	232581	101114	9965	84944	100965	74533	5058	30614
21125	14220	4722	448	2806	2974	5056	265	1098
25972	16834	8507	5615	-2255	-2037	7130	138	647
36997	16783	12806	1732	4170	4241	9573	899	596
41394	25424	9792	591	8012	8077	10327	623	2191
242229	98856	65537	15479	77655	84677	45340	2469	18522
198475	74920	58267	13461	63676	71677	38348	2070	15193
61272	58435	16201	1556	16106	16827	17716	482	4009
6257	5409	2121	74	-257	-775	1082	69	15
12843	9052	3977	17	371	996	2660	176	172

8－08 全市限额以上住宿业和餐饮业

Main Financial Indicators of Living and Catering Services

单位：万元

项 目	Item	企业数（个） Number of Enterprises (unit)	年末资产负债 Assets and Liabilities 流动资产合计 Circulating Funds	# 存 货 Inventory	固定资产原价 Orginal Value of Fixed Assets
总 计	**Total**	**693**	**1080835**	**52882**	**1315539**
（一）按登记注册类型分组	**Grouped By Registered Type**				
1. 内资企业	**Domestic－funded Enterprises**	**657**	**767262**	**39276**	**982784**
国有企业	State－owned Enterprises	66	88226	4495	156628
集体企业	Collective－owned Enterprises	28	25488	685	62410
股份合作企业	Cooperative Enterprises	3	1063	44	1284
联营企业	Joint Ownership Enterprises	2	3178	150	2794
国有联营企业	State Joint Ownership Enterprises	－	－	－	－
集体联营企业	Collective Joint Enterprises	1	511	66	－
国有与集体联营企业	Joint State－collective Enterprises	1	2667	84	2794
其他联营企业	Other Joint Ownership Enterprises	－	－	－	－
有限责任公司	Limited Liability Corporations	172	221535	11373	358333
国有独资公司	State－funded Corporations	4	10184	1451	29618
其他有限责任公司	Other Limited Liability Corporations	168	211351	9922	328714
股份有限公司	Share－holding Corporations Ltd.	17	86836	2935	87022
私营企业	Private Enterprises	364	333636	19380	309990
私营独资企业	Private－funded Enterprises	30	10864	893	6961
私营合伙企业	Private Partnership Enterprises	14	7384	162	5773
私营有限责任公司	Private Limited Liability Corporations	302	271225	12823	274163
私营股份有限公司	Private Share－holding Corporations Ltd.	18	44163	5503	23094
其他企业	Other Enterprises	5	7301	215	4324
2. 港、澳、台商投资企业	**Enterprises With Investment from Hong Kong, Macao and Taiwan**	**20**	**265624**	**5595**	**237343**
合资经营企业（港或澳、台资）	Joint－venture Enterprises (With Funds from Hong Kong, Macao and Taiwan)	14	260093	5342	212637
合作经营企业（港或澳、台资）	Coorperative Enterprises (With Funds from Hong Kong, Macao and Taiwan)	－	－	－	－
港、澳、台商独资经营企业	Enterprises With Sole Investment from Hong Kong, Macao and Taiwan	6	5530	254	24707
港、澳、台商投资股份有限公司	Share－holding Corporations Ltd. With Investment from Hong Kong, Macao and Taiwan	－	－	－	－
3. 外商投资企业	**Enterprises With Foreign Investment**	**16**	**47950**	**8011**	**95411**
中外合资经营企业	Joint－venture Enterprises	8	38131	7301	74865
中外合作经营企业	Cooperation Enterprises	2	4251	436	16799
外资企业	Enterprises With Sole Foreign Investment	5	4383	243	3580
外商投资股份有限公司	Share－holding Corporations Ltd. With Foreign Investment	1	1185	31	167
（二）按国民经济行业分组	**Grouped By Sector**				
正餐	Dinner	288	2244061	190734	1525917
快餐	Short Order	19	243153	69490	607677
饮料及冷饮服务	Beverages and Services	16	174598	12099	30820
其他餐饮业	Others	7	38938	1718	53205

财务状况按注册类型、行业分(2009 年)

Enterprises Above Designated Size by Status of Registration and Sector(2009)

(10000 yuan)

累计折旧 Accumulated Depreciation	#本年折旧 Depreciation	资产合计 Total Assets	负债合计 Total Liabilities	所有者权益 Creditors' Equity	实收资本 Capital Hold	#国家资本 State Capital
717783	**109571**	**2933748**	**1973366**	**960382**	**843362**	**242629**
537545	**77252**	**2197805**	**1445195**	**752610**	**691758**	**215186**
113095	11502	290428	132460	157968	113419	109919
37478	5123	105789	70140	35649	36821	50
927	74	1586	882	704	784	–
3394	377	6159	1512	4647	6791	5691
–	–	–	–	–	–	–
–	–	511	736	-225	1100	–
3394	377	5648	776	4871	5691	5691
–	–	–	–	–	–	–
201974	28152	795721	508135	287585	258830	49025
19987	3214	136630	105001	31629	42100	8100
181988	24939	659091	403135	255957	216730	40925
48966	5222	201519	87308	114211	76056	47501
125972	26093	783262	639101	144161	193768	–
2792	662	18364	12898	5466	6784	–
2647	399	14305	13800	505	3120	–
114354	22671	670109	560953	109156	169130	–
6178	2362	80484	51450	29035	14734	–
5739	708	13341	5656	7685	5290	3000
138414	**18805**	**561590**	**401249**	**160341**	**106718**	**27443**
129174	16467	529748	364885	164863	92528	27443
–	–	–	–	–	–	–
9239	2338	31843	36364	-4522	14191	–
–	–	–	–	–	–	–
41825	**13513**	**174353**	**126922**	**47431**	**44885**	**–**
33884	13168	139491	76103	63388	33127	–
6876	618	24192	42111	-17919	3496	–
931	-280	9137	8301	835	7302	–
135	6	1533	407	1126	960	–
525994	118154	4182573	2894998	1287575	1048411	65210
294041	126112	1099202	762723	336479	236354	1210
18035	5258	226530	81541	144989	52793	2450
28146	2159	66525	24662	41863	17905	11970

项　目	Item	营业收入 Revenue of Business	主营业务收入 Main Revenue of Business	主营业务成本 Main Cost of Business	主营业务税金及附加 Business Tax and Extra Charges
总　计	**Total**	**2076085**	**2047612**	**936524**	**93846**
(一)按登记注册类型分组	**Grouped By Registered Type**				
1.内资企业	**Domestic-funded Enterprises**	**1264611**	**1242574**	**526688**	**67473**
国有企业	State-owned Enterprises	164028	161937	45885	8143
集体企业	Collective-owned Enterprises	32447	32161	9147	1895
股份合作企业	Cooperative Enterprises	3883	3883	2332	176
联营企业	Joint Ownership Enterprises	5826	5826	929	355
国有联营企业	State Joint Ownership Enterprises	-	-	-	-
集体联营企业	Collective Joint Enterprises	2544	2544	279	167
国有与集体联营企业	Joint State-collective Enterprises	3282	3282	650	188
其他联营企业	Other Joint Ownership Enterprises	-	-	-	-
有限责任公司	Limited Liability Corporations	346759	341296	115852	19345
国有独资公司	State-funded Corporations	12873	10866	2914	597
其他有限责任公司	Other Limited Liability Corporations	333886	330431	112939	18748
股份有限公司	Share-holding Corporations Ltd.	91648	90128	36234	4484
私营企业	Private Enterprises	609760	597272	313568	32471
私营独资企业	Private-funded Enterprises	23989	23964	12723	1432
私营合伙企业	Private Partnership Enterprises	10408	10323	5390	631
私营有限责任公司	Private Limited Liability Corporations	424163	411977	189363	23448
私营股份有限公司	Private Share-holding Corporations Ltd.	151201	151009	106093	6961
其他企业	Other Enterprises	10261	10071	2738	604
2.港、澳、台商投资企业	**Enterprises With Investment from Hong Kong, Macao and Taiwan**	**452106**	**447346**	**281021**	**8050**
合资经营企业(港或澳、台资)	Joint-venture Enterprises(With Funds from Hong Kong, Macao and Taiwan)	439727	435372	277423	7430
合作经营企业(港或澳、台资)	Coorperative Enterprises (With Funds from Hong Kong, Macao and Taiwan)	-	-	-	-
港、澳、台商独资经营企业	Enterprises With Sole Investment from Hong Kong, Macao and Taiwan	12379	11974	3598	620
港、澳、台商投资股份有限公司	Share-holding Corporations Ltd. With Investment from Hong Kong, Macao and Taiwan	-	-	-	-
3.外商投资企业	**Enterprises With Foreign Investment**	**359369**	**357693**	**128815**	**18324**
中外合资经营企业	Joint-venture Enterprises	313646	312951	110896	16076
中外合作经营企业	Cooperation Enterprises	33975	33786	12323	1693
外资企业	Enterprises With Sole Foreign Investment	9745	8964	3826	439
外商投资股份有限公司	Share-holding Corporations Ltd. With Foreign Investment	2003	1992	1771	116
(二)按国民经济行业分组	**Grouped By Sector**				
正餐	Dinner	5680852	5654698	334777	307887
快餐	Short Order	3360212	3344978	121327	173369
饮料及冷饮服务	Beverages and Services	341382	339468	16965	16443
其他餐饮业	Others	91398	84806	4984	2162

continued (10000 yuan)

主营业务利润 Main Profits of Business	营业费用 Expenses of Business	管理费用 Administration Cost	财务费用 Financial Cost	营业利润 Management Profits	利润总额 Total Profits	本年应付工资总额 Total Wages Payable	本年应付福利费总额 Total Welfare Expenses Payable	本年应交所得税 Income Tax
1017242	**558736**	**335650**	**54456**	**92742**	**123765**	**215719**	**13587**	**34462**
648413	**354468**	**263139**	**38236**	**11344**	**32447**	**153175**	**8672**	**11803**
107909	52642	45451	1286	10680	11453	26610	1884	2634
21118	12498	10141	758	-2058	-1984	4521	155	123
1375	535	731	4	106	769	507	15	211
4542	1824	2946	-34	-195	-195	1137	-	2
-	-	-	-	-	-	-	-	-
2098	916	1384	23	-225	-225	732	-	-
2444	908	1562	-57	30	30	405	-	2
-	-	-	-	-	-	-	-	-
206099	106217	89136	12588	883	3296	49399	3766	2777
7356	4559	5571	1383	-2879	-2519	3808	441	11
198744	101657	83565	11206	3761	5815	45592	3324	2765
49409	30896	14625	1481	3895	19420	15663	593	1372
251232	148095	95616	22051	-2518	-1068	53529	1936	4393
9809	7105	2277	238	225	338	2437	28	153
4302	3221	1011	356	-222	-169	1129	20	44
199166	114385	86926	20685	-11091	-9827	40355	1853	1785
37956	23385	5402	772	8570	8590	9609	35	2412
6728	1761	4494	102	551	755	1810	323	292
158274	**48589**	**55923**	**11907**	**46252**	**56292**	**25366**	**1448**	**11753**
150519	44724	50602	9860	49373	59379	23749	1311	11753
-	-	-	-	-	-	-	-	-
7756	3865	5321	2047	-3121	-3087	1617	137	-
-	-	-	-	-	-	-	-	-
210554	**155679**	**16588**	**4314**	**35145**	**35026**	**37178**	**3467**	**10906**
185980	134275	12601	2199	37279	37254	33046	3263	10847
19771	17684	1441	1985	-1152	-1295	999	204	-
4699	3720	2289	99	-804	-815	2856	-	59
105	-	258	30	-178	-119	278	-	-
1999040	1316381	520552	79620	96242	240320	529886	13483	49874
1958338	1440462	86115	21814	419344	413973	300990	26918	114403
153378	122041	32283	992	-136	5037	59429	7395	689
32800	16767	10150	3	12460	11832	11673	477	3589

8－09　全市限额以上住宿业和餐饮业经营按登记注册类型分(2009年)

Management Conditions of Living and Catering Services Enterprises Above Designated Size by Status of Registration(2009)

单位:万元　　　　(10000 yuan)

项　目	Item	法人企业(个) Number of Enterprises (unit)	营业收入 Revenue of Business	#客房收入 Revenue of Guest Rooms	#餐饮收入 Revenue of Catering Services	#商品销售收入 Revenue of Goods Sales
总　计	**Total**	**693**	**1710269**	**410379**	**1226177**	**12116**
1. 内资企业	**Domestic－funded Enterprises**	**657**	**1222495**	**341439**	**819089**	**9674**
国有企业	State－owned Enterprises	66	158394	73208	66861	3523
集体企业	Collective－owned Enterprises	28	32229	18392	10464	105
股份合作企业	Cooperative Enterprises	3	4251	754	2918	－
联营企业	Joint Ownership Enterprises	2	4978	2847	1897	－
国有联营企业	State Joint Ownership Enterprises	－	－	－	－	－
集体联营企业	Collective Joint Enterprises	1	2544	1533	777	－
国有与集体联营企业	Joint State－collective Enterprises	1	2434	1314	1120	－
其他联营企业	Other Joint Ownership Enterprises	－	－	－	－	－
有限责任公司	Limited Liability Corporations	172	324652	124463	177624	3666
国有独资公司	State－funded Corporations	4	12304	7304	4320	33
其他有限责任公司	Other Limited Liability Corporations	168	312348	117158	173304	3634
股份有限公司	Share－holding Corporations Ltd.	17	86056	19022	62524	883
私营企业	Private Enterprises	364	601675	98248	491677	1376
私营独资企业	Private－funded Enterprises	30	24067	2298	21191	44
私营合伙企业	Private Partnership Enterprises	14	10398	1762	8552	1
私营有限责任公司	Private Limited Liability Corporations	302	416337	90665	314975	1330
私营股份有限公司	Private Share－holding Corporations Ltd.	18	150873	3522	146959	2
其他企业	Other Enterprises	5	10261	4506	5125	121
2. 港、澳、台商投资企业	**Enterprises With Investment from Hong Kong, Macao and Taiwan**	**20**	**128647**	**61640**	**61185**	**90**
合资经营企业(港或澳、台资)	Joint－venture Enterprises(With Funds from Hong Kong, Macao and Taiwan)	14	116269	57680	53279	89
合作经营企业(港或澳、台资)	Coorperative Enterprises (With Funds from Hong Kong, Macao and Taiwan)	－	－	－	－	－
港、澳、台商独资经营企业	Enterprises With Sole Investment from Hong Kong, Macao and Taiwan	6	12379	3961	7906	1
港、澳、台商投资股份有限公司	Share－holding Corporations Ltd. With Investment from Hong Kong, Macao and Taiwan	－	－	－	－	－
3. 外商投资企业	**Enterprises With Foreign Investment**	**16**	**359127**	**7300**	**345902**	**2352**
中外合资经营企业	Joint－venture Enterprises	8	313562	5744	303309	2269
中外合作经营企业	Cooperation Enterprises	2	33814	753	33034	－
外资企业	Enterprises With Sole Foreign Investment	5	9748	804	7568	83
外商投资股份有限公司	Share－holding Corporations Ltd. With Foreign Investment	1	2003	－	1992	－

8-10 全市限额以上住宿业和餐饮业经营按国民经济行业分(2009年)

Management Conditions of Living and Catering Services Enterprises Above Designated Size by Sector(2009)

单位:万元 (10000 yuan)

项　目	Item	法人企业(个) Number of Enterprises (unit)	营业收入 Revenue of Business	#客房收入 Revenue of Guest Rooms	#餐饮收入 Revenue of Catering Services	#商品销售收入 Revenue of Goods Sales
总　计	**Total**	**693**	**1710269**	**410379**	**1226177**	**12116**
住宿业	**Acommodations**	**363**	**765929**	**396369**	**307767**	**9269**
旅游饭店	Restaurants for Junketing	261	689135	341803	290265	9103
一般旅馆	General Hotel	102	76795	54566	17503	166
其他住宿服务	Other Acommodations	–	–	–	–	–
餐饮业	**Catering Services**	**330**	**944339**	**14010**	**918409**	**2847**
正餐	Dinner	288	566039	13864	545513	510
快餐	Short Order	19	335976	–	335086	–
饮料及冷饮服务	Beverages and Services	16	33648	–	29841	2337
其他餐饮业	Others Catering Services	7	8676	147	7970	–

8 – 11 个体工商业登记注册情况(2009 年末)
Statistics of Individual Owned Business(End of 2009)

项 目	Item	全 市 Whole Municipality		市 区 Urban District	
		合 计 Total	#城 镇 Urban	合 计 Total	#城 镇 Urban
户数(户)	**Number of Households (household)**	**284561**	**210015**	**199407**	**164973**
农、林、牧、渔业	Farming, Forestry, Animal Husbandry and Fishery	3379	1433	2369	1191
采矿业	Mining and Quarrying	139	44	17	8
制造业	Manufacturing	20219	7692	11041	4672
电力、燃气及水的生产和供应业	Production and Supply of Electricity, Gas and Water	104	65	64	55
建筑业	Construction	723	389	450	285
交通运输、仓储和邮政业	Transportation, Storage and Post	8343	4329	5704	3122
信息传输、计算机服务和软件业	Information Transmission, Computer Services and Software	537	431	370	339
批发和零售业	Wholesale and Retail Trade & Catering Services	194234	151192	141028	121927
住宿和餐饮业	Accommodations and Catering	21782	16658	13382	11653
房地产业	Real Estate	245	236	196	193
租赁和商务服务业	Renting and Business Service	1706	1398	1301	1077
居民服务和其他服务业	Service for the Residents and Other Service Sector	31239	24536	22232	19326
卫生、社会保障和社会福利业	Health Care, Sports & Social Welfare	263	190	129	112
文化、体育和娱乐业	Culture, Sports and Entertainment	1417	1222	938	850
其他行业	Others	231	200	186	163
从业人员(人)	**Employed Persons(person)**	**597761**	**420766**	**348500**	**292408**
农、林、牧、渔业	Farming, Forestry, Animal Husbandry and Fishery	30231	3104	4521	2221
采矿业	Mining and Quarrying	730	207	38	13
制造业	Manufacturing	66159	22001	25164	10306
电力、燃气及水的生产和供应业	Production and Supply of Electricity, Gas and Water	168	89	75	64
建筑业	Construction	2426	983	1295	556
交通运输、仓储和邮政业	Transportation, Storage and Post	11224	6081	6858	3985
信息传输、计算机服务和软件业	Information Transmission, Computer Services and Software	1140	936	740	691

8－11 续表 continued

项 目	Item	全 市 Whole Municipality		市 区 Urban District	
		合 计 Total	#城 镇 Urban	合 计 Total	#城 镇 Urban
批发和零售业	Wholesale and Retail Trade & Catering Services	316577	244067	220895	194300
住宿和餐饮业	Accommodations and Catering	59330	47879	35233	31927
房地产业	Real Estate	399	382	318	312
租赁和商务服务业	Renting and Business Service	3567	3003	2705	2306
居民服务和其他服务业	Service for the Residents and Other Service Sector	100489	87431	47405	42726
卫生、社会保障和社会福利业	Health Care, Sports & Social Welfare	722	565	411	381
文化、体育和娱乐业	Culture, Sports and Entertainment	3947	3481	2344	2181
其他行业	Others	652	557	498	439
注册资金(万元)	**Capital Registered(10000 yuan)**	**1335548**	**986126**	**866618**	**723215**
农、林、牧、渔业	Farming, Forestry, Animal Husbandry and Fishery	66395	27664	41261	20335
采矿业	Mining and Quarrying	6071	2073	218	170
制造业	Manufacturing	148727	58535	70707	33352
电力、燃气及水的生产和供应业	Production and Supply of Electricity, Gas and Water	493	218	203	168
建筑业	Construction	14242	4480	5648	2148
交通运输、仓储和邮政业	Transportation, Storage and Post	65017	39853	40100	27662
信息传输、计算机服务和软件业	Information Transmission, Computer Services and Software	3064	2352	1275	1206
批发和零售业	Wholesale and Retail Trade & Catering Services	712597	592583	518645	467404
住宿和餐饮业	Accommodations and Catering	143536	121553	81328	75504
房地产业	Real Estate	810	647	698	547
租赁和商务服务业	Renting and Business Service	11923	9165	8359	6427
居民服务和其他服务业	Service for the Residents and Other Service Sector	137472	103825	84996	75883
卫生、社会保障和社会福利业	Health Care, Sports & Social Welfare	2825	2207	1358	1238
文化、体育和娱乐业	Culture, Sports and Entertainment	21247	20055	11032	10556
其他行业	Others	1129	916	790	615

8－12 私营企业登记注册情况(2009 年末)
Statistics of Private Owned Business(End of 2009)

项目	Item	全市 Whole Municipality		市区 Urban District	
		合计 Total	#城镇 Urban	合计 Total	#城镇 Urban
户数(户)	**Number of Households (household)**	**140938**	**98296**	**116690**	**89984**
农、林、牧、渔业	Farming, Forestry, Animal Husbandry and Fishery	1734	598	1053	438
采矿业	Mining and Quarrying	221	39	36	15
制造业	Manufacturing	37685	12923	24791	10245
电力、燃气及水的生产和供应业	Production and Supply of Electricity, Gas and Water	344	78	99	43
建筑业	Construction	6316	4833	5468	4369
交通运输、仓储和邮政业	Transportation, Storage and Post	2520	1641	2207	1506
信息传输、计算机服务和软件业	Information Transmission, Computer Services and Software	7670	7162	7283	6918
批发和零售业	Wholesale and Retail Trade & Catering Services	46949	37712	41613	35418
住宿和餐饮业	Accommodations and Catering	2093	1700	1703	1463
房地产业	Real Estate	3681	2827	2935	2325
租赁和商务服务业	Renting and Business Service	16295	15186	15357	14462
居民服务和其他服务业	Service for the Residents and Other Service Sector	6752	5575	5994	5104
卫生、社会保障和社会福利业	Health Care, Sports & Social Welfare	258	207	223	177
文化、体育和娱乐业	Culture, Sports and Entertainment	687	624	603	570
其他行业	Others	7733	7191	7325	6931
从业人员(人)	**Employed Persons(person)**	**1309253**	**917568**	**988274**	**826842**
农、林、牧、渔业	Farming, Forestry, Animal Husbandry and Fishery	12209	4893	6210	3214
采矿业	Mining and Quarrying	3428	670	724	206
制造业	Manufacturing	429553	147821	202952	112964
电力、燃气及水的生产和供应业	Production and Supply of Electricity, Gas and Water	2800	880	704	515
建筑业	Construction	63271	51833	51020	44346
交通运输、仓储和邮政业	Transportation, Storage and Post	22514	16442	17269	13272
信息传输、计算机服务和软件业	Information Transmission, Computer Services and Software	66904	63658	64967	62307

8－12 续表 continued

项　　目	Item	全市 Whole Municipality 合计 Total	全市 Whole Municipality #城镇 Urban	市区 Urban District 合计 Total	市区 Urban District #城镇 Urban
批发和零售业	Wholesale and Retail Trade & Catering Services	377369	325493	342484	306125
住宿和餐饮业	Accommodations and Catering	23158	20650	19070	17625
房地产业	Real Estate	31322	26794	24620	21484
租赁和商务服务业	Renting and Business Service	145529	138510	137891	132162
居民服务和其他服务业	Service for the Residents and Other Service Sector	51669	45262	45921	41436
卫生、社会保障和社会福利业	Health Care, Sports & Social Welfare	2170	1814	1835	1532
文化、体育和娱乐业	Culture, Sports and Entertainment	6347	5778	5430	5218
其他行业	Others	71010	67070	67177	64436
注册资金（万元）	**Capital Registered (10000 yuan)**	**32369376**	**23721138**	**26671504**	**21022946**
农、林、牧、渔业	Farming, Forestry, Animal Husbandry and Fishery	297181	108360	187644	74767
采矿业	Mining and Quarrying	80538	33354	22707	21132
制造业	Manufacturing	8761217	3397918	5931138	2614472
电力、燃气及水的生产和供应业	Production and Supply of Electricity, Gas and Water	80449	31021	27803	17983
建筑业	Construction	2374865	1822667	2062235	1599888
交通运输、仓储和邮政业	Transportation, Storage and Post	458252	324474	396026	297153
信息传输、计算机服务和软件业	Information Transmission, Computer Services and Software	1044916	1028151	1023736	1012935
批发和零售业	Wholesale and Retail Trade & Catering Services	7601264	6660819	6865395	6239659
住宿和餐饮业	Accommodations and Catering	391379	325946	267564	242519
房地产业	Real Estate	2967478	2491097	2281949	1958597
租赁和商务服务业	Renting and Business Service	4902812	4365112	4649604	4165901
居民服务和其他服务业	Service for the Residents and Other Service Sector	799190	705803	676545	622720
卫生、社会保障和社会福利业	Health Care, Sports & Social Welfare	34703	34059	25263	24679
文化、体育和娱乐业	Culture, Sports and Entertainment	135856	125488	119177	118424
其他行业	Others	2439276	2266869	2134818	2012117

主要统计指标解释

社会消费品零售额 指各种经济类型的批发零售贸易业、住宿餐饮业和其他行业对城乡居民和社会集团的消费品零售额总和。这个指标反映通过各种商品流通渠道向居民和社会集团供应的生活消费品来满足他们生活需要，是研究人民生活，社会消费品购买力、货币流通等问题的重要指标。社会消费品零售额包括：(1)售给城乡居民作为生活用的商品和修建房屋用的建筑材料；(2)售给机关、团体、学校、部队、企业、事业单位的职工食堂和旅店（招待所）附设专门供本店旅客食用，不对外营业的食堂和各种食品、燃料；企业、单位和国营农场直接售给本单位职工和职工食堂的自己生产的产品；(3)售给部队干部、战士生活用的粮食、副食品、衣着品、日用品、燃料；(4)售给来华的外国人、华侨、港澳台同胞的消费品；(5)居民自费购买的中、西药品、中药材及医疗用品；(6)报社、出版社直接售给居民和社会集团的报纸、图书、杂志、集邮公司出售的新、旧纪念邮票、特种邮票、首日封、集邮册、集邮工具等；(7)旧货寄售商店自购、自销部分的商品；(8)煤气公司、液化石油气站售给居民和社会集团的煤气灶具和罐装液化石油气；(9)售给社会集团的办公用品、纸张、帐册、文印用品、计算工具、书刊杂志和奖品；公共用品和纺织品、针织品；学校用的教学用具；文体用品；非专用的劳动保护用品，如工作服、套袖、围群、手套、毛巾、肥皂等；日用百货和杂品，包括职工食堂用的餐具、炊具、设备和清洁卫生工具等；家具、设备、日用电器、电讯设备、电影器材和照相器材等；取暖用的设备和燃料、防暑、降温的饮料；非生产经营用的交通工具如小轿车、面包车、工具车、卡车和油料；零星修理的各种零配件、材料、工具、建筑材料等；举办各种招待会、茶话会、宴会用的烟酒茶和各种食品及馈赠的礼品；从公费医疗经费中开支的中、西药品、中药材和医疗器材以及其他非生产性设备和用品。

限额以上批发零售贸易业 指批发贸易业年销售额在2000万元及以上，零售贸易业年销售额在500万元及以上的各种经济类型商贸企业。

商品销售总额 指对本企业（单位）以外的单位和个人出售（包括对国（境）外直接出口）的商品金额。这个指标反映批发零售贸易业在国内市场上销售商品以及出口商品的总量。商品销售总额包括：(1)售给城乡居民和社会集体团消费用的商品；(2)售给工业、农业、建筑业、运输邮电业、批发零售贸易业、餐饮业、服务业等作为生产、经营使用的商品；(3)售给批发零售贸易业作为转卖或加工后转卖的商品；(4)对国（境）外直接出口的商品，不包括：出售本企业（单位）自用的废旧包装用品，未通过买卖行为付出的商品，经本单位介绍，由买卖双方直接结算，本单位只收取手续费的业务，购货退出的商品以及商品损耗和损失等。

Explanatory Notes on Main Statistical Indicators

Total Retail Sales of Consumer Goods refer to the sum of retail sales of consumer goods sold by wholesale and retail, catering and other sectors to urban and rural residents and social groups. This indicator is used to show the supply of consumer goods through various channels to households and institutions, and is very important for the study on people' s livelihood, on the purchasing power of consumer goods and on the circulation of money. The retail sales of consumer goods include: (1) commodities sold to urban and rural residents for their daily use and building materials sold to them for the construction or repair of houses; (2) food and fuels sold to canteens of institutions, enterprises, schools, military units and to canteens of hotels and hostels that only serve their guest, and commodities produced by enterprises, institutions or state farms and sold directly to their employees or their canteens; (3) grains and non – staple food, clothing, daily articles and fuels sold to military personnel; (4) consumer goods sold to foreigners, overseas Chinese, and Chinese compatriots form Taiwan, Hong Kong and Macao during their stay in the mainland of China; (5) Chinese and Western medicines, herbs and medical facilities purchased by residents; (6) newspapers, books and magazines directly sold to residents and social groups by publishers, new and old commemorative stamps, special stamps, first – day covers, stamp albums and other stamp – collection articles sold by stamp companies; (7) consumer goods purchased and then sold by second – hand shops; (8) stoves and other heating facilities and liquefied gas sold by gas companies to households and institutions; and (9) commodities sold to social groups. included under this heading are : office appliances, paper, account books, printing articles, calculaters, newspapers, magazines and prizes; public articles, textiles and knitgoods; realias for schools; cultural and sports articles; working articles for unspecial use i. e. working clothes, raglan sleeves, gloves, towels and soaps; commidities and miscellaneous goods for daily use i. e. dishwares, cookers and cleaning articles for canteens of institutions, enterprises, schools; furnishings, appliances, communications facilities , film and photograph equipments and materials; heating facilities, fuels and beverages; vehicles (exclude for business use) such as cars, microbuses, trucks and oils; parts , fittings, instruments and building materials, tobaccoes, alcohols, teas, foods for all kinds of reception meetings and banquets and prizes for presenting; Chinese and Western medicines, herbs and medical facilities expenditured by medical insurance fund and other non – production goods and equipments.

Wholesale And Retail Trade Above Designated Size wholesale trade, with annual sales over 20 million yuan of different status of registration; retail sale trade, with annual sales over 5 million yuan of different status of registration.

Total Sales of Commodities refer to selling of commodities by the establishments to other establishments and individuals (including direct export). This indictor is used to show the total value of sales of commodities at domestic markets and export. The total sales include: (1) commodities sold to urban and rural residents and social groups for their consumption; (2) commodities sold to establishments in industry, agriculture, construction, transportation, post and telecommunications, wholesale and retail trades, catering trade and public utility for their production and operation; (3) commodities sold to wholesale and retail establishment for re – selling, with or without further processing; and (4) commodities for direct export to other countries. Excluded are selling of waste packaging materials used by the establishments (units) themselves, commodities transferred without buying or selling procedures, commission income from brokerage in transactions whose settlement is directly handled by buyers and sellers, rejected commodities in the purchase, loss in commodities, etc.

第九篇
CHAPTER-9

对外经济、旅游
FOREIGN TRADE AND TOURISM

对外经济、旅游
Foreign Trade and Tourism

主要统计指标
Major Statistical Indicators

协议利用外资金额	Total Contracted Foreign Investments	69.65	亿美元	(USD 100 million)
为上年	As Compared with the Preceding Year	111.8	%	(%)
实际利用外资金额	Foreign Investments Actually Used	40.14	亿美元	(USD 100 million)
为上年	As Compared with the Preceding Year	121.2	%	(%)
进出口总额	Total Imports and Exports	404.17	亿美元	(USD 100 million)
为上年	As Compared with the Preceding Year	84.1	%	(%)
# 出口总额	Total Exports	271.80	亿美元	(USD 100 million)
为上年	As Compared with the Preceding Year	80.9	%	(%)
接待境外旅游	Number of Foreign Tourists	230.40	万人次	(10000 person-times)
为上年	As Compared with the Preceding Year	104.1	%	(%)
旅游外汇收入	Total Foreign Exchange Earnings from International Tourism	13.80	亿美元	(USD 100 million)
为上年	As Compared with the Preceding Year	106.5	%	(%)

9-01 主要年份外商直接投资情况
Foreign Direct Investment in Main Years

单位:万美元 (USD 10000)

年份 Year	项目个数(个) Number of Projects (unit)	协议总投资额 Total Investments of Agreements	协议利用外资金额 Foreign Investments of Agreements	实际利用外资金额 Foreign Investments Actually Used
1978	–	–	–	–
1979	–	–	–	–
1980	3	153	128	–
1981	–	–	–	–
1982	–	–	–	–
1983	2	356	100	–
1984	9	6932	2697	–
1985	21	6638	1731	907
1986	9	5722	2017	683
1987	10	2685	1256	1470
1988	23	6781	2734	696
1989	34	3897	1569	1860
1990	68	7817	3951	751
1991	121	11107	5551	2129
1992	583	125224	60915	9678
1993	1078	222325	121947	35713
1994	624	174406	110541	41098
1995	427	136662	90207	42659
1996	221	108150	70982	53651
1997	174	51682	27888	41187
1998	216	98219	51400	38425
1999	212	83416	56742	42025
2000	315	89781	64548	43093
2001	483	154447	103023	50324
2002	587	247888	96720	52186
2003	869	432660	200104	100850
2004	802	629727	307746	140982
2005	756	770941	400503	171274
2006	747	1080602	537986	225536
2007	574	854907	558059	280181
2008	483	862523	622788	331154
2009	554	948323	696486	401370

注:2002 年起协议外资和实际外资按新口径计算。

a) From 2002, investments of agreements and foreign investments actually uesd counted with new standard.

9－02 外商投资企业分国别(地区)情况(2009年)
Foreign－Funded Enterprises by Region or Territory(2009)

单位:万美元 (USD 10000)

国别(地区)	Country (territory)	历年累计 Accumulated 项目(个) Projects (unit)	历年累计 Accumulated 总投资额 Total Investments	历年累计 Accumulated 协议外资金额 Total Contracted Foreign Investments	2009年 In Year 2009 项目(个) Projects (unit)	2009年 In Year 2009 总投资额 Total Investments	2009年 In Year 2009 协议外资金额 Total Contracted Foreign Investments
合计	**Total**	**10036**	**7130482**	**4203584**	**554**	**948323**	**696486**
#香港	#Hong Kong	4059	3520640	2136916	263	581853	413670
澳门省	Macao	64	38397	25752	－	－33	8
台湾	Taiwan	1318	290181	157179	41	12288	6746
日本	Japan	648	335484	169444	23	26288	10984
美国	U. S. A	1338	689197	394208	68	97846	75802
新加坡	Singapore	256	260274	138527	13	39611	20956
澳大利亚	Australia	162	73894	46056	11	14523	14014
泰国	Thailand	36	12799	3483	1	－959	194
意大利	Italy	182	101252	53244	4	9860	9804
荷兰	Netherlands	75	63087	25841	3	9853	6187
西班牙	Spain	58	52807	19740	4	19730	5822
马来西亚	Malaysia	67	27699	15598	4	1118	978
韩国	Republic of Korea	256	67872	37141	13	6138	5130
法国	France	101	61767	31176	4	4924	4592
玻利维亚	Bolivia	12	1770	1262	－	－	－
加拿大	Canada	165	62548	37355	11	4409	4773
英国	Britain	143	135764	68957	21	17778	14047
奥地利	Austria	19	9286	5328	－	－	1500
波兰	Poland	4	240	147	－	－	－
洪都拉斯	Honduras	6	1118	563	－	－	－
德意志联邦国	Federal states	171	86804	43231	6	4224	3798
英属维尔京群岛	The British Virgin Islands	471	840848	473258	29	85484	35569

9-03 外商直接投资分区县(市)情况
Foreign Direct Investment by Region

单位:万美元　　　　(USD 10000)

区域	Region	批准项目数(个) Number of Projects(unit)		协议利用外资金额 Total Contracted Foreign Investments		实际利用外资金额 Foreign Investments Actually Used	
		2009年 In Year 2009	历年累计 Accumulated Until the End of 2009	2009年 In Year 2009	历年累计 Accumulated Until the End of 2009	2009年 In Year 2009	历年累计 Accumulated Until the End of 2009
全市	**Total**	**554**	**10036**	**696486**	**4203584**	**401370**	**2110143**
市区	Urban District	483	8289	598376	3624514	355179	1851705
上城	Shangcheng	36	513	42199	228460	32018	118147
下城	Xiacheng	37	599	42579	202753	18218	89811
江干	Jianggan	25	538	43057	234752	18703	84415
拱墅	Gongshu	46	738	42594	248661	20001	105848
西湖	Xihu	55	694	44198	234770	23493	127272
高新(滨江)区	Hi-Tech(Binjiang)	53	799	82377	431390	52756	272205
萧山	Xiaoshan	68	1174	67400	380240	47296	198382
余杭	Yuhang	81	1140	63930	348605	28068	154915
桐庐	Tonglu	15	419	19934	101644	10470	46916
淳安	Chun'an	13	150	19000	99499	9170	43362
建德	Jiande	10	183	2774	65012	572	22469
富阳	Fuyang	22	621	33227	193071	15516	91692
临安	Lin'an	11	374	23175	119844	10463	53999

9－04 国内招商引资分区县(市)情况
Domestic Attract Investment by Region

单位:亿元 (100 million yuan)

区 域	Region	批准项目数(个) Number of Projects(unit)		协议引进资金 Total Contracted Foreign Investments		实际引进资金 Foreign Investments Actually Used	
		2009 年 In Year 2009	2008 年 In Year 2008	2009 年 In Year 2009	2008 年 In Year 2008	2009 年 In Year 2009	2008 年 In Year 2008
全 市	**Total**	**5451**	**5210**	**1287.02**	**1090.7**	**560.55**	**473.13**
市 区	Urban District	5133	4922	1090.05	924.53	475.32	399.04
上 城	Shangcheng	471	501	143.29	121.09	61.23	51.28
下 城	Xiacheng	876	642	167.78	140.37	71.71	57.14
江 干	Jianggan	490	580	139.28	110.42	62.76	52.2
拱 墅	Gongshu	1796	2076	165.03	128.79	70.54	59.44
西 湖	Xihu	832	658	124.12	120.62	64.62	53.76
高新(滨江)区	Hi－Tech(Binjiang)	238	132	121.01	98.59	57.16	47.57
萧 山	Xiaoshan	257	202	83.77	71.43	37.47	33.04
余 杭	Yuhang	41	68	74.21	70.35	28.44	25.67
桐 庐	Tonglu	117	49	39.91	34.94	16.96	16.15
淳 安	Chun'an	59	56	38.95	32.22	16.96	13.81
建 德	Jiande	37	105	39.25	33.18	16.58	13.67
富 阳	Fuyang	72	41	39.51	33.61	17.67	16.01
临 安	Lin'an	33	37	39.35	32.22	17.06	14.45

9-05 国家级开发区建设发展情况(2009 年末)
The Construction of National - Class Development Zones(End of 2009)

项目	Item	合计 Total	杭州经济技术开发区 Hangzhou Economic and Technological Development Zone	杭州高新技术开发区 Hangzhou High - tech Development Zone	杭州之江国家旅游度假区 Hangzhou Zhijiang National Tourism and Holiday Resort	萧山经济技术开发区 Xiaoshan Economic and Technological Development Zone
规划面积(平方公里)	Area of planning (sq. km)	224.74	34	12.64	156	22.1
已开发面积(平方公里)	Area of Development (sq. km)	86.63	37.94	12.64	10.45	25.6
有偿出让土地面积(平方公里)	Area of Being Sold (sq. km)	46.07	17.42	6.76	8.23	13.66
累计由开发区投入基础设施款(亿元)	Investments in Infrastructure (100 million yuan)	313.35	166.01	104.51	29.41	13.42
年末批准进区企业(个)	Number of Enterprises Approved (unit)	7026	2894	3231	82	819
其中:三资企业 (个)	Foreign Investments Enter - prises (unit)	1634	559	518	69	488
累计协议利用外资(亿美元)	Foreign Investments of Agree-ments (USD 100 million)	165.4	76.55	44.16	10.52	34.17
累计实际利用外资(亿美元)	Foreign Investments Actually Used (USD 100 million)	87.43	35.71	26.22	6.44	19.06
年末投产企业个数(个)	Number of Enterprises in Pro-duction or Operation (unit)	4977	2426	1476	20	1055
当年销售收入(亿元)	Sales Revenue (100 million yuan)	3282.83	1202.83	1450	4	626
当年工业总产值(现价) (亿元)	Gross Industrial Output Value (100 million yuan)	2579.04	1078.97	980	48.07	472
当年实现利税(亿元)	Fulfilled Profits and Tax (100 million yuan)	153.9	61.9	72	-	20
当年出口创汇(亿美元)	Foreign Exchange Earmings of Export (USD 100 million)	72	35	22	-	15
当年财政收入(亿元)	Financial Revenue (100 million yuan)	181.21	69.4	71.9	9.29	30.62

9－06　主要年份进出口情况

Imports and Exports in Main Years

单位:亿美元　　(USD 100 million)

年　份 Year	进出口 Exports And Imports		出口 Exports		进口 Imports	
	总值 Total Value	为上年% As Compared with the Preceding Year(%)	总值 Total Value	为上年% As Compared with the Preceding Year(%)	总值 Total Value	为上年% As Compared with the Preceding Year(%)
1978	-	-	-	-	-	-
1979	-	-	-	-	-	-
1980	-	-	-	-	-	-
1981	-	-	-	-	-	-
1982	-	-	-	-	-	-
1983	-	-	-	-	-	-
1984	-	-	-	-	-	-
1985	-	-	-	-	-	-
1986	-	-	-	-	-	-
1987	-	-	-	-	-	-
1988	-	-	-	-	-	-
1989	0.84	-	0.50	-	0.34	-
1990	1.45	172.6	0.99	198.0	0.46	135.3
1991	2.18	150.3	1.48	149.5	0.70	152.2
1992	3.42	156.9	2.16	146.0	1.26	180.0
1993	8.73	255.3	4.92	227.8	3.81	302.4
1994	34.96	400.5	26.11	530.7	8.85	232.3
1995	45.18	129.2	33.18	127.1	12.00	135.6
1996	43.52	96.3	31.11	93.8	12.41	103.4
1997	48.83	112.2	37.43	120.3	11.40	91.8
1998	59.73	122.3	44.16	118.0	15.57	136.6
1999	73.40	122.9	50.79	115.0	22.61	145.3
2000	104.76	142.7	69.65	137.1	35.11	155.3
2001	112.98	107.9	72.84	104.6	40.14	114.3
2002	131.07	116.0	84.81	116.4	46.26	115.3
2003	182.38	139.2	109.55	129.2	72.83	157.4
2004	244.96	134.3	151.75	138.6	93.21	128.0
2005	298.70	121.9	198.04	130.5	100.66	108.0
2006	389.09	130.3	262.28	132.4	126.81	126.0
2007	434.26	111.7	299.66	114.3	134.60	106.2
2008	480.65	110.7	336.14	112.2	144.51	107.4
2009	404.20	84.1	271.80	80.9	132.40	91.6

9-07 进出口情况(2009 年)
Imports and Exports(2009)

单位:亿美元 (USD 100 million)

项目	Item	2009 年 In Year 2009	2008 年 In Year 2008	为上年(%) As Compared with year 2008 (%)
全市进出口总值(海关口径)	Total Exports And Imports	404.20	480.47	84.1
一、出口总额	Exports	271.80	335.99	80.9
1. 国有企业	State-owned Enterprises	67.63	89.36	75.7
2. 三资企业	Foreign Investment Enterprises	94.20	120.48	78.2
(1)中外合作企业	Cooperation Enterprises	0.80	1.14	69.7
(2)中外合资企业	Joint-Venture Enterprises	46.19	62.55	73.8
(3)外商独资企业	Enterprises With Sole Foreign Investment	47.22	56.78	83.2
3. 集体企业	Collective-owned Enterprises	13.10	19.99	65.5
4. 私营企业	Private Enterprises	96.49	105.88	91.1
二、进口总额	Imports	132.40	144.47	91.6

9－08 外贸出口分区县(市)情况(2009 年)
Export of Foreign Trade by Region(2009)

单位:万美元 (USD 10000)

区 域 Region		出口总值 Exports of This Year	为上年(%) As Compared with the Preceding Year(%)	进口总值 Imports of This Year	为上年(%) As Compared with the Preceding Year(%)
全市合计	**Total**	**2717961**	**80.9**	**1332030**	**91.6**
#不含省属	#Non－provincial	2121432	81.1	992989	82.6
上 城	Shangcheng	74658	90.5	63616	90.3
下 城	Xiacheng	86353	73.8	65848	53.1
江 干	Jianggan	95064	85.7	14314	83.2
拱 墅	Gongshu	52077	93.6	25584	99.2
西 湖	Xihu	112939	83.7	25531	82.2
高新(滨江)区	Hi－Tech(Binjiang)	164559	85.4	66854	81.0
萧 山	Xiaoshan	561665	83.5	268162	95.6
余 杭	Yuhang	257195	86.1	28301	116.1
桐 庐	Tonglu	52824	81.9	7240	99.8
淳 安	Chun'an	8918	88.3	3121	114.5
建 德	Jiande	59281	66.3	18189	140.2
富 阳	Fuyang	56165	87.4	59993	95.9
临 安	Lin'an	61133	100.1	9322	65.3

9－09　出口企业自营出口前20位排名(2009年)

The List of First Twenty Foreign Trade Enterprises(2009)

单位:万美元　　(USD 10000)

企业名称	Name of Enterprises	位次 Ranks	出口额 Export Value
东芝信息机器(杭州)有限公司	Toshiba Information Equipment (Hangzhou) Co., Ltd.	1	73582
杭州中策橡胶有限公司	Hangzhou Zhongce Rubber Co. Ltd.	2	56848
杭州市轻工工艺纺织品进出口有限公司	Hangzhou Hardicrafts and Textiles Import and Export Corporation	3	25658
杭州巨星科技有限公司	Hangzhou Greatstar Indnserial Co.,Ltd.	4	22137
杭州东信移动电话有限公司	Hangzhou Eastcom Cellular Phone Co.,Ltd.	5	20509
浙江新安化工集团股份有限公司	Zhejiang Wynca Chemical Group Co., Ltd.	6	19391
博世电动工具(中国)有限公司	Bosch Power Tools(China) Co.,Ltd	7	18748
杭州市矢崎配件有限公司	HZ YAZAKI	8	17105
杭州华三通信技术有限公司	H3C	9	16514
杭州余杭国际贸易有限公司	Hangzhou Yuhang International Trade Co. Ltd.	10	15900
杭州摩托罗拉移动通信设备有限公司	Hangzhou Motorola Mobile Telecomunications Equipment Co. Ltd.	11	15733
杭州松下家用电器有限公司	Hangzhou Panasonic Home Appliances Washing Machine Co.,Ltd.	12	14400
杭州余杭对外贸易有限公司	Hangzhou Yuhang Foreign Trade Co.,Ltd.	13	14321
汉帛(中国)有限公司	Hempel (China) Co. Ltd.	14	12522
万向进出口有限公司	Wanxiang Import and Export Co.,Ltd	15	11082
UT斯达康通讯有限公司	UT－Starcom Co. Ltd.	16	10934
杭州市对外经济贸易服务有限公司	Hangzhou Foreign Economic Relations&Trade Service Co.,Ltd	17	10742
泰尔茂医疗产品(杭州)有限公司	TERUMO Medical Prodrlts(Hangzhou)Co.,Ltd	18	10148
杭州松下住宅电器设备有限公司	Hangzhou Panasonic Home Appliances Co.,Ltd.	19	9691
杭州市粮油食品土畜产进出口有限公司	Hangzhou Grain,Oil, Food, Native Products and Livestock Products Import and Export Co. Ltd.	20	9385

9－10 外贸出口主要国别(地区)情况
Export of Trade by Main Country or Territory

单位:万美元 (USD 10000)

国 别(地区)	Country (territory)	2009 年 In Year 2009	2008 年 In Year 2008	为上年(%) As Compared with the Preceding Year(%)
合 计	**Total**	**2717961**	**3359819**	**80.9**
#香港	#Hong Kong	96597	94395	102.3
台湾	Taiwan	28897	38696	74.7
德国	The Federal Republic of Germany	171904	202326	85.8
日本	Japan	248159	278938	89.0
美国	U. S. A	577419	750802	76.9
新加坡	Singapore	26237	48108	54.5
澳大利亚	Australia	62193	73224	84.9
泰国	Thailand	27684	30507	90.7
意大利	Italy	89900	115552	77.8
荷兰	Netherlands	85084	101666	83.7
西班牙	Spain	58407	82281	71.0
马来西亚	Malaysia	24850	27664	89.8
韩国	Republic of Korea	58721	105285	55.8
法国	France	69533	77047	90.2
比利时	Belgium	37556	43894	85.6
加拿大	Canada	56509	71390	79.2
英国	Britain	107030	116995	91.5
印度尼西亚	Indonesia	31339	38880	80.6
丹麦	Denmark	22797	32063	71.1
俄罗斯	Russia	37108	57890	64.1

9－11　主要年份旅游事业发展情况
Development of Tourism in Main Years

年　份 Year	旅游总收入（亿元）Total Tourism Revenue（100 million yuan）	国内旅游收入（亿元）Domestic Earnings（100 million yuan）	旅游外汇收入（亿美元）Foreign Exchange Earnings from International Tourism（USD 100 million）	旅游总人数（万人次）Total Tourists（10000 person－times）	国内游客人数（万人次）Domestic Tourists（10000 person－times）
1978	－	－	0.07	－	－
1979	－	－	0.10	－	－
1980	－	－	0.11	－	－
1981	－	－	0.13	－	－
1982	－	－	0.13	－	－
1983	－	－	0.14	－	－
1984	－	－	0.15	－	－
1985	－	－	0.23	－	－
1986	－	－	0.36	－	－
1987	－	－	0.38	－	－
1988	－	－	0.47	－	－
1989	－	－	0.23	－	－
1990	－	－	0.48	－	－
1991	－	－	0.66	－	－
1992	－	－	0.86	－	－
1993	－	－	0.80	－	－
1994	－	－	1.01	－	－
1995	106.0	94.3	1.45	2148	2104
1996	136.5	122.6	1.67	2055	2009
1997	158.8	142.1	2.01	2150	2100
1998	163.4	146.0	2.10	2172	2121
1999	186.0	166.7	2.37	2266	2207
2000	214.3	190.0	2.92	2376	2305
2001	249.7	218.9	3.37	2592	2510
2002	294.4	254.8	4.77	2758	2652
2003	325.9	290.9	4.22	2862	2776
2004	410.1	361.2	5.97	3139	3016
2005	465.1	403.6	7.58	3417	3266
2006	543.7	471.2	9.09	3864	3682
2007	630.1	548.6	11.19	4320	4112
2008	707.2	617.2	12.96	4773	4552
2009	803.1	708.9	13.80	5324	5094

9-12 主要年份境外旅游者人数

Number of International Tourists in Main Years

单位:人次 (person-times)

年份 Year	合计 Total	外国人 Foreigners	华侨 Overseas Chinese	港澳台同胞 Compatriots from Hong Kong, Macao and Taiwan	平均逗留天数 Average days of Staying
1978	53475	728	728	26648	-
1979	84914	44714	1069	39131	2.59
1980	124960	61710	1868	61382	2.70
1981	154745	87727	2004	65014	2.71
1982	152897	89100	2483	61314	2.49
1983	160564	97803	3136	59625	2.18
1984	179200	105771	2514	70915	2.12
1985	238385	156311	7011	75063	2.18
1986	266370	170960	8318	87092	2.38
1987	300603	183477	17048	100078	2.38
1988	349246	149512	39989	159745	2.08
1989	248502	66094	18819	163589	2.08
1990	388345	86621	33593	268131	2.09
1991	390197	136809	23698	229690	2.00
1992	489578	183781	38541	267256	2.03
1993	459620	199796	25184	234640	2.06
1994	337362	201692	11324	124346	2.10
1995	441262	249418	14608	177236	2.06
1996	462313	273477	9991	178845	2.07
1997	504276	288949	10060	205267	2.20
1998	507243	261353	14281	231609	2.20
1999	591853	324625	9250	257978	2.09
2000	707148	400906	-	306242	2.15
2001	819438	447689	-	371749	2.41
2002	1056266	631576	-	424690	2.50
2003	861163	482073	-	379090	2.72
2004	1234063	791616	-	442447	2.59
2005	1513585	1020840	-	492745	2.63
2006	1820171	1236792	-	583379	2.57
2007	2085997	1453650	-	632347	2.67
2008	2213329	1543665	-	669654	2.73
2009	2304045	1572838	-	731207	2.87

注:从1995年起为全市数。

a) Data in this table has included the tourists of whole minicipality since 1995.

9－13　接待境外游客及旅游外汇收入情况

Number of International Tourists and Foreign Exchange Earnings

项　　目	Item	2009年 In Year 2009	2008年 In Year 2008	为上年(%) As Compared with year(%)
全年接待人数总计(人)	**Number of Foreign Tourists(person)**	**2304045**	**2213319**	**104.1**
#外国人	#Foreigners	1572838	1543665	101.9
港澳台同胞	Compatriots From Hong Kong, Macao and Taiwan	731207	669654	109.2
全年接待人天数(人天)	**Total Person－days (person－days)**	**6617700**	**6033256**	**109.7**
#外国人	#Foreigners	4381824	4076108	107.4
港澳台同胞	Compatriots From Hong Kong, Macao and Taiwan	2235876	1957148	114.2
平均逗留天数(天)	**Average Days of Staying (days)**	**2.87**	**2.73**	**105.1**
#外国人	#Foreigners	2.79	2.64	105.7
港澳台同胞	Compatriots From Hong Kong, Macao and Taiwan	3.06	2.92	104.8
旅游外汇总收入(万美元)	**Total Foreign Exchange Earnings From International Tourism (USD 10000)**	**137995**	**129610**	**106.5**

9－14 接待境外游客分国别(地区)情况

Number of International Tourists by Country or Territory

单位:人次 (person－times)

国 别(地区)	Country (territory)	2009 年 In Year 2009	2008 年 In Year 2008	为上年(%) As Compared with the Preceding Year(%)
合 计	**Total**	**1572838**	**2213319**	**101.2**
#香港	#Hong Kong	278358	264195	105.4
澳门	Macao	17106	11990	142.7
台湾	Taiwan	435743	393469	110.7
日本	Japan	293732	292575	100.4
美国	U. S. A	126360	127849	98.8
新加坡	Singapore	48472	45181	107.3
澳大利亚	Australia	28340	30273	93.6
泰国	Thailand	58284	57932	100.6
意大利	Italy	22635	21679	104.4
荷兰	Netherlands	13124	14096	93.1
西班牙	Spain	21824	22166	98.5
马来西亚	Malaysia	80939	78556	103.0
韩国	Republic of Korea	418922	436562	96.0
法国	France	34561	32495	106.4
德国	Germany	49787	43220	115.2
加拿大	Canada	26807	29621	90.5
英国	Britain	32789	28967	113.2
印度尼西亚	Indonesia	22821	30216	75.5
印度	India	17795	16388	108.6
菲律宾	Filipine	11631	9279	125.4

主要统计指标解释

外商直接投资 是指外国企业和经济组织或个人(包括华侨、港澳台胞以及我国在境外注册的企业)按我国有关政策、法规,用现汇、实物、技术等在我国境内开办外商独资企业、与我国境内的企业或经济组织共同举办中外合资经营企业、合作经营企业或者合作开发资源的投资(包括外商投资收益的再投资)以及经政府有关部门批准的项目投资总额内,企业从境外借入的资金。

进出口总额 海关进出口总额指实际进出我国国境的货物总金额。包括对外贸易实际进出口货物,来料加工装配进出口货物,国家间、联合国及国际组织无偿援助物资和赠送品,华侨、港澳台同胞和外籍华人捐赠品,租赁期满归承租人所有的租赁货物,进料加工进出口货物,边境地方贸易及边境地区小额贸易进出口货物(边民互市贸易除外),中外合资经营企业、中外合作经营企业、外商独资经营企业进出口货物和公用物品,到、离岸价格在规定限额以上的进出口货样和广告品(无商业价值、无使用价值和免费提供出口的除外),从保税仓库提取在中国境内销售的进口货物,以及其他进出口货物。进出口总额以观察一个国家在对外贸易方面的总规模。我国规定出口货物按离岸价格统计,进口货物按到岸价格统计。

境外旅游人数 指来我国参观、访问、旅行、探亲、访友、休养、考察、参加会议和从事经济、科技、文化、教育、体育、宗教等活动的外国人、华侨、港澳和台湾同胞的人数。不包括外国在我国的常驻机构,如使领馆、通讯社、企业办事处的工作人员;来我国常住的外国专家、留学生以及在岸逗留不过夜人员。

境外旅游(外汇)收入 指入境旅游的外国人、华侨、港澳台同胞在中国大陆旅游过程中发生的一切旅游支出,对国家来说就是境外旅游(外汇)收入。

Explanatory Notes on Main Statistical Indicators

Direct Investment by Foreign Entrepreneurs refers to the investments inside China by foreign enterprises and economic organizations or individuals (including overseas Chinese, compatriots from Hong Kong, Macao and Taiwan, and Chinese enterprises registered abroad), following the relevant policies and laws of China, for the establishment of ventures exclusively with foreign own investment, Sino – foreign joint ventures and cooperative enterprises or for co – operative exploration of resources with enterprises or economic organizations in China. It includes the re – investment of the foreign entrepreneurs with the profits gained from the investment and the funds that enterprises borrow from abroad in the total investment of projects which are approved by the relevant department of the government.

Total Imports and Exports at Customs refer to the value of commodities imported into and exported from the boundary of China. They include the actual imports and exports through foreign trade, imported and exported goods under the processing and assembling trades and materials, supplies and gifts as aid given gratis between governments and by the United Nations and other international organizations, and contributions donated by overseas Chinese, compatriots in Hong Kong, Macao and Chinese foreign citizenship, leasing commodities owned by tenant at the expiration of leasing period, the imported and exported commodities processed with imported materials, commodities trading in border areas (excluding mutual exchange goods), the imported and exported commodities and articles for public use of the Sino – foreign joint ventures, cooperative enterprises and ventures exclusively with foreign own investment. Also included are import or export of samples and advertising goods for whose CIF or FOB value are beyond the permitted ceiling (excluding goods of no trading or use value and free commodities for export), imported goods sold in China from bonded warehouses and other imported or exported goods. The indicator of the total imports and exports at customs can be used to observe the total size of external trade in a country. In accordance with the stipulation of Chinese government, imports are calculated at CIF, while exports are calculated at FOB.

International Tourists refer to foreigners, overseas Chinese compatriots from Hong Kong, Macao and Taiwan coming to China for sightseeing, visits, tours, family reunions, vacations, study tours, conferences and other activities of a business, scientific and technological, cultural, educational and religious nature. It does not include representatives and employees of resident institutions of foreign countries in China such as embassies, consulates, news agencies and offices of foreign companies and organizations, nor does it include long – term foreign experts or students residing in China, or persons in transition without spending a night in China.

Foreign Exchange Earnings from International Tourism refer to the total expenditures of foreigners, overseas Chinese, Chinese compatriots from Hong Kong, Macao and Taiwan during their stay in the mainland of China, which are earnings of foreign exchange form international tourism from the point of vies from China.

第十篇
CHAPTER-10

财政、金融、保险
FINANCE,BANKING AND INSURANCE

财政、金融、保险
Finance, Banking and Insurance

主要统计指标
Major Statistical Indicators

全市财政总收入	Total Financial Revenue	1019.43	亿元	(100 million yuan)
为上年	As Compared with the Preceding Year	112.0	%	(%)
地方财政收入	Financial Revenue of Local Government	520.79	亿元	(100 million yuan)
为上年	As Compared with the Preceding Year	114.4	%	(%)
地方财政支出	Financial Expenditure of Local Government	490.40	亿元	(100 million yuan)
为上年	As Compared with the Preceding Year	116.9	%	(%)
年末金融机构各项存款余额	Balance of Deposits of Financial Institutions at Year-end	14284.21	亿元	(100 million yuan)
为上年	As Compared with the Preceding Year	126.0	%	(%)
#城乡居民储蓄存款余额	Balance of Savings Deposits of Rural and Urban Residents at Year-end	4286.92	亿元	(100 million yuan)
为上年	As Compared with the Preceding Year	123.3	%	(%)
年末金融机构各项贷款余额	Balance of Loans of Financial Institutions at Year-end	13113.30	亿元	(100 million yuan)
为上年	As Compared with the Preceding Year	130.3	%	(%)

10-01 主要年份财政收入及支出

Financial Revenue and Expenditure in Main Years

单位:万元 (10000 yuan)

年份 Year	财政收入 Financial Revenue		财政支出 Financial Expenditure	
	全市 Total	市区 Urban District	全市 Total	市区 Urban District
1978	94102	73396	16170	7779
1979	103259	81885	20334	11289
1980	118529	94015	21726	11867
1981	128564	100645	23964	13891
1982	140510	107298	24945	13687
1983	153941	116559	32765	17822
1984	172996	130757	46937	28710
1985	186472	131923	57710	35435
1986	205952	141943	73213	43959
1987	226262	152268	70717	41011
1988	246961	161208	95655	53031
1989	255003	156649	113571	61534
1990	252503	149904	118167	62587
1991	267597	158130	123134	62403
1992	286394	168341	132814	65984
1993	394946	233670	185168	90545
1994	484597	300014	215415	102430
1995	551262	339828	249050	120084
1996	635334	414557	302390	151016
1997	740725	485650	363834	197054
1998	869824	585615	424478	237221
1999	1026577	689394	563524	335243
2000	1428519	970937	734328	445698
2001	1884608	1612225	1049330	849479
2002	2571408	2235021	1410199	1166298
2003	3297091	2861459	1635948	1340463
2004	3957516	3488744	1956282	1602303
2005	5207930	4584112	2383344	1957619
2006	6244906	5484645	2754809	2254347
2007	7884237	6929667	3357153	2747060
2008	9105489	7991043	4196674	3454599
2009	10194264	8965758	4903983	4000324

注:从 2001 年起市区数据包括萧山区和余杭区。

a) Data of urban district include Xiaoshan and Yuhang district since 2001.

10－02 分县(市)

Local Financial

单位:万元

指标 Item \ 年份 year	全市 Total 2009	全市 Total 为上年(%) As Compared with Year 2008(%)	市区 Urban District 2009	市区 Urban District 为上年(%) As Compared with Year 2008(%)
合计 Total	**10194264**	**112.0**	**8965758**	**112.2**
一、地方财政收入 Local Financial Revenue	5207899	114.4	4535191	114.2
(一)税收收入 Tax Revenue	5043428	113.6	4416399	113.5
1.增值税 Value added Tax	856311	112.1	723591	112.7
2.营业税 Business Tax	1764472	122.8	1578220	122.6
3.企业所得税 Enterprises´Income Tax	747259	91.7	679992	92.3
4.企业所得税退税 Company Income Tax Rebates	－51	37.0	－51	37.0
5.个人所得税 Individual Income Tax	321063	117.8	286066	118.9
6.城市维护建设税 City Construction and Maintenance Tax	306234	106.0	268910	106.6
7.耕地占用税 Tax on the Use of Arable Land	67004	134.8	49444	123.1
8.契税 Contract Tax	483118	135.9	427102	134.2
9.房产税 Real Estate Tax	162043	109.9	143100	108.7
10.其他税收 Others Tax	335975	109.1	260025	106.7
(二)非税收入 Non－tax Revenue	164471	142.0	118792	147.9
1.专项收入 Special Revenue	134919	113.0	111200	114.7
其中:教育费附加 Revenue from Extra－Charges for Education	120509	113.4	101544	113.5
排污费 Revenue for Permitting Pollution	14339	110.8	9656	128.2
2.行政事业性收费收入 Income from Administrative Fees	9320	382.0	7524	－
3.罚没收入 Penalty and Confiscatory Income	119330	116.9	86593	111.4
4.国有资本经营收入 Seate－owned Assets Profits	－105678	90.4	－91978	90.1
其中:国有计划亏损补贴 Subsides to Loss－making of state－owned Enterprises	－105678	90.4	－91978	90.1
5.国有资源(资产)有偿使用收入 Compensation for the Use of Seate－owned Assets Income	6517	75.0	5419	72.9
6.其他收入 Others Revenue	63	32.0	34	37.8
二、上划中央二税 Revenue of Central Government	3383959	115.8	2981555	116.8
1.消费税 Consumption Tax	815026	129.2	810784	129.5
2.国内增值税 Value－added Tax	2568933	112.1	2170771	112.7
三、中央所得税 Central Government Income Tax	1602406	98.3	1449012	98.9
1.企业所得税 Enterprises Income Tax	1120812	91.7	1019913	92.3
2.个人所得税 Individual Income Tax	481594	117.8	429099	118.9

注:发展速度按同口径计算。

财政收入(2009 年)
Revenue by Region(2009)

(10000 yuan)

#萧山区 Xiaoshan	#余杭区 Yuhang	桐庐县 Tonglu	淳安县 Chun'an	建德市 Jiande	富阳市 Fuyang	临安市 Lin'an
1370808	**1000679**	**176351**	**95695**	**200336**	**501056**	**255068**
695281	596701	95011	55893	105736	275699	140369
659637	577711	87778	49614	100684	254469	134484
165806	85638	19350	7530	23021	56348	26471
201874	211613	27880	20387	25733	71648	40604
74683	69982	10307	6403	10068	25145	15344
-34	-	-	-	-	-	-
34687	24832	5143	2929	6645	12166	8114
41092	31430	4569	2258	6162	15292	9043
3906	14167	1852	588	6852	7579	689
50123	71143	8344	3313	7255	21236	15868
30706	9575	2448	2019	3054	8232	3190
56794	59331	7885	4187	11894	36823	15161
35644	18990	7233	6279	5052	21230	5885
19687	12985	3171	1455	3474	10882	4737
16052	11483	2693	1261	2717	8525	3769
3635	1502	478	194	757	2286	968
-	-	-	779	780	42	195
21728	12042	3903	3731	5387	12933	6783
-6779	-6999	-	-	-4700	-3000	-6000
-6779	-6999	-	-	-4700	-3000	-6000
974	962	159	285	111	373	170
34	-	-	29	-	-	-
511523	261757	58166	25805	69531	169391	79511
14106	4844	116	3214	468	347	97
497417	256913	58050	22591	69063	169044	79414
164004	142221	23174	13997	25069	55966	35188
111973	104973	15460	9604	15102	37717	23016
52031	37248	7714	4393	9967	18249	12172

a) The developing speed is calculated with the same standard.

单位:万元

指 标 Item	全 市 Total		市 区 Urban District	
	2009	为上年(%) As Compared with Year 2008(%)	2009	为上年(%) As Compared with Year 2008(%)
合 计 Total	**4903983**	**116.9**	**4000324**	**115.8**
一、一般公共服务 Expenditure for General Public Services	710542	109.6	573202	110.9
二、外交 Expenditure for Foreign Affairs	－	－	－	－
三、国防 Expenditure for National Defense	6772	110.7	5574	108.6
四、公共安全 Expenditure for Public Security	341886	110.2	281782	109.7
其中:公安 Public Security Departments	251964	110.9	212112	110.5
五、教育 Expenditure for Education	862769	116.2	633369	116.2
其中:教育费附加支出 Expenditure on Extra－Charges for Educations	88854	100.4	77502	109.0
六、科学技术 Expenditure for Science and Technology	220721	119.0	186783	117.8
七、文化体育与传媒 Expenditure for Culture,Sports and Media	121959	90.0	105530	87.5
八、社会保障和就业 Expenditure for Social Safety Net and Employment Effort	485469	120.4	409177	120.4
其中:行政事业单位离退休 Retired Persons in Adminiserative Department	154700	146.6	136987	147.6
九、医疗卫生 Expenditure for Medical and Health Care	323644	124.7	247574	124.0
十、环境保护 Expenditure for Environmental Protection	97518	130.3	62682	134.7
其中:排污费支出 Sewage Expenses	14302	110.3	7023	74.2
自然生态保护 Nataral Ecological Proteceion	40095	167.6	25427	214.6
十一、城乡社区事务 Expenditure for Urban and Rural Community Affairs	789148	115.6	746105	114.8
十二、农林水事务 Expenditure for Agriculture, Forestry and water Conservancy	254489	119.2	142277	114.2
十三、交通运输 Expenditure for Trarssportation	188390	－	157238	－
十四、采掘电力信息等事务 Expenditure for Mining,Power,Information and Others	264084	118.6	244471	115.4
十五、粮油物资储备等管理事务 Expenditure for Grrain and Ovl Reservation,and Other Materials Management Services	79848	135.9	67215	123.1
十六、金融监管支出 Expenditure for Financial Supervision	93	66.0	－	－
十七、地震灾后恢复重建支出 Expenditure for Post－earthquake Recorery and Reconstruction	25165	136.6	21641	140.5
十八、其他支出 Other Expenditure	131486	71.9	115704	70.8

财政支出(2009 年)
Expenditure by Region(2009)

(10000 yuan)

#萧山区 Xiaoshan	#余杭区 Yuhang	桐庐县 Tonglu	淳安县 Chun'an	建德市 Jiande	富阳市 Fuyang	临安市 Lin'an
650678	**580629**	**142678**	**151915**	**146030**	**273521**	**189515**
80854	76562	20566	25225	21984	36151	33414
–	–	–	–	–	–	–
1746	993	424	64	361	–	349
40008	31780	10012	9511	9198	18380	13003
32464	24175	6867	6435	6231	12352	7967
159813	115032	29485	35748	36229	81621	46317
17484	10531	2937	672	3010	29	4704
19312	19390	4744	3000	7058	10913	8223
12393	12191	3536	2748	2546	4309	3290
48765	42740	10345	10184	9552	29826	16385
2296	83	23	1546	183	13758	2203
50548	36679	12325	14156	12680	22606	14303
10597	17369	5479	7396	4887	9601	7473
833	1586	767	100	399	5164	849
6008	4285	1856	4378	3088	2342	3004
91483	56495	9106	5239	8375	11082	9241
48309	42948	17193	21072	20059	33862	20026
38293	51399	8553	6113	4119	5261	7106
32042	29464	6058	1709	1099	5666	5081
6685	12810	2350	3031	2252	1354	3646
–	–	47	–	46	–	–
6318	–	–	–	–	2358	1166
3512	34777	2455	6719	5585	531	492

10－04　主要年份全市金融机构存、贷款余额

Balance of Deposits and Loans of Financial Institutions in Main Years

单位：万元　　(10000 yuan)

年份 Year ＼ 项目 Item	各项存款 Deposits	#城乡储蓄存款 Savings Deposits Of Urban and Rural Residents	#城镇储蓄存款 Savings Deposits of Urban Residents	各项贷款 Loans
1978	86824	20714	17056	136759
1979	108998	28937	22640	135713
1980	180707	40447	30896	174153
1981	226949	51440	38889	236678
1982	262156	67192	50113	216040
1983	303130	86635	64736	236203
1984	388305	115766	85439	329195
1985	484999	159596	115592	580180
1986	635514	222110	153572	769841
1987	776105	302762	207505	967477
1988	839680	351943	241839	1145989
1989	1017087	501592	346318	1338984
1990	1646165	697515	479031	1803266
1991	2036334	904490	616308	2136903
1992	2652966	1144737	763309	2651983
1993	3469954	1563328	1048413	3415527
1994	5061345	2394370	1642498	4450932
1995	7079650	3423379	2448787	5672105
1996	9619291	4638458	3459439	7434243
1997	12251840	5583306	4229591	9388500
1998	14948225	6701158	5155548	11620537
1999	17886717	7425967	5760527	14937506
2000	20884723	7885579	6151084	16866431
2001	26215100	9418400	7396800	20877000
2002	33731500	11834000	9492300	27523800
2003	46527300	15899600	13079600	38187000
2004	57072000	18351700	15016100	48000400
2005	67487200	21916600	17960100	55453000
2006	78555500	25552400	20789600	66038600
2007	93109600	26348300	21154300	84306800
2008	113333500	34765900	27584600	100690500
2009	142842104	42869189	34027871	131133023

注：1989 年以前数据均为银行机构存贷款，1990 年及以后年份数据为调整后金融机构存贷款，2003 年始金融机构存贷款为本外币合并数据。2007 年起金融机构数据含国家开发银行。2008 年起为含外资金融机构存贷款本外币合并数据。

a) Data before 1989 belongs to banking system, data after 1990 adjusted for deposits and loans of financial institutions, data of 2003 include both RMB and foreign currency. The data of financial institutions included the State Development Bank since 2007. The date in this table cornhined RMB and foreign currency deposits and loans including foreign financial institutions since day.

10－05　主要年份市区金融机构存、贷款余额

Balance of Deposits and Loans of Financial Institutions of Urban District in Main Years

单位:万元　(10000 yuan)

年份 Year ＼ 项目 Item	各项存款 Deposits	#城乡储蓄存款 Savings Deposits of Urban and Rural Residents	#城镇储蓄存款 Savings Deposits of Urban Residents	各项贷款 Loans
1978	58372	13774	13246	101144
1979	73720	18055	17241	98792
1980	134275	24702	23282	121231
1981	172721	31358	29345	170539
1982	198350	39756	37047	142091
1983	226160	50439	46833	155297
1984	293145	66108	61934	194977
1985	359825	89114	82868	418214
1986	458142	115818	106703	557763
1987	565429	156704	142642	714313
1988	610601	180341	163466	846998
1989	737388	256238	229518	1000731
1990	1062574	354316	297390	1271779
1991	1309462	451756	397322	1469671
1992	1695011	572660	479248	1774158
1993	2263969	762234	662234	2298124
1994	3383877	1242379	1085363	3033010
1995	4851774	1853512	1639875	3907199
1996	6828786	2734904	2371657	5350499
1997	8831147	3287475	2873638	6772221
1998	10785066	3905602	3440607	8615412
1999	13051806	4336058	3835542	11462505
2000	15436286	4620235	4101716	13105849
2001	23765400	7976400	6460200	19237800
2002	30638400	10139800	8370100	25476700
2003	42522000	13834200	11693000	30297500
2004	52542100	16014700	13479900	44517600
2005	62249500	19231800	16208400	51455900
2006	72269600	22391800	18737800	61190700
2007	86197300	23124600	19132300	78456200
2008	104930100	30665200	24996500	93838100
2009	131800234	37837816	30801878	121473548

注:1989 年以前数据均为银行机构存贷款,1990 年及以后年份数据为调整后金融机构存贷款。2003 年始金融机构存贷款为本外币合并数据。2007 年起金融机构数据含国家开发银行。2008 年起为含外资金融机构存贷款本外币合并数据。

a) Data before 1989 belongs to banking system, data after 1990 adjusted for deposits and loans of financial institutions. data of 2003 include both RMB and foreign currency. The data of financial institutions included the State Development Bank since 2007. The date in this table cornhined RMB and foreign currency deposits and loans including foreign financial institutions since day.

10－06 金融机构

Balance of Deposits and

单位:万元

指 标	Item	全 市 Total		市 区 Urban District	
		2009 年末 At the End of Year 2009	为上年(%) As Compared with the Preceding Year(%)	2009 年末 At the End of Year 2009	为上年(%) As Compared with the Preceding Year(%)
一、各项存款	**Deposits**	**142842104**	**126.0**	**131800234**	**125.6**
1. 企事业单位存款	Deposits of Enterprises	68763637	146.5	65157025	146.5
(1)活期存款	Current Deposits	33620272	142.1	31369824	141.4
(2)定期存款	Fixed Deposits	35143365	151.0	33787201	151.5
2. 储蓄存款	Savings Deposits	42869189	123.3	37837816	123.4
(1)活期储蓄	Current Deposits	14739214	130.3	12543478	130.6
(2)定期储蓄	Fixed Deposits	28129975	119.9	25294338	120.1
3. 信托存款	Trust Deposits	-	-	-	-
4. 委托存款	Entrusting Deposits	1762822	129.6	1753128	129.6
5. 其他存款	Other Deposits	29446456	97.3	27052265	95.2
二、各项贷款	**Loans**	**131133023**	**130.3**	**121473548**	**129.5**
1. 短期贷款	Short－term Loans	56943814	118.8	51675944	117.6
2. 中长期贷款	Medium and Long term Loans	63547623	144.0	59498163	143.3
3. 信托贷款	Trust Loans	-	-	-	-
4. 委托贷款	Entrusting Loans	1136477	143.8	1136477	143.8
5. 其他贷款	Other Loans	3879306	131.1	3831817	130.9
6. 票据融资	Note Financing	5458237	114.8	5168832	113.5
7. 各项垫款	Advance Money	167566	209.4	162315	200.4

本外币存、贷款余额(2009年)
Loans of Financial Institutions(2009)

(10000 yuan)

#萧山区 Xiaoshan	#余杭区 Yuhang	桐庐县 Tonglu	淳安县 Chun'an	建德市 Jiande	富阳市 Fuyang	临安市 Lin'an
19080059	**9799782**	**1703888**	**1229195**	**1773213**	**4044174**	**2291400**
7328477	3943091	489979	363347	565138	1416707	771441
3531625	2246094	322165	288385	379806	799214	460878
3796852	1696997	167814	74962	185332	617493	310563
7035886	3735637	864375	548408	931597	1669455	1017538
2086295	1192999	341460	233787	347623	750720	522146
4949591	2542638	522915	314621	583974	918735	495392
–	–	–	–	–	–	–
47997	12962	532	1829	667	5953	713
4667699	2108092	349002	315611	275811	952059	501708
16332204	**7704354**	**1339181**	**886847**	**1343813**	**3956108**	**2133526**
11861868	3926906	617838	336686	615859	2470173	1227314
3776024	3492805	691788	536342	679226	1259842	882262
–	–	–	–	–	–	–
–	–	–	–	–	–	–
326240	9132	15557	4576	10566	13800	2990
345069	267726	13188	9243	38162	208232	20580
23003	7785	810	–	–	4061	380

10－07 金融机构人民币

Balance of RMB Deposits, RMB Loans, Cash Income

单位:万元

指 标	Item	全 市 Total		市 区 Urban District	
		2009 年	为上年(%) As Compared with the Preceding Year(%)	2009 年	为上年(%) As Compared with the Preceding Year(%)
一、年末各项存款余额	**Deposits(End of 2009)**	**140591584**	**126.1**	**129624478**	**125.7**
1. 企业存款	Deposits from Enterprises	67289917	147.1	63732967	147.0
2. 财政存款	Treasury Deposits	4465148	115.0	4150812	111.3
3. 机关团体部队存款	Deposits from Government, Groups Troops	4530511	138.7	3933228	133.8
4. 城乡储蓄存款	Agencies and Organizations from Rural and Urban	42235849	123.5	37227915	123.6
5. 农业存款	Agricultural Deposits	3498636	137.5	2863143	134.8
6. 委托存款	Entrusting Deposits	1753313	129.2	1743629	129.2
7. 其他存款	Other Deposits	16818210	82.2	15972784	81.9
二、年末各项贷款余额	**Loans(End of 2009)**	**126878624**	**129.7**	**117272536**	**128.8**
1. 短期贷款	Short－term Loans	55950197	118.2	50688225	117.0
#工业贷款	#Loans for Industrial	15917834	109.2	13963435	106.7
商业贷款	Commercial Loans	5925903	108.3	5724345	107.5
建筑业贷款	Constructional Loans	2318888	119.2	2219233	119.6
农业贷款	Agricultural Loans	2588057	100.3	1683333	97.2
乡镇企业贷款	Loans to Township Enterprises	5882181	125.7	4947768	125.6
三资企业贷款	Loans to Sino－foreign Joint Venture and Cooperative Enterprises and Foreign－funded Enterprises	1424882	98.5	1355377	97.7
私营企业及个体贷款	Loans to Private Enterprises and Individuals	3440423	139.5	3317575	138.4
2. 中长期贷款	Medium and Long Term Loans	62279871	142.8	58230410	142.0
#基本建设贷款	#Loans for Capital Construction	26951900	126.9	25173848	124.9
技术改造贷款	Loans for Innovation	357108	124.3	325158	134.6
其他中长期贷款	Other Medium and Long Term Loans	34970863	158.3	32731404	158.8
3. 委托贷款	Entrusting Loans	1134620	143.9	1134620	143.9
4. 票据融资	Note Financing	5456945	114.8	5167541	113.5
5. 其他贷款	Other Loans	2056991	153.1	2051740	152.6
附:个人消费贷款	Loans for Individual Consumption	19678781	156.6	17906727	156.9
三、现金收入	**Cash Income**	**169840598**	**105.0**	**139688647**	**106.3**
其中:商品销售收入	Income from Commodity sales	18856212	105.8	15459569	103.8
四、现金支出	**Cash Expenditure**	**168165624**	**105.2**	**137284186**	**106.7**
其中:工资性支出	Wsges	8493780	98.3	7169003	94.7
五、货币投放(＋)回笼(－)	**Currency Issuance (withdraw)**	**－1674974**	**85.4**	**－2404461**	**86.2**

存、贷款余额及现金收支(2009 年)

and Expenditure of Financial Institutions(2009)

(10000 yuan)

#萧山区 Xiaoshan	#余杭区 Yuhang	桐庐县 Tonglu	淳安县 Chun'an	建德市 Jiande	富阳市 Fuyang	临安市 Lin'an
18862621	**9734308**	**1695718**	**1219630**	**1761808**	**4027737**	**2262213**
7158903	3895490	486812	356268	558506	1408508	746856
331398	137424	48138	75200	40143	76796	74059
376509	410411	83389	147489	80931	148445	137029
6996163	3722889	859388	545923	927595	1661638	1013390
1020807	511098	126097	76061	57418	278742	97175
47768	12881	532	1829	667	5943	713
2931073	1044115	91362	16860	96548	447665	192991
15909005	**7693726**	**1323624**	**882062**	**1330310**	**3939555**	**2130537**
11782070	3926564	617837	336478	612923	2467420	1227314
4549651	846284	163855	52524	224637	1017481	495902
529732	344022	26014	17231	19491	99794	39028
503550	59484	12040	1910	18165	53155	14385
738912	396637	162985	147342	136861	234819	222717
1941097	912838	123381	44689	69327	566582	130434
485706	137075	–	–	–	69505	–
653044	329533	14084	11923	14124	60824	21893
3775064	3492805	691788	536342	679226	1259842	882263
1226300	1227528	302840	237200	386593	501478	349941
59900	37000	10600	–	5500	10800	5050
2488864	2228277	378348	299142	287133	747564	527272
–	–	–	–	–	–	–
345070	267726	13189	9242	38161	208232	20580
6801	6631	810	–	–	4061	380
1203524	1130708	256019	254848	219787	622461	418939
31543231	**15900698**	**4783326**	**2123168**	**4122753**	**12070639**	**7052065**
4304973	1834184	245260	124024	318877	1976599	731883
32107994	**16135628**	**4855220**	**2081461**	**4138259**	**12520006**	**7286492**
1416941	1017728	206878	111680	247912	418675	339632
564763	**234930**	**71894**	**-41707**	**15506**	**449367**	**234427**

10－08　城乡居民储蓄存款余额(2009 年)

Balance of Savings Deposits of Rural and Urban Residents(2009)

单位:万元　　　　(10000 yuan)

地区	Region	总计 Total		城镇居民 Urban Residents		农村居民 Rural Residents	
		2009 年末 At the End of Year 2009	为上年(%) As Compared with the Preceding Year(%)	2009 年末 At the End of Year 2009	为上年(%) As Compared with the Preceding Year(%)	2009 年末 At the End of Year 2009	为上年(%) As Compared with the Preceding Year(%)
全　市	**Total**	**42869189**	**123.3**	**34027871**	**123.4**	**8841318**	**123.1**
市　区	Urban District	37837816	123.4	30801878	123.2	7035938	124.1
萧山区	Xiaoshan	7035886	126.5	4370556	126.8	2665330	126.0
余杭区	Yuhang	3735637	123.9	2223991	124.9	1511646	122.5
桐庐县	Tonglu	864375	119.5	560980	120.2	303395	118.1
淳安县	Chun'an	548408	120.4	338054	122.6	210354	117.0
建德市	Jiande	931597	126.8	681944	128.7	249653	121.9
富阳市	Fuyang	1669455	125.3	1012293	128.4	657162	120.9
临安市	Lin'an	1017538	119.0	632722	120.0	384816	117.4

注:2003 年始为本外币合并储蓄存款余额。

a) Data in this table include both RMB and foreign currency since 2003.

10－09 保险业务情况(2009 年)
Development of Insurance Business(2009)

单位:万元 (10000 yuan)

指 标	Item	保险费收入 Premium	赔付金额 Indemnity Expenditure
全市总计	**Total**	**1596920**	**498892**
为上年%	As Compared with the Preceding Year＝100(%)	109.2	104.4
一、财产保险	Property Insurance	595627	301359
企业财产险	Enterprise Property Insurance	47776	21469
家庭财产险	Family Property Insurance	1655	989
机动车辆险	Transportation Equipment Insurance	462797	233587
工程险	Project Insurance	6947	1279
责任险	Responsibilihty Insurance	12128	5865
信用险	Export Credit Insurance	39395	24346
保证险	Guarantee Insurance	－1872	925
船舶险	Shipping Insurance	8159	3153
货运险	Cargo Insurance	11544	5810
特殊风险保险	Special Pisks Insurance	3105	2233
农业保险	Agriculture Insurance	3548	1714
其他险	Other	445	－11
二、人身险	Personal Insurance	1001293	197533
寿险	Life Insurance	889904	163362
意外伤害险	Accidental Insurance	35879	7763
健康险	Health Insurance	75510	26408

主要统计指标解释

财政收入 包括:(1)各项税收。主要有增值税、营业税、土地增值税、城市维护建设税、资源税、城市土地使用税、印花税、个人所得税、企业所得税、关税和耕地占用税等。

(2)专项收入包括征收排污费、征收城市水资源费收入,教育费附加收入等。

存款 企业、机关、团体或居民根据可以收回的原则,把货币资金存入银行或其他信用机构保管并取得一定利息的一种信用活动形式。根据存款对象的不同可划分为企业存款、财政存款、机关团体存款、基本建设存款、城镇储蓄存款、农村存款等科目。它是银行信贷资金的主要来源。

贷款 银行或其他信用机构根据必须归还的原则,按一定利率,为企业、个人等提供资金的一种信用活动形式。我国银行贷款分为流动资金贷款、固定资产贷款、城乡个体工商户贷款城乡个体工商户贷款以及农业贷款等科目。

Explanatory Notes on Main Statistical Indicators

Financial Revenue It includes the following main items: (1) various tax revenues, including value added tax, business tax, land value added tax, tax on city maintenance and construction, resources tax, tax on use of urban land, stamp tax, personal income tax, enterprise income tax and tax on occupancy of cultivated land, etc. (2) Special revenues, including revenue collected from imposing fee on sewage treatment, revenue collected from imposing fee on urban water resources, and extra – charges for education, etc.

Deposit is a form of credit by which enterprises, institutions, organizations or households can put money into banks and other credit institutions for safekeeping and interest earning under the principle of free withdrawal. According to different depositors, deposits are divided into enterprise deposits, treasury deposits, deposits of government agencies and organizations, capital construction deposits, urban savings deposits, rural deposits and other deposits. Deposits are major sources of the credit funds of banks.

Loan is a form of credit by which banks and other credit institutions provide funds at certain interest rate to enterprises and individuals in the light of the principle of unconditional repayment. Loans from Chinese banks include circulating capital loans, fixed assets loans, loans to urban and rural individuals engaged in industrial and commercial business and agricultural loans.

第十一篇
CHAPTER-11

城市建设、环境保护
URBAN CONSTRUCTION AND ENVIRONMENTAL PROTECTION

城市建设、环境保护
Urban Construction and Environmental Protection

主 要 统 计 指 标
Major Statistical Indicators

市区建成区面积	Developed Area in Urban District	392.73	平方公里	(sq.km)
市区实有道路面积	Area of Roads in Urban District at Year-end	4485	万平方米	(10000 sq.m)
市区用电量	Electricity Consumption of Urban District	346.93	亿千瓦时	(100 million kw/h)
# 工业用电	Industrial Electricity Consumption	230.20	亿千瓦时	(100 million kw/h)
生活用电	Electricity Consumption for Residential Use	45.31	亿千瓦时	(100 million kw/h)
市区供水能力	Water-supply Capacity of Urban District	320	万吨 / 日	(10000 tons/day)
市区供水总量	Annual Volume of Tap Water Supplied in Urban District	69499	万吨	(10000 tons)
市区气化率	Percentage of Population with Access to Gas in Urban District	100	%	(%)
市区公共绿地面积	Public Green Area in Urban District	4676	公顷	(hectare)
工业废水排放达标率	Upto-standard Rate of Industrial Waste Water Discharge	96.21	%	(%)

11－01 主要年份市区城市公共交通
Urban Public Transportation in Main Years

指 标	Item	2000	2005	2006	2007	2008	2009
年末运营线路条数（条）	Number of Operating Routes (year－end) (unit)	163	368	381	393	425	441
年末运营线路总长度（公里）	Length of Operating Routes (year－end) (km)	2016	4902	5172	5416	6190	6462
年末运营公共汽车（辆）	Number of Public Transportation Vehicles(year－end) (unit)	1781	3997	4396	4578	5785	6150
年末运营无轨电车（辆）	Number of Operating Trolleys (unit)	223	189	118	118	118	118
客运总量 （万人次）	Passenger Traffic (10000 person－times)	57986	70653	78027	88362	102579	112844
全年票款收入（万元）	Income of Tickets (10000 yuan)	43604	86448	98416	105773	120975	127746
平均耗油（升/百公里）	Average Gasoline Consumption (litre/100km)	27.75	33.92	32.66	35.34	38.11	38.65
平均耗电（千瓦时/百公里）	Average Electricity Consumption (kwh/100km)	80.52	102.80	106.87	116.13	118.69	132.67

注：本表为主城区系统内数据（不含萧山、余杭）。客运总量2000年起按新口径计算。

a) Data in this table only include public transportation system (exclude Xiaoshan and Yuhang district). Number of passengers traffic counted with new standard since 2000.

11－02 主要年份市区城市供电、供水

Urban Electricity and Water Supply in Main Years

指 标	Item	2000	2005	2006	2007	2008	2009
一、城市供电	**Urban Electricity Supply**						
全年用电总量（亿千瓦时）	Total Electricity Consumption (100 million kwh)	60.19	244.78	279.94	313.47	325.75	346.93
工业（亿千瓦时）	Industrial Electricity Consumption (100 million kwh)	33.52	172.56	197.61	219.92	221.28	230.20
生活（亿千瓦时）	Electricity Consumption for Residential Use (100 million kwh)	9.86	27.98	32.53	36.86	41.15	45.31
二、城市供水（自来水）	**Urban Water Supply**						
总售水量（万吨）	Total Annual Volume of Tap Water Saled (10000 tons)	27510	58332	57518	56906	58452	59291
平均日供水（万吨）	Per Capita Daily Consumption of Tap Water (10000 tons)	92	201	177	183	187	190
供水能力（万吨/日）	Capacity of Water Supply (10000 tons/day)	146	253	256	274	299	320
供水总量（万吨）	Total Annual Volume of Tap Water Supplied (10000 tons)	33725	73331	64734	66753	68178	69499
其中：生产用水（万吨）	For Productive Use (10000 tons)	8100	27327	20258	19519	19354	16671
生活用水（万吨）	For Residential Use (10000 tons)	19410	35220	33979	33682	35902	37274
用水普及率（%）	Percentage of Population with Access to Tap Water (%)	100	100	100	100	100	100

注：从2001年起市区数据包括萧山区和余杭区。

a) Data of urban include Xiaoshan and Yuhang district since 2001.

11－03 主要年份市区市政建设
Public Utilities in Urban District in Main Years

指 标	Item	2000	2005	2006	2007	2008	2009
一、市政建设	**Urban Infrastructure**						
年末实有道路面积（万平方米）	Area of Roads (year－end) (10000 sq. m)	1183	3175	4216	4185	4258	4485
年末实有道路长度（公里）	Length of Roads(year－end) (km)	1050	1782	1942	1993	2030	2117
年末实有桥梁数（座）	Number of Bridges(year－end) (unit)	291	991	857	848	917	1063
排水管道长度（公里）	Length of Drainage Pipelines (km)	1431	2945	2419	3115	3286	3650
城市污水排放量（万立方米）	Volume of Sewage Drained (10000 cu. m)	27010	55141	44108	47952	61330	57132
城市污水处理总量（万立方米）	the Total Volume of Urban Sewage Treatment (10000 cu. m)	－	43352	37758	36918	51808	51433
二、城市液化气	**Urban Liquefied Petroleum Gas**						
供气总量 （万吨）	Total Volume of Liquefied Petroleum Gas Supply (10000 tons)	7.47	15.28	8.54	5.91	8.96	10.11
其中：家庭用气（万吨）	Supply for Residential Use (10000 tons)	5.08	9.51	5.53	3.52	6.63	6.25
三、人工煤气及天然气	**Coal Gas and Natural Gas**						
家庭用气总量（万立方米）	Total Volume of Coal Gas Consumed (10000 cu. m)	4367	3225	3101	4010	4917	7285
家庭用气户数（万户）	Residential Households with Access to Gas (10000 households)	14.46	25.48	29.50	37.46	43.58	51.84
四、全社会气化率 %	**Percentage of Population with Access to Gas** (%)	95.70	99.17	100	100	100	100

注：从2001年起市区数据包括萧山区和余杭区。

a) Data of urban include Xiaoshan and Yuhang district since 2001.

11－04 主要年份市区园林绿化

Urban Forestation in Main Years

指　标	Item	2000	2005	2006	2007	2008	2009
一、园林绿化	**Urban Forestation**						
建城区绿化覆盖面积（公顷）	The Green Areas Coveraged in Constructed Areas (hectare)	6083	11734	12490	13284	14177	15686
园林绿地面积（公顷）	Total Area of Parks, Gardens and Green Areas (hectare)	6035	10774	11309	12141	12971	14366
其中:公共绿地（公顷）	Public Green Area (hectare)	976	2564	2926	3486	4078	4676
建城区绿化覆盖率（%）	Rate of the Green Areas Coveraged in Constructed Areas (%)	34.33	37.31	38.14	38.55	38.60	39.94
公园景点个数　（个）	Number of Parks and Scenic Resorts (unit)	70	184	106	138	150	165
公园景点面积（公顷）	Area of Parks and Scenic Resorts (hectare)	489	997	852	1412	1430	1688
二、收费公园、风景点游人量（万人次）	**Number of Visitors to Parks and Scenic Resorts (10000 persontimes)**	1916	2396	2994	2976	3726	3985

注:园林绿化 1995 年的数据统计口径为普查口径。从 2001 年起市区数据包括萧山区和余杭区。

a) Data in 1995 came from census. Data of urban include Xiaoshan and Yuhang district since 2001.

11-05 工业"三废"排放及处理率(2009年)

Discharge and Disposal Rate of Industrial "Three Waste" (2009)

单位:% (%)

指标	Item	全市 Whole Municipality	市区 Urban District
工业废水排放达标率	Up to-standard Rate of Indusurial Waste Water Discharge	96.21	95.58
工业废水重复用水率	Industrial Waste Water Reused	72.43	81.64
工业废水化学需氧量排放降低率	The Lower Rate of COD Emission from Industrial Waste Water	4.10	-
工业废气二氧化硫去除率	Rate of Sulphur Dioxide Removed from Industrial Waste Gas	46.48	42.31
工业废气烟尘去除率	Rate of Soot Removed from Industrial Waste Gas	97.16	97.47
工业废气粉尘去除率	Rate of Industrial Dust Removed from Industrial Waste Gas	98.08	98.93
工业废气二氧化硫排放达标率	Up to-standard Rate of Sulphru Dioxide Emission	99.48	99.28
工业废气二氧化硫排放降低率	The Lower Rate of SO_2 Emission from Industrial Waste Gas	3.70	-
工业废气烟尘排放达标率	Up to-standard Rate of Industrial Soot Emission	98.56	96.62
工业废气粉尘排放达标率	Up to-standard Rate of Industrial Dust Emission	99.84	99.68
工业固体废物综合利用率	Rate of Industrial Solid Wastes Utilized in a Comprehensive Way	95.43	97.64
工业固体废物贮存率	Rate of Industrial Solid Wastes Stored	0.02	0.03
工业固体废物处置率	Rate of Industrial Solid Wastes Treated	4.50	2.33
工业固体废物排放率	Rate of Industrial Solid Wastes Discharged	0.04	-
工业锅炉烟尘排放达标率	Up to-standard Rate of Industrial Boilers' Soot Emission	100	100
工业炉窑烟尘排放达标率	Up to-standard Rate of Industrial Furnaces & Kilns' Soot Emission	97.95	96.41
城市污水处理率	Rate of Urban Waste Water Treated	89.28	90.02

主要统计指标解释

自来水生产能力 指年底城建部门管理的自来水厂实际生产能力。

生活用水量 指居民日常生活与公共福利设施的用水量。包括居民、饮食店、旅馆、医院、理发店、浴池、洗衣店、游泳池、商店、学校、机关、部队等单位的用水量。

供气总量 指全年售给各类用户的全部煤气量。包括工业用量、家庭用量和其他用量。

年末实有道路长度 指除土路外,路面经过铺装宽度在3.5米以上的道路,包括高级、次高级道路和普通道路。

城市桥梁 指城市范围内,修建在河道上的桥梁和道路与道路立交、道路跨越铁路的立交桥,以及人行天桥。包括永久性桥和半永久性桥,不包括临时性桥、铁路桥、涵洞。

营运线路长度 指设置的固定营运线路的长度,包括郊区营运线路长度。不包括临时行驶的线路长度。

用水普及率 指城市用水的非农业人口数(不包括临时人口和流动人口)与城市非农业人口总数之比。计算公式为:

$$用水普及率 = \frac{城市用水非农业人口数}{城市非农业人口数} \times 100\%$$

城市园林绿地面积 指城市公共绿地、专用绿地、生产绿地、防护绿地、郊区风景名胜区的全部面积。

公共绿地面积 指供游览休息的各种公园、动物园、植物园、陵园以及花园、游园和供游览休息用的林荫道绿地、广场绿地。不包括一般栽植的行道树及林荫道的面积。

Explanatory Notes on Main Statistical Indicators

Production Capacity of Tap Water refers to the actual comprehensive production capacity of the waterworks administered by the urban construction department.

Consumption of water for Residential Use refers to the water consumption of households for daily life and the water consumption of public welfare facilities, including the consumption of restaurants, hotels, hospitals, barber shops, public bathhouses, laundries, swimming pools, shops, schools, institutions, army units and other units.

Volume of Gas Supply refers to the total volume of gas Sold to users in a year, including the volume for industrial use, residential use and other uses.

Length of Roads at the Year - end refers to the length of roads with a paved surface, and with a width of more than 3 - 5 meters, including high quality, medium quality and ordinary roads.

Urban Bridges refers to bridges over river courses, great separated junctions and overpasses in urban areas. Permanent bridges and semi - permanent bridges are included. Temporary bridges, railway bridges and culverts are excluded.

Length in Operation refers to the length of the roads in fixed operation, including the suburb one, but excluding the tomporary ones.

Percentage of Urban Population with Access to Tap Water refers to the ratio of the urban non - agricultural population (excluding temporary and mobile population) with access to tap water to the tolal urban non - agricultural population. The formula is:

$$\text{Percentage of Poputalion with Access to Tap Water} = \frac{\text{Urban Non - agricultural Population with Access to Tap Water}}{\text{Urban Non - agricultural Population}} \times 100\%$$

Area of Urban Gardens and Green Areas refers to the total area of urban public green land, special green land, production green land, protection green land and suburban scenic spots.

Public Green Area refers to green area of various parks, zoos, botanical gardens, cemeteries, amusement parks, tree - flanked boulevards Greenland squares for tourism and relaxing. Areas with trees planted along - side the streets and boulevards are excluded.

第十二篇
CHAPTER-12

科技、教育、文化、卫生、体育
SCIENCE AND TECHNOLOGY, EDUCATION, CULTURE, PUBLIC HEALTH AND SPORTS

科技、教育、文化、卫生、体育
Science and Technology, Education, Culture, Public Health and Sports

主要统计指标
Major Statistical Indicators

高等学校数	Number of Regular Institution of Higher Education	36	个	(unit)
高等学校在校学生数	Students Enrollment of Regular Institution of Higher Education	429774	人	(person)
中等学校在校学生数	Students Enrollment of Secondary Schools	4016	人	(person)
高中在校学生数	Students Enrollment of Senior High Schools	118057	人	(person)
初中在校学生数	Students Enrollment of Junior High Schools	241899	人	(person)
小学在校学生数	Students Enrollment of Primary Schools	445132	人	(person)
医疗病床数	Number of Beds in Health Institutions	40226	张	(bed)
# 医院	Number of Beds in Hospitals	33094	张	(bed)
卫生技术人员数	Number of Medical Technical Personnel	56270	人	(person)
# 执业(助理)医师	Number of Registered (Assistant) Doctors	22753	人	(person)
公共图书馆	Public Library	16	个	(unit)

12－01 分县(市)城镇单位年末人才资源

Trained Personnel Resource of Urban Units by Region

单位:人 (person)

地 区	Region	人才资源数 Number of Trained Personnel Resources		#专业技术人员 Technical Personnel	
		2009	2008	2009	2008
全市	**Whole Municipality**	**1140129**	**994220**	**482215**	**430341**
市区	Urban District	988551	854013	413580	367598
萧山区	Xiaoshan	189158	153014	66000	53089
余杭区	Yuhang	83503	74060	31752	26750
桐庐县	Tonglu	24660	23153	9940	9532
淳安县	Chun'an	19381	16820	9307	8725
建德市	Jiande	23254	25018	11850	11007
富阳市	Fuyang	44887	41238	19809	18366
临安市	Lin'an	39396	33978	17729	15113

12－02　分行业城镇单位专业技术人员(2009年)
Technical Personnel of Urban Units by Sector(2009)

单位:人　(person)

行　业	Sector	合计 Total	国有 State－owned	集体 Collective－owned Units
全市	**Total**	**482215**	**203393**	**14267**
农、林、牧、渔业	Farming, Forestry, Animal Husbandry and Fishery	397	190	13
采矿业	Mining & Quarrying	293	－	49
制造业	Manufacture	98821	3303	842
电力、燃气及水的生产和供应业	Production and Supply of Electricity, Gas and Water	5278	2590	3
建筑业	Construction	49960	3834	518
交通运输、仓储和邮政业	Transportation, Storage, Post & Telecommunications	7316	3743	419
信息传输、计算机服务和软件业	Information Transmission, Computer Services and Software	33560	3590	31
批发和零售贸易	Wholesale & Retail Trade	18537	2546	445
住宿和餐饮业	Accommodations and Catering	5952	989	431
金融业	Banking	32309	7144	17
房地产业	Real Estate	10520	1296	289
租赁与商务服务业	Renting and Business Service	12457	3524	883
科学研究、技术服务与地质勘查业	Scientific Research, Technical Service and Geological Prospecting	37062	19676	708
水利、环境和公共设施管理业	Water Conservancy, Environment and Public Utility	2855	1434	202
居民服务和其他服务业	Service for the Residents and Other	862	389	61
教育	Education	97751	90534	3638
卫生、社会保障和社会福利业	Health Care, Sports & Social Welfare	52955	45219	5514
文化、体育和娱乐业	Culture, Sports and Entertainment	10928	10098	55
公共管理和社会组织	Public Management and Social Organzations	4402	3294	149

12－03 按经济类型分的城镇单位专业技术人员(2009年)

Technical Personnel of Urban Units by Ownership(2009)

单位:人

(person)

地　区	Region	合计 Total	国有 State－owned	集体 Collective－owned Units	其他 Others
总计	**Total**	**482215**	**203393**	**14267**	**264555**
市区	Urban District	413580	163944	11251	238385
萧山区	Xiaoshan	66000	18703	3914	43383
余杭区	Yuhang	31752	13209	1643	16900
桐庐县	Tonglu	9940	6103	343	3494
淳安县	Chun'an	9307	6245	305	2757
建德市	Jiande	11850	7450	747	3653
富阳市	Fuyang	19809	10928	552	8329
临安市	Lin'an	17729	8723	1069	7937

12－04　文化事业
Number of Institutions

单位：个

指　标	Item	全　市 Total	市　区 Urban District	#萧山区 Xiaoshan
剧　　场	Theaters	12	11	-
剧　　团	Opera Troupes	20	16	1
文 化 馆	Cultural Centers	13	8	1
文 化 站	Cultural Stations	198	95	27
图 书 馆	Libraries	16	11	1
博 物 馆	Museums	35	34	3
展 览 馆	Exhibition Buildings	1	1	-

12－05　分县(市)艺术表演团体
Basic Statistics on Performance of

指　标	Item	全　市 Total		市　区 Urban District	
		2009	为上年(%) As Compared with the Preceding Year(%)	2009	为上年(%) As Compared with the Preceding Year(%)
艺术表演场所演出场次（场）	Number of Performances in Artistic Performance Place (scene)	2751	91.43	2251.00	93.44
艺术表演场所演出收入（万元）	Income of Performances in Artistic Performance Place (10000 yuan)	2063	77.04	2043.00	77.01
剧团演出场次（场）	Number of Performances of Opera Troupes (scene)	6720	100.03	5654.00	102.33
#农　村（场）	#Rural Areas (scene)	3471	106.96	2523.00	118.34
剧团演出观众人数(万人次)	Number of Spectators of Opera Troupes (10000 person－times)	575	47.36	445.00	41.47
剧团演出收入（万元）	Income of Performances of Opera Troupes (10000 yuan)	4468	141.39	4203.00	146.19

单位数(2009 年)
for Culture(2009)

(unit)

#余杭区 Yuhang	桐庐县 Tonglu	淳安县 Chun'an	建德市 Jiande	富阳市 Fuyang	临安市 Lin'an
2	–	–	–	–	1
1	1	–	1	1	1
1	1	1	1	1	1
19	13	23	16	25	26
1	1	1	1	1	1
4	1	–	–	–	–
–	–	–	–	–	–

演出情况(2009 年)
Art Troupes by Region(2009)

		桐庐县 Tonglu	淳安县 Chun'an	建德市 Jiande	富阳市 Fuyang	临安市 Lin'an
#萧山区 Xiaoshan	#余杭区 Yuhang					
–	479	–	–	–	–	500
–	44	–	–	–	–	20
100	132	160	–	276	200	430
78	100	102	–	226	190	430
49	22	32	–	41	40	17
69	87	72	–	55	121	17

12－06 全市专利申请与授权情况
Patent Application and Granted

单位:件　　(item)

地　区	Region	专利申请合计 Patent Applications	专利申请发明 Inventions	专利申请实用新型 Utility Models	专利申请外观设计 Designs	专利授权合计 Patent Applications Granted	专利授权发明 Inventions	专利授权实用新型 Utility Models	专利授权外观设计 Designs
全市	**Whole Municipality**	**26077**	**6703**	**9806**	**9568**	**15507**	**2535**	**5806**	**7166**
市区	Urban District	21543	6286	7871	7386	12285	2400	4770	5115
上城区	Shangcheng	596	121	267	208	436	61	180	195
下城区	Xiacheng	1958	689	645	624	1092	271	391	430
江干区	Jianggan	3577	872	1355	1350	2443	253	895	1295
拱墅区	Gongshu	998	221	440	337	512	65	233	214
西湖区	Xihu	5405	2478	1981	946	3008	1146	1113	749
高新(滨江)区	Hi－Tech(Binjiang)	2069	1363	511	195	1280	431	479	370
萧山区	Xiaoshan	4135	273	1488	2374	1755	66	781	908
余杭区	Yuhang	2805	269	1184	1352	1759	107	698	954
桐庐县	Tonglu	874	42	407	425	846	12	255	579
淳安县	Chun'an	202	19	81	102	112	5	54	53
建德市	Jiande	560	70	104	386	480	22	55	403
富阳市	Fuyang	1578	141	874	563	986	32	358	596
临安市	Lin'an	1320	145	469	706	798	64	314	420

12－07 主要年份市区文化事业单位数
Cultural Institutions of Urban District in Main Years

单位：个 (unit)

年 份 Year	电影院 Cinemas	剧 团 Opera Troupes	剧 场 Theaters	文化馆 Cultural Centers	文化站 Cultural Stations	图书馆 Libraries	博物馆 Museums
1978	7	13	6	5	–	2	1
1979	8	14	7	5	27	2	1
1980	8	15	7	5	37	2	1
1981	8	17	7	6	40	2	1
1982	9	17	7	6	45	3	1
1983	9	15	3	6	46	3	1
1984	9	15	4	6	49	3	1
1985	8	16	9	6	47	3	2
1986	8	15	8	6	48	3	2
1987	8	15	9	6	38	3	2
1988	7	14	9	6	50	3	2
1989	7	14	9	6	48	2	2
1990	9	14	9	5	48	3	2
1991	10	14	8	5	48	3	2
1992	11	14	8	5	48	3	6
1993	10	14	9	5	42	3	6
1994	11	13	9	5	48	3	6
1995	11	13	9	5	67	3	6
1996	10	13	8	5	55	3	6
1997	10	13	8	5	52	3	6
1998	9	13	8	6	55	3	7
1999	9	13	6	6	52	3	8
2000	8	12	6	6	52	3	9
2001	49	14	11	8	89	5	11
2002	–	14	10	8	90	4	11
2003	19	14	11	13	92	4	11
2004	18	14	14	8	93	5	12
2005	16	15	10	8	94	7	12
2006	16	15	10	8	94	8	12
2007	16	15	10	8	92	9	12
2008	18	15	11	8	92	9	13
2009	15	16	11	8	95	11	34

注：从 2001 年起市区数据包括萧山区和余杭区。

a) Data of urban include Xiaoshan and Yuhang district since 2001.

12－08　主要年份高等学校基本情况

Basic Statistics on Regular Institutions of Higher Education in Main Years

单位:人　　　　　　　　　　　　　　　　　　　　　　　　(person)

年　份 Year	学校数(个) Number of Schools(unit)	在校学生数 Students Enrollment	教职员工数 Teachers and Staff	#专职教师 Number of Full－time Teachers
1978	9	13319	8966	3946
1979	12	17518	10182	4458
1980	13	23545	12400	5278
1981	13	28936	13090	5359
1982	13	25821	14363	6067
1983	14	27443	15267	6172
1984	16	31384	15889	6387
1985	20	36996	17507	7247
1986	22	40051	18968	7845
1987	21	39922	18965	7876
1988	21	40787	19582	8133
1989	21	40330	19680	8107
1990	21	39866	19495	8075
1991	21	42192	19489	7737
1992	19	43787	19841	7561
1993	19	51063	19787	7561
1994	19	59109	19903	7703
1995	20	63124	19883	7799
1996	20	66023	19693	7824
1997	20	69391	19540	7793
1998	17	76546	19320	7723
1999	18	89109	20136	8135
2000	32	122386	23791	10477
2001	33	174894	25805	11866
2002	34	224048	27307	13605
2003	35	269798	34508	18141
2004	36	313599	33325	18445
2005	36	351918	34816	19583
2006	36	373563	36929	21375
2007	36	392770	38843	23197
2008	36	409559	39762	24017
2009	36	429774	40420	24765

注:在校学生数包括各高校研究生。

a) Number of students enrollment include graduate students in all schools.

12－09 主要年份中等专业学校基本情况

Basic Statistics on Specialized Secondary Schools in Main Years

单位:人 (person)

年 份 Year	学校数(个) Number of Schools(unit)	在校学生数 Students Enrollment	教职员工数 Teachers and Staff	#专职教师 Number of Full－time Teachers
1978	26	8711	3044	1080
1979	27	11093	2601	1124
1980	26	9453	2450	1101
1981	35	7309	3122	1276
1982	37	8284	3694	1529
1983	37	10516	3716	1604
1984	42	13419	4194	1758
1985	46	16527	5095	1959
1986	50	19114	5641	2336
1987	52	20929	6081	2623
1988	51	22117	6144	2741
1989	54	23302	6602	2888
1990	55	23564	6679	2948
1991	55	23331	6584	2770
1992	55	26373	6786	2825
1993	56	30336	6732	2780
1994	57	36079	6881	2840
1995	57	42784	6851	2888
1996	58	49593	6789	2904
1997	57	51752	6731	2896
1998	56	55796	6554	2746
1999	50	52272	5023	2272
2000	28	45238	2950	1421
2001	26	32763	2053	1051
2002	14	26255	1251	566
2003	13	21735	1058	457
2004	11	21262	869	416
2005	10	20344	893	443
2006	8	12540	410	184
2007	8	8927	414	194
2008	8	5514	345	152
2009	8	4016	233	65

12－10　主要年份高中基本情况

Basic Statistics on Senior High Schools in Main Years

单位:人　　　　(person)

年　份 Year	学校数(个) Number of Schools(unit)	在校学生数 Students Enrollment	专职教师数 Number of Full－time Teachers
1978	352	102815	5235
1979	182	58866	3471
1980	151	43661	3173
1981	118	34606	2825
1982	113	35136	2740
1983	111	38580	2740
1984	105	43167	2781
1985	104	47510	3016
1986	95	46379	2972
1987	92	44697	3006
1988	89	42196	2947
1989	88	39994	2898
1990	86	39829	2922
1991	82	37809	2896
1992	74	34620	2791
1993	72	32483	2641
1994	75	35720	2673
1995	72	40771	2880
1996	70	43692	3135
1997	69	47975	3388
1998	75	55688	3693
1999	82	64459	4172
2000	85	73049	4745
2001	88	79632	5262
2002	81	91635	6126
2003	77	108116	6879
2004	81	115303	7510
2005	80	120883	8041
2006	82	124177	8421
2007	80	122939	8542
2008	76	120294	8646
2009	75	118057	8751

12－11　主要年份初中基本情况

Basic Statistics on Junior Middle Schools in Main Years

单位:人　　(person)

年　份 Year	学校数(个) Number of Schools(unit)	在校学生数 Students Enrollment	专职教师数 Number of Full－time Teachers
1978	254	247209	11978
1979	363	208484	11020
1980	369	204073	10695
1981	359	194024	10015
1982	367	193135	10107
1983	370	190221	9948
1984	368	192971	9679
1985	361	196889	9799
1986	376	199638	9821
1987	385	195426	10264
1988	380	170079	10055
1989	376	151223	9825
1990	382	160111	9564
1991	387	185590	10020
1992	367	212022	10603
1993	365	203896	10876
1994	371	205388	11495
1995	373	216300	12058
1996	374	229466	12810
1997	368	227809	13370
1998	359	222191	13493
1999	339	239174	13723
2000	330	269484	14529
2001	314	285203	15685
2002	315	282951	15758
2003	316	268824	15836
2004	303	252291	16042
2005	289	241374	16205
2006	263	235527	16374
2007	262	238252	16591
2008	260	244464	16965
2009	252	241899	17317

12－12　主要年份小学基本情况

Basic Statistics on Primary Schools in Main Years

单位:人　　　　(person)

年　份 Year	学校数(个) Number of Schools(unit)	在校学生数 Students Enrollment	教职员工数 Teachers and Staff	#专职教师数 Number of Full－time Teachers
1978	4959	605137	24103	22291
1979	4850	577811	25089	23220
1980	4781	560244	25388	22902
1981	4668	525503	22468	20832
1982	4528	479264	22213	20289
1983	4417	444301	20842	18945
1984	4345	427763	20496	18500
1985	4286	414839	20945	18415
1986	4250	413507	20796	18464
1987	4205	405856	21067	18751
1988	4137	426842	21658	19236
1989	4106	459162	22660	20177
1990	4077	460514	20542	18099
1991	3972	453055	20781	18369
1992	3654	450496	21452	19067
1993	3473	477026	22141	19775
1994	3352	504867	22751	20462
1995	3172	513988	23743	21380
1996	3006	525674	24553	22197
1997	2762	538390	25269	23022
1998	2395	532845	25718	23499
1999	1996	512874	26350	24120
2000	1659	485679	25938	23876
2001	1354	467982	25535	23179
2002	1197	456535	25425	23138
2003	1044	448969	25304	22955
2004	897	447971	25396	23066
2005	791	458942	25793	23541
2006	605	459529	26040	23848
2007	437	456152	26455	24251
2008	418	452143	26894	24743
2009	417	445132	27445	25424

12－13 主要年份幼儿园基本情况

Basic Statistics on Kindergartens in Main Years

单位:人　　　　(person)

年　份 Year	园　数(个) Kindergartens(unit)	在园幼儿数 Kindergarteners Enrollment	教职员工数 Teachers and Staff	#教　师 Number of Full－time Teachers
1978	266	37597	2570	1439
1979	216	59245	3731	2201
1980	518	82182	4763	3398
1981	676	82808	5275	3691
1982	853	95733	6357	4269
1983	1034	95676	6271	4135
1984	1749	112095	7238	4900
1985	1743	115766	7360	5278
1986	1607	118792	7898	5659
1987	1678	133773	8622	6335
1988	1541	139883	9221	6608
1989	1397	132947	9595	6849
1990	1526	136277	9808	7167
1991	1422	150982	10472	7388
1992	1431	133773	9240	6487
1993	1328	171005	10779	7886
1994	1470	165860	10718	7891
1995	1493	149497	10102	7943
1996	1437	150587	10203	7625
1997	1504	146530	10480	7743
1998	1695	153035	10691	7956
1999	1787	156372	10719	8107
2000	2037	168414	11740	8770
2001	1249	174204	11447	7880
2002	1268	175891	11988	8086
2003	1285	176862	13702	9076
2004	1098	186472	14991	9544
2005	1188	188991	16161	10288
2006	1188	195552	17550	11053
2007	1071	212754	19330	12168
2008	1037	235867	21193	12917
2009	972	246336	22970	14211

12－14　高等学校

Basic Statistics on Regular

单位:人

单位名称	Item	在校学生数 Students Enrollment	
		2009	为上年(%) As Compared with the Preceding Year(%)
全　　市	**Total**	**394087**	**103.8**
市　　区	**Urban District**	**375075**	**103.8**
其中:1.浙江大学	Zhejiang University	22260	100.1
2.杭州电子科技大学	Hangzhou Dianzi University	16290	97.2
3.浙江工业大学	Zhejiang Univesity of Technology	21422	100.5
4.浙江理工大学	Zhejiang Sci－Tech University	15932	108.1
5.浙江林学院	Zhejiang Forestry University	12588	103.0
6.浙江中医学院	Zhejiang College of Traditional Chinese Medicine	4781	102.2
7.浙江工商大学	Zhejiang Gongshang University	14706	101.4
8.中国美术学院	China Academy of Art	8486	102.9
9.中国计量学院	China Institute of Metrology	11384	109.1
10.浙江科技学院	Hangzhou Application Engineering and Technology College	13857	103.7
11.浙江广播电视大学	Zhejiang Radio & TV University	10236	114.2
12.浙江水利水电专科学校	Zhejiang Water Conservancy and Hydroelectricity College	7288	95.0
13.浙江财经学院	Zhejiang Institute of Finance and Economics	11057	111.1
14.浙江警察学院	Zhejiang Police College	2943	83.1
15.浙江传媒学院	Zhejiang Institute of Media and Communications	9245	104.8
16.浙江树人大学	Zhejiang Shuren University	13998	104.3
17.杭州师范大学	Hangzhou Normal University	11263	105.5
18.浙江大学城市学院	Zhejiang University City College	13281	104.7

注:本表不含在校研究生。

基本情况(2009年)

Institutions of Higher Education(2009)

(person)

本年招生数 Number of New Students Enrollment	本年毕业生数 Number of Graduates	教职员工数 Teachers and Staff 合计 Total	其中:专职教师 Full - time Teachers	2009年预计毕业生 Number of Students Will Graduate in 2009
114568	**96101**	**40420**	**24765**	**106594**
109370	**91746**	**38584**	**23509**	**102117**
5465	5170	8203	3471	5844
3934	4329	1532	1065	4549
5485	5025	2607	1558	5385
4054	2921	1653	1137	3562
3423	2884	1376	906	2959
1187	1104	706	528	1009
3659	3568	1629	1039	3817
2331	1969	1041	644	2160
3277	2257	1163	769	2460
3760	2953	1182	802	3108
4496	3380	235	116	3425
1884	2155	570	419	3007
3358	2201	1174	704	2520
522	1106	387	282	767
2546	2016	800	564	2263
3778	3096	773	524	3536
3193	2619	1889	1097	2687
3498	2452	940	712	2798

a) Data in this table does not contain post - graduate students.

12-15 普通中学及职业

Basic Statistics on Senior, Junior

单位:人

指 标	Item	全 市 Total	市 区 Urban District	#萧山区 Xiaoshan
高　　中	**Senior High Schools**			
学校数(所)	Number of Schools(unit)	75	52	10
在校学生数	Students Enrollment	118057	70363	22381
为上年(%)	As Compared with the Preceding Year (%)	98.14	98.41	99.52
本年招生数	Number of New Students Enrollment	39298	23324	7308
本年毕业生数	Number of Graduates	41408	24193	8023
#专职教师	#Full-time Teachers	8751	5466	1643
2010年预计毕业生数	Number of Students Will Graduate in 2010	39644	23515	7685
初　　中	**Junior High Schools**			
学校数(所)	Number of Schools(unit)	252	150	43
在校学生数	Students Enrollment	241899	148105	50524
为上年(%)	As Compared with the Preceding Year (%)	98.95	100.74	100.24
本年招生数	Number of New Students Enrollment	79652	50021	17135
本年毕业生数	Number of Graduates	77268	45222	14850
#专职教师	#Full-time Teachers	17317	10996	3436
2010年预计毕业生数	Number of Students Will Graduate in 2010	79681	47786	16168
职业中学	**Vocational Schools**			
学校数(所)	Number of Schools(unit)	37	20	4
在校学生数	Students Enrollment	68316	42217	13314
为上年(%)	As Compared with the Preceding Year (%)	97.71	100.05	98.19
本年招生数	Number of New Students Enrollment	25400	15765	5068
本年毕业生数	Number of Graduates	22599	13622	4252
专职教师数	Full-time Teachers	3709	2202	502
2010年预计毕业生数	Number of Students Will Graduate in 2010	20851	13009	3940

中学基本情况(2009 年)
High Schools and Vacational Schools(2009)

(person)

#余杭区 Yuhang	桐庐县 Tonglu	淳安县 Chun'an	建德市 Jiande	富阳市 Fuyang	临安市 Lin'an
9	3	4	5	6	5
13201	7087	7767	9600	13284	9956
99.19	97.03	93.15	97.92	97.67	102.11
4513	2538	2469	3446	4207	3314
4381	2688	3006	3487	4619	3415
929	520	497	642	987	639
4313	2223	2763	3129	4637	3377
37	14	17	24	21	26
29655	14613	15497	18772	26773	18139
99.61	98.46	98.29	95.03	98.42	91.20
10152	4714	5164	5919	8375	5459
9011	4728	5294	6827	8350	6847
2279	970	1095	1243	1721	1292
9559	4760	5082	6431	9009	6613
4	2	4	3	4	4
9036	2619	4524	4152	9050	5754
103.90	89.42	86.47	87.15	104.77	93.48
3459	861	1399	1636	3508	2231
2736	944	1910	1635	2570	1918
446	172	203	219	558	355
2916	980	1653	1048	2546	1615

12－16 小学、幼儿园及特殊

Basic Statistics on Primary Schools,

单位：人

指 标	Item	全 市 Total	市 区 Urban District	#萧山区 Xiaoshan
小 学	**Primary Schools**			
学校数(所)	Number of Schools(unit)	417	234	80
班数(班)	Number of Classes(unit)	11741	7719	2427
在校学生数	Students Enrollment	445132	303264	101939
为上年(%)	As Compared with the Preceding Year (%)	98.45	101.01	96.75
本年招生数	Number of New Students Enrollment	71465	50553	16446
本年毕业生数	Number of Graduates	80441	50498	18334
教职员工数	Number of Teachers and Staff	27445	17827	4790
#专职教师	#Full－time Teachers	25242	16458	4596
2010年预计毕业生数	Number of Students Will Graduate in 2010	76679	49908	17733
幼儿园	**Kindergartens**			
园数(个)	Number of Kindergartens(unit)	972	593	216
班数(班)	Number of Classes(unit)	8199	5726	1639
在园幼儿数	Kinders Enrollment	246336	174660	50040
教职员工数	Number of Teachers and Staff	22970	17615	4563
#教师	#Full－time Teachers	14211	10575	2792
盲聋哑学校	**Schools for the Blind, Deaf and Deaf－mute**			
学校数(个)	Number of Schools(unit)	5	2	1
在校学生数	Students Enrollment	758	389	140
本年招生数	Number of New Students Enrollment	97	36	13
本年毕业生数	Number of Graduates	83	21	－
专职教师	Number of Full－time Teachers	201	108	36
弱智学校	**Schools for Weaken in Intelligence**			
学校数(个)	Number of Schools(unit)	5	4	
在校学生数	Students Enrollment	534	505	
本年招生数	Number of New Students Enrollment	87	82	
本年毕业生数	Number of Graduates	54	52	
专职教师	Number of Full－time Teachers	110	106	
工读学校	**Reformatory Schools**			
学校数(个)	Number of Schools(unit)	1	1	
在校学生数	Students Enrollment	140	140	
本年招生数	Number of New Students Enrollment	60	60	
本年毕业生数	Number of Graduates	70	70	
专任教师总数	Number of Full－time Teachers	36	36	

教育基本情况(2009 年)

Kindergartens and Special Education(2009)

(person)

#余杭区 Yuhang	桐庐县 Tonglu	淳安县 Chun'an	建德市 Jiande	富阳市 Fuyang	临安市 Lin'an
45	23	37	26	57	40
1536	630	673	644	1286	789
63489	22682	21715	25506	43349	28616
106.69	92.67	90.04	89.92	95.97	96.05
11393	3468	2873	3231	6832	4508
10074	4978	5102	5904	8500	5459
3744	1423	1846	1653	2823	1873
3379	1228	1714	1532	2545	1765
9925	4198	4366	5270	7926	5011
66	87	61	36	118	77
955	412	303	452	724	582
31629	11584	11320	12143	21694	14935
2698	887	544	917	1781	1226
1726	547	392	649	1176	872
–	–	–	–	2	1
–	–	–	–	280	89
–	–	–	–	49	12
–	–	–	–	24	38
–	–	–	–	78	15
–	1	–	–	–	–
–	29	–	–	–	–
–	5	–	–	–	–
–	2	–	–	–	–
–	4	–	–	–	–
–	–	–	–	–	–
–	–	–	–	–	–
–	–	–	–	–	–
–	–	–	–	–	–
–	–	–	–	–	–

12－17 各级成人教育

Basic Statistics on

单位:人

指 标	Item	成人高等学历教育 Higher Education for Adults	职工大学 Staff and Workers College	广播电视大学 Broadcasting and Television College	教育学院 Educational Institute
全 市	**Total**				
学校数(所)	Number of Schools(unit)	5	3	1	1
在校学生数	Students Enrollment	130954	5677	10236	2375
为上年(%)	As Compared with the Preceding Year (%)	83.58	37.73	114.2	73.51
本年招生数	Number of New Students Enrollment	49902	2751	4496	1018
本年毕业生数	Number of Graduates	65541	4854	3380	1687
教职员工数	Number of Teachers and Staff	1113	372	235	506
#专职教师	#Full－time Teachers	653	225	116	312
市 区	**Urban District**				
学校数(所)	Number of Schools(unit)	5	3	1	1
在校学生数	Students Enrollment	128994	5677	10236	2375
为上年(%)	As Compared with the Preceding Year(%)	83.18	37.73	114.2	73.51
本年招生数	Number of New Students Enrollment	48924	2751	4496	1018
本年毕业生数	Number of Graduates	64945	4854	3380	1687
教职员工数	Number of Teachers and Staff	1113	372	235	506
#专职教师	#Full－time Teachers	653	225	116	312

基本情况(2009 年)
Various Adult Education(2009)

(person)

普通高校举办函大夜大 Correspondence School and Night School Held by Regular Higher Education	普通高校举办脱产班 Training Classes Be Released form Production	成人中等学历教育 Specialized Secondary Education	成人中等专业 Specialized Secondary Schools for Adults	成人中学 Secondary Schools for Adults	成人技术培训学校 Technical Schools for Adults
–	–	101	17	84	353
50071	6914	33715	25390	8325	429661
81.42	51.46	107.1	103.86	118.39	77.11
19977	–	11740	11740	–	–
25945	7771	15816	9217	6599	487445
–	–	1433	987	446	4065
–	–	929	574	355	1984
–	–	41	12	29	207
49266	6739	25941	24397	1544	341133
81.71	51.7	107.94	104.82	204.23	85.68
19650	–	11705	11705	–	–
25645	7543	9599	9017	582	393904
–	–	1033	811	222	3497
–	–	691	499	192	1617

12－18　主要年份医疗卫生机构数

Number of Health Institutions in Main Years

单位:个　　　　(unit)

年 份 Year	全市合计 Total	#医 院 Hospitals	市区合计 Urban District	#医 院 Hospitals
1978	1361	421	689	45
1979	1390	426	696	50
1980	1381	425	675	51
1981	1476	424	749	51
1982	1540	432	798	56
1983	1540	435	800	58
1984	1574	437	807	54
1985	1582	404	787	47
1986	1636	407	826	53
1987	1693	420	865	55
1988	1710	438	878	55
1989	1721	443	882	57
1990	1738	440	890	58
1991	1789	441	889	58
1992	1767	436	885	58
1993	1730	403	882	68
1994	1717	416	882	72
1995	1712	414	883	72
1996	1712	416	893	83
1997	1711	411	891	81
1998	1491	419	757	89
1999	1530	400	789	85
2000	1599	396	853	85
2001	1496	391	1072	191
2002	1817	116	1277	88
2003	1901	99	1323	73
2004	1985	114	1396	87
2005	2196	127	1604	97
2006	2570	134	1886	107
2007	2607	138	1872	104
2008	2544	141	1813	108
2009	2687	144	1887	111

注:从2001年起市区数据包括萧山区和余杭区。2002年起医院数据不包括卫生院。

a) Data of urban include Xiaoshan and Yuhang district since 2001. From 2002, the figures of hospitals exclude health centers.

12-19 主要年份医疗病床数

Number of Beds in Health Institutions in Main Years

单位:张 (bed)

年 份 Year	全 市 Total	#医 院 Hospitals	市 区 Urban District	#医 院 Hospitals
1978	14042	11704	6588	5789
1979	15124	12682	7335	6282
1980	16317	13478	8244	6940
1981	17408	13576	9646	7185
1982	17179	14350	9194	7580
1983	17338	14584	9411	7833
1984	17694	14691	9536	7867
1985	19637	15010	11095	7933
1986	20555	16035	11657	8448
1987	21465	16770	12203	8863
1988	23394	17954	13204	9651
1989	24111	18363	13581	9773
1990	24121	18879	13219	10041
1991	24966	19444	13968	10437
1992	25606	20243	14206	10821
1993	25653	20884	14058	10982
1994	25984	20870	14231	11045
1995	26684	21360	14731	11336
1996	28141	22217	15427	12132
1997	26616	22341	15076	12190
1998	27327	23110	15530	12766
1999	26713	22952	14988	12691
2000	27166	23303	15496	13068
2001	27063	23520	20523	17770
2002	27609	22797	21200	18667
2003	29144	22036	22641	18205
2004	31738	24444	25008	20338
2005	33251	25907	26732	21931
2006	33972	27186	27172	23184
2007	36928	29987	29884	25664
2008	38114	31416	30663	26882
2009	40226	33094	32412	28031

注:从2001年起市区数据包括萧山区和余杭区。

a) Data of urban include Xiaoshan and Yuhang district since 2001.

12－20 医疗卫生
Number of Health

单位:个

指　　标	Item	全　　市 Total	市区 Urban District
总　　计	**Total**	**2687**	**1887**
一、医院	Number of Hospitals	144	111
1. 综合医院	General Hospitals	83	64
2. 中医医院	Hospitals of Chinese Medicine	21	11
3. 中西医结合医院	Chinese Therapeutics with Western	3	3
4. 专科医院	Specialized Hospitals	35	31
口腔医院	Hospitals for Mouth	6	6
眼科医院	Hospitals for Eye	－	－
肿瘤医院	Tumor Hospitals	1	1
妇产(科)医院	Hospitals for Pregnant Woman	5	4
儿童医院	Children Hospitals	1	1
精神病医院	Mental Hospitals	3	2
传染病医院	Hospitals for Infectious Diseases	1	1
骨科医院	Orthopaedics Hospitals	5	3
康复医院	Healing Hospitals	4	4
整型外科医院	Plastic Hospitals	2	2
美容医院	Beauty Hospitals	2	2
其他专科医院	Other Special Hospitals	5	5
5. 护理院	Nursing Centers	2	2
二、疗养院	Sanatoriums	9	6
三、社区卫生服务中心(站)	Health Service Centers for Community	898	716
1. 社区卫生服务中心	Health Service Centers	95	79
2. 社区卫生服务站	Health Service Stations	803	637
四、卫生院	Health Service Centers	180	49
1. 街道卫生院	Rural Township Hospitals in Subdistrict	14	4
2. 乡镇卫生院	Rural Township Hospitals in Country	166	45
五、门诊部	Clinics	187	147
六、诊所、卫生所、医务室、护理站	Other Health Care Institutions	1158	806
七、急救中心(站)	First－aid Centers(stations)	8	4
八、采供血机构	Blood Supplying Agencies	3	2
九、妇幼保健院(所、站)	Maternity and Child Care Centers(stations)	9	4
十、专科疾病防治所(所、站)	Specialized Centers for Disease Prevention and Control(stations)	7	1
十一、疾病预防控制中心	Centers for Disease Prevention and Control	15	10
十二、卫生监督所	Institutions of Public Health Inspection	14	9
十三、医学科学研究机构	Research Institutions of Medical Science	1	1
十四、医学在职培训机构	Medical Training Organization for Incumbent	7	4
十五、健康教育所(站、中心)	Education Center for Health(stations)	2	1
十六、其他卫生机构	Other Health Care Institutions	45	16

机构数(2009 年)
Institutions(2009)

(unit)

#萧山区 Xiaoshan	#余杭区 Yuhang	桐庐县 Tonglu	淳安县 Chun'an	建德市 Jiande	富阳市 Fuyang	临安市 Lin'an
466	**354**	**109**	**134**	**177**	**196**	**184**
25	7	5	5	7	6	10
18	4	4	3	5	2	5
3	1	1	2	1	4	2
–	–	–	–	–	–	–
2	2	–	–	1	–	3
1	–	–	–	–	–	–
–	–	–	–	–	–	–
–	–	–	–	–	–	–
–	–	–	–	–	–	1
–	–	–	–	–	–	–
–	1	–	–	1	–	
–	–	–	–	–	–	
–	1	–	–	–	–	2
–	–	–	–	–	–	–
–	–	–	–	–	–	–
–	–	–	–	–	–	–
1	–	–	–	–	–	–
2	–	–	–	–	–	–
1	–	–	–	–	3	–
183	211	50	52	37	43	–
2	33	2	–	1	13	–
181	178	48	52	36	30	–
49	–	11	21	28	29	42
4	–	–	–	1	6	3
45	–	11	21	27	23	39
17	–	–	1	14	8	17
182	131	40	47	82	76	107
2	1	–	3	1	–	–
1	–	–	–	1	–	–
–	1	1	1	1	1	1
–	–	–	1	1	2	2
1	1	1	1	1	1	1
1	1	1	1	1	1	1
–	–	–	–	–	–	–
1	1	–	1	1	–	1
1	–	–	–	–	–	1
2	–	–	–	2	26	1

12－21 医疗病床
Number of Beds in

单位:张

指　　标	Item	全　市 Total	市区 Urban District
总　　计	**Total**	**40226**	**32412**
一、医院	Number of Hospitals	33094	28031
1. 综合医院	General Hospitals	21322	17618
2. 中医医院	Hospitals of Chinese Medicine	5610	4471
3. 中西医结合医院	Chinese Therapeutics with Western	535	535
4. 专科医院	Specialized Hospitals	5587	5367
口腔医院	Hospitals for Mouth	48	48
眼科医院	Hospitals for Eye	－	－
肿瘤医院	Tumor Hospitals	1374	1374
妇产(科)医院	Hospitals for Pregnant Woman	836	816
儿童医院	Children Hospitals	830	830
精神病医院	Mental Hospitals	1250	1120
传染病医院	Hospitals for Infectious Diseases	500	500
骨科医院	Orthopaedics Hospitals	200	130
康复医院	Healing Hospitals	273	273
整型外科医院	Plastic Hospitals	125	125
美容医院	Beauty Hospitals	41	41
其他专科医院	Other Special Hospitals	110	110
5. 护理院	Nursing Centers	40	40
二、疗养院	Sanatoriums	1317	817
三、社区卫生服务中心(站)	Health Service Centers for Community	2362	2148
1. 社区卫生服务中心	Health Service Centers	2292	2148
2. 社区卫生服务站	Health Service Stations	70	－
四、卫生院	Health Service Centers	1738	559
1. 街道卫生院	Rural Township Hospitals in Subdistrict	247	40
2. 乡镇卫生院	Rural Township Hospitals in Country	1491	519
五、门诊部	Clinics	727	707
六、诊所、卫生所、医务室、护理站	Other Health Care Institutions	－	－
七、急救中心(站)	First－aid Centers(stations)	－	－
八、采供血机构	Blood Supplying Agencies	－	－
九、妇幼保健院(所、站)	Maternity and Child Care Centers(stations)	540	150
十、专科疾病防治所(所、站)	Specialized Centers for Disease Prevention and Control(stations)	448	－

数(2009 年)

Health Institutions(2009)

(bed)

#萧山区 Xiaoshan	#余杭区 Yuhang	桐庐县 Tonglu	淳安县 Chun'an	建德市 Jiande	富阳市 Fuyang	临安市 Lin'an
4446	**2636**	**1009**	**859**	**1909**	**2441**	**1596**
3776	1966	665	613	1284	1234	1267
3129	1116	529	489	960	739	987
567	250	136	124	194	495	190
–	–	–	–	–	–	–
40	600	–	–	130	–	90
–	–	–	–	–	–	–
–	–	–	–	–	–	–
–	–	–	–	–	–	–
–	–	–	–	–	–	20
–	–	–	–	–	–	–
–	520	–	–	130	–	–
–	–	–	–	–	–	–
–	80	–	–	–	–	70
–	–	–	–	–	–	–
–	–	–	–	–	–	–
–	–	–	–	–	–	–
40	–	–	–	–	–	–
40	–	–	–	–	–	–
60	–	–	–	–	500	–
32	520	97	–	33	84	–
32	520	27	–	33	84	–
–	–	70	–	–	–	–
559	–	167	196	262	293	261
40	–	–	–	8	98	101
519	–	167	196	254	195	160
19	–	–	–	–	20	–
–	–	–	–	–	–	–
–	–	–	–	–	–	–
–	–	–	–	–	–	–
–	150	80	50	30	230	–
–	–	–	–	300	80	68

12－22 卫生事业
Number of Medical

单位：人

指　　标	Item	全　市 Total	市　区 Urban District
总　　计	**Total**	**68374**	**55287**
一、卫生技术人员	Number of Medical Technical Personnel	56270	45219
1. 执业(助理)医师	Registered (Assistant) Doctor	22753	17996
执业医师	Registered Doctor	20436	16559
助理医师	Assistant Doctor	2317	1437
2. 注册护士	Registered Nurse	20997	17530
3. 药剂师	Druggist	3985	3005
4. 技师人员	Checking Member	3452	2782
5. 其他	Others	5083	3906
二、其他技术人员	Other Medical Technical Personnel	3068	2625
三、管理人员	Managerial Personnel	3830	3164
四、工勤人员	Logistics Worker	5206	4279

人员数(2009 年)
Technical Personnel(2009)

(person)

萧山区 Xiaoshan	余杭区 Yuhang	桐庐县 Tonglu	淳安县 Chun'an	建德市 Jiande	富阳市 Fuyang	临安市 Lin'an
7588	**4962**	**2114**	**1652**	**2957**	**3701**	**2663**
6394	4338	1814	1473	2487	2964	2313
2735	1763	744	655	951	1325	1082
2314	1482	588	509	815	1080	885
421	281	156	146	136	245	197
2167	1409	561	418	877	939	672
470	338	162	145	240	219	214
356	277	125	93	166	160	126
666	551	222	162	253	321	219
403	129	58	33	23	195	134
321	152	129	63	199	175	100
470	343	113	83	248	367	116

12－23 主要年份卫生技术人员

Number of Medical Technical Personnel in Main Years

单位:人 (person)

年 份 Year	全 市 Total	执业(助理)医师 Number of Registered (Assistant) Doctors	护士(师) Senior and Junior Nurses	市 区 Urban District	执业(助理)医师 Number of Registered (Assistant) Doctors	护士(师) Senior and Junior Nurses
1978	19059	7375	3483	10867	4346	2510
1979	20060	7539	3536	11779	4733	2632
1980	21110	8311	3885	12376	5179	2804
1981	22737	9284	4139	13697	5946	3032
1982	23558	9883	4369	14221	6204	3193
1983	24914	10833	4562	15213	6990	3352
1984	25648	11291	4817	15807	7393	3487
1985	25593	11503	5071	15840	7644	3705
1986	26489	12623	5391	16543	8239	3940
1987	27663	12369	5805	17361	8329	4156
1988	28676	13674	6938	18022	8710	4801
1989	29791	14177	7348	18619	9146	5085
1990	30990	14483	7822	19231	9374	5397
1991	32169	14858	8153	19630	9494	5610
1992	32628	14842	8417	19690	9373	5736
1993	33172	15181	8643	19708	9499	5797
1994	33964	15465	8979	19907	9472	5940
1995	34245	16465	9531	19943	9607	6249
1996	34946	16789	9794	20695	9889	6508
1997	35423	17112	10019	20728	9902	6571
1998	35857	16022	10577	21035	9452	6788
1999	35256	16668	10587	20519	9610	6856
2000	35487	16317	11186	20344	9050	7300
2001	36643	16994	11576	28293	12968	9343
2002	37193	16092	11922	28818	12332	9653
2003	39019	16614	12460	30299	12731	10161
2004	39816	16770	13248	30886	12894	10840
2005	42353	17833	14514	33206	13802	12034
2006	45375	18831	15557	35904	14689	12986
2007	49780	20701	17455	39860	16290	14601
2008	52379	21223	18702	42015	16747	15556
2009	56270	22753	20997	45219	17996	17530

注:从 2001 年起市区数据包括萧山区和余杭区。
a) Data of urban include Xiaoshan and Yuhang district since 2001.

12－24 体育运动情况(2009 年)

Basic Statistics on Sports Activities(2009)

单位:人 (person)

指　　标	Item	2009 年	为上年(%) As Compared with the Preceding Year(%)
一、体委工作人员数	**Workers in Sports Commissions**	**923**	**90.1**
#教练员	#Full－time Coaches	75	68.2
二、等级裁判员发展人数	**Number of Referees in Grades**	**194**	**131.1**
#女	#Female	54	91.5
一级裁判员	First Grade Referees	－	－
二级裁判员	Second Grade Referees	194	131.1
三级裁判员	Third Grade Referees	－	－
三、等级运动员发展人数	**Number of Athletes in Grades**	**441**	**110.0**
#女	#Female	134	108.1
一级运动员	First Grade Athlete	－	－
二级运动员	Second Grade Athlete	441	110.0
三级运动员	Third Grade Athlete	－	－
少年级运动员	Youngster Athlete	－	－
四、县级以上运动竞赛次数 (次)	**Number of Sports Meets above County Level (time)**	**2920**	**178.5**
参加运动会人数	Number of Persons Attending Sports Meets	766752	98.3

主要统计指标解释

文化事业机构 指从事专业文化工作和为专业文化工作服务的独立建制的单独核算的单位。不包括这些单位另外举办独立核算的其他机构和各部门的业余文化组织。

艺术表演团体 指从事戏曲、音乐、舞蹈、杂技等专业艺术表演,有独立帐户,实行单独核算的团体。不包括半工半艺、半农半艺和民间职业剧团。

普通高等学校 指按照国家规定的设置标准和审批程序批准举办,通过国家统一招生考试,招收高中毕业生为主要培养对象,实施高等教育的全日制大学、独立设置的学院和高等专科学校、短期职业大学。

成人高等学校 指按照国家有关规定审批,招收通过全国成人高教统一招生考试的具有高中毕业或同等学历的在职从业人员利用脱产、半脱产、业余或函授等多种形式对其实施高等学历教育,培养高等教育专科或本科毕业水平的专门人才,修业年限、课程设置和总学时数均按高等学历教育要求付诸实施的学校。包括广播电视大学、职工高等学校、农民高等学校、管理干部学院、教育学院、独立设置的函授学院等。

小学学龄儿童入学率 指调查范围内已入小学学习的学龄儿童占校内外学龄儿童总数(包括弱智儿童在内,但不包括盲聋哑儿童)的比重。计算公式:

$$小学学龄儿童入学率 = \frac{已入学的小学学龄儿童数}{校内外小学学龄儿童总数} * 100\%$$

等级运动员人数 指经考核正式批准授予等级运动员称号的人数。运动员等级分为国际级运动健将、运动健将、一级运动员、二级运动员、三级运动员、少年级运动员。

等级裁判员人数 指经考核正式批准授予等级裁判员称号的人数。裁判员等级分为国际裁判、国家级裁判、一级裁判、二级裁判、三级裁判。

卫生机构 卫生机构是指从卫生行政部门取得《医疗机构执业许可证》,或从民政、工商行政、机构编制管理部门取得法人单位登记证书,为社会提供医疗保健、疾病控制、卫生监督等服务或从事医学科研、医学教育等卫生单位和卫生社会团体。不包括卫生行政机构、香港和澳门特别行政区以及台湾所属卫生机构。

卫生技术人员 卫生技术人员包括执业(助理)医师、注册护士、药剂人员、检验和影像技师(士、员)等卫生专业人员。

执业(助理)医师、执业(中)药师和注册护士 执业(助理)医师、执业(中)药师和注册护士是指领取医师、药师执业证书和注册护士证书的人员。不包括从事管理工作的医师、药师和护士。

Explanatory Notes on Main Statistical Indicators

Cultural Institutions refer to units which have their own organizational system and independent accounting system and specialize in or serve cultural development. They exclude other establishments run by these cultural institutions and amateur cultural groups established by various departments.

Art Troupe refers to the troupe which is engaged in drama, opera, music, dance, acrobatics or other art performance, opens independent accounts with banks and has self – supporting accounting system; excluding the troupes which are engaged partly in industrial or agricultural activities, partly in art performance and the professional troupes organized by the people.

Regular Institutions of Higher Learning refer to educational establishments set up according to the government evaluation and approval procedures, enrolling graduates from senior secondary schools and providing higher education courses and training for senior professionals, They include full – time universities, colleges, high professional schools and short – term professional universities.

Institutions of Higher Learning for Adults refer to educational establishments, set up in line with relevant rules approved by the government, enrolling staff and workers with senior secondary school or equivalent education, and providing higher education courses in many forms of full – time, part – time, space – time, or correspondence for adults. Professionals thus trained receive a qualification equivalent to graduates studying regular courses at regular universities, colleges and professional colleges. Institutions of higher learning for adults include Radio and TV universities, schools of high education for staff and workers and peasants, colleges for management cadres, pedagogical colleges, independent correspondence colleges.

Enrollment Rate of Primary School – age Children refer to the proportion of school – age children enrolled at schools to the total number of school – age children both in and outside schools (including retarded children, but excluding blind, deaf and mute children). The formula is:

$$\text{Enrollment Rate of Primary School – age Children} = \frac{\text{Total primary School – age Children at Schools}}{\text{Total Primary School – age Children Both at and Outside Schools}}$$

Number of Athletes in Grades refers to the number of athletes who have been given titles through examination. The titles of athletes include international masters of sports, masters of sports, first – grade, second – grade and third – grade sportsmen and young athletes.

Number of Referees in Grades refers to the number of referees who have been given titles after examination. They are classified as international referees, national referees and referees of the first, second and third grades.

Health Institutions refers to the Institutions and Society organization that get the registered license of health and medical institution from the health adiministration department, or get the registered license of units from civil administration department, industry and business administration and organization management department, and offers medical treatment, controlling of disease, supervision of sanitation. Health institution excludes health administration department and Institutions of Hong Kong, Macao, and Taiwan.

Medical Technical Personnel include registered (Assistant) doctor, registered nurse, druggist, checking members and photo artificer.

Registered (Assistant) Doctor, Registered Druggist and Registered Nurse refers to the personnel who get the licence of doctor, druggist and nurse, the management staff excluded.

第十三篇
CHAPTER-13

人民生活、物价、民政
PEOPLE'S LIVELIHOOD, PRICE INDICES AND CIVIL ADMINISTRATION

人民生活、物价、民政
People's Livelihood, Price Indices and Civil Administration

主要统计指标
Major Statistical Indicators

全市城镇单位在岗职工工资总额	Total Wages of Staff and Workers of Urban Units	754.91	亿元	(100 million yuan)
#国有单位	State-owned Units	287.11	亿元	(100 million yuan)
全市城镇单位在岗职工平均工资	Annual Average Wages of Staff and Workers of Urban Units	43947	元	(yuan)
#国有单位	State-owned Units	63602	元	(yuan)
市区城镇居民人均年可支配收入	Per Capita Annual Disposable Income of Urban Households of Urban District	26864	元	(yuan)
为上年	As Compared with the Preceding Year	111.5	%	(%)
农民人均年纯收入	Per Capita Annual Net Income of Rural Households	11822	元	(yuan)
为上年	As Compared with the Preceding Year	110.6	%	(%)
市区居民消费价格指数	Consume Price Index of Urban District	98.6	上年=100	(Preceding Year=100)
市区商品零售价格指数	Commodity Retail Price Index of Urban District	98.6	上年=100	(Preceding Year=100)
工业品出厂价格指数	Ex-factory Price Index of Industrial Products	95.1	上年=100	(Preceding Year=100)

13－01 主要年份市区城镇住户调查情况

Basic Conditions of Urban Households in Main Years

年 份 Year	调查户数（户） Number of Households Surveyed（household）	平均每户人口（人） Average Household Size（person）	平均每户就业人数（人） Average Number of Employed Persons Per Household（person）	年人均可支配收入（元） Per Capita Annual Disposable Income（yuan）	年人均消费性支出（元） Per Capita Annual Living Expenditure（yuan）	人均住房使用面积（平方米） Per Capita Living Space in City Areas（sq. m）
1978	28	4.20	2.89	338	301	–
1979	28	4.19	2.77	396	365	–
1980	28	4.18	2.79	521	491	–
1981	100	3.97	2.37	540	513	–
1982	100	3.90	2.35	532	532	–
1983	100	3.90	2.42	578	535	8.8
1984	100	3.90	2.36	729	679	9.3
1985	150	3.53	2.26	1026	908	9.7
1986	150	3.49	2.27	1169	1072	9.9
1987	150	3.42	2.25	1260	1118	10.6
1988	200	3.41	2.16	1565	1515	10.6
1989	200	3.40	2.15	1764	1615	10.6
1990	200	3.37	2.15	1985	1685	10.9
1991	200	3.40	2.20	2128	1894	10.8
1992	200	3.28	2.14	2580	2296	11.1
1993	200	3.21	2.10	3525	3183	11.2
1994	200	3.31	2.10	5249	4559	11.9
1995	200	3.20	2.05	6301	5559	11.7
1996	200	3.20	2.00	7206	6095	11.9
1997	200	3.14	1.99	7896	6766	12.4
1998	300	3.12	1.93	8465	7235	14.1
1999	300	3.11	1.92	9085	7424	14.6
2000	300	3.10	1.83	9668	7790	14.9
2001	440	2.98	1.72	10896	8968	15.5
2002	500	2.93	1.53	11778	9215	16.3
2003	500	2.92	1.51	12898	9950	17.2
2004	500	2.92	1.48	14565	11213	17.8
2005	600	2.84	1.42	16601	13438	20.7
2006	600	2.81	1.44	19027	14472	21.0
2007	600	2.72	1.45	21689	14896	21.6
2008	600	2.75	1.29	24104	16719	22.4
2009	600	2.68	1.25	26864	18595	23.1

注：从 2001 年起市区数据包括萧山区和余杭区。

a) Data of urban include Xiaoshan and Yuhang district since 2001.

13－02 市区城镇居民家庭平均每人全年现金收支

Per Capita Annual Cash Income and Expenditure of Urban Residents

单位:元 (yuan)

项目 Item	1995	2000	2005	2006	2007	2008	2009
家庭总收入 Total Income	**9120.88**	**9709.45**	**18761.51**	**21367.13**	**24474.89**	**27034.76**	**30337.78**
其中:可支配收入 Disposable Income	9085	9668	16601	19026.86	21689.36	24103.58	26863.93
一、工薪收入 Income from Wages	6776.28	7074.79	12961.40	14427.48	16293.33	16948.94	18769.76
1.工资及补贴收入 Bonus and Subsidy	6446.59	6702.84	12235.25	13915.20	15904.55	16572.54	18515.37
2.其他劳动收入 Other Income of Staff & Workers From Their Working Units	329.69	371.95	726.15	512.27	388.78	376.40	254.38
二、经营净收入 Income of Staff & workers in Other－owned Units	277.48	235.69	1041.05	1101.51	2027.13	1406.95	1596.66
三、财产性收入 Property Income	131.78	116.93	585.72	1137.67	584.11	1939.01	2147.08
四、转移性收入 Transfer Income	1935.34	2282.04	4173.33	4700.48	5570.31	6739.87	7824.28
#养老金或离退休金 Annuities & Retirement Pension	1705.17	1751.49	3384.69	3788.36	4461.22	5409.92	6517.65
#赡养收入 Supporting Income	15.07	23.99	47.71	41.22	54.70	104.03	197.19
#捐赠收入 Income from Donation	118.51	230.73	353.99	473.76	474.42	676.41	563.84
借贷收入 Credit Income	**1680.13**	**2157.36**	**4289.05**	**5475.29**	**6882.79**	**4854.84**	**8797.72**
#提取储蓄存款 Money Drawn from Bank	1464.73	1869.60	3779.11	4947.88	6044.00	4719.70	6885.49
#借入款 Money Borrowed	85.35	62.28	118.70	302.43	228.68	36.32	110.88
家庭总支出 Total Expenditure	**6531.96**	**9169.32**	**17260.06**	**19513.14**	**21545.09**	**23289.70**	**29159.11**
消费性支出 Living Expenditure	5558.62	7789.68	13437.58	14471.74	14895.75	16719.10	18594.75
其中:服务性消费支出 Service Living Expenditure	－	－	3832.72	4230.84	4038.27	4820.91	5141.30
非消费性支出 Other Non－Living Expenditure	973.34	1379.64	3822.48	5041.40	6649.34	6570.60	10564.36
1.购买商品住宅及建房支出 Expenditure for House－purchasing	731.72	751.68	435.25	950.79	1565.53	947.29	4464.89
2.赡养支出 Supporting Expenditure	54.52	108.60	345.31	557.90	756.19	722.52	871.86
3.捐赠支出 Living Expenditure	123.79	455.76	920.25	1005.27	1246.70	1438.34	1459.77
4.各种非储蓄性保险支出 Expenditure for Non－saving Insurance	4.99	28.80	42.99	169.95	211.19	330.88	214.92
5.社会保障支出 Expenditure for Social Security	－	－	1739.65	1924.93	2288.50	2463.66	2854.86
#个人交纳的养老基金 Annuities	－	－	618.20	717.70	895.82	893.33	1016.32
#个人交纳的住房公积金 Accumulated Expenditure for House－purchasing	－	－	872.86	955.39	1060.40	1201.48	1412.36
#个人交纳的医疗基金 Expenditure for Medical Treatment	－	－	199.24	204.37	280.42	300.53	342.60
借贷支出 Expenditure for Credit	**1319.42**	**2154.60**	**4547.79**	**8215.12**	**9259.10**	**8542.02**	**10988.78**
#存入储蓄款 Saving in Bank	1007.63	1658.52	3298.06	6184.50	6341.17	6993.63	9319.94
#借出款 Money Lent	54.89	42.00	28.10	17.77	163.93	40.87	4.61
#储蓄性保险支出 Expenditure for Saving Insurance	25.99	109.80	190.63	256.15	279.31	437.27	389.03
期末手存现金 Per Capita Cash in Hand at Year－end	**512.68**	**1374.96**	**2255.52**	**1963.45**	**2770.43**	**1743.08**	**1282.59**

13－03　2009年市区城镇居民家庭人均现金收支(按收入水平分组)

Per Capita Annual Cash Income and Expenditure of Urban Residents in 2009(Grouped by Income Level)

单位:元　　　　(yuan)

项　目 Item	总平均 Average	按可支配收入分组 Grouped by Disposable Income				
		20%低收入户 20% Lowest Income House－holds	20%较低收入户 20% Low Income House－holds	20%中间收入户 20% Middle Income House－holds	20%较高收入户 20% High Income House－holds	20%最高收入户 20% Highest Income House－holds
家庭总收入 Total Income	**30337.78**	**13394.67**	**20401.04**	**25935.55**	**34523.53**	**61085.48**
其中:可支配收入 Disposable Income	26863.93	11453.63	18163.09	23655.81	30943.22	53401.77
一、工薪收入 Income from Wages	18769.76	7599.45	9729.73	12323.63	20417.75	46354.91
二、经营净收入 Income of Staff & workers in Other－owned Units	1596.66	1007.51	978.26	1159.82	1557.99	3417.27
三、财产性收入 Property Income	2147.08	815.02	1808.08	2289.31	2408.53	3655.39
四、转移性收入 Transfer Income	7824.28	3972.69	7884.97	10162.79	10139.26	7657.90
借贷收入 Credit Income	**8797.72**	**1711.08**	**9268.22**	**4450.54**	**6136.89**	**23413.57**
家庭总支出 Total Expenditure	**29159.11**	**11939.30**	**23880.83**	**21291.14**	**28163.73**	**63647.28**
消费性支出 Living Expenditure	18594.75	9431.07	17868.25	15970.95	20028.61	31318.82
其中:服务性消费支出 Service Living Expenditure	5141.30	2323.04	4535.30	4318.28	5618.85	9442.53
非消费性支出 Other Non－Living Expenditure	10564.36	2508.23	6012.58	5320.19	8135.12	32328.46
1. 购买商品住宅及建房支出 Expenditure for House－purchasing	4464.89	0	2599.25	704.81	1531.56	18176.03
2. 赡养支出 Supporting Expenditure	871.86	180.87	256.89	842.49	756.87	2457.06
3. 捐赠支出 Living Expenditure	1459.77	493.53	1002.38	1466.26	2115.21	2447.39
4. 各种非储蓄性保险支出 Expenditure for Non－saving Insurance	214.92	11.83	68.67	101.76	180.98	752.09
5. 社会保障支出 Expenditure for Social Security	2854.86	1704.84	1934.04	1942.61	2973.78	5987.40
借贷支出 Expenditure for Credit	**10988.78**	**2834.75**	**5892.67**	**9255.16**	**12290.50**	**26380.31**
期末手存现金 Per Capita Cash in Hand at Year－end	**1282.59**	**894.52**	**1089.65**	**1199.39**	**1715.54**	**1614.34**

13 – 04 主要年份市区城镇居民家庭人均消费性支出

Per Capita Annual Living Expenditure of Urban Residents in Main Years

单位:元 (yuan)

项目 Item	1995	2000	2005	2006	2007	2008	2009
消费性支出 Total Living Expenditure	**5558.62**	**7789.68**	**13437.58**	**14471.74**	**14895.75**	**16719.10**	**18594.75**
食品类 Food	2774.32	3303.48	4682.40	4817.63	5526.10	6410.16	6972.89
粮食 Grain	235.38	206.76	249.84	261.17	281.37	326.91	346.10
油脂类 Oil and Fats	49.08	56.88	72.50	77.18	118.54	162.29	137.53
肉禽及制品 Meat, Poultry and Related Products	554.87	514.56	574.29	554.89	729.53	959.13	880.45
蛋类 Eggs	57.23	43.80	55.16	52.42	65.29	73.73	79.93
水产品类 Aquatic Products	395.19	514.20	466.42	500.68	581.65	633.72	702.21
菜类 Vegetables	266.63	302.88	364.56	404.51	444.28	467.75	529.66
酒和饮料 Liquor and Beverage	146.63	192.12	298.47	259.11	308.87	381.41	439.49
干鲜瓜果类 Dried and Fresh Melons and Fruits	211.93	214.44	335.20	365.87	428.02	433.91	508.37
在外用餐 Out – dining	368.60	531.00	1232.68	1285.90	1366.37	1684.34	1820.50
衣着类 Clothing	665.02	645.00	1298.53	1354.58	1512.81	1656.81	1818.07
家庭设备用品及服务 Facilities, Articles and Service	491.46	626.50	673.50	584.66	678.22	762.43	1096.70
医疗保健 Medicine and Medical Service	145.11	444.12	983.06	884.82	955.53	1132.49	961.47
交通和通信 Transportation and Communication	280.01	547.51	2234.02	2876.37	2549.38	2589.77	3008.68
教育文化娱乐服务 Education, Cultural and Recreation Service	433.13	1079.11	1970.11	2010.54	1689.63	1782.02	1956.94
居住 Residence	488.03	701.04	1150.69	1478.91	1508.88	1814.01	2046.72
杂项商品和服务 Miscellaneous Commodities and Service	281.53	442.92	445.26	464.22	475.20	571.41	733.28

13-05 2009年市区城镇居民家庭人均全年消费性支出(按收入水平分组)

Per Capita Annual Living Expenditure of Urban Residents in 2009(Grouped by Income Level)

单位:元 (yuan)

项 目 Item	总平均 Average	按可支配收入分组 Grouped by Disposable Income				
		20%低收入户 20% Lowest Income House-holds	20%较低收入户 20% Low Income House-holds	20%中间收入户 20% Middle Income House-holds	20%较高收入户 20% High Income House-holds	20%最高收入户 20% Highest Income House-holds
消费性支出 Total Living Expenditure	**18594.75**	**9431.07**	**17868.25**	**15970.95**	**20028.61**	**31318.82**
食品类 Food	6972.89	4699.47	7052.88	7022.13	7600.98	8881.09
粮食 Grain	346.10	296.84	360.85	391.79	373.62	314.82
油脂类 Oil and Fats	137.53	126.43	155.71	165.49	127.13	111.89
肉禽及制品 Meat, Poultry and Related Products	880.45	796.69	950.41	975.65	916.84	771.33
蛋类 Eggs	79.93	72.2	76.23	84.49	85.48	82.94
水产品类 Aquatic Products	702.21	530.14	805.59	710.02	825.49	669.39
菜类 Vegetables	529.66	457.55	546.67	615.69	568.14	470.68
酒和饮料 Liquor and Beverage	439.49	234.31	484.65	415.14	415.33	675.85
干鲜瓜果类 Dried and Fresh Melons and Fruits	508.37	314.04	451.79	505.70	564.81	743.18
在外用餐 Out-dining	1820.50	675.26	1829.88	1611.13	2063.91	3123.18
衣着类 Clothing	1818.07	768.01	1305.26	1444.00	2105.73	3692.78
家庭设备用品及服务 Facilities, Articles and Service	1096.70	303.52	1238.35	983.39	1444.63	1657.50
医疗保健 Medicine and Medical Service	961.47	605.53	993.29	936.53	992.84	1335.24
交通和通信 Transportation and Communication	3008.68	974.40	2050.27	1628.71	3547.78	7295.43
教育文化娱乐服务 Education, Cultural and Recreation Service	1956.94	898.36	1317.01	1550.15	2068.41	4172.53
居住 Residence	2046.72	982.65	3354.49	2030.55	1605.86	2313.39
杂项商品和服务 Miscellaneous Commodities and Service	733.28	199.12	556.70	375.49	662.38	1970.85

13－06 主要年份市区城镇居民家庭平均每百户耐用消费品拥有量

Number of Major Durable Consumer Goods Owned Per 100 Urban Households in Main Years

项目 Item		1995	2000	2005	2006	2007	2008	2009
摩托车 Motorcycle	(辆) (unit)	1.50	3.60	11.00	11.67	10.02	4.89	4.78
助力电动车 Electric－bicycle	(辆) (unit)	－	－	28.67	33.33	35.96	36.05	38.78
家用汽车 Family Car	(辆) (unit)	－	0.70	12.83	14.00	15.44	17.84	21.65
微波炉 Micro－wave Oven	(个) (unit)	－	39.00	68.17	67.17	66.50	69.06	74.62
影碟机 Video Player	(台) (unit)	－	54.00	69.67	68.33	－	－	－
普通电话 Telephone	(部) (set)	－	95.00	99.83	97.00	97.37	92.33	89.64
移动电话 Mobile Phone	(部) (set)	－	19.00	178.67	176.83	187.19	180.87	178.5
淋浴热水器 Water Heater	(台) (unit)	43.50	81.30	92.33	91.50	94.91	93.34	94.95
排油烟机 Smoke Exhauster	(台) (unit)	34.50	72.67	83.33	85.33	－	－	－
洗衣机 Washing Machine	(台) (unit)	93.50	96.33	94.17	96.50	95.73	89.80	94.60
电冰箱 Refrigerator	(台) (unit)	103.50	101.67	100.00	99.50	100.82	98.15	100.30
电炊具 Electric Cooking Appliances	(个) (unit)	79.50	88.00	100.50	106.33	－	－	－
家用电脑 Personal Computer	(台) (unit)	－	23.00	74.50	74.50	82.10	81.74	86.87
彩色电视机 Color TV Set	(台) (unit)	102.30	146.67	182.67	180.67	181.28	167.27	173.96
吸尘器 Dust Collector	(台) (unit)	21.00	23.33	20.67	20.00	－	－	－
组合音响 Music Center	(套) (set)	12.00	28.67	37.83	34.83	33.00	32.27	31.15
摄像机 Video Recorder	(架) (unit)	－	3.33	7.50	7.00	9.03	9.20	10.31
照相机 Camera	(架) (unit)	54.00	64.67	59.00	56.67	54.02	51.50	53.73
空调器 Air Conditioner	(台) (unit)	43.00	104.00	183.33	187.83	191.30	195.53	203.87

13－07　主要年份全市农村住户调查情况

Basic Conditions of Whole Municipality Rural Households in Main Years

年份 Year	调查户数(户) Number of Households Surveyed (household)	平均每户人口(人) Average Number of Residents per Household (person)	平均每户劳动力(人) Average Number of Laborers Per Household (person)	农民人均年纯收入(元) Per Capita Annual Net Income of Rural Households (yuan)	人均生活费支出(元) Per Capita Annual Living Expenditure (yuan)	人均居住面积(平方米) Per Capita Floor Space (sq. m)
1978	–	–	–	162	–	–
1979	–	–	–	204	–	–
1980	60	4.72	2.93	250	287	23.3
1981	60	4.60	2.70	333	294	25.2
1982	60	4.43	2.73	405	328	26.3
1983	170	4.55	2.85	395	355	29.9
1984	170	4.44	2.81	510	416	31.7
1985	420	4.40	2.88	624	542	29.9
1986	620	4.39	2.88	675	601	31.3
1987	620	4.34	2.86	820	714	33.1
1988	620	4.26	2.87	996	925	35.5
1989	620	4.17	2.85	1117	1011	36.8
1990	620	4.16	2.89	1171	923	39.6
1991	620	4.03	2.81	1308	1018	38.0
1992	620	4.01	2.81	1493	1129	37.5
1993	540	3.91	2.76	1748	1276	37.1
1994	630	3.85	2.35	2267	1884	37.8
1995	630	3.87	2.30	3012	2373	40.5
1996	630	3.81	2.77	3482	2772	42.2
1997	630	3.87	2.86	3785	2762	42.0
1998	630	3.87	2.88	4006	2858	46.2
1999	630	3.80	2.80	4209	2851	48
2000	630	3.61	2.59	4894	3393	49
2001	630	3.57	2.53	5330	3909	52
2002	630	3.53	2.53	5708	4444	52.7
2003	670	3.48	2.53	6250	5142	54.7
2004	670	3.48	2.54	6950	5608	58.9
2005	1100	3.34	2.34	7655	6004	66.0
2006	1100	3.63	2.52	8515	6901	66.5
2007	1100	3.60	2.61	9549	7568	68.0
2008	1100	3.56	2.58	10692	8446	69.7
2009	1100	3.57	2.59	11822	9065	70.74

13－08 主要年份全市农村居民家庭人均纯收入

Per Capita Annual Gross and Net Income of Whole Municipality Rural Households in Main Years

单位:元 (yuan)

项目 Item	1995	2000	2005	2006	2007	2008	2009
全年纯收入 Net Income	**3012**	**4894**	**7655**	**8515**	**9549**	**10692**	**11822**
1. 劳动者的工资性收入 Laborers´Remuneration	896	2045	3347	4772	5401	6318	6967
2. 家庭经营收入 Income from Household Business Operation	1960	2363	3358	3011	3318	3363	3694
#农业收入 Income from Farming	578	1016	1588	777	784	836	885
林业收入 Income from Forestry	142	71	311	306	338	328	395
牧业收入 Income from Animal Husbandry	397	382	310	234	235	151	212
渔业收入 Income from Fishery	24	31	185	94	135	71	77
工业收入 Income from Industry	112	262	392	295	328	406	441
建筑业收入 Income from Construction	77	102	228	225	297	326	306
交通、运输、仓储及邮电业收入 Transportation, Posts, Storage and Telecommunication	136	163	483	334	329	367	395
批发和零售贸易、餐饮业收入 Income from Retail Wholesale & Trade and Catering Services	118	150	391	471	523	550	638
社会服务业收入 Social Serve Trade	59	73	127	125	138	146	177
3. 转移性收入 Transfer Income	83	312	481	346	330	419	553
#在外人口寄回或带回 Income of Going out to Work	5	21	93	75	41	53	72
农村外部亲友赠送 Present from Rural Friends and Relatives	9	7	133	13	10	31	25
4. 财产性收入 Property Income	73	174	469	386	500	592	609
#土地征用补偿收入 #Compensation for Confiscating Land	6	100	243	156	198	208	192

13－09 主要年份全市农村居民家庭人均支出

Per Capita Gross Expenditure of Whole Municipality Rural Households in Main Years

单位:元 (yuan)

项目 Item	1995	2000	2005	2006	2007	2008	2009
全年总支出 Gross Expenditure	**3457.32**	**3789**	**8043**	**9308**	**9661**	**11223**	**11632**
生活消费支出 Living Expenditure	**2373**	**3393**	**6004**	**6901**	**7568**	**8446**	**9065**
1. 食品 Food	1212.66	1392	2145	2418	2636	3031	3067
#在外饮食 #Out－dining	42.65	83	221	302	311	399	436
食品加工费 Food－processing	13.18	15	11	10	12	11	12
2. 衣着 Clothing	169.19	169	381	438	476	527	530
3. 居住 Residence	395.77	694	1143	1481	1637	1856	2157
#住房 #Housing	284.49	509	724	1033	1103	1223	1500
电费 Electricity	21.99	56	110	140	172	201	221
燃料 Fuel	53.12	38	77	94	108	116	102
4. 家庭设备、用品及服务 Household Facilities, Articles and Services	154.52	163	307	326	361	385	445
5. 医疗保健 Medicines and Medical Services	99.06	329	474	478	505	589	570
#医药卫生保健用品 #Medicines	39.21	99	189	170	264	264	247
医疗保健服务费 Medicines Services	58.45	64	256	292	241	325	323
6. 交通和通讯 Transportation and Communications	102.24	204	680	793	948	1065	1182
#交通工具 #Vehicles	66.93	123	158	252	354	418	567
交通费 Traffic	17.91	36	83	79	82	88	80
邮电费 Postage	4.43	62	219	218	247	270	258
7. 文教娱乐用品及服务 Cultural, Educational and Recreational Articles and Services	155.83	318	735	823	836	828	936
文化教育娱乐用品 Cultural, Educational and Recreational Articles	42.60	70	114	167	174	176	223
文化教育娱乐服务 Culrural, Educational and Recreational Services	113.23	248	621	656	662	652	712

项目 Item	1995	2000	2005	2006	2007	2008	2009
#学杂费 #Tuition and Incidental Expenses	93.59	210	430	442	384	334	355
技术培训费 Technical Training Expenses	5.29	5	32	31	47	34	44
文娱费 Recreational and Cultural Expenses	10.88	9	22	23	33	44	53
8.其他商品和服务 Other Commodities and Services	83.73	124	139	144	169	165	178
家庭经营费用支出 Expenditure of Household Business Operation	**680.56**	**427**	**1157**	**1226**	**1017**	**1217**	**1025**
种植业生产支出 Expenditure of Farming	198.70	183	245	277	283	271	220
林业生产支出 Expenditure of Forestry	2.76	10	71	99	68	62	75
牧业生产支出 Expenditure of Animal Husbandry	266.83	121	168	162	181	248	162
渔业生产支出 Expenditure of Fishery	3.83	10	116	71	32	30	28
工业生产支出 Expenditure of Industry	61.98	61	276	310	181	303	249
建筑业生产支出 Expenditure of Construction	2.98	3	35	31	39	69	92
运输业生产支出 Expenditure of Transportation	63.60	29	141	224	234	235	143
批发和零售贸易、餐饮业支出 Expenditure of Wholesale and Retail Trade & Catering Services	52.69	6	84	28	50	53	39
服务业支出 Expenditure of Services Trade	5.06	1	9	15	12	11	5
其他经营支出 Others	22.13	3	12	9	8	4	12
购置生产用固定资产支出 Expenditure of Purchasing Fixed Assets	**134.66**	**86**	**202**	**152**	**66**	**124**	**138**
税费支出 Expenditure of Taxes	**23.32**	**50**	**31**	**20**	**23**	**12**	**10**
其他非借贷性支出 Others Expenditure not for Loans	**235.30**	**206**	**649**	**344**	**383**	**712**	**710**
#寄给和带给在外人口 Posting and Giving to People Outside	6.26	23	396	158	172	181	132
赠送农村外部亲友 Present to Rural Friends and Relatives	7.12	8	7	7	7	6	6
附:生产用固定资产累计折旧 Depreciation of Fixed Assets for Production	**63.46**	**79**	**218**	**235**	**–**	**–**	**–**

13－10 主要年份全市农村居民家庭平均每百户耐用消费品拥有量
Number of Major Durable Consumer Goods Owned Per 100 Rural Households in Main Years

项　　目	Item	1995	2000	2005	2006	2007	2008	2009
自行车　（辆）	Bicycle （Unit）	209	183	124	127	127	126	127
电风扇　（台）	Electric Fan （Unit）	211	258	267	291	－	－	－
洗衣机　（台）	Washing Machine （Unit）	14	34	62	72	74	78	82
电冰箱　（台）	Refrigerator （Unit）	23	46	72	83	88	91	95
摩托车　（辆）	Motorcycle （Unit）	13	38	73	80	71	71	70
黑白电视机（台）	Black and White TV Set （Unit）	73	57	17	13	10	6	6
彩色电视机（台）	Color TV Set （Unit）	34	86	141	156	163	170	177
录像机　（台）	Video Cassette Recorder （Unit）	3	7	7	8	－	－	－
收录机　（台）	Radio Cassette Player （Unit）	26	28	16	14	－	－	－
照相机　（架）	Camera （Unit）	4	7	14	17	17	19	22
抽油烟机　（台）	Smoke Exhauster （Unit）	4	17	39	49	52	55	59
吸尘器　（台）	Dust Collector （Unit）	2	3	5	6	6	6	8
空调机　（台）	Air Conditioner （Unit）	1	8	12	70	83	91	100

13－11 主要年份全市城镇单位在岗职工工资总额
Total Wages of Fully Employed Staff and Workers in Main Years

单位:万元 (10000 yuan)

年　份 Year	总　计 Total	国有经济单位 State－owned Units	城镇集体经济单位 Collective－owned Units	其他经济单位 Units of Other Types of Ownership
1978	43775	32730	11045	－
1979	52127	38651	13476	－
1980	67918	49461	18457	－
1981	72896	52581	20315	－
1982	75584	55325	20259	－
1983	78336	57716	20620	－
1984	102223	72149	29385	689
1985	130114	90643	38482	989
1986	157471	111010	45230	1231
1987	180077	127353	50512	2212
1988	230868	163863	63525	3480
1989	253956	180706	68230	5020
1990	277910	203212	70253	4445
1991	313906	227438	78827	7641
1992	377614	272098	89429	16087
1993	534537	367062	118634	48841
1994	772236	525936	159864	86436
1995	890488	598524	170638	121326
1996	973592	647327	171227	155038
1997	1073862	722182	173502	178178
1998	1112718	719249	127584	265885
1999	1180947	755073	102906	322968
2000	1267524	784396	80911	402217
2001	1481659	899920	65534	516205
2002	1614676	1026645	65820	522211
2003	1867776	1174126	64820	628830
2004	2188159	1367229	71112	749818
2005	2970200	1617671	88226	1264303
2006	3811735	1825613	99009	1887113
2007	4954813	2202920	130443	2621450
2008	6416424	2551401	149362	3715661
2009	7549145	2871075	171367	4506703

注:1998 年以前为全市职工工资总额。

a) Data on total wage bill before 1998 refer to wages of staff and workers.

13－12　主要年份市区城镇单位在岗职工工资总额

Total Wages of Fully Employed Staff and Workers of Urban District in Main Years

单位:万元　(10000 yuan)

年　份 Year	总　计 Total	国有经济单位 State－owned Units	城镇集体经济单位 Collective－owned Units	其他经济单位 Units of Other Types of Ownership
1978	28256	21727	6529	－
1979	34318	26164	8154	－
1980	45574	33920	11654	－
1981	48809	35856	12953	－
1982	50959	37898	13061	－
1983	52909	39848	13061	－
1984	69135	51057	17498	580
1985	87774	63830	23100	844
1986	105995	77989	26936	1070
1987	121003	89233	29728	2042
1988	152859	113227	36474	3158
1989	167055	123862	38759	4434
1990	182985	139337	40061	3587
1991	209052	157279	45778	5995
1992	253653	186961	52890	13802
1993	359041	254742	63921	40378
1994	521669	360273	87807	73589
1995	615450	422101	92980	100369
1996	683244	462364	94061	126819
1997	762957	521029	84456	147472
1998	803264	532561	74852	195851
1999	864418	559707	61417	243294
2000	949872	594435	47580	307857
2001	1279749	756669	49687	473393
2002	1398222	866806	48691	482724
2003	1617504	996961	44920	575624
2004	1859164	1162299	50943	645921
2005	2584779	1380262	64558	1139959
2006	3338568	1562198	72670	1703700
2007	4317965	1882616	101388	2333961
2008	5679543	2180009	117583	3381951
2009	6665279	2425106	147894	4092280

注:从2001年起市区数据包括萧山区和余杭区,1998年以前为职工工资总额。

a) Data of urban include Xiaoshan and Yuhang district since 2001, data on total wage bill before 1998 refer to wages of staff and workers.

13－13　主要年份全市城镇单位在岗职工年平均工资

Annual Average Wages of Fully Employed Staff and Workers in Main Years

单位:元　　(yuan)

年　份 Year	总　计 Total	国有经济单位 State－owned Units	城镇集体经济单位 Collective－owned Units	其他经济单位 Units of Other Types of Ownership
1978	597	634	509	－
1979	643	694	531	－
1980	777	832	660	－
1981	783	824	693	－
1982	791	823	714	－
1983	813	840	745	－
1984	1036	1080	943	1006
1985	1266	1302	1188	1287
1986	1469	1531	1336	1561
1987	1616	1682	1469	1685
1988	1986	2063	1806	2129
1989	2173	2259	1961	2416
1990	2382	2504	2078	2582
1991	2586	2710	2252	3123
1992	3071	3236	2600	3571
1993	4220	4479	3404	4949
1994	6118	6565	4750	6936
1995	7156	7546	5604	8266
1996	7966	8336	6178	9199
1997	9108	9522	6905	10519
1998	10555	11180	7720	10826
1999	12187	12972	8938	11883
2000	14257	15441	10150	13401
2001	18319	21119	13831	15394
2002	21418	24739	15090	17685
2003	24668	29121	18154	19757
2004	28891	35507	24010	21879
2005	31069	40483	23964	24332
2006	32791	44664	21845	26641
2007	36496	53343	26095	29300
2008	40193	56802	30698	33823
2009	43947	63602	36625	36953

注:1998 年以前为全市职工年平均工资。

a) Data on total wage bill before 1998 refer to average wages of staff and workers.

13－14　主要年份市区城镇单位在岗职工年平均工资

Annual Average Wages of Fully Employed Staff and Workers of Urban District in Main Years

单位:元　　　　(yuan)

年　份 Year	总　计 Total	国有经济单位 State－owned Units	城镇集体经济单位 Collective－owned Units	其他经济单位 Units of Other Types of Ownership
1978	642	673	558	－
1979	692	730	593	－
1980	814	868	688	－
1981	810	847	724	－
1982	809	845	719	－
1983	835	869	746	－
1984	1071	1119	954	1012
1985	1316	1348	1235	1290
1986	1536	1589	1401	1519
1987	1690	1744	1545	1692
1988	2073	2135	4897	2119
1989	2261	2340	2031	2381
1990	2486	2587	2179	2691
1991	2706	2812	2350	3233
1992	3233	3385	2719	3658
1993	4561	4816	3565	5115
1994	6597	7024	4978	7254
1995	7786	8154	5928	8658
1996	7851	9032	6689	9888
1997	10048	10319	7624	11299
1998	11512	11865	8298	12339
1999	13225	13698	9391	13545
2000	15454	16373	10370	15017
2001	18962	21916	14573	16018
2002	22091	25720	15295	18279
2003	25535	30334	18074	20563
2004	30719	37585	24291	23488
2005	32166	41977	24220	25440
2006	33967	46509	21971	27751
2007	37991	55675	25774	30746
2008	41501	58696	31097	35252
2009	45149	65118	38096	38423

注:从 2001 年起市区数据包括萧山区和余杭区,1998 年之前为市区城镇单位职工年平均工资。

a) Data of urban include Xiaoshan and Yuhang district since 2001, data on total wage bill before 1998 refer to average wages of staff and workers of urban collective－owned units.

13－15 全市城镇单位从业人员劳动报酬(2009 年)

Laborers´Remuneration of Employed Persons in Urban Units(2009)

单位:万元 (10000 yuan)

行业 Sector / 地区 Region	年末单位从业人员劳动报酬 Laborers´Remuneration of Employed Persons at Year－end	在岗职工工资总额 Total Wages of Fully Employed Staff and Workers	其他从业人员劳动报酬 Laborers´Remuneration of Other Employed Persons	#在岗职工平均工资(元/人) Average Wage of Fully Employed Staff and Workers (yuan/person)
全市总计 Total	**8321164**	**7549145**	**772019**	**43947**
其中:企业 Enterprises	6141842	5448245	693597	39092
事业 Institutions	1474872	1410810	64062	63610
机关 Agencies and Organizations	660821	650111	10710	73950
民间非营利组织 Non－profit Organizations	18268	15859	2409	29002
其他 Other	25361	24121	1240	27072
市区总计 Urban District	**7395770**	**6665279**	**730491**	**45149**
其中:企业 Enterprises	5609536	4949162	660373	40515
事业 Institutions	1221047	1161998	59049	65972
机关 Agencies and Organizations	525938	518346	7592	78760
民间非营利组织 Non－profit Organizations	15649	13313	2335	28393
其他 Other	23601	22459	1142	27724
上城区 Shangcheng	**954617**	**879039**	**75578**	**62541**
下城区 Xiacheng	**1142032**	**1040868**	**101164**	**63772**
江干区 Jianggan	**446501**	**413574**	**32926**	**35752**
拱墅区 Gongshu	**564647**	**466171**	**98476**	**41772**
西湖区 Xihu	**1043732**	**869496**	**174236**	**44822**
高新(滨江)区 Hi－Tech (Binjiang)	**764771**	**721673**	**43098**	**57166**
萧山区 Xiaoshan	**1340024**	**1263514**	**76509**	**33987**
余杭区 Yuhang	**558717**	**533346**	**25370**	**37375**
桐庐县 Tonglu	**144519**	**135799**	**8719**	**33561**
淳安县 Chun´an	**102800**	**100497**	**2304**	**38656**
建德市 Jiande	**150725**	**146713**	**4011**	**41789**

单位:万元 13-15 续表 continued (10000 yuan)

行业 Sector / 地区 Region	年末单位从业人员劳动报酬 Laborers´Remuneration of Employed Persons at Year-end	在岗职工工资总额 Total Wages of Fully Employed Staff and Workers	其他从业人员劳动报酬 Laborers´Remuneration of Other Employed Persons	#在岗职工平均工资(元/人) Average Wage of Fully Employed Staff and Workers (yuan/person)
富阳市 Fuyang	**306207**	**285811**	**20396**	**38131**
临安市 Lin´an	**221144**	**215046**	**6098**	**33106**
按国民经济行业分组 Grouped by Sector				
农、林、牧、渔业 Farming, Forestry, Animal Husbandry and Fishery	5672	5559	113	32681
采矿业 Mining and Quarrying	5736	5727	9	25085
制造业 Manufacturing	2195825	2028674	167151	31261
电力、煤气及水的生产和供应业 Production and Supply of Electricity, Gas and Water	145379	134030	11349	72445
建筑业 Construction	1007272	724877	282395	28318
交通运输、仓储及邮政业 Transportation, Storage and Post	343726	310663	33063	45740
信息传输、计算机服务和软件业 Information Transmission Computer Service and Software	409347	375765	33582	83483
批发与零售业 Wholesale & Retail Trade	446582	422181	24402	43150
住宿和餐饮业 Accommodations and Catering	169085	157232	11853	26559
金融业 Banking and Insurance	712847	648808	64039	130687
房地产业 Real Estate	177410	164487	12922	47257
租赁与商务服务业 Renting and Business Service	244131	221619	22512	34233
科学研究、技术服务与地质勘查业 Scientific Research, Technical Service and Geological Prospecting	293242	269440	23803	61143
水利、环境和公共设施管理业 Water Conservany, Environment and Public Utility	75250	69319	5931	35522
居民服务和其他服务业 Service for the Residents and Other	23024	20922	2102	29850
教育 Education	791686	766184	25502	65345
卫生、社会保障和社会福利业 Health Care, Sports and Social Welfare	432907	405551	27356	67969
文化、体育与娱乐业 Culture, Sports and Entertainment	102000	91316	10684	59062
公共管理与社会组织 Public Management and Social Organzations	740043	726793	13250	67148

13－16　全市国有单位从业人员劳动报酬(2009 年)

Laborers´Remuneration of Employed Persons for State－owned Units(2009)

单位:万元　　(10000 yuan)

行业 Sector / 地区 Region	年末单位从业人员劳动报酬 Laborers´Remuneration of Employed Persons at Year－end	在岗职工工资总额 Total Wages of Fully Employed Staff and Workers	其他从业人员劳动报酬 Laborers´Remuneration of Other Employed Persons	#在岗职工平均工资(元/人) Average Wage of Fully Employed Staff and Workers (yuan/person)
总计 Total	**3035865**	**2871075**	**164790**	**63602**
按隶属关系分 Grouped by Subordination				
中央属 Central	572632	524449	48183	82713
省　属 Provincial	873404	812647	60757	64400
市　属 Municipal	458641	435152	23489	60116
县及县以下 At and below County Level	1118277	1086942	31335	58113
其他 Other	12911	11885	1025	49667
按企业、事业、机关分组 Grouped by Enterprises, Institutions and Agencies				
企业 Enterprises	963885	870501	93385	56701
事业 Institutions	1407782	1347600	60181	64481
机关 Agencies and Organizations	660469	649759	10710	73950
民间非营利组织 Non－profit Organizations	2737	2241	497	28043
其他 Other	992	975	17	42212
按国民经济行业分组 Grouped by Sector				
农、林、牧、渔业 Farming, Forestry, Animal Husbandry and Fishery	2990	2885	105	33905
采矿业 Mining & Quarrying	－	－	－	－
制造业 Manufacturing	80481	78681	1801	42233

单位:万元 13－16 续表 continued (10000 yuan)

地 区 Region / 行 业 Sector	年末单位从业人员劳动报酬 Laborers´Remuneration of Employed Persons at Year－end	在岗职工工资总额 Total Wages of Fully Employed Staff and Workers	其他从业人员劳动报酬 Laborers´Remuneration of Other Employed Persons	#在岗职工平均工资(元/人) Average Wage of Fully Employed Staff and Workers (yuan/person)
电力、煤气及水的生产和供应业 Production and Supply of Electricity, Gas and Water	95735	85510	10225	90871
建筑业 Construction	72750	68038	4712	42425
交通运输、仓储及邮政业 Transportation, Storage and Post	216067	192840	23226	47225
信息传输、计算机服务和软件业 Information Transmission Computer Service and Software	78730	64900	13831	108947
批发与零售业 Wholesale & Retail Trade	60616	56524	4092	75921
住宿和餐饮业 Accommodations and Catering	28368	26218	2149	28234
金融业 Banking and Insurance	131146	123339	7807	131998
房地产业 Real Estate	17791	17162	630	47487
租赁与商务服务业 Renting and Business Service	90569	76035	14534	35005
科学研究、技术服务与地质勘查业 Scientific Research, Technical Service and Geological Prospecting	167011	156686	10325	65746
水利、环境和公共设施管理业 Water Conservany, Environment and Public Utility	51087	47032	4055	37596
居民服务和其他服务业 Service for the Residents and Other	11508	10550	958	42609
教育 Education	738756	717459	21297	67540
卫生、社会保障和社会福利业 Health Care, Sports and Social Welfare	388603	365356	23247	71274
文化、体育与娱乐业 Culture, Sports and Entertainment	88394	78553	9841	63626
公共管理与社会组织 Public Management and Social Organzations	715266	703309	11958	70593

13－17 全市城镇集体单位从业人员劳动报酬(2009年)

Laborers´Remuneration of Employed Persons for Collective－owned Units(2009)

单位:万元 (10000 yuan)

行业 Sector / 地区 Region	年末单位从业人员劳动报酬 Laborers´Remuneration of Employed Persons at Year－end	在岗职工工资总额 Total Wages of Fully Employed Staff and Workers	其他从业人员劳动报酬 Laborers´Remuneration of Other Employed Persons	#在岗职工平均工资(元/人) Average Wage of Fully Employed Staff and Workers (yuan/person)
总计 Total	**181463**	**171367**	**10096**	**36625**
按企业、事业分组 Grouped by Enterprises and Institutions				
企业 Enterprises	112142	106003	6139	31762
事业 Institutions	67091	63210	3881	49398
机关 Agencies and Organizations	352	352	－	73375
民间非营利组织 Non－profit Organizations	853	778	75	32157
其他 Other	1025	1023	2	31103
按国民经济行业分组 Grouped by Sector				
农、林、牧、渔业 Farming, Forestry, Animal Husbandry and Fishery	389	389	－	21854
采矿业 Mining & Quarrying	1480	1478	2	20329
制造业 Manufacturing	16311	16024	286	26034
电力、煤气及水的生产和供应业 Production and Supply of Electricity, Gas and Water	88	88	－	18354
建筑业 Construction	6326	5256	1069	30037
交通运输、仓储和邮政业 Transportation, Storage and Post	26805	25104	1700	52784
信息传输、计算机服务和软件业 Information Transmission Computer Service and Software	1458	1370	88	48246
批发与零售业 Wholesale & Retail Trade	7490	6727	764	35459
住宿和餐饮业 Accommodations and Catering	6948	6594	354	21769
金融业 Banking and Insurance	128	128	－	55783
房地产业 Real Estate	7096	6555	541	61549
租赁与商务服务业 Renting and Business Service	31096	30076	1020	25259
科学研究、技术服务与地质勘查业 Scientific Research, Technical Service and Geological Prospecting	6131	5645	485	58318
水利、环境和公共设施管理业 Water Conservany, Environment and Public Utility	6567	6130	438	29370
居民服务和其他服务业 Service for the Residents and Other	2229	2159	71	22464
教育 Education	27150	25964	1186	59524
卫生、社会保障和社会福利业 Health Care, Sports and Social Welfare	30419	28363	2056	50847
文化、体育与娱乐业 Culture, Sports and Entertainment	407	389	18	30406
公共管理与社会组织 Public Management and Social Organzations	2946	2928	18	33045

13－18　全市其他单位从业人员劳动报酬(2009 年)

Laborers´Remuneration of Employed Persons for Other Ownership Units(2009)

单位:万元　　(10000 yuan)

行业 Sector / 地区 Region	年末单位从业人员劳动报酬 Laborers´Remuneration of Employed Persons at Year－end	在岗职工工资总额 Total Wages of Fully Employed Staff and Workers	其他从业人员劳动报酬 Laborers´Remuneration of Other Employed Persons	#在岗职工平均工资(元/人) Average Wage of Fully Employed Staff and Workers (yuan/person)
合计 Total	**5103836**	**4506703**	**597133**	**36953**
按登记注册类型分 Grouped by Ownership				
内资 Domestic－funded Enterprises	3418517	2987451	431066	37982
港、澳、台商投资 Enterprises with Investment from Hong Kong, Macao and Taiwan	722367	671210	51157	35161
外商投资 Enterprises with Foreign Investment	962952	848042	114910	35024
按企业、事业分组 Grouped by Enterprises, Institutions and Agencies				
企业 Enterprises	5065814	4471741	594074	37055
民间非营利组织 Non－profit Organizations	14678	12840	1838	29003
其他 Other	23344	22123	1221	26494
按国民经济行业分组 Grouped by Sector				
农、林、牧、渔业 Farming, Forestry, Animal Husbandry and Fishery	2293	2285	8	33999
采矿业 Mining and Quarrying	4256	4249	7	27307
制造业 Manufacturing	2099033	1933969	165065	30985
电力、煤气及水的生产和供应业 Production and Supply of Electricity, Gas and Water	49557	48433	1124	53558
建筑业 Construction	928196	651583	276614	27356

单位:万元　　　　13－18　续表　continued　　　　(10000 yuan)

行业 Sector / 地区 Region	年末单位从业人员劳动报酬 Laborers´Remuneration of Employed Persons at Year－end	在岗职工工资总额 Total Wages of Fully Employed Staff and Workers	其他从业人员劳动报酬 Laborers´Remuneration of Other Employed Persons	#在岗职工平均工资(元/人) Average Wage of Fully Employed Staff and Workers (yuan/person)
交通运输、仓储和邮政业 Transportation, Storage and Post	100855	92719	8136	41524
信息传输、计算机服务和软件业 Information Transmission Computer Service and Software	329159	309495	19664	79828
批发与零售业 Wholesale & Retail Trade	378477	358930	19546	40558
住宿和餐饮业 Accommodations and Catering	133770	124420	9350	26537
金融业 Banking and Insurance	581573	525341	56232	130425
房地产业 Real Estate	152522	140771	11752	46724
租赁与商务服务业 Renting and Business Service	122466	115508	6958	37128
科学研究、技术服务与地质勘查业 Scientific Research, Technical Service and Geological Prospecting	120101	107108	12993	55592
水利、环境和公共设施管理业 Water Conservany, Environment and Public Utility	17596	16157	1439	32859
居民服务和其他服务业 Service for the Residents and Other	9287	8213	1074	22993
教育 Education	25780	22761	3019	34160
卫生、社会保障和社会福利业 Health Care, Sports and Social Welfare	13886	11833	2053	41841
文化、体育与娱乐业 Culture, Sports and Entertainment	13199	12374	825	41425
公共管理与社会组织 Public Management and Social Organzations	21831	20557	1274	26621

13－19 主要年份市区价格指数
Price Indices of Urban District in Main Years

（上年＝100）　　（Preceding Year＝100）

年　份 Year	居民消费价格指数 General Consumer Price Index	商品零售价格指数 General Retail Price Index
1978	100.1	100.1
1979	100.4	100.9
1980	100.8	109.3
1981	102.0	102.0
1982	102.0	102.3
1983	102.1	102.3
1984	103.1	103.1
1985	117.2	117.5
1986	106.0	106.1
1987	110.5	111.3
1988	121.9	123.4
1989	117.8	118.2
1990	104.6	104.4
1991	107.5	106.9
1992	110.4	110.2
1993	121.4	117.3
1994	121.5	118.8
1995	116.5	113.3
1996	110.5	107.2
1997	106.7	102.4
1998	101.8	99.8
1999	100.4	98.2
2000	100.8	98.3
2001	99.5	95.3
2002	98.8	97.9
2003	99.5	98.1
2004	102.5	101.6
2005	101.7	100.3
2006	101.2	100.2
2007	103.5	103.1
2008	104.9	106.0
2009	98.6	98.6

13－20　市区居民消费价格指数(2009年)

Consumer Price Indices in Urban District(2009)

(上年＝100)　　(Preceding Year＝100)

项　目	Item	指数 Indices
居民消费价格总指数	**Consumer Price Indices**	**98.6**
一、食品	**Food**	**101.7**
1. 粮食	Grain	105.1
2. 淀粉	Starches and Tubers	108.4
3. 干豆类及豆制品	Bean and Its Products	102.2
4. 油脂	Oil and Fat	77.8
5. 肉禽及其制品	Meal Poultry and Their Products	92.5
6. 蛋	Eggs	104.2
7. 水产品	Aquatic Products	105.2
8. 菜	Vegetables	105.2
9. 调味品	Flavoring	100.7
10. 糖	Sugar	100.8
11. 茶及饮料	Tea and Beverages	105.1
12. 干鲜瓜果	Dried and Fresh Melons and Fruits	110.7
13. 糕点饼干	Cake、Biscuit and Bread	100.9
14. 液体乳及乳制品	Milk and Its Products	99.5
15. 在外用膳食品	Outward Dinner	102.9
16. 其他食品	Other Food	99.4
二、烟酒及用品	**Tobacco、Liquor and Articles**	**100.7**
1. 烟草	Tobacco	100.1
2. 酒	Liquor	102.4
3. 吸烟饮酒用品	Articles	100.2
三、衣着	**Clothing**	**100.6**
1. 服装	Garments	102.6
2. 衣着材料	Clothing Material	101

(上年=100) 13-20 续表 continued (Preceding Year=100)

项目	Item	指数 Indices
3.鞋袜帽	Shoes, Socks and Hats	93.3
4.衣着加工服务	Clothing Processing Service	100.2
四、家庭设备用品及维修服务	**Household Facilities, Articles and Repair Service**	**100.9**
1.耐用消费品	Durable Consumer Goods	100.2
2.室内装饰品	Interior Decorations	102.6
3.床上用品	Bed Articles	100.4
4.家庭日用杂品	Daily Use Household Articles	102.5
5.家庭服务及加工维修服务	Household and Repair Service	100.9
五、医疗保健和个人用品	**Medical Articles and Personal Articles**	**100.6**
1.医疗保健	Medical Care	100.7
2.个人用品及服务	Personel Articles and Service	100.3
六、交通和通信	**Transportation and Communication**	**95.2**
1.交通	Transportation	95.5
2.通信	Communication	94.6
七、娱乐教育文化用品及服务	**Recreation, Education and Culture Articles**	**96.9**
1.文娱用耐用消费品及服务	Durable Consumer Goods and Recreation Service	93
2.教育	Education	100.3
3.文化娱乐类	Cultural and Recreational Articles	101.4
4.旅游	Tourism and Outgoing	88.6
八、居住	**Residence**	**91.8**
1.建房及装修材料	Construction and Upholstery Materials	99.1
2.租房	House Renting	101.3
3.自有住房	Private Owned Houses	75.7
4.水、电、燃料	Water, Electricity and Fuels	97

13-21 市区零售价格指数(2009年)
Retail Price Indices in Urban District(2009)

(上年=100) (Preceding Year=100)

项目	Item	指数 Indices
商品零售价格总指数	**Retail Price Indices**	**98.6**
一、食品	**Food**	**101.6**
1.粮食	Grain	105.1
2.淀粉	Starches and Tubers	108.4
3.干豆类及豆制品	Bean and Its Products	102
4.油脂	Oil and Fat	77.9
5.肉禽及其制品	Meal Poultry and Their Products	91.6
6.蛋	Eggs	104.2
7.水产品	Aquatic Products	104.7
8.菜	Vegetables	105
9.调味品	Flavoring	100.4
10.糖	Carbohydrate	100.3
11.干鲜瓜果	Dried and Fresh Melons and Fruits	111.1
12.糕点饼干面包	Cake、Biscuit and Bread	100.9
13.液体乳及乳制品	Milk and Its Products	99.5
14.在外用膳食品	Outward Dinner	103.1
15.其他食品	Other Food	99.4
二、饮料、烟酒	**Beverages, Tobacco and Liquor**	**101.7**
1.茶及饮料	Tea and Beverages	104.9
2.烟草	Tobacco	100.1
3.酒	Liquor	102.6
三、服装、鞋帽	**Garments, Shoes and Hats**	**100.1**
1.服装	Garments	102.8
2.鞋袜帽	Shoes, Socks and Hats	93.6
3.其他	Other	94.5
四、纺织品	**Textiles**	**100.7**
1.衣着材料	Clothing Material	101.9
2.床上用品	Bed Articles	99.9
五、家用电器及音像器材	**Household Electric Appliances, Audio and Video Equipment**	**96.4**
1.家庭设备	Household Equipment	99.2
2.文娱用耐用消费品	Durable Consumer Goods for Entertainment	89.1

（上年＝100）　　13－21　续表　continued　　（Preceding Year＝100）

项　目	Item	指数 Indices
3. 音像器材	Audio and Video Equipment	100.4
六、文化办公用品	**Stationery and Office Supplies**	**98.8**
七、日用品	**Commodities**	**99.3**
1. 日用百货	General Merchandise for Daily Use	96.6
2. 日用杂品	Sundries for Daily Use	99.2
3. 洗涤用品	Washing Articles	104.8
4. 其他日用品	Other Commodity	99.4
八、体育娱乐用品	**Sports and Entertainment Goods**	**102.4**
1. 体育用品	Sports Goods	100.6
2. 娱乐用品	Entertainment Goods	103.1
九、交通、通信用品	**Transportation and Communications Articles**	**93.2**
1. 交通运输机械	Transportation Vehicles	95.1
2. 通讯器材	Equipment of Communication	81.3
十、家具	**Funishings**	**100.5**
十一、化妆品	**Cosmetics**	**99.3**
十二、金银珠宝	**Jewellery**	**93.5**
十三、中西药品及医疗保健用品	**Chinese and Western Medicine, Health Care Articles**	**100.8**
1. 医疗器具及用品	Medical Instruments and Articles	105.4
2. 中药材及中成药	Chinese Medicinal Materials and Chinese Traditional Medicine	100.5
3. 西药	Western Medicine	100.4
4. 保健品及器具	Articles for Health Care	100.6
十四、书报杂志及电子出版物	**Books, Newspapers, Magazines and Electron Publications**	**101.3**
1. 教材及参考书	Teaching Materials and Reference Books	103.3
2. 书报杂志	Books, Newspapers and Magazines	102
3. 电子音像制品	Electronic Music and Film Products	96.7
十五、燃料	**Fuels**	**89.7**
1. 煤炭及制品	Coal and Coal Products	97.7
2. 石油及制品	Oil and Oil Products	88.5
十六、建筑材料及五金电料	**Construction Materials and Hardware**	**96.8**
1. 建筑装潢材料	Construction and Upholstery Materials	96.7
2. 五金电料	Hardware and Electric Materials	97.4

13－22 主要工业品出厂价格分类指数

Ex－Factory Price Indices of Industrial Products in Main Years

（上年＝100）　　　　　　　　　　　　　　　　　　　　　　　　（Preceding Year＝100）

项　　目 Item	1999	2000	2005	2006	2007	2008	2009
工业品出厂价格总指数 Ex－factory Price Indices of Industrial Products	**96.9**	**100.3**	**103.5**	**103.1**	**103.6**	**105.9**	**95.1**
一、按轻重工业分 Grouped by Industries							
轻工业 Light Industry	**95.8**	**99.3**	**101.8**	**101.7**	**102.0**	**103.2**	**96.5**
以农产品为原料 Made from Agricultural Products	96.9	99.9	102.0	101.8	100.6	102.5	98.5
以非农产品为原料 Made from Non－agricultural Products	95.3	98.0	101.7	101.6	103.4	103.8	94.7
重工业 Heavy Industry	**98.0**	**101.1**	**105.6**	**104.9**	**105.4**	**109.2**	**93.1**
采掘业 Mining & Quarrying Industry	－	99.5	103.0	140.0	124.0	104.9	83.5
原料工业 Raw Materials Industry	99.0	104.4	107.7	104.8	107.2	112.6	93.3
加工业 Manufacturing Industry	97.6	98.9	104.3	102.6	103.4	108.1	93.6
二、按二大部类分 Grouped by Means of Producting and Consumer Goods							
生产资料 Means of Production	**97.9**	**101.9**	**104.8**	**103.7**	**104.4**	**107.0**	**93.2**
采掘 Mining	－	99.6	103.0	131.6	120.7	104.9	83.5
原料 Raw Materials	98.4	103.8	110.7	104.4	107.6	108.0	90.7
加工 Manufacture	97.7	100.3	101.6	102.2	102.8	106.8	94.4
生活资料 Consumer Goods	**95.7**	**97.5**	**101.2**	**101.6**	**101.0**	**102.8**	**100.2**
食品 Foods	98.8	96.4	101.6	101.8	101.0	102.2	100.2
衣着 Clothing	95.2	101.1	101.4	101.1	100.6	101.5	100.1
一般日用品 Articles for Daily Use	94.9	97.8	101.7	103.3	101.8	106.1	100.1
耐用消费品 Durable Consumer Goods	94.8	94.5	99.5	99.9	100.5	102.2	100.4

项 目 Item	1999	2000	2005	2006	2007	2008	2009
三、按工业部门分 Grouped by Industrial Sector							
冶金工业 Metallurgical Industry	95.6	104.0	104.8	107.2	112.9	117.3	87.0
电力工业 Power Industry	99.8	96.0	106.2	102.1	102.2	105.4	101.5
煤炭及炼焦工业 Coal and Coking Industry	99.8	107.9	102.1	101.5	108.8	99.3	-
石油工业 Petroleum Industry	108.1	131.6	124.7	114.0	103.1	120.7	92.3
化学工业 Chemical Industry	97.2	101.1	106.0	102.4	107.0	109.8	87.2
机械工业 Machine Building Industry	94.9	96.7	102.9	103.2	101.5	102.6	97.3
建材工业 Building Materials Industry	103.1	103.0	91.7	99.6	104.1	106.0	96.5
森林工业 Timber Industry	96.6	96.9	101.4	100.8	101.6	100.9	98.3
食品工业 Food Industry	98.0	95.8	100.6	101.0	101.3	102.8	100.2
纺织工业 Textile Industry	97.3	107.3	103.4	104.4	99.8	100.3	97.8
缝纫工业 Tailoring Industry	96.3	100.5	101.5	101.0	100.7	101.5	99.9
皮革工业 Leather Industry	91.6	98.0	101.4	101.3	100.3	100.2	99.7
造纸工业 Paper Industry	96.2	102.9	100.3	98.8	100.6	109.8	94.8
文教艺术 Cultural, Educational & Handicrafts Articles	90.4	98.7	99.7	98.8	99.2	103.5	98.4
其 他 Others	101.1	103.6	102.2	108.5	103.3	103.4	101.7

13－23　主要原材料、燃料、动力购进价格分类指数

Purchasing Price Indices of Raw Materials, Fuels and Power in Main Years

(上年＝100)　　(Preceding Year＝100)

项　目 Item	1999	2000	2005	2006	2007	2008	2009
原材料购进价格指数 Raw Materials Purchasing Price Index	**97.2**	**107.4**	**106.9**	**106.1**	**104.6**	**110.8**	**92.2**
燃料动力类 Fuel and Power	103.0	108.0	116.4	107.4	104.5	126.1	91.5
黑色金属材料类 Ferrous and Metals	96.3	102.7	105.2	94.2	109.7	123.9	83.6
其中:钢材 Rolled －steel	94.9	103.2	104.9	94.2	108.6	120.3	82.9
其它 Other	98.2	101.0	105.7	94.0	114.0	137.4	86.2
有色金属材料和电线类 Non－ferrous Metals and Electric Wire	97.6	108.0	111.2	129.8	113.4	95.6	85.2
化工原料类 Chemical Raw Materials	97.6	111.0	110.1	106.3	108.1	106.3	88.5
木材及纸浆类 Wood and Paper Pulps	95.5	104.5	101.0	102.7	106.6	104.4	91.4
建筑材料及非金属类 Building Materials	98.2	100.6	102.3	98.9	103.6	114.8	98.5
其它工业原材料及半成品 Other Industrial Raw Materials and Semi－products	97.2	111.0	103.6	110.5	102.5	107.3	96.1
农副产品类 Farm and Sideline Products	95.0	104.0	103.9	112.2	100.2	107.6	101.5
纺织原料类 Textile Raw Materials	89.4	104.7	99.9	103.3	98.5	99.2	96.6

13－24 房地产销售价格指数
Saling Price Indices of Houses in Main Years

(上年＝100)　　(Preceding Year＝100)

项目	Item	2000	2005	2006	2007	2008	2009
总　计	**Total**	**104.9**	**109.7**	**102.6**	**107.3**	**108.6**	**102.8**
一、新建房	**New Building**	**105.7**	**110.1**	**102.9**	**107.8**	**110.0**	**102.0**
(一)住宅	**Residential Buildings**	**104.7**	**109.7**	**103.2**	**108.3**	**109.9**	**102.1**
1. 经济适用房	Economical and Livable Living Houses	99.5	100.0	100.0	100.0	100.0	100.0
2. 普通住宅	Common Residence	104.9	112.1	103.0	108.3	107.8	102.1
(1)多层住宅	Multi－layer Residence	106.2	115.5	103.0	106.1	108.2	98.9
(2)高层住宅	Higher Level Residence	101.2	110.6	102.8	108.3	107.8	102.4
3. 高档住宅	Luxury Buildings	105.6	110.2	105.5	114.0	123.7	103.5
(1)别墅	Villas	105.6	112.9	103.5	–	100.1	100.1
(2)高档公寓	Flats	–	109.8	105.6	114.0	123.7	104.1
(二)非住宅	**Non－residential Buildings**	**110.5**	**111.0**	**102.0**	**105.9**	**110.9**	**101.6**
1. 办公楼	Office Buildings	103.1	112.6	102.5	106.6	114.7	102.9
2. 商业营业用房	Buildings for Commercial and Entertainment Use	117.1	105.3	101.2	105.4	107.1	99.2
3. 其他用房	Other	–	113.2	102.8	101.3	100.0	101.9
二、二手房	**Second－hand Housing**	**107.1**	**108.4**	**102.0**	**106.0**	**104.2**	**104.6**
(一)非住宅	Non－residential Buildings	–	110.6	104.0	106.9	102.2	102.0
(二)住　宅	Residential Buildings	107.1	107.6	101.6	105.8	104.5	105.3

13－25 房地产租赁价格指数
Renting Price Indices of Houses in Main Years

（上年＝100） (Preceding Year＝100)

项目	Item	2000	2005	2006	2007	2008	2009
总计	**Total**	**103.3**	**102.4**	**101.1**	**102.7**	**102.5**	**101.8**
一、住宅	**Residential Buildings**	**118.8**	**101.1**	**101.0**	**102.2**	**106.0**	**101.9**
（一）廉租房	Low－cost Housing	119.0	－	－	－	100.0	87.5
（二）商品住宅	Commercial Residential Buildings	98.8	101.1	101.0	102.2	106.3	102.5
二、非住宅	**Non－residential Buildings**	**103.4**	**101.0**	**102.0**	**104.2**	**101.2**	**101.8**
（一）办公楼	Office	106.5	101.2	102.2	105.8	102.7	103.8
（二）商业营业用房	Commercial Business Buildings	110.3	103.2	100.6	102.5	100.5	100.7
（三）其他	Else	99.5	101.2	100.0	100.0	100.0	100.0

13－26 社会办福利院情况(2009 年)
Basic Statistics on Welfare Homes(2009)

指标 Item	单位(个) Homes (unit)	年末职工人数(人) Staff and Workers (person)	年末床位数(张) Beds (bed)	年末在院人数(人) Persons Housed (person)	#老人(人) Seniors(person)
全市 Total	**208**	**1909**	**22430**	**11729**	**10556**
市区 Urban District	111	1514	15057	7676	6756
#萧山区 Xiaoshan	30	274	3916	1844	1776
余杭区 Yuhang	23	164	2302	757	692
桐庐县 Tonglu	12	64	1281	1056	1024
淳安县 Chun'an	21	56	1034	718	696
建德市 Jiande	15	93	1523	841	809
富阳市 Fuyang	23	80	1428	680	636
临安市 Lin'an	26	102	2107	758	635

13－27 优抚对象
Number of Persons Enjoying

单位：人

指　　标 Item	全　　市 Total	市　　区 Urban District	#萧山区 Xiaoshan
享受定期抚恤金人数 Number of Persons Receiving Periodical Commiseration	630	187	86
烈属 Number of Martyr Kinsfolk	287	67	30
牺牲军人家属 Number of the Sacrifice Soldiers	106	30	9
病故军人家属 Number of Kinsfolks of the Illness－died Soldiers	237	90	47
享受定期补助人数 Number of Persons Enjoying Regular Subsidies	13599	3408	1539
其中：红军失散人员 Number of Persons be Scattered of the Red Army	3	－	－
在乡复员军人 Rural Demobilized Soldier	4244	1316	516
抗日 The War of Resistance Against Japan	43	24	3
优待优抚对象带病回乡退伍军人 Number of Rural Veterans with Illness Receiving Subsiders	5146	857	548
优待优抚对象户数 Number of Households Receiving Subsiders	29603	18165	2926
优待军属户数 Number of Households Sacrifice Soldiers	6783	3548	1105

人员情况（2009 年）

Public Subsidies（2009）

（person）

#余杭区 Yuhang	桐庐县 Tonglu	淳安县 Chun'an	建德市 Jiande	富阳市 Fuyang	临安市 Lin'an
54	94	93	87	106	63
18	39	54	55	37	35
11	25	7	12	24	8
25	30	32	20	45	20
1290	1473	1494	1884	2976	2364
–	–	3	–	–	–
597	537	526	390	778	697
5	4	–	1	3	11
209	563	809	1029	509	1379
2552	2415	2418	3113	758	2734
826	648	534	646	758	649

13－28 市、县级社会

Basic Statistics on Institutions and

单位：个

指 标	Item	全 市 Total	市 区 Urban District	#萧山区 Xiaoshan
合 计	**Total**	**2177**	**1499**	**223**
按活动区域分	**Grouped by Region**			
地级社团	City－level Societies	616	616	－
县级社团	County－level Societies	1561	883	223
按性质分	**Grouped by Category**			
科技与研究	Technology and Research	115	70	－
生态环境	Ecological Envirenment	25	11	2
教育	Education	77	58	2
卫生	Health	98	67	12
社会服务	Social Services	256	170	14
文化	Culture	197	128	29
体育	Sport	163	134	8
法律	Law	19	15	－
工商业服务	Industry and Business Services	387	255	19
宗教	Religion	34	21	5
农业及农村发展	Agricure and Rural Development	163	56	23
职业及从业组织	Vocational and Business Organizations	193	107	1
国际及涉外组织	International and Foreign Organizations	6	－	－
其他	**Other**	**444**	**407**	**108**

团体机构情况(2009 年)
Organizations at County Level(2009)

(unit)

#余杭区 Yuhang	桐庐县 Tonglu	淳安县 Chun'an	建德市 Jiande	富阳市 Fuyang	临安市 Lin'an
213	**113**	**104**	**157**	**169**	**135**
213	113	104	157	169	135
2	11	3	5	13	13
5	2	2	7	2	1
15	3	3	7	1	5
6	6	6	8	5	6
60	20	31	15	18	2
8	8	6	20	27	8
22	2	2	14	7	4
3	–	1	1	2	–
84	28	9	19	37	39
3	4	3	2	3	1
5	16	27	7	39	18
–	13	11	38	4	20
–	–	–	4	2	–
–	**–**	**–**	**10**	**9**	**18**

13－29　社会保障分县(市)情况(2009 年)

Social Security by Region(2009)

单位:万人　(10000 persons)

指标 Item	基本养老保险参保人数 Number of Persons in the Basic Pension Program	基本养老保险参保职工 Number of Employed Persons in the Basic Pension Program	基本医疗保险参保人数 Number of Persons in the Basic Medical Insurance Program	工伤保险参保人数 Number of Persons in the Work－injure Insurance Program	生育保险参保人数 Number of Persons in the Bear Insurance Program	职工失业保险人数 Number of Persons in the Unemployment Insurance Program
全　市 Total	**342.24**	**288.29**	**298.31**	**274.15**	**199.80**	**215.68**
市　区 Urban District	279.83	235.21	255.12	218.85	167.55	189.78
#萧山区 Xiaoshan	67.53	61.05	41.27	55.41	37.62	38.03
余杭区 Yuhang	32.55	27.87	29.59	29.20	17.75	21.22
桐庐县 Tonglu	9.91	8.38	8.15	8.70	4.96	3.93
淳安县 Chun'an	6.85	5.69	6.38	6.21	3.13	2.91
建德市 Jiande	11.66	9.07	7.86	7.90	5.44	5.52
富阳市 Fuyang	21.51	19.18	9.52	21.36	12.28	9.89
临安市 Lin'an	12.48	10.75	11.28	11.13	6.44	3.65

13－30 近年来社会保障情况

Social Security in Recent Years

单位:万人 (10000 persons)

指 标 Item	2001	2002	2003	2004	2005	2006	2007	2008	2009
城镇登记失业人员 Number of the Registered Unemployed Persons in Urban Units	6.97	6.85	7.09	7.27	6.09	6.30	5.96	5.45	5.64
城镇登记失业率(%) The Registered Rate of Unemployment in Urban Units(%)	4.48	4.43	4.39	4.33	3.71	3.46	3.21	3.02	2.99
失业人员再就业 The Re－employed Persons of Unemployment	21.61	17.65	15.75	17.96	13.09	12.08	13.1	12.59	15.56
基本养老保险参保人数 Number of Persons in the Basic Pension Program	144.08	164.37	190.85	209.36	227.58	253.34	280.49	318.11	342.24
#基本养老保险参保职工 Number of Employed Persons in the Basic Pension Program	109.31	127.99	152.5	169.06	185.32	208.87	233.15	267.6	288.29
失业保险参保人数 Number of Persons in the Unemployment Insurance Program	95.52	96.93	98.71	105.73	118.36	145.77	170.09	202.41	215.68
基本医疗保险参保人数 Number of Persons in the Basic Medical Insurance Program	-	139.75	155.66	172.35	187.71	208.5	237.74	274.59	298.31
工伤保险参保人数 Number of Persons in the Work－injure Insurance Program	47.77	52.24	64.29	88.45	111.03	132.09	201.64	245.82	274.15
生育保险参保人数 Number of Persons in the Bear Insurance Program	60.48	62.25	69.2	79.78	96.41	128.89	155.64	181.68	199.80
参加农村合作医疗人数 Number of Persons in the Rural Medical Cooperative Service System	-	-	170.6	324.14	350.6	370.65	369.7	369.18	346.95

主要统计指标解释

从业人员劳动报酬　指各单位在一定时期内直接支付给本单位全部从业人员的劳动报酬总额。

在岗职工工资总额　指各单位在一定时期内直接支付给本单位全部在岗职工的劳动报酬总额。

工资总额的计算原则应以直接支付给职工的全部劳动报酬为根据。各单位支付给本单位全部职工的劳动报酬,不论是计入成本的还是不计入成本的,不论是以货币形式支付还是以实物形式支付的,不论是单位自筹的资金还是上级(或政府财政部门)下拨的资金,不论是厂级单位筹集的资金还是下属车间(科室)及附属经营单位筹集的资金,均应列入工资总额计算的范围。

在岗职工平均工资　指各单位的在岗职工在一定时期内平均每人所得的货币工资额。它表明一定时期内在岗职工工资收入的高低程度,是反映在岗职工工资水平的主要指标。计算公式为:

$$\text{在岗职工平均工资} = \frac{\text{报告期实际支付的全部在岗职工工资总额}}{\text{报告期全部在岗职工平均人数}}$$

城镇居民家庭总收入　指被调查的城镇居民家庭全部收入。包括经常或固定得到的收入和一次性收入,不包括周转性收入。如:提取银行存款、向亲友借入款、收回借出款以及其他各种暂收款。

城镇居民家庭可支配收入　指被调查的城镇居民家庭在支付个人所得税、个人交纳的社会保障支出之后,所余下的实际收入。

计算公式为:可支配收入 = 总收入 - 个人所得税 - 个人交纳的社会保障支出

城镇居民家庭消费性支出　指被调查的城镇居民家庭用于日常生活的全部支出,包括购买商品支出和文化生活、服务等非商品性支出。不包括罚没、丢失款和缴纳的各种税款(如个人所得税、牌照税、房产税等),也不包括个体劳动者生产经营过程中发生的各项费用。

农村居民家庭纯收入　指农村常住居民家庭总收入中,扣除从事生产和非生产经营费用支出、缴纳税款和上交承包集体任务金额以后剩余的,可直接用于进行生产性、非生产性建设投资、生活消费和积蓄的那一部分收入。它是反映农民家庭实际收入水平的综合性的主要指标。农民家庭纯收入,既包括从事生产性和非生产性的经营收入,又包括取自在外人口寄回带回和国家财政救济、各种补贴等非经营性收入;既包括货币收入,又包括自产自用的实物收入。但不包括向银行、信用社和向亲友贷款等属于借贷性的收入。

计算公式为:

纯收入 = 总收入 - 家庭经营费用支出 - 生产用固定资产折旧 - 税收 - 上交集体承包任务 - 调查补贴 - 集体提留和摊派。

离休、退休、退职人员　指正式办理了离休、退休、退职手续,并享受相应的离休、退休、退职待遇的人员。

保险福利费用　指企业、事业、机关单位在工资以外实际支付给职工和离休、退休、退职人员个人以及用于集体的劳动保险和福利费用。

社会福利事业单位　指集中收养社会孤、老、残、幼的机构。包括由民政部门管理的社会福利院、儿童福利院、精神病人福利院和城镇集体办的福利院,以及农村集体举办的敬老院。

社会福利事业单位收养人数　包括民政部门管理和城镇及农村集体举办的社会福利事业单位中收养的老人,少年儿童,缺乏生活自理能力的残疾人员和精神病人。

商品零售价格指数　是反映城乡商品零售价格变动趋势的一种经济指数。零售物价的调整变动直接影响到城乡居民的生活支出和国家的财政收入,影响居民购买力和市场供需平衡,影响消费与积累的比例。因此,计算零售价格指数,可以从一个侧面对上述经济活动进行观察和分析。

居民消费价格指数　是反映一定时期内城乡居民所购买的生活消费品价格和服务项目价格变动趋势和程度的相对数。是综合了城市居民消费价格指数和农民消费价格指数计算取得。利用居民消费价格指数,可以观察和分析消费品的零售价格和服务价格变动对城乡居民实际生活支出的影响程度。

工业品出厂价格指数　是反映全部工业产品出厂价格总水平的变动趋势和程度的相对数。其中除包括工业企业售给商业、外贸、物资部门的产品外,还包括售给工业和其他部门的生产资料以及直接售给居民的生活消费品。通过工业生产价格指数能观察出厂价格变动对工业总产值的影响。

Explanatory Notes on Main Statistical Indicators

Labour Remuneration refers to total payment by various units to their employees during a certain period of time, including total wage bill of permanent workers and staff and remuneration payment to other employees.

Total Wages of Fully Employed Staff and Workers refer to the total remuneration payment to fully employed staff and workers in various units during a certain period of time. The calculation of total wages is based on the total remuneration payment to the staff and workers. Therefore, all the wages and salaries and other payments to staff and workers are included in the total wages regardless of their sources, category, and forms (in kind or cash). (Total wages of staff and workers in this yearbook include only total wages of fully employed staff and workers, excluding the living allowances distributed to those who have left their working units while keeping their labour contract/employment relation unchanged).

Average Wage of Fully Employed Staff and Workers refers to the average wage in money terms per person during a certain period of time for fully employed staff and workers in enterprises, institutions, and government agencies, which reflects the general level of wage income during a certain period of time and is calculated as follows:

$$\text{Average Wage of Fully Employed Staff and Workers} = \frac{\text{Total wages of Fully employed staff and workers in Reference Period}}{\text{Average Number of Fully employed Staff and workers in Reference period}}$$

Total Income of Urban Households refers to the total actual income of the sample households, including regular or fixed income and occasional income. The income of a circulating nature such as withdrawal from bank deposit, loans borrowed from relatives or friends, repayment of loans received and various temporary collection of many is excluded.

Disposable Income of Urban Households refers to total income minus income tax, personal contribution to social security and subsidy for keeping diaries in being a sample household. The following formula is used:

Disposable Income = total households income − income tax − personal contribution to social security

Expenditure for Consumption of Urban Households refers to total expenditure of the sample households for consumption in daily life, including expenditure for various commodities and expenses for non – commodity items such as culture and service, etc., but excluding fines and confiscation, loss, tax payments (such as income tax, license tax, real estates tax, etc.) and various expenses by individual laborers for business purposes.

Net Income of Rural Households refers to the total income of the permanent residents of the rural households during a year after the deduction of the expenses for productive and non – productive business operation, the payment for taxes and productive constriction, for consumption in daily life and for savings deposit. It is a comprehensive indicator to show the actual level of the income of the peasants' household. The net income of the rural households includes not only the income from the productive and non – productive business operation, but also the income from the non – business operation, such as the money remitted or brought back by the members of the household who are in other places, the government relief payment and various subsidies. It includes not only the money income, but also the income in kind. But the income from borrowing from banks, friends and relatives is excluded.

Retired and Resigned Person refers to the persons who have form ally gone through the formalities for their retirement or quitting work and enjoy the corresponding treatments.

Insurance an d welfare Funds refers to labour insurance and welf are funds paid by enterprises, organizations and institutions to their staff and workers as well as retired and resigned persons in addition to their wages and salaries.

Social Welfare Institutions refer to institutions taking care of old people without children, handicapped people and orphans. They include social welfare institutions run by civil affairs departments, children welfare institutions, social welfare institutions for mental patients, and collective – owned old people's home in rural areas.

Number of People Taken in by social welfare Institutions refers to the number of old people, children, totally dependent handicapped people and mental patients taken in by social welfare institutions run by civil affairs departments and those run by collective units in urban and rural areas.

Retail price Index reflects the general change in retail prices of commodities. The change and adjustment in retail prices directly affect the living expenditure of urban and rural residents, government revenue, purchasing power of residents and the equilibrium of market supply and demand, and the ratio of consumption to accumulation. Therefore, the calculation of retail price index is useful to analyze the changes of the above economic activities.

Consumer Price Index reflects the trend and degree of changes in prices of consumer goods and services purchased by urban and rural residents, and is a composite index derived from the urban consumer price index and the rural consumer price index. Consumer price index can be used to analyze the impact of consumer price change on actual expenditure for living cost of urban and rural residents.

Ex – factory price index of Industrial Products reflects the trend and degree of changes in general ex – factory prices of all industrial products, including sales of industrial products by and industrial enterprise to all units outside the enterprise, as well as sales of consumer goods to residents. It can be used to analyze the impact of ex – factory prices on gross industrial output value.

中国统计出版社最新图书简目

（仅供参考，以最后出书为准）

统计资料

中国统计年鉴－2010

2010 中国发展报告

中国劳动统计年鉴－2010

中国建筑业统计年鉴－2010

中国商品交易市场统计年鉴－2010

中国民政统计年鉴－2010

中国科技统计年鉴－2010

中国高技术产业统计年鉴－2010

全国农产品成本收益资料汇编－2010

第二次全国残疾人抽样调查资料系列

中国县（市）社会经济调查年鉴－2010

中国国内生产总值核算历史资料（1952－2004）

大中型批发零售和住宿餐饮企业统计年鉴－2010

中国统计摘要－2010

中国第三产业统计年鉴－2010

中国社会统计年鉴－2010

中国人口和就业统计年鉴－2010

中国房地产统计年鉴－2010

中国贸易外经统计年鉴－2010

中国农村统计年鉴－2010

中国教育经费统计年鉴－2009

中国科学技术协会统计年鉴－2010

中国棉花年鉴－2008/2009

中国农村住户调查年鉴－2010（中、英文）

中国季度国内生产总值核算历史资料（1992－2005）

国际统计年鉴－2010

中国区域经济统计年鉴－2010

中国城市统计年鉴－2009

中国工业经济统计年鉴－2010

中国能源统计年鉴－2010

2010 中国地区经济监测报告

中国农产品价格调查年鉴－2010

中国农村贫困监测报告－2010

工业企业科技活动资料－2010

中国城市（镇）生活与价格年鉴－2010

中国农村全面建设小康监测报告－2010

中国零售和餐饮业连锁企业统计年鉴－2010

2005 年中国 1% 人口抽样调查系列资料

2010 年省级综合统计年鉴系列

北京　天津　河北　山西　内蒙古

河南　湖北　湖南　广东　广西

新疆　新疆生产建设兵团

辽宁　吉林　黑龙江　上海　江苏

海南　重庆　四川　贵州　云南

浙江　安徽　福建　江西　山东

西藏　陕西　甘肃　青海　宁夏

2010 年市（县）级综合统计年鉴系列

天津滨海新区

运城　忻州　临汾　呼和浩特

黑龙江垦区　上海浦东新区

宁波　绍兴　台州　舟山　温州

厦门经济特区　南昌　上饶

十堰　荆州　黄冈　长沙　广州

贵阳　昆明　西安　庆阳　银川

石家庄　唐山　邯郸　太原　大同

包头　沈阳　大连　长春　吉林市

苏州　无锡　常州　徐州　南通

金华　嘉兴　衢州　安庆　福州

济南　青岛　潍坊　东营　郑州

东莞　惠州　深圳　桂林　南宁

乌鲁木齐　吐鲁番

长治　阳泉　晋城　朔州　晋中

四平　延吉　哈尔滨　齐齐哈尔

盐城　镇江　江阴　丹阳　杭州

福州经济技术开发区

洛阳　三门峡　南阳　武汉　宜昌

柳州　来宾　河池　海口　成都

“十一五”规划教材

非参数统计　医学统计学

多元统计分析　经济计量学教程

统计数据处理概论

企业经营管理统计

统计学：从数据到结论

概率论与数理统计　统计学

应用时间序列分析

质量管理统计方法　社会统计学

市场调查与预测

国民经济核算教程（国民经济统计学）

现代金融投资统计分析

统计指数理论及应用

多元统计分析实验

统计学原理（非统计专业使用）

概率论与数理统计（经济、管理类专业使用）

重点图书

新中国六十年

挑大学选专业 2010—高考志愿填报指南

挑大学选专业 2010—考研择校指南